Frugal Innovation and the New Product Development Process

This book explores the new product development process of firms developing frugal innovation for the base-of-the-pyramid (BOP) markets in developing countries. Frugal innovations are products characterised by an affordable price-point, durability, usability and core functionalities that are highly adapted to BOP consumers' needs. Frugal products have the potential to drive the development progress and living standards of low-income consumers.

With an innovation framework developed from worldwide frugal case studies, this book provides detailed insights through two in-depth start-up firms in Indonesia that have successfully launched frugal products for the low-income market. These two start-ups have addressed two major development challenges for not just Indonesia, but also the global BOP market – traditional methods of cooking and access to clean drinking water.

A detailed roadmap is developed from insights into the processes and management decisions of these two start-ups and combined with previous studies on frugal products. Providing a detailed roadmap across the different phases and stages of the new product development process when developing frugal products, this book will be insightful to not only innovators but also investors and government agencies supporting their activities.

Stephanie B.M. Cadeddu is a Research Associate at Swinburne University of Technology, Melbourne, Australia. She has extensive experience working with start-ups, including through field research in Indonesia. Her research and teaching interests include frugal innovation, social impact and community development.

Jerome D. Donovan is a Senior Lecturer in Entrepreneurship and Innovation at Swinburne University of Technology in Melbourne, Australia. He is also a Principal Advisor in Technology Entrepreneurship and Commercialisation Development with the Ministry of Science and Technology (Vietnam). His research interests include innovation and entrepreneurship, sustainability and development.

Cheree Topple is the Deputy Chair of Management and Marketing at Swinburne University of Technology in Melbourne, Australia. Her research interests span issues of human resource development and sustainability, with recent publications in *Environmental Impact Assessment Review*, *Transnational Corporations* and *Impact Assessment and Project Appraisal*.

Gerrit A. de Waal is a Senior Lecturer in Entrepreneurship and Innovation at RMIT University in Melbourne, Australia. His current research is in frugal innovation, having published in *R&D Management*, *IEEE Transactions on Engineering Management* and the *International Journal of Innovation Management*.

Eryadi K. Masli is a Lecturer in Entrepreneurship and Innovation at Swinburne University of Technology, Melbourne, Australia. He was a former investment banker, working across Southeast Asia. He is also a Principal Advisor to MANIFEX, a private equity fund. His research interests include start-up funding and innovation.

Routledge Advances in Management and Business Studies

For more information about this series, please visit www.routledge.com/Routledge-Advances-in-Management-and-Business-Studies/book-series/SE0305

Frugal Innovation and the New Product Development Process

Insights from Indonesia

Stephanie B.M. Cadeddu,
Jerome D. Donovan,
Cheree Topple,
Gerrit A. de Waal and
Eryadi K. Masli

Routledge
Taylor & Francis Group

LONDON AND NEW YORK

First published 2019
by Routledge
2 Park Square, Milton Park, Abingdon, Oxon OX14 4RN

and by Routledge
52 Vanderbilt Avenue, New York, NY 10017

First issued in paperback 2020

Routledge is an imprint of the Taylor & Francis Group, an informa business

British Library Cataloguing-in-Publication Data
A catalogue record for this book is available from the British Library

Library of Congress Cataloging-in-Publication Data
Names: Cadeddu, Stephanie B. M., author.
Title: Frugal innovation and the new product development process : insights from Indonesia / by Stephanie B.M. Cadeddu [and four others].
Description: Abingdon, Oxon ; New York, NY : Routledge, 2019. | Series: Routledge advances in management and business studies ; 81
Identifiers: LCCN 2018045821 | ISBN 9780367029319 (hardback) | ISBN 9780429000980 (ebook)
Subjects: LCSH: New products—Indonesia. | Low-income consumers—Indonesia. | Technological innovations—Economic aspects—Indonesia.
Classification: LCC HF5415.153 .C33 2019 | DDC 658.5/75—dc23
LC record available at https://lccn.loc.gov/2018045821

ISBN 13: 978-0-367-66268-4 (pbk)
ISBN 13: 978-0-367-02931-9 (hbk)

Typeset in Galliard
by Apex CoVantage, LLC

Contents

Figures

Tables

Acknowledgements

This book is based on a study conducted into two Indonesian start-ups in 2015. We would like to thank the participants of this study who were so willing to open their doors, share their personal insights and provide detailed feedback to a series of follow-ups we have had with them in developing this book. Thank you to both Prime Cookstoves and Tirta Indonesia Mandiri Foundation for their time and effort.

We would also like to thank Pak Bens P. and his wife as well as Anti and Yulius for facilitating the research journey in Indonesia. Your support has made this book possible, and we deeply appreciate your willingness to help. Similarly, we wish to acknowledge the Indonesian Danone Institute Foundation and their financial support that also made the field research in Indonesia possible.

1 Base-of-the-pyramid markets and the need for frugal innovation

Introduction

> Poverty is not just a lack of money; it is not having the capability to realize one's full potential as a human being.
>
> (Sen 1999)

Base-of-the-pyramid (BOP) markets are mass markets in developing countries where at least four billion people, despite low disposable incomes, are inclined to buy new products to improve their everyday lives (Banerjee & Duflo 2011; Pitta, Subrahmanyan & Tomas Gomez-Arias 2008; Prahalad 2012; Tiwari, Fischer & Kalogerakis 2016). Developing and emerging countries such as India, China, Brazil, South Africa or Indonesia have these mass markets who need product innovations related to basic health, food and water, housing, sanitation and/or education needs (Alkire 2002; Cadeddu et al. 2016; Prahalad 2009).

Offering new market opportunities, Western and emerging market firms such as General Electric, Godrej and Boyce, Tata Group and Jaipur Foot have been tapping into these under-served billions of BOP consumers (Agarwal et al. 2017; Govindarajan & Trimble 2013). These firms have also faced significant challenges in altering products, practices and processes to suit these markets (Prahalad 2012; Simanis 2012; Subramaniam, Ernst & Dubiel 2015; Winter & Govindarajan 2015). One particular reason for this is BOP consumers do not necessarily want cheaper and simplified premium products, as often thought; they generally have preferences for better, pricier and more suitable products and services to address their needs (London 2016; Nakata 2012; Subrahmanyan & Tomas Gomez-Arias 2008).

To reach these consumers, modern new product development (NPD) trends are emerging from these firms' practices. The literature discussing one of the most relevant NPD approaches in these new socio-economic contexts in developing countries[1] points to frugal innovation (e.g. Pisoni, Michelini & Martignoni 2018; Radjou & Prabhu 2014; Rao 2014; Weyrauch & Herstatt 2017). Frugal innovation aims to develop new products characterised by their affordability, usability, durability and core functionality, which offer alternative solutions to existing products that are incompatible with BOP markets' needs (Petrick & Jun-tiwasarakij 2011; Weyrauch & Herstatt 2017).

A well-known example illustrating the suitability of frugal innovation NPD for BOP markets in developing countries is Godrej and Boyce's ChotuKool, an alternative to standardised refrigerators that are generally too expensive and unsuitable for Indian BOP consumers. The ChotuKool cooling device is highly suitable to these consumers as it is affordable (nearly 70 USD) and can store food and water for up to seven days without electricity. The ChotuKool is also portable, allowing transportable fresh water in rural areas, and fits into Indian BOP consumers' houses (Agnihotri 2015; ChotuKool 2014).

The success of these frugal innovations' NPD not only comes from their performance and suitability to local BOP markets but also stems from these firms' different approaches to the NPD process (NPDP). In particular, this study highlights that these successful NPD in BOP markets is reliant not only on a firm's ability to provide such innovation, but also on different NPD management practices throughout firms' NPDP (Cunha et al. 2014; Pisoni, Michelini & Martignoni 2018; Radjou & Prabhu 2015; Zeschky, Winterhalter & Gassmann 2014). The next section discusses how frugal innovation and the NPDP are two fields that, when connected, clarify on the key decisions, tools and techniques necessary for the NPDP of frugal innovation, addressing BOP consumers' needs.

NPD process (NPDP) and frugal innovation

The main question has shifted from why firms should innovate to how to innovate and adapt practices to the socio-economic context of developing countries. These alterations generally occurring in the context of innovation management practices emphasised firms' NPDP as one of the most influencing factors for successful NPD (Barczak, Griffin & Kahn 2009; Markham & Lee 2013). Trott (2012) reinforced this, arguing that effective management practices have a critical effect on the direction and likely efficiency of firms' processes. Actually, many studies have defined best-practice NPD as inclusive of NPDP aspects (e.g. Barczak, Griffin & Kahn 2009; Cooper 2013).

Yet while such NPD practices are well-researched, these studies have generally occurred in the context of high-income markets in developed countries. This leads to most well-established NPDP models integrating theories and practices based on high-income market contexts that are not necessarily suitable to guide firms innovate for BOP markets in developing countries (Le Bas 2016a; Radjou, Prabhu & Ahuja 2012; Viswanathan & Sridharan 2012).

Many scholars (e.g. Prahalad 2012; Radjou & Prabhu 2015; Viswanathan & Sridharan 2012) highlight the necessity to modify firms' traditional mindset when undertaking NPDP for BOP markets, including the process by which the innovation is "conceived of, executed, and delivered" (Petrick & Juntiwasarakij 2011, p. 24). Léger and Swaminathan (2007, p. 22) proposed "the innovation process could follow a different pattern in developing countries". Frugal innovation literature suggests such NPD approaches are emerging from a market-driven process comprising cheaper, simpler and resource-constrained innovation activities (Cunha et al. 2014; Sehgal, Dehoff & Panneer 2010).

One of the main reasons suggested by Radjou and Prabhu (2014) is traditional NPDP approaches are "bloated Western innovation model[s] [that are] . . . wasteful and out of sync with market realities", and in particular for BOP markets. Indeed, the NPDP for frugal products involves significant adjustments for these consumers' needs. It includes products' attributes and features as well as development, manufacturing and delivery processes, which challenge the argument that only de-featuring premium products addresses poor people's needs (Anderson & Markides 2007; Pisoni, Michelini & Martignoni 2018; Sehgal, Dehoff & Panneer 2010).

Despite such assertions, little research has explored the NPDP for BOP markets in developing countries (Lee et al. 2011; Subramaniam, Ernst & Dubiel 2015). Correspondingly, Cunha et al. (2014, p. 2) asserted that "[p]roduct innovation in resource-poor environments is as old as creativity itself, but as an academic field it is nascent and immature". Agarwal et al. (2017, p. 11) recently highlighted gaps between NPDP for BOP markets and relevant industry research:

> The ambiguity in the prescriptive variables exhibits limited research focus on the innovation process and different means or approaches toward achieving the required product characteristics.

Within this context, this raises questions on whether the current body of knowledge provides sufficient guidelines for academics and practitioners to drive successfully the NPDP for frugal innovation in BOP markets. The following section discusses a promising NPDP framework for frugal innovation from two key research areas, which highlights the importance of NPDP as a management practices for successful innovation.

NPDP framework for frugal innovation

New contexts of innovation often destabilise firms' conventional ways of innovating (Sharma & Jha 2016), as they are required to move away from well-known practices (Le Bas 2016a; Nobelius 2004). This is especially true when undertaking NPD for BOP markets in developing countries (Ernst et al. 2015; Nakata 2012). Some scholars support that if a firm is willing to address BOP markets' needs, numerous changes must be considered at its NPDP level (Léger & Swaminathan 2007; Radjou & Prabhu 2014; Sharma & Jha 2016). For example, in comparison with NPDP for high-income markets, using traditional market research or relying on existing infrastructure is not appropriate when targeting BOP markets (Prahalad 2012; Ramamurti & Singh 2009).

As frugal innovation literature has an increasing prominence in the innovation management field, the need for further studies to examine concepts, theories and practices of frugal innovators' NPDP has thus become evident. Few scholars (e.g. Radjou & Prabhu 2015; Viswanathan & Sridharan 2012; Zeschky,

Winterhalter & Gassmann 2014) have given attention to how to manage the development of a frugal innovation, though there is poor research on the management of frugal innovation from a new idea to a final scalable frugal product structured around NPDP (Agarwal et al. 2017; Subramaniam, Ernst & Dubiel 2015). This underpins the focus of this study, including the focus on developing a NPDP framework for frugal innovation.

In this vein, Ulrich (2011, p. 395) suggests developing NPDP models by "focusing on what decisions must be made, and then consider what information, perspectives, and tools are most relevant to those decisions". To help understand the decisions made and tools used by frugal innovators across their NPDP, a consolidated NPDP framework is built through existing conceptualisations of NPDP models and well-established cross-functional activities embedded within phases and stages. While this framework acknowledges existing holistic models, it is not supposed to be comprehensive; it leverages the most common NPDP stages only. This search has included literature in relation to firms' NPDP decisions serving developed countries, related to product innovation management, R&D management, engineering and design, marketing and operation management.

Figure 1.1 depicts the basis of this study's consolidated NPDP framework upon which frugal innovation literature has been mapped out in Chapter 3. This consolidated NPDP provides a broad structure of the four NPDP phases and nine

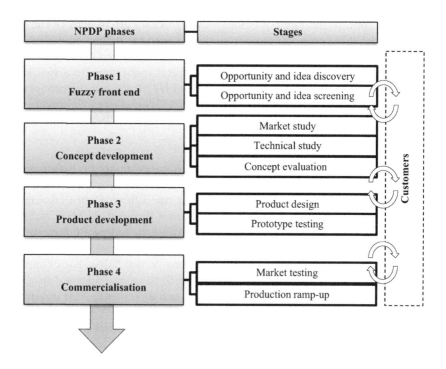

Figure 1.1 Consolidated NPDP: four phases and nine stages

associated stages involved in the management of NPD to build the basis for the NPDP for frugal innovation. Chapter 3 provides more details about the stages characteristics, tools and techniques that portray the specificities of each stage.

The use of tools and techniques was included as, in practice, these are not exclusive from decision-making such as decisions related to design (Lutters et al. 2014). The multidisciplinary character of NPDP is also observed across different activities, for example marketing activities at the market study stage, or engineering activities at the product design stage in Figure 1.1. Furthermore, the iterative nature of NPDP is represented by circulating arrows, allowing back and forth iteration as the most recent NPDP models suggest.

Chapter 3 will establish the basis for this study's NPDP framework for frugal innovation, which is further explored through two Indonesian case studies in Chapter 4 and Chapter 5. To establish this NPDP framework, the frugal innovation literature is mapped on the consolidated NPDP. By mapping out the frugal innovation literature in the consolidated NPDP framework, the outcome is the development of 15 key frugal innovation practices to examine related to the decisions, tools and techniques preferred by frugal innovators. Frugal innovators in this study focused on those within developing and emerging countries, as these countries have often been observed as innovation hubs where such new products can emerge (Agarwal et al. 2017; Lee et al. 2011; Prahalad 2012). In particular, Indonesia is this study's key focus due to its highly relevant settings detailed ahead.

Indonesia: a potential frugal innovation hub

Indonesia stands out as the largest economy in the Association of Southeast Asian Nations (ASEAN) and also ranks as the world's tenth largest economy (based on Purchasing Power Parity, or PPP) (Asian Development Bank 2017; World Bank 2017e). Indonesia Gross Domestic Product (GDP) per capita was about 830 USD in 2002 and had risen to nearly 3,570 USD in 2016 (World Bank 2017b). Indonesia has moved from being a developing country to standing up as an emerging market due to shifting its focus on increasing the population's well-being and seeking to become more industrialised (Amadeo 2018).

The economic growth illustrates not only the potential of this market, but also its innovation prospects. Indonesia is not without its own challenges either, being the fourth most populated country in the world with more than 260 million inhabitants (CIA 2017; World Bank 2017e) and more than 31 per cent still live on less than 3.20 USD a day (as per 2011 PPP) in 2016 (World Bank 2017a). Poverty is decreasing, however, with the population living under the national poverty line (below 0.82 USD) representing more than 43 million of the population (16.6 per cent) in 2007, decreasing to around 27.5 million (10.64 per cent) in 2017 (Central Statistics Agency BPS 2017; World Bank 2017c). While poverty is decreasing, the amount of people living under the national poverty line remains relatively high as well as the next level of 'near-poor' represent almost 40 per cent of the Indonesian population (approximately 104 million) (World Bank 2017a).

This suggests that firms targeting the Indonesian BOP market should embed cost constraints in their NPD, which is a major characteristic of frugal innovation being affordable.

Furthermore, a high number of Indonesians who have low disposable income also encounter difficulties addressing their basic needs (UNDP 2015; World Bank 2017a). While the 16,000 islands that constitute Indonesian geography bring up complex problems of infrastructure (Prasetya 2017), another challenge is the large proportion of the population living in rural areas. These people account for approximately 45 per cent of the total inhabitants, according to the World Bank (2017d). In the aim to address rural and related problems such as difficult access to institutional and basic needs, the Indonesian Government implemented a development plan with a focus on education and healthcare issues related to those with low-income and living in rural areas (World Bank 2017e). This implies that the low-income and rural population not only create cost constraints on innovators, but also their geographical and institutional constraints, like under-developed healthcare, water access, sanitation or education, require NPD to embed more than just affordability features. With such constraints on firms innovating in Indonesia, it is critical that innovation also responds to Indonesia's environment with accessible, durable and usable products like the concept of frugal innovation offers.

With this in mind, frugal innovation appears as an appropriate NPD approach that could support to meet the Indonesian population's basic needs. In particular, frugal offers a distinct opportunity to address the challenges in Indonesia with a focus on low-income and rural population's basic needs. Two distinct problems experienced by this group in Indonesia are the toxic smoke emitted by stoves used for cooking and heating homes, and the difficult access to clean drinking water. Despite the necessity to address these issues, alternative solutions have been difficult to develop in Indonesia, implying that there are significant opportunities for frugal innovation locally. The next two sections discuss these problems and how frugal innovation could address this issue.

Frugal cooking appliances

The World Health Organization (WHO) (2016) identifies that nearly three billion people cook and heat their homes using open fires or traditional stoves. These are run on solid biomass such as wood, dung and coconut shells. These methods are, however, highly toxic and have created significant health risks due to air pollution that is detrimental for households exposed to stoves' smoke (WHO 2016; World Bank 2015).

Looking at Indonesia, almost 40 per cent of the rural and peri-urban Indonesian population (about 24.5 million households) are biomass users, which the related cooking appliance have shown to be responsible for nearly 165,000 deaths every year (ASTAE [Asia Sustainable and Alternative Energy Program] 2013). Initiatives from the Indonesian government, such as the 2008 conversion program changing kerosene to LPG fuel and stoves, show clear support to address costs and health issues related to cooking habits in Indonesia (Afrida 2010). The aim was to offer a LPG stove and subsidise a 3kg gas bottle.

However, at the initial stage of the program, subsidised LPG bottles were not extended outside the major areas of Java Island (Pertamina & WLPGA 2015), making subsidised LPG spread unevenly around Indonesia. Additionally, a growing number of deadly explosions emerged from using the LPG stoves, which was mainly due to lack of product training, leading people to fear the use of these products. Finally, the Government's program also had limited funding. This meant that subsidies for the gas bottle would reduce substantially over time, leaving low-income and rural people with an unsustainable solution to toxic cooking (IEA 2015).

The Indonesian Government also decided to explore alternatives options to LPG stoves in 2009, which opened the doors for NPD in clean biomass cookstove. In fact, a more recent World Bank initiative, the Clean Stove Initiative, has encouraged the development of more efficient and less toxic cookstove products (World Bank 2014). As a result, numerous firms have initiated the development and the scaling of several thousand of their new improved cookstoves, such as Prime cookstoves, Envirofit, Philips cookstove, Xunda Field Dragon, Rocket Works Rocket Stove and Ace 1.

Among these new products, Prime Cookstoves is one of the main successful firms, achieving product entry in the Indonesian BOP market and at the international level. The stoves developed by Prime Cookstoves are clean and energy-efficient with low CO_2 emissions, operating on top-lit updraft (TLUD) technology that uses "preheating, counter-flow and co-firing burning mechanism" (Primestoves 2017). It can be fuelled with a wide variety of wood biomass such as coconut shell, wood sticks or agricultural by-products. Prime cookstoves also have all the qualifying characteristics to be classified as frugal innovation (see Chapter 4 for further details). The successful entry and market adoption of Prime cookstoves as a frugal innovation is evidence of the presence and compatibility of frugal innovation for the Indonesian BOP market.

With a focus on low-income and rural population's basic needs, another distinct problem experienced by this group in Indonesia is the difficult access to clean drinking water. While solutions to address this basic human right are increasing around the world, there are huge opportunities for frugal innovation in Indonesia due to its unique settings, with a variety of water problems across the numerous Indonesian islands. The next section discusses problems related to available water filter devices in Indonesia and how frugal innovation could address this issue.

Frugal drinking appliances

Turning to the issue of accessing clean water, the United Nations General Assembly (2010) has recently recognised this as a basic human right. Despite this recognition, the prevalence of this global challenge is evident with some 2.1 billion people lacking access to "safely managed drinking water services" (WHO/

UNICEF 2017). It is estimated that over 1.8 billion people drink water contaminated with faecal matter (Bain et al. 2014), with approximately 340,000 children under 5 years old dying annually in 2013 from associated illnesses including diarrheal diseases (WHO 2015).

In Indonesia alone, the number of children dying under 5 years old is staggering, with some 150,000 children dying every year; no access to clean drinking water is a key cause (UNICEF 2014). In 2018, there are still 3.4 million Indonesian people lacking access to safe water (DFAT 2018). The Asian Development Bank (2016) pinpointed that the role of water access related to the well-being of Indonesian people and has been added as one of the key priorities in preparing the Masterplan for the Acceleration and Expansion of Indonesia Economic Development, 2011–2025 (MP3EI). According to WHO/UNICEF (2017), Indonesia is one of the key countries that is on track to reach universal basic water services by 2030.

The ability to access clean water has been established under the sixth Sustainable Development Goals (United Nations 2018), with the number of people accessing clean water in Indonesia clearly increasing within the last few years (Patunru 2015). Nonetheless, low-income people find it difficult to acquire safe water, in particular in Indonesia where there are poorly managed drinking water services. Low-income families have access to other options, such as boiling water or buying refill water, which, however, raise their daily expenses (Prathama 2018).

With the aim to address this basic human right, a number of solutions have appeared in Indonesia such as the Tirta CupuManik (TCM) water filter, Nazava water filter, Pureit and Folia Water. The TCM water filter has emerged as one of the key devices, with a silver enhanced ceramic 'pot' water filter produced locally that is affordable and can be used at home and filter up to 99.88 per cent of bacteria. The TCM water filter has also been developed in collaboration with the Ministry of Research & Technology (Indonesia). The TCM water filter is classified as a frugal innovation by its qualifying characteristics (see Chapter 5 for further details). This book thus focuses on these two case studies in Indonesia in these two product categories, cooking appliances and water filters, with the next section detailing the research strategy underpinning this study.

Case study research approach

This exploratory study seeks to illustrate management practices undertaken by frugal innovators throughout all different NPDP stages. In particular, this book identifies and explores the key decisions, tools and techniques of frugal innovators across the nine stages of the NPDP. With this in mind, a case study strategy has been chosen with a single-level firm analysis and with the frugal innovators' NPDP as the unit of analysis. Such a strategy allows in-depth digging into 'how' a phenomenon occurs, in other words how firms develop frugal products for the BOP markets in developing countries. Through this approach, this study investigates the decision-makers' choices throughout the various NPDP phases and stages.

As the focus of this study is on firms' developing new frugal products, the sample chosen, refined through purposive sampling, led to the identification of two start-up firms in Indonesia that have developed a frugal innovation – Prime Cookstoves and Tirta Indonesia Mandiri Foundation. As a result of this in-depth case study approach, there were six observational visits as well as 13 interviews with managers across key functional areas – top management, production manager, marketing manager, product development manager and additional ones across logistics, product testing, sales management and distribution, including product trainers.

While more organisations could have been suitable, the choice of two local firms provides a unique and richer basis to comprehend and illuminate the NPDP framework for frugal innovation. This allows the comprehensive investigation and documentation of each element of the four NPDP phases. A final considera-tion as part of this study's methodology is to ensure a careful assessment of qual-ity criteria in relation to qualitative studies.

Book structure

This book is structured in six chapters. This chapter, Chapter 1 – "Base-of-the-pyramid markets and the need for frugal innovation" – introduces the background to this study, including the relevance of frugal innovation to NPD adapted to BOP markets in developing countries. This chapter has also introduced Indonesia as a potential innovation hub, in particular highlighting problems with cooking and drinking appliances, which frugal innovation has the potential to address. The significance of this study was also justified in this chapter, highlighting a general lack of research on frugal innovation from a NPDP lens, an influencing factor for firms' success.

Chapter 2 – "Critical reflections on the state of innovation research" – provides a broad overview of past and more contemporary innovation research by review-ing the innovation literature refined to NPD and the NPDP literature for the last 60 years. This section leads to the development of a consolidated NPDP frame-work and creates the foundations of the NPDP framework for frugal innovation which will be discussed in Chapter 3. The final section of this chapter defines fru-gal innovation and questions how such innovations are developed, highlighting a critical area to investigate linked to the NPDP for frugal innovation.

Chapter 3 – "Mapping NPDP for frugal innovation" – proposes a NPDP framework for frugal innovation, which is the underpinning basis of this study. The framework for frugal innovation is developed by leveraging the four NPDP phases and associated nine stages, including characteristics, tools and techniques of the consolidated NPDP for developed countries. This chapter contextual-ises frugal innovation and identifies frugal innovators' management preferences across their NPDP (using conceptual and frugal case studies). This results in 15 key areas to examine that present essential managerial practices at each NPDP stage. This chapter concludes with an overview of the methodology and research approach utilised in this study.

Chapter 4 – "Prime Cookstoves: cooking with frugal innovation" – investigates and documents the frugal innovation practices of Prime Cookstoves in their development of the Prime cookstove cooking device. This chapter is structured around each phase of the NPDP and the 15 key areas as identified in Chapter 3. This provides valuable insights into the practices, decision-making dilemmas and context for the development of the Prime cookstove. It provides a roadmap for frugal innovators on how to better structure and develop frugal products to address BOP consumers' needs.

Chapter 5 – "Tirta Indonesia Mandiri Foundation: drinking with frugal innovation" – is similarly structured like the Prime Cookstoves chapter, examining each phase of the NPDP and the 15 key areas identified in Chapter 3. This provides additional insights into the practices, decision-making dilemmas and context for the development of the TCM water filter. This provides a comparative case study for examining frugal innovators practices, extending from the first case study on Prime Cookstoves.

Chapter 6 – "The NPDP for frugal innovation" – integrates Prime Cookstoves' and Tirta Indonesia Mandiri Foundation's management practices and insights from their frugal innovation experiences and the frugal innovation literature, and reinforces the role and elements of each phase of the NPDP framework for frugal innovation. It brings together the evidence and insights from not only Prime Cookstoves' and Tirta Indonesia Mandiri Foundation's activities and decision-making, but also the broader sample of case studies referred to within this study. It reinforces the "Roadmap of NPDP for Frugal Innovation" developed in Chapter 3. Following the development of this model, utilising both deductive and inductive methods, this chapter reviews some of the key limitations from this study focusing on two case studies within Indonesia. This chapter concludes with a discussion of the NPDP framework for frugal innovation, limitations of this research, theoretical and practical implications and further research opportunities.

Note

1 And more recently researched in the developed countries (Bhatti et al. 2017; Le Bas 2016b).

References

Afrida, N 2010, 'Recall pressure mounts as more injured in LPG explosions', *The Jakarta Post*, viewed 4 December 2016, <www.thejakartapost.com/news/2010/07/03/recall-pressure-mounts-more-injured-lpg-explosions.html>.

Agarwal, N, Grottke, M, Mishra, S & Brem, A 2017, 'A systematic literature review of constraint-based innovations: State of the art and future perspectives', *IEEE Transactions on Engineering Management*, vol. 64, no. 1, pp. 3–15.

Agnihotri, A 2015, 'Low-cost innovation in emerging markets', *Journal of Strategic Marketing*, vol. 23, no. 5, pp. 399–411.

Alkire, S 2002, 'Dimensions of human development', *World Development*, vol. 30, no. 2, pp. 181–205.

Amadeo 2018, *What are emerging markets? Five defining characteristics*, viewed 28 April 2018, <www.thebalance.com/what-are-emerging-markets-3305927>.

Anderson, J & Markides, C 2007, 'Strategic innovation and the base of the pyramid', *MIT Sloan Management Review*, vol. 49, no. 1, pp. 82–88.

Asian Development Bank 2016, *Indonesia country water assessment*, Manilla, Philippines, Asian Development Bank, viewed 1 September 2018, <www.adb.org/sites/default/files/institutional-document/183339/ino-water-assessment.pdf>.

Asian Development Bank 2017, *Indonesia and ADB*, viewed 15 January 2018, <www.adb.org/countries/indonesia/main>.

ASTAE (Asia Sustainable and Alternative Energy Program) 2013, *Indonesia: Toward universal access to clean cooking*, East Asia and Pacific Clean Stove Initiative Series, World Bank, Washington, DC.

Bain, R, Cronk, R, Wright, J, Yang, H, Slaymaker, T & Bartram, J 2014, 'Fecal contamination of drinking-water in low-and middle-income countries: A systematic review and meta-analysis', *PLoS Medicine*, vol. 11, no. 5, p. e1001644.

Banerjee, AV & Duflo, E 2011, *Poor economics: A radical rethinking of the way to fight global poverty*, Public Affairs, New York.

Barczak, G, Griffin, A & Kahn, KB 2009, 'Perspective: Trends and drivers of success in NPD practices: Results of the 2003 PDMA best practices study*', *Journal of Product Innovation Management*, vol. 26, no. 1, pp. 3–23.

Bhatti, YA, Prime, M, Harris, M, Wadge, H, McQueen, J, Patel, H, Carter, AW, Parston, G & Darzi, A 2017, 'The search for the holy grail: Frugal innovation in healthcare from low-income or middle-income countries for reverse innovation to developed countries', *BMJ Innovations*, vol. 3, no. 4, pp. 1–9.

Cadeddu, SBM, Donovan, JD, de Waal, GA, Masli, EK & Topple, C 2016, 'Frugal innovation and the new product development process', ISPIM Innovation Symposium, The International Society for Professional Innovation Management (ISPIM), 1.

Central Statistics Agency (BPS) 2017, *The overview of poverty in Indonesia on March 2017*, viewed 12 January 2018, <www.bps.go.id/website/brs_eng/brsEng-2017 0717114702.pdf>.

ChotuKool 2014, *Evolution of ChotuKool*, viewed 10 November 2018, <http://chotu kool.com/evolution_chotuKool.aspx>.

CIA 2017, *The World Factbook. East & Southeast Asia – Indonesia*, Central Intelligence Agency, viewed 11 November 2018, <https://www.cia.gov/library/publications/the-world-factbook/geos/print_id.html>.

Cooper, RG 2013, 'New products: What separates the winners from the losers and what drives success', in KB Kahn, *PDMA handbook of new product development*, 3rd edn, John Wiley & Sons, Hoboken, NJ, pp. 3–34.

Cunha, MPE, Rego, A, Oliveira, P, Rosado, P & Habib, N 2014, 'Product innovation in resource-poor environments: Three research streams', *Journal of Product Innovation Management*, vol. 31, no. 2, pp. 202–210.

DFAT 2018, *Increasing access to clean water and sanitation in Indonesia*, viewed 10 August 2018, <https://dfat.gov.au/aid/who-we-work-with/ngos/ancp/news/Pages/increasing-access-to-clean-water-and-sanitation-in-indonesia.aspx>.

Ernst, H, Kahle, HN, Dubiel, A, Prabhu, J & Subramaniam, M 2015, 'The antecedents and consequences of affordable value innovations for emerging markets', *Journal of Product Innovation Management*, vol. 32, no. 1, pp. 65–79.

Govindarajan, V & Trimble, C 2013, *Reverse innovation: Create far from home, win everywhere*, Harvard Business Review Press.

IEA 2015, *Energy and climate change*, International Energy Agency, viewed 5 October 2017, <www.iea.org/publications/freepublications/publication/WEO2015Spe cialReportonEnergyandClimateChange.pdf>.

Le Bas, C 2016a, 'Frugal innovation, sustainable innovation, reverse innovation: Why do they look alike? Why are they different?' *Journal of Innovation Economics & Management*, vol. 21, no. 3, pp. 9–26.

Le Bas, C 2016b, 'The importance and relevance of frugal innovation to developed markets: Milestones towards the economics of frugal innovation', *Journal of Innovation Economics & Management*, no. 3, pp. 3–8.

Lee, Y, Lin, BW, Wong, YY & Calantone, RJ 2011, 'Understanding and managing international product launch: A comparison between developed and emerging markets', *Journal of Product Innovation Management*, vol. 28, no. s1, pp. 104–120.

Léger, A & Swaminathan, S 2007, 'Innovation theories: Relevance and implications for developing country innovation', *IDEAS Working Paper Series from RePEc*, vol. 743, no. DIW Discussion Papers.

London, T 2016, *The base of the pyramid promise: Building businesses with impact and scale*, Stanford University Press, Stanford.

Lutters, E, van Houten, FJAM, Bernard, A, Mermoz, E & Schutte, CSL 2014, 'Tools and techniques for product design', *CIRP Annals – Manufacturing Technology*, vol. 63, no. 2, pp. 607–630.

Markham, SK & Lee, H 2013, 'Product development and management association's 2012 comparative performance assessment study', *Journal of Product Innovation Management*, vol. 30, no. 3, pp. 408–429.

Nakata, C 2012, 'From the special issue editor: Creating new products and services for and with the base of the pyramid', *Journal of Product Innovation Management*, vol. 29, no. 1, pp. 3–5.

Nobelius, D 2004, 'Towards the sixth generation of R&D management', *International Journal of Project Management*, vol. 22, no. 5, pp. 369–375.

Patunru, AA 2015, 'Access to safe drinking water and sanitation in Indonesia', *Asia & the Pacific Policy Studies*, vol. 2, no. 2, pp. 234–244.

Pertamina & WLPGA 2015, *Kerosene to LP gas conversion programme in Indonesia: A case study of domestic energy*, viewed 7 February 2018, <www.wlpga.org/wp-content/uploads/2015/09/kerosene-to-lp-gas-conversion-programme-in-indonesia.pdf>.

Petrick, IJ & Juntiwasarakij, S 2011, 'The rise of the rest: Hotbeds of innovation in emerging markets', *Research Technology Management*, vol. 54, no. 4, pp. 24–29.

Pisoni, A, Michelini, L & Martignoni, G 2018, 'Frugal approach to innovation: State of the art and future perspectives', *Journal of Cleaner Production*, vol. 171, no. Supplement C, pp. 107–126.

Pitta, D, Subrahmanyan, S & Tomas Gomez-Arias, J 2008, 'Integrated approach to understanding consumer behavior at bottom of pyramid', *Journal of Consumer Marketing*, vol. 25, no. 7, pp. 402–412.

Prahalad, CK 2009, *The fortune at the bottom of the pyramid, revised and updated 5th anniversary edition: Eradicating poverty through profits*, FT Press.

Prahalad, CK 2012, 'Bottom of the pyramid as a source of breakthrough innovations', *Journal of Product Innovation Management*, vol. 29, no. 1, pp. 6–12.

Prasetya, E 2017, *Of 17,504 Islands in Indonesia, 16,056 have been UN verified*, viewed <www.merdeka.com/peristiwa/dari-17504-pulau-di-indonesia-16056-telah-diverifikasi-pbb.html>.

Prathama, KA 2018, *Testing the waters for affordable water filters in Indonesia*, viewed 1 September 2018, <https://kopernik.info/en/news-events/news/testing-the-waters-for-affordable-water-filters-in-indonesia>.

Primestoves 2017, *Prime cookstoves, highly efficient, ultra clean biomass cookstoves: Product specifications*, viewed 2 December 2017, <www.primestoves.com/img/docs/product%20spec%20sheet_2.2_low.pdf>.

Radjou, N & Prabhu, J 2014, '4 CEOs who are making frugal innovation work', *Harvard Business Review*, vol. 11, no. 4.

Radjou, N & Prabhu, J 2015, *Frugal innovation: How to do more with less*, Profile Books, London.

Radjou, N, Prabhu, J & Ahuja, S 2012, *Jugaad innovation: Think frugal, be flexible, generate breakthrough growth*, John Wiley & Sons, Inc.

Ramamurti, R & Singh, JV 2009, *Emerging multinationals in emerging markets*, Cambridge University Press.

Rao, BC 2014, 'Alleviating poverty in the twenty-first century through frugal innovations', *Challenge*, vol. 57, no. 3, pp. 40–59.

Sehgal, V, Dehoff, K & Panneer, G 2010, 'The importance of frugal engineering', *Strategy + Business*, Summer, no. 59, pp. 1–4.

Sen, A 1999, *Development as freedom*, Knopf, New York.

Sharma, A & Jha, S 2016, 'Innovation from emerging market firms: What happens when market ambitions meet technology challenges?' *Journal of Business & Industrial Marketing*, vol. 31, no. 4, pp. 507–518.

Simanis, E 2012, 'Reality check at the bottom of the pyramid', *Harvard Business Review*, vol. 90, no. 6, pp. 120–124.

Subrahmanyan, S & Tomas Gomez-Arias, J 2008, 'Integrated approach to understanding consumer behavior at bottom of pyramid', *Journal of Consumer Marketing*, vol. 25, no. 7, pp. 402–412.

Subramaniam, M, Ernst, H & Dubiel, A 2015, 'From the special issue editors: Innovations for and from emerging markets', *Journal of Product Innovation Management*, vol. 32, no. 1, pp. 5–11.

Tiwari, R, Fischer, L & Kalogerakis, K 2016, 'Frugal innovation in scholarly and social discourse: An assessment of trends and potential societal implications', Joint working paper of Fraunhofer MOEZ Leipzig and Hamburg University of Technology in the BMBF-ITA project, Leipzig, Hamburg.

Trott, P 2012, *Innovation management and new product development*, 5th edn., Financial Times, Prentice Hall, Harlow.

Ulrich, KT 2011, 'Design is everything?' *Journal of Product Innovation Management*, vol. 28, no. 3, pp. 394–398.

UNDP 2015, *About Indonesia*, viewed 2 February 2018, <www.id.undp.org/content/indonesia/en/home/countryinfo.html>.

UNICEF 2014, *Water and sanitation: Challenges*, viewed 7 August 2018, <www.unicef.org/indonesia/wes.html>.

United Nations 2018, *Sustainable development goal 6: Ensure availability and sustainable management of water and sanitation for all*, viewed 15 August 2018, <https://sustainabledevelopment.un.org/sdg6>.

United Nations General Assembly 2010, *General assembly adopts resolution recognizing access to clean water, sanitation as human right, by recorded vote of 122 in favour, none against, 41 abstentions*, viewed 8 August 2018.

Viswanathan, M & Sridharan, S 2012, 'Product development for the BoP: Insights on concept and prototype development from university-based student projects in India', *Journal of Product Innovation Management*, vol. 29, no. 1, pp. 52–69.

Weyrauch, T & Herstatt, C 2017, 'What is frugal innovation? Three defining criteria', *Journal of Frugal Innovation*, vol. 2, no. 1, pp. 1–17.

WHO 2015, *Key facts from JMP 2015 report*, viewed 1 September 2018, <www.who.int/water_sanitation_health/publications/JMP-2015-keyfacts-en-rev.pdf>.

WHO 2016, *Household (Indoor) air pollution*, viewed 2 April 2018, <www.who.int/indoorair/en/>.

WHO/UNICEF 2017, *Progress on drinking water, sanitation and hygiene 2017: Update and SDG baselines*, viewed 8 August 2018, <www.who.int/mediacentre/news/releases/2017/launch-version-report-jmp-water-sanitation-hygiene.pdf>.

Winter, A & Govindarajan, V 2015, 'Engineering reverse innovations: Principles for creating successful products for emerging markets', *Harvard Business Review*, vol. 93, no. 7–8, pp. 80–89.

World Bank 2014, *Cleaner cook stoves for a healthier Indonesia*, viewed 28 April 2018, <www.worldbank.org/en/news/feature/2014/11/03/cleaner-cook-stoves-for-a-healthier-indonesia>.

World Bank 2015, *Social marketing plan for Indonesia clean stove initiative results based financing pilot program*, viewed 28 April 2018, <http://documents.worldbank.org/curated/en/510701468040586520/pdf/939180BRI0Box30ative0marketing0plan.pdf>.

World Bank 2017a, *Country poverty brief East Asia & Pacific: Indonesia*, viewed 15 January 2018, <http://databank.worldbank.org/data/download/poverty/B2A3A7F5-706A-4522-AF99-5B1800FA3357/9FE8B43A-5EAE-4F36-8838-E9F58200CF49/60C691C8-EAD0-47BE-9C8A-B56D672A29F7/Global_POV_SP_CPB_IDN.pdf>.

World Bank 2017b, *GDP per capita (current US$)*, viewed 2 February 2018, <https://data.worldbank.org/indicator/NY.GDP.PCAP.CD?locations=ID>.

World Bank 2017c, *Poverty headcount ratio at national poverty lines (% of population)*, viewed 15 January 2018, <https://data.worldbank.org/indicator/SI.POV.NAHC?locations=ID>.

World Bank 2017d, *Rural population (% of total population)*, viewed 15 January 2018, <https://data.worldbank.org/indicator/SP.RUR.TOTL.ZS?locations=ID>.

World Bank 2017e, *The world bank in Indonesia*, viewed 2 April 2018, <www.worldbank.org/en/country/indonesia/overview>.

Zeschky, MB, Winterhalter, S & Gassmann, O 2014, 'From cost to frugal and reverse innovation: Mapping the field and implications for global competitiveness', *Research-Technology Management*, vol. 57, no. 4, pp. 20–27.

2 Critical reflections on the state of innovation research

Introduction

Innovation, in particular product innovation, or new product development (NPD), is vital in driving firms' competitive advantage both nationally and across borders. However, successful product innovation does not happen in isolation; there are underlying processes that firms need to manage, control, inform and/or direct NPD outcomes (Tao, Probert & Phaal 2010). Adams, Bessant and Phelps (2006, p. 21) highlight the importance of this, suggesting "competitive success is dependent upon an organization's management of the innovation process", or the NPD process (NPDP).

With the aim to guide scholars and practitioners undertaking frugal innovation practices, an understanding of the innovation phenomenon in developed and developing countries is necessary. This book provides this context divided in two chapters. Chapter 2 provides a broader context of innovation, focused on NPD, frugal innovation and the NPDP. The aim is to examine the frugal innovation literature and to position this within the broader NPDP research domain. Chapter 3 focuses on developing a NPDP framework for frugal innovation which will guide this study, addressing an existing shortcoming in frugal innovation research.

This chapter is divided into three sections, with the first section discussing broadly the role and specific nature of innovation in modern firms that have led to finding new ways of innovating globally. This section also specifically focuses on product-based innovation. The second section defines frugal innovation and contextualises this through two key underlying aspects that should be considered. The first aspect is the context of frugal innovation and the targeted market – that is, BOP markets. The second aspect focuses on four characteristics that define a frugal product: affordability, core functionality, usability and durability.

Essential for managing product innovation in organisations of any size, the third section looks at NPDP practices, which forms the foundation of this study. This section is divided into four parts, with the first one highlighting the evolution of NPDP models over 60 years, before moving on to a review of the current clusters of research observed in the more modern NPDP literature. The third section draws from this well-established NPDP literature to consolidate key NPDP phases and stages into a generic NPDP framework for developed countries.[1] This creates the foundations against which the frugal innovation literature is reviewed in Chapter 3. In line with reviewing the most common elements of firms' NPDP, the final section of this chapter examines the literature detailing the processes underlying frugal product development. This section highlights a significant knowledge gap in relation to the NPDP for frugal innovation and establishes the basis of this study's contribution.

Innovation: what is it and why is it important?

With an increasing body of knowledge on frugal innovation in developing and developed countries, an obvious question relates to the definition of innovation and its role at a broader level. Its contemporary context has been mainly attributed to the theories developed by economist Joseph Schumpeter (1939), despite the term 'innovation' embracing different aspects (Adams, Bessant & Phelps 2006; Crossan & Apaydin 2010).

Schumpeter argued that innovation is a system of changes stimulating 'creative destruction' to renew existing assets, including creation, change and launch. Here, it is also distinguished between invention and innovation by relating the former with the technical development of new products/processes and the latter with their application to markets. This difference highlights the way in which innovation also incentivises firms' existence, corporate renewal and success.

Many prominent scholars have suggested different definitions of innovation. For example, Veryzer (1998, p. 306) described innovation as "the creation of a product, service, or process". Tidd, Bessant and Pavitt (2005, p. 40) suggested a broader definition of innovation as "a core process concerned with renewing what the organization offers and the ways in which it generates and delivers these".

More recently, Kahn et al. (2012, p. 455) embraced both these perspectives to define innovation as "a new idea, method, or device . . . the act of creating a new product or process, which includes invention and the work required to bring an idea or concept to final form". Garud, Tuertscher and Van de Ven (2013, p. 774) alternatively recommended employing phases that shape the innovation process, "the invention, development, and implementation of new ideas". McKinley, Latham and Braun (2014, p. 91) defined innovation as being "manifested in significant modifications of production processes or product or service architectures and sometimes by the introduction of an entirely new product, service, or production process".

Perhaps the most comprehensive definition in the literature, from which this study has founded its understanding of innovation, is by Crossan and Apaydin (2010, p. 1155), who stated that it occurs at several levels:

> the production or adoption, assimilation, and exploitation of a value-added novelty in economic and social spheres; renewal and enlargement of products, services, and markets; development of new methods of production; and establishment of new management systems.

This definition factors in the breadth of innovation occurring both as an outcome (e.g. product) and as a process (e.g. production; management system). These authors also believe that innovation can happen from both inside the firm through 'production' and outside through 'adoption'. The inclusion of the beneficial and multi-level impact and value of innovating (e.g. economic and social) along with the novelty and innovation types further compounds the breadth of their definition. It also goes beyond the creativity process embedded in firms' innovation processes by including its operational exploitation.

What is clear from these more contemporary definitions of innovation is that the role of innovation, be it a process, an outcome or both, is vital in driving firms' competitive advantage both nationally and across borders, and has social and economic effects (Cadeddu, Donovan & Masli 2013; Govindarajan & Ramamurti 2011; Shum & Lin 2007; Von Stamm 2008). As the innovation field has mostly focused on developed countries, this section has defined it within this context. In this study, it was surmised that innovation, as well as frugal innovation, can be defined ruled by three characteristics: the type, the novelty and the impact of the innovation, which is briefly described ahead and refined to product innovation type.

Type, novelty and impact of innovation

The range of type, novelty and impact of innovation can inform whether innovation occurs as an outcome or as a process, influencing the way firms innovate. First, different types of innovation can occur on the basis of what firms want to change or innovate. Such innovation can be a renewal or improvement of a process and technology, changes in marketing approach and firms' strategy, organisational structure or product (see Figure 2.1) (Gunday et al. 2011; Kotelnikov 2018; OECD 2005). Depending on their innovation strategy, firms' competitiveness will be enhanced when pursuing a relevant type of innovation, which will be embedded in their system (Gunday et al. 2011).

Despite these various types of innovation, product-based innovation is frequently identified in the literature as "a key component of the sustainable success of a business' operations" (Henard & Szymanski 2001, p. 362) and is, therefore, the focus of this study. Product innovation, or NPD, is "the development of new and improved products and services" (Cooper 2013, p. 3) and has been identified as a significant driver of innovation performance (Cooper 2013; Gunday et al. 2011). NPD is often critical in generating and maintaining firms' business success, particularly via additional income streams and markets (Tidd 2013).

Product innovation can vary on the basis of the level of novelty of the object being innovated. The *Oslo Manual* (OECD 2005), an influential international guide that helps firms define and assess innovation, suggests these different levels can occur through the use of new materials, new intermediate products, new functional parts, radically new technology or fundamentally new functions (new products). When the desired outcome is the improvement of existing products, it is generally referred to as 'product development' while the development of

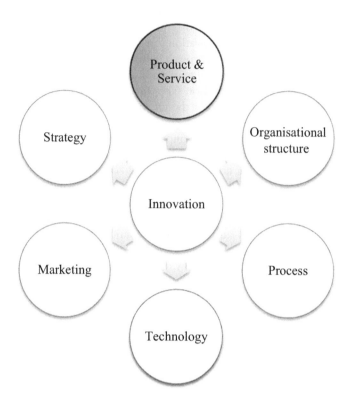

Figure 2.1 Innovation types at the firm level

Sources: Adapted from Kotelnikov (2018) and OECD (2005)

new products refers to 'NPD'. It is important to note that these two terms are often used interchangeably in the literature, despite holding different meanings (e.g. Kahn et al. 2012; Ulrich & Eppinger 2012).

Similarly, at a more macro-level, the newness of the product innovation can be relative and be new to the firm, new to the world and/or new to the market (Davila, Epstein & Shelton 2012; Holahan, Sullivan & Markham 2014). Such newness reflects the 'final' classification of innovation, which can range from incremental to radical changes on the basis of the extent of newness (Holahan, Sullivan & Markham 2014; Verworn, Herstatt & Nagahira 2008). Radical innovation relates to breakthrough changes, whereas incremental innovation refers to continuous changes and improvements of an existing technology or processes that are used differently (Dodgson, Gann & Phillips 2013; Garcia & Calantone 2002; Tidd 2001).

The impact that a product innovation outcome creates on the receiver (e.g. industry, market, firm) can be referred to as sustainable or disruptive in nature. According to Christensen and Raynor (2013, p. 2), sustainable innovations mainly target consumers, requiring "better performance than previously available, whether that performance is an incremental improvement or a breakthrough, leapfrog-over-competitors variety". In contrast, disruptive innovation is new products that are successful due to their simpler, more adapted and more affordable aspects, to which frugal innovation can also be often associated (e.g. Ramdorai & Herstatt 2017; Rao 2013; Ray & Ray 2011). As the concept of innovation has been clarified, the next section describes what frugal innovation is in the context of the nascent frugal innovation literature.

What is frugal innovation?

As introduced in Chapter 1, a key emerging phenomenon in the innovation literature, and in particular in modern innovation management practices, relates to the development of frugal innovation for BOP markets[2] (Agarwal et al. 2017; Bound & Thornton 2012; Radjou & Prabhu 2015; Weyrauch & Herstatt 2017; Wooldridge 2010; Zeschky, Winterhalter & Gassmann 2014). Its relevance to these markets emerges from its core tenet, "doing more and better with less", meaning the development of more affordable and core functional products for the consumers living in BOP markets (Banerjee & Leirner 2013; Radjou & Prabhu 2015; Zeschky, Winterhalter & Gassmann 2014).

Before reviewing the diverse definitions of frugal innovation, clarifications are required around the diverse frugal innovation terminologies applied to this phenomenon targeting BOP markets (Agarwal et al. 2017; Brem & Wolfram 2014). These innovations have been synonymously referred to as Jugaad innovation (Krishnan 2010; Radjou, Prabhu & Ahuja 2012), good-enough innovation (Zeschky, Widenmayer & Gassmann 2014), inclusive innovation (George, McGahan & Prabhu 2012) and resource-constrained innovation (Pansera & Owen 2015; Zeschky, Widenmayer & Gassmann 2011). Other terms include affordable value innovation (Ernst et al. 2015), BOP innovation (London & Hart 2010; Prahalad 2012), low-cost innovation (Agnihotri 2015) and cost-innovation (Williamson 2010).

Previous research on frugal innovation has, however, highlighted the importance of distinguishing the different meanings of these terms (e.g. Agarwal et al. 2017; Brem & Wolfram 2014; Weyrauch & Herstatt 2017; Zeschky, Winterhalter & Gassmann 2014). This is because critical differences exist between terms such as low-cost and cost-innovation. For example, Agnihotri (2015) described the term 'low-cost innovation' as embracing frugal innovation, Jugaad innovation and reverse innovation.

In contrast, when firms implement cost-innovation, the focus is on adopting a cost-reduction mindset across their NPDP, leading to the development of a low-cost version of a product (Williamson 2010). Cost-innovation resembles a stripped-down version of a premium product, without the core functionality and performance adapted to BOP markets like frugal innovation proposes (Agnihotri 2015; Tiwari & Herstatt 2014; Zeschky, Widenmayer & Gassmann 2011; Zeschky, Winterhalter & Gassmann 2014).

In addition to these different terminologies, as scholars define frugal innovation differently across the literature, accurately defining frugal innovation is also essential to such a nascent field to avoid overlaps with other types of innovation (Bhatti & Ventresca 2013; Brem & Wolfram 2014; Le Bas 2016a). For example, Zeschky, Winterhalter and Gassmann (2014) examined and distinguished the central tenets of four types of NPD innovation that are generally present in emerging markets (cost, good-enough, frugal and reverse innovation). They differentiate frugal innovation from other NPD by its development of new product architecture as well as new product application at a much more affordable price than existing alternatives.

Weyrauch and Herstatt (2017) reviewed the different perspectives taken by the literature when discussing frugal innovation and categorised the findings as the foundations for three criteria to ensure this type of innovation can be distinguished from other phenomena. As a result, these authors suggest that an NPD can be named frugal innovation if three criteria are met: substantial cost reduction, concentration on core functionalities and optimised performance level.

Additionally, these definitions (upon which this study will build its own definition at the end of this section) often rely on a defined targeted market and product characteristics – two underlying aspects of frugal innovation (e.g. Lehner & Gausemeier 2016; Pisoni, Michelini & Martignoni 2018). This section is thus based on these two aspects, divided in two sections ahead. The first focuses on an overview of BOP markets characteristics, including their income, the resource-constrained environment and geographical locations. The second aspect relates to the four product level characteristics attributed to frugal products: affordability, usability, core functionality and durability.

BOP markets: low-income consumers in a resource-constrained environment

The frugal innovation literature is often associated with the concept of BOP markets in developing countries,[3] which are also known as 'resource-constrained markets' (Gibbert, Hoegl & Valikangas 2014; Zeschky, Winterhalter & Gassmann 2014). BOP markets consist of the largest but poorest socio-economic group of consumers. These are often associated with low disposable income and a highly constrained environment that limits consumer resources and capabilities to realise their human potential and alleviate their poverty (Karnani 2017; Kolk, Rivera-Santos & Rufin 2014; Prahalad 2012). This section first focuses on BOP consumers' income, before describing the resource-constrained environment in which they live and building the definition for BOP markets in this study.

First, there are inconsistencies between income ranges attributed to BOP markets as well as the interchanged use of the term 'BOP markets/consumers' and 'emerging markets'. When looking at the inconsistent income ranges from previous research, a frequent income attributed to BOP consumers is those consumers living with less than 2 USD a day (Karnani 2017; Prahalad 2009). This is because it originated from the seminal work of Prahalad (2005) *The Fortune at the Bottom of the Pyramid: Eradicating Poverty through Profits*, which identified four billion low-income consumers on the basis of the idea that they could offer firms opportunities in these untapped mass markets.

In contrast, Hammond et al. (2007) identified the low-income bracket as those living under 8 USD a day, which is similar to the BOP Innovation Center's definition of "4.5 billion people who have to live on less than US $8 per day" (BOP Innovation Center 2017). In more industry-led research like Gassmann et al. (2017), BOP consumers targeted by frugal innovators are broadly perceived as a combination of low-end and middle markets. The description of BOP consumers' income has clearly evolved inconsistently, as can be seen in Figure 2.2. The BOP markets worldwide can include poor and low-income people earning between 2 USD or less a day and 10 USD a day. For this study, the range of income accepted to describe the BOP markets is similar to Hammond et al.'s (2007) definition of 8 USD per day, as any low-income market could need a frugal innovation NPD that is adapted to meet their income level.

In addition to inconsistencies in income ranges, BOP markets/consumers are terms used interchangeably across the literature with 'emerging markets' without consistent classifications (Karnani 2017; Kolk, Rivera-Santos & Rufin 2014). One can argue that these two terms (i.e. emerging markets and BOP markets) both refer to the low-income population in countries deemed as emerging economies or to those emerging markets with the populations gradually moving out

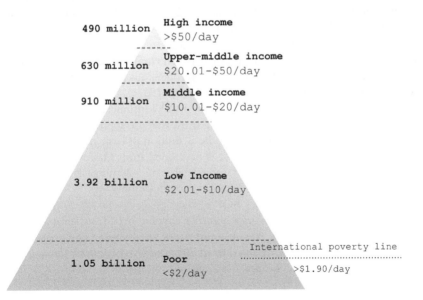

Figure 2.2 The world income pyramid in USD in 2011 (per capita income, and 2011 purchasing power parity)

Sources: World Bank (2015) and Kochhar (2015)

of the BOP bracket to more disposable income (e.g. Sehgal, Dehoff & Panneer 2010; Zeschky, Widenmayer & Gassmann 2011).

In other words, the term 'emerging markets' often denotes a huge under-served market incorporating billions of low-income consumers with rising dis-posable income, hence a high-growth market opportunity for innovators and businesses (Gassmann et al. 2017; Hammond et al. 2007; Prahalad 2009). In line with this, the targeted consumers of frugal innovation in this study relates to BOP markets in developing and emerging countries, similar to the definition of IMF (2013, p. 121).

In addition to their low levels of income, the resource-constrained and geo-graphic environment in which BOP consumers live also define this market for frugal innovation with restricted access to products that meet certain basic needs (Cunha et al. 2014; Hammond et al. 2007). These are critical factors to consider, as these can change BOP consumers' perceptions of new products as well as limit firms from conducting NPD the traditional way (Karnani 2017; Kotler 2016; Nakata & Berger 2011). Not only poor but also often geographically and socially disconnected, BOP consumers have restricted access to, for example, healthcare, water or transport infrastructure and finance services as well as education, tech-nology and knowledge (Jagtap et al. 2014; Khanna & Palepu 2010; Nakata & Weidner 2012).

In addition to this resource-constrained environment, geographic conditions are likely to differ between nations irrespective of whether they are developed or developing, which can also limit BOP consumers to address their basic needs (Gollakota, Gupta & Bork 2010; Mukerjee 2012; Sen 1999). This can be, for example, through geographic isolation, remoteness of their location or difficulty in accessing mainstream service provision due to difficult terrain. Such con-strained environments can be dissimilar between rural and urban areas of devel-oping countries due to the high level of heterogeneous populations in a country (Collier 2008; Subramaniam, Ernst & Dubiel 2015).

Undeniably, this environment affects the BOP consumers' access to products that can meet their basic needs, including those that are appropriately adapted to address their distinct problems. While the definition of basic needs varies across studies (Alkire 2002), in this study, it is developed from Maslow's hierarchy of needs (Maslow 1943) (i.e. food and water, shelter and clothing) along with more modern basic needs (i.e. health, sanitation and education issues).

In summary, this study defines BOP markets as *the low-income bracket of con-sumers in developing and emerging countries earning 8 USD or less a day. BOP markets are also defined by a resource-constrained environment and geography in which these consumers live, affecting their ability to address basic needs through prod-ucts such as food, housing, healthcare and energy.*

Frugal product characteristics

Frugal innovation research emphasises the need for products to be of acceptable value for BOP markets as well as responding to specific criteria (e.g. Gollakota,

Table 2.1 Frugal innovation characteristics

Frugal characteristics	Description	References
Affordability	Cost-effective; economical; adapted to BOP's affordability price-point; cost-reduced compared with premium counterparts; reduced cost of ownership	Basu, Banerjee and Sweeny (2013); Bound and Thornton (2012); Tiwari, Kalogerakis and Herstatt (2014); Weyrauch and Herstatt (2017)
Core functionality	Focus on core (primary) functionality; optimised performance	Weyrauch and Herstatt (2017); Zeschky, Winterhalter and Gassmann (2014)
Usability	Easy-to-use; adaptable; user-friendly; practical	Agarwal et al. (2017); Tiwari and Herstatt (2013)
Durability	Robust; easy to maintain	Agarwal et al. (2017); Petrick (2011); Tiwari and Herstatt (2013)

Gupta & Bork 2010; Kumar & Puranam 2012; Weyrauch & Herstatt 2017). In particular, the following characteristics have been highlighted as essential for successful frugal innovation NPD: affordability, core functionality, usability and durability, with unique features relevant to BOP consumers' needs. For the purpose of this study, this research has built on a range of studies (see Table 2.1) to define frugal innovation as

New products for BOP markets with optimised core functionalities at affordable price-point, embracing usability and durability. Frugal products offer alternative solutions to existing products developed for high-income consumers.

With the main question reflecting how to innovate, it is correct to say that the type of innovation a firm pursues, including frugal innovation NPD, influences the way it is managed and the control methods used. One of these includes the processes underlying the generation and development of new products, formally named the NPD process (NPDP) (Holahan, Sullivan & Markham 2014). NPDP has been identified within existing research as a key influencing factor in successful NPD outcomes (Barczak, Griffin & Kahn 2009; Cooper 2012; Markham & Lee 2013). As the understanding of such process is important for the emergent frugal innovation trend observed in modern innovation management studies, the NPDP and its characteristics are further discussed ahead.

Different models for NPDP and why they are not relevant to BOP markets

This section focuses on the process specific to product innovation, which has been deemed as one of the most important elements of innovation management – the actual innovation process (or NPDP)[4] along with relevant tools and techniques adopted to manage it within the firm (Rothwell 1994; Tao, Probert & Phaal 2010). The NPDP is a set of "phases that describe the normal means by which a company repetitively converts embryonic ideas into salable products" (Kahn et al. 2012, p. 458). A variety of studies has emphasised the importance of implementing a formal process for firms' NPD efforts as a critical element for improving innovation performance (e.g. Barczak, Griffin & Kahn 2009; Holahan, Sullivan & Markham 2014; Kahn et al. 2012).

The role of NPDP in firms' innovation performance has also been highlighted across different business activities, such as marketing (e.g. Kotler 1997), operations management (e.g. Krishnan & Ulrich 2001) and design and engineering (e.g. Bhuiyan 2011). The importance of managing the NPDP is also apparent from the increasing number of firms collaborating with and joining supportive organisations that assist with implementing NPD and in particular NPDP best practices. For example, the Product Development Institute (PDI) has worked with more than 1,000 multinationals for the past 20 years (PDI 2017), and the Product Development and Management Association (PDMA) has more than 2,000 members today (PDMA 2017).

The diversity of firms undertaking NPD and the development of the NPDP field has led to more practical and consistent NPDP models in the literature and across disciplines (Lawson 2015). While this is a substantial benefit, it also highlights the necessity of continuous improvement to NPDP models/frameworks to suit changing environments (Barczak, Griffin & Kahn 2009; Rothwell 1994). This is also necessary when considering the context of frugal innovation. As Kotsemir and Meissner (2013, p. 17) argue, new innovation trends such as frugal innovation "require appropriate models for the description and explaining of their development".

With both the broadening interest in, and evolution of, NPDP models, it is nevertheless worthwhile clarifying the historical contexts and progression of these models, in particular to create a strong foundation to the development of the NPDP for frugal innovation. This forms the first part of this section, which establishes strong grounding for better understanding the decrease in NPDP literature post-2000s. The second part of this section will discuss the contemporary clusters of literature and practices within NPDP, before concluding with a review of commonly accepted elements (phases and stages) of firms' NPDP, which is the final part of the section. These NPDP elements will shape the consolidated NPDP that is the foundation of the NPDP framework for frugal innovation in Chapter 3.

NPDP models: 60 years in evolution (1950s–2000s)

Literature on the NPDP emerged in the 1950s, building from the broader NPD area and from the way firms managed and organised innovation at the time. However, the organisational management of innovation began to receive significant scholar attention only from the early 1980s (e.g. Booz, Allen & Hamilton 1982;

Calantone & di Benedetto 1988; Cooper & Kleinschmidt 1986; Takeuchi & Nonaka 1986). It is also evident from the 1980s and 1990s, when articles began to consolidate the NPDP elements (e.g. phases, stages, activities) shaping these NPDP models (e.g. Cooper 1994; Mahajan & Wind 1992; Murphy & Kumar 1997; Poolton & Barclay 1998; Veryzer 1998; Zirger & Maidique 1990).

The main reason for this gradual evolution in NPDP practices arose from changes in markets in the Western world. According to Rothwell (1994), the evolutionary aspects of the Western world and its socio-economic history impacted on the progressive elaboration of NPDP models. Competitive markets, economic and industrial growth, and firms' strategic priorities were the changes that increased the need to refine the understanding of the NPDP (Brown & Eisenhardt 1995; Schilling & Hill 1998). Such changes were clearly reflected in how innovative firms structured their NPDP.

To better understand this evolution, we leverage Rothwell's (1994) framework to structure the 60-year evolution of these models. This has also been frequently used in other contemporary research (e.g. Abdulsomad 2013; Cagnazzo, Botarelli & Taticchi 2008; Gaubinger et al. 2014; Marinova & Phillimore 2003). Rothwell (1994) strategically framing the gradual change of the innovation models into five generations.

From the 1950s to early 1980s, there were three generations, with an initial shift from the first generation of 'technology-push' model (see Figure 2.3) to the second generation, the 'market-pull' model in the 1960s (see Figure 2.4). The technology-push model demonstrated that innovation started with a basic science stage, where firms' R&D and engineering activities were the main source of innovation (Godin 2006). From the 1960s, the influence of consumers' needs resulted in the 'market needs' stage driving innovation in firms with the 'market-pull' model (Booz, Allen & Hamilton 1982; Poolton & Barclay 1998; Rothwell 1994). A particular aspect of these models is their distinctive stages; however,

Figure 2.3 Technology-push model (first generation)

Source: Adapted from Rothwell (1994, p. 8)

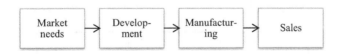

Figure 2.4 Market-pull model (second generation)

Source: Adapted from Rothwell (1994, p. 9)

they did not provide much detail about the activities occurring at each of those NPDP stages (Hobday 2005).

While these two models were defined by a linear and sequential process, the 1970s saw the rise of the third generation, the 'coupled' model (see Figure 2.5), which integrated interdependency between stages and firms' external elements. This model comprised a linear process (in the middle) of five stages that dually interacted with external market and technology drivers (on the outside). More general and pragmatic than the previous models, the coupled model replicated interactions or 'feedback loops' (represented by the two-way arrows) that occurred in real life between firms' functional departments and stages of development (Rothwell 1994).

With competition expanded from outside the United States, the fourth and fifth generations of innovation processes started to appear from the end of the 1980s to the early 2000s, mainly driven by product successes of Japanese automotive firms and their particular fast entry in markets (Nobelius 2004; Rothwell 1994). Japanese firms' success stemmed from the simultaneous and collaborative approaches as well as speed and flexibility in their NPDP phases and stages, which generated multidimensional models (e.g. Nonaka 1990; Poolton & Barclay 1998; Rothwell 1994; Takeuchi & Nonaka 1986). The structure of the fourth generation models enhanced not only in-house NPDP stages that were now executed in a parallel way, but also teamwork cross-functionality (Rothwell 1994).

The two most common models representing the cross-functionality of the fourth generation were Cooper's (1983) and Cooper and Kleinschmidt's (1986) stage-gate model, further improved by Cooper (1994) and Kline and Rosenberg's (1986) chain-linked model. As shown in Figure 2.6, the seminal work of Cooper (e.g. Cooper 1983, 1994; Cooper & Kleinschmidt 1986) shows the division of the NPDP into five overlapping stages (inclusive of idea generation) and gates representing a 'go/kill' decisions checkpoint. These gates enable feedback loops within and across the stages, indicating flexibility of decisions across

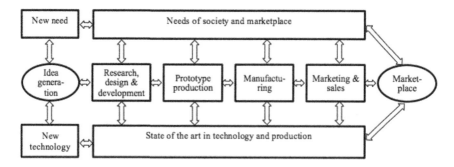

Figure 2.5 Coupled model (third generation)

Source: Adapted from Rothwell (1994, p. 10)

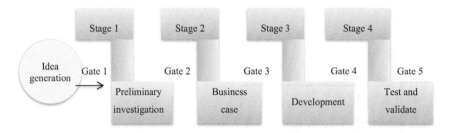

Figure 2.6 Cooper's stage-gate model
Source: Adapted from Cooper (1994)

cross-functional activities throughout the NPDP (Cooper 2010; Trott 2012). Such cross-functional overlap between stages was illustrated via the aggregation of NPDP activities into each stage, such as 'prototype production' and 'manufacturing' into the 'development' stage. Among contemporary NPDP models, this way of managing firms' NPD via these updated approaches (e.g. Cooper 2008, 2014) has remained a key milestone (Gaubinger et al. 2014).

The second most common model is the chain-linked adapted fourth generation model of Kline and Rosenberg (1986) (see Figure 2.7). They further illuminated the different iterations that can occur throughout five main NPDP stages including via feedback loops (represented by the F and f) and research and knowledge (the K-R links) in Figure 2.7. Their model demonstrated the complex interactions occurring throughout the various NPDP stages including cross-functionality between R&D and non-technological contributors such as suppliers, consumers and collaborators (Kline & Rosenberg 1986).

The final fifth generation model originated in the 1990s from the pressure of global competition for faster market entry at lower costs, due to prioritising the use of electronic tools during the product development phase (Rothwell 1994). For example, the concept of 'concurrent engineering' (CE) was subsequently introduced to allow the trade-off between product development time versus costs. Such tools allowed different teams to work simultaneously on finalising the product, allowing efficient time and cost management of an NPD project (Rothwell 1994; Ulrich & Eppinger 2012).

This additional collaboration (intra or extra firms) also characterised the fifth generation of NPDP model through the idea of 'open linkages' (Hobday 2005; Rothwell 1994). Enabling open collaboration to occur led to a more controlled and time-efficient diffusion of information between and within entities within wider integrated systems (Chesbrough, Vanhaverbeke & West 2006; Nobelius 2004). For example, the 'open innovation' model of Chesbrough (2003) (see Figure 2.8) emphasised the possibility throughout the NPDP to add inflow and outflow linkages of knowledge to the internal innovation processes. According to Chesbrough (2003) and Chesbrough, Vanhaverbeke and West (2006), this internal and external flow can originate from either technology-based actors or

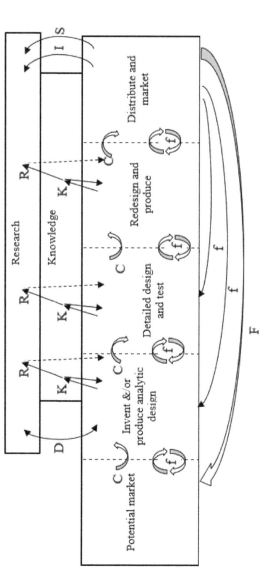

K-R Links = Links through knowledge to research and return paths. If problem solved at node K, link to R not activated. Return from research (dashed line) is problematic – therefore dashed line.

f/F = Feedback loops

D = Direct link to and from research from problems in invention and design.

I = Support of scientific research by instruments, machines, tools and procedures of technology.

S = Support of research in science underlying product area to gain information directly and by monitoring outside work. The information obtained may apply anywhere along the chain.

Figure 2.7 Chain-linked model (fourth generation)

Source: Adapted from Kline and Rosenberg (1986)

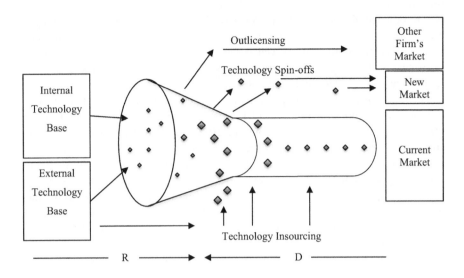

Figure 2.8 Open innovation model (example of fifth generation)
Source: Adapted from Chesbrough (2003)

from the marketplace, allowing the participation of different co-operators as part of the NPDP.

This collaborative model has consequently raised awareness among researchers about the complexity of this multidisciplinary process and the associated contextual elements shaping NPD practices (Griffin 1997; McCarthy et al. 2006; Schilling & Hill 1998; Veryzer 1998). This study's review of NPDP models pinpoints that these adaptations have occurred in accordance with the models' respective socio-economic and generation context (Salerno et al. 2015).

According to Kotsemir and Meissner (2013), the development of new NPDP models has slowed down since the late 2000s as the existing models such as open innovation can adapt with modern firms and their NPD strategy. The first reason for this slowdown could stem from the modern literature on NPDP that has instead contributed towards intrinsic practices, creating more contemporary clusters of research, which are introduced in the following section. A second possibility is that new product innovation trends like frugal innovation require adapted innovation models (Agarwal et al. 2017; Kotsemir & Meissner 2013), and this will be discussed further in the last section of this chapter.

Contemporary clusters of influence in the NPDP literature

The literature has shown a decrease in studies further developing NPDP models (Biemans, Griffin & Moenaert 2010; Di Benedetto 2013) and has highlighted the existence of diverse clusters of influence. That is, modern research around NPDP practices illustrates the prevalence of clusters focusing on project management tools, specific phases such as the fuzzy front end and tools and techniques specific to each NPDP phase as well as the effects of innovation success or failure of specific NPDP stages. This section will briefly describe each of these four contemporary clusters identified in the literature.

The first cluster focuses on project management tools such as agile methods, inspired by the fifth generation model structure (Chen, Ravichandar & Proctor 2016; Cooper 2017; Cooper & Sommer 2016). Agile methods such as scrums and sprints are increasingly considered in the literature as allowing leaner and faster progress across the product development phase (Cooper 1994, 2011, 2017). These methods allow for spiral development through 'build-test-revise cycles' (Cooper 2017, p. 48) where product requirements, project planning and deliverables evolve and adapt across early and later development phases (Chen, Ravichandar & Proctor 2016; Cooper 2017; Cooper & Sommer 2016). This cluster has emerged from increased interest in enabling firms' quick reactions towards market, technical and contextual situations (Cooper & Sommer 2016).

A second cluster focuses on the application of tools and techniques that enable effective management over firms' innovation outcomes (Adams, Bessant & Phelps 2006). This cluster shows a rising interest in specific tools and techniques and their role in firms' NPDP (e.g. Belliveau, Griffin & Somermeyer 2004; de Waal & Knott 2016; Graner & Mißler-Behr 2014; Kawakami, Barczak & Durmuşoğlu 2015; Van Kleef, van Trijp & Luning 2005). There is also an increasing interest in categorising NPDP tools and techniques by disciplines such as marketing and engineering tools (de Waal & Knott 2010; Markham & Lee 2013).

A third cluster observed in the literature is the degree of impact that each NPDP stage has on a firm's innovation performance, with studies exploring new product performance. These studies recognise that technical, marketing and financial performance and decisions made across idea generation, conceptualisation, product development and commercialisation are critical moderators to the development of successful new products (e.g. Fu 2010; Henard & Szymanski 2001; Lawson 2015; Millson & Wilemon 2006; Yin, Kaku & Liu 2012). Acknowledging the importance of such decisions across the NPDP provides firms with better control over their NPDP and reinforces the role of each phase and stage with earlier studies seen in the previous section.

The final cluster reviews the fuzzy front end phase, which is the initial phase of the NPDP. It relates to the generation, selection and organisation of NPD project(s) before firms further commit more resources (Kim & Wilemon 2002; Koen et al. 2002; Verworn, Herstatt & Nagahira 2008). The importance of these activities early in firms' NPDP was first highlighted by Cooper (1988) and empirically validated by Cooper (1990). The fuzzy front end has since become a major focus of more recent NPDP literature (e.g. Brem & Voigt 2009; Frishammar & Florén 2008; Koen, Bertels & Kleinschmidt 2014; Markham 2013; van den Ende, Frederiksen & Prencipe 2015; Verworn, Herstatt & Nagahira 2008).

The common ground such studies share are scholars' and practitioners' incentives to investigate the moderators of market success and failure. These clusters provide an in-depth focus on NPDP practices, contributing to the community of academia and managers innovating in the developed countries. However, this more contemporary literature is mostly scattered and contextual, concentrating on more specific aspects of the NPDP. Hence, there is less focus on the continuing adaptation of NPDP frameworks based on changing environments (Barczak, Griffin & Kahn 2009; Rothwell 1994), more particularly within the frugal innovation context.

In line with this, scholars have also questioned firms' NPDP practices in developing countries and the way they generate, design and develop new products for these emerging markets (Agarwal et al. 2017). For example, in a special edition of the *Journal of Product Innovation Management*, the following question was put forward: "How do EMNCs [Emerging Multinational Companies] that continue dominating low-end markets in emerging and developed markets manage their innovation processes?" (Subramaniam, Ernst & Dubiel 2015, p. 10).

This raises additional questions about drawing a more adapted approach to modern NPDP frameworks for frugal innovation via existing NPDP foundations. It also shows a critical gap in knowledge regarding the management of NPD in the context of developing countries, which is the foundation of this study. To this end, this study has refined and consolidated the current theoretical NPDP knowledge including the contemporary clusters for a more comprehensive structure for reviewing the frugal innovation literature. It also includes narrowing the scope of the NPDP to contextual moderators (frugal innovation perspective) in Chapter 3 to shape the conceptual NPDP framework for frugal innovation. The next section provides an overview of these foundations for the consolidated NPDP.

Reviewing NPDP phases and stages: preview of the consolidated NPDP

Taking into account that "[a] formal process for NPD is now the norm" (Barczak, Griffin & Kahn 2009, p. 7), it is critical to ensure the efficient management of the elements shaping it, including processes, phases, stages and tools and techniques (as discussed earlier). These are designed to guide a firm in managing, understanding and developing innovative products, and to increase the chance of success in targeted markets (Graner & Mißler-Behr 2013; Henard & Szymanski 2001).

Contemporary NPD is commonly thought to rely on overlapping NPDP phases and stages that integrate cross-functional NPDP activities across multiple disciplines (e.g. marketing, product management, design and engineering, manufacturing, operation management) (Crawford & Di Benedetto 2014; Krishnan & Loch 2005; Ulrich & Eppinger 2012). The adaptation of the evolutionary NPDP models across multi-disciplines illustrates a diversity of terms describing each NPDP phase and stage, as observed in Table 2.2. For example, the "business economic analysis" activity (Nijssen & Lieshout 1995) of an NPD project against

Table 2.2 Examples of NPDP elements

Authors	Number and names of elements shaping the NPDP	
Nijssen and Lieshout (1995)	8 stages	Idea generation, idea screening, concept development and testing, marketing strategy, business economic analysis, product development, market testing, commercialisation
Schilling and Hill (1998)	5 stages	Opportunity identification, concept development, product design, process design, commercial production
Cooper (2011)	6 stages	Discovery, scoping, business case, development, testing and validation, launch
Ulrich and Eppinger (2012)	6 phases	Planning, concept development, system-level design, detail design, testing and refinement, production ramp-up
Koen, Bertels and Kleinschmidt (2014)	3 phases	Front end of innovation, new product development, commercialisation
Crawford and Di Benedetto (2014)	5 phases	Opportunity identification and selection, concept generation, concept/project evaluation, development, launch

the 'system-level design' activity (Ulrich & Eppinger 2012) of a working concept showcases the multidisciplinary nature of NPDP.

The main reason for these disparities stems from scholars, firms and practitioners designing their NPDP according to the purpose and perspective of their research and discipline (e.g. De Waal et al. 2014). This can challenge further conceptualisation of NPDP models (Crawford & Di Benedetto 2014; Tatikonda & Montoya-Weiss 2001; Trott 2012). While such unilateral perspectives have an advantageous position through a limited focus on NPDP, as well as remaining within the boundaries set by the authors, they also support a need for this study to consolidate the NPDP elements around the innovation process. This is especially true when conceptualising a nascent concept like frugal innovation.

In order to build a strong grounding for developing the NPDP for frugal innovation, the consolidated NPDP is built upon existing conceptualisations of NPDP models including well-established cross-functional NPDP activities embedded within phases and stages. In line with this, Ulrich (2011, p. 395) suggests developing NPDP models by "focusing on what decisions must be made, and then consider what information, perspectives, and tools are most relevant to those decisions".

In this vein, the literature search has included literature focused on firms' NPDP decisions for serving developed countries related to product innovation management, R&D management, engineering design, marketing and operations management.[5] The use of tools and techniques was included as, in practice, these are not excluded from decision-making such as decisions related to design (Lutters et al. 2014). Figure 2.9 depicts the basis of this study's consolidated NPDP upon which frugal innovation literature has been mapped out in Chapter 3.

This consolidated NPDP provides a broad structure of the four NPDP phases and nine associated stages of NPD management to build the basis for the NPDP for frugal innovation. The multidisciplinary character of the NPDP is observed across the different NPDP activities, such as marketing via the market study stage and engineering via the product design stage. Furthermore, like the most recent NPDP models, circulating arrows represent the iterative nature of NPDP, allowing back and forth iteration and spirals between stages, phases and customers.

While this figure acknowledges existing holistic models, the consolidated NPDP is not meant to be comprehensive. Chapter 3 provides more details about the stages' characteristics and tools and techniques, which portray the specificities of each NPDP stage (both for developed and developing countries). Now that innovation has been contextualised to NPDP, the following section will deepen the understanding of how current frugal innovation studies are linked to NPDP practices. The next section reviews the underlying processes involved in the development of frugal products, revealing an important gap around NPDP for frugal innovation.

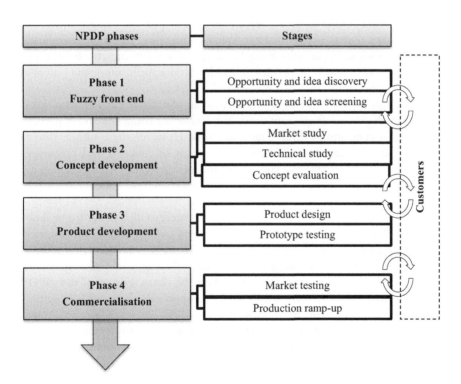

Figure 2.9 Consolidated NPDP: four phases and nine stages

How to develop frugal innovation NPD?

The adequacy of frugal innovation to suit BOP consumers as a product offering emphasises the importance of understanding how to conceptualise frugal innovation NPD (Agarwal et al. 2017; Pansera 2013; Subramaniam, Ernst & Dubiel 2015). However, the frugal innovation literature is also characterised by disparities in how this is conceptualised. It has been approached as a mindset, an outcome and/or a process, without clear guidance for practitioners and researchers undertaking this phenomenon (Pisoni, Michelini & Martignoni 2018; Soni & Krishnan 2014). This section, therefore, reviews existing literature on frugal innovation, with a focus on studies discussing frugal innovation NPD.

The main question is: How to develop and manage frugal innovation NPD? From an NPDP angle, studies that could answer this question are scarce, despite an increasing body of literature that highlight "the crucial role played by the innovation process in defining/framing frugal approaches to innovation" (Pisoni, Michelini & Martignoni 2018, p. 122). Few studies investigating the NPDP from a holistic perspective exist, and a special edition by Subramaniam, Ernst and Dubiel (2015) clearly points out the significance of answering how firms manage innovation for the BOP markets in developing countries.

Despite providing a better understanding of the underlying processes of frugal innovation, the majority of studies looking at the process of managing innovation (or NPDP) concentrate exclusively on specific phases or stages within the NPDP. Agarwal et al. (2017, p. 10) emphasise this point, based on a systematic literature review of frugal innovation, "[e]xcept for some studies, the emphasis of the research so far has been on idea generation, conceptualization, and potential exploitation of constraint-based innovation".

An example of such studies is Viswanathan and Sridharan (2012), who investigated the NPDP for frugal innovation for developing countries, and in particular India, by generating a three-stage framework. However, these authors discuss key managerial decisions across the development of concepts and prototypes only, and remained within the context of students' projects. Other examples are Rao (2013) on product design and Jagtap et al. (2014) and Šoltés et al. (2017) on the design process.[6]

While other scholars have also studied how to successfully achieve frugal innovation NPD, the literature seems dispersed across various innovation activities[7] and angles (Tiwari, Kalogerakis & Herstatt 2016). For example, frugal innovation has been discussed as being achievable via embracing a new strategic mindset on NPD efforts (strategy), understanding the characteristics of the NPDP outcome (frugal product) and applying a frugal approach on the underlying processes (process) (see examples in Table 2.3).

This study argues that these innovation activities are not irrelevant to comprehend the development of successful frugal products. For example, Wooldridge (2010, p. 18) supported that frugal innovation is developed by embracing diverse innovation activities, as it is "not just about redesigning products; it involves rethinking entire production processes and business models". Similarly, Bhatti

Table 2.3 Examples of innovation activities to achieve frugal innovation

Innovation activities	Types	Illustrative references
Frugal engineering	Process	Brem and Wolfram (2014); Kumar and Puranam (2012); Rajadurai and Parameshwari (2014); Rosca and Bendul (2017); Sehgal, Dehoff and Panneer (2010)
Frugal product's design criteria/context	Process	Aranda-Jan, Jagtap and Moultrie (2016); Basu, Banerjee and Sweeny (2013); Bingham, Whitehead and Evans (2016); Campbell, Lewis and Mattson (2011); Lehner and Gausemeier (2016); Mattson and Wood (2014); Whitney (2010); Zeschky, Winterhalter and Gassmann (2014)
Business model	Strategy	Eyring, Johnson and Nair (2011); Rosca, Arnold and Bendul (2017); Winterhalter et al. (2017); Wood and Mattson (2016); Yunus, Moingeon and Lehmann-Ortega (2010)
Value chains and marketing through local collaboration	Process	Anderson and Markides (2007); London (2016); London and Hart (2004); Nakata and Weidner (2012); Payaud (2014)
Supply chains through collaboration with local businesses	Process	Rosca, Arnold and Bendul (2017); Viswanathan and Sridharan (2012)
Management philosophy	Strategy	Radjou & Prabhu (2015); Radjou et al. (2012)
Social innovation, social entrepreneurship and inclusive growth	Strategy	George, McGahan and Prabhu (2012); Kahle et al. (2013); Pansera (2013)

(2012, p. 18) noted the concept of frugal innovation as potentially encompassing and redefining "business models, reconfigur[ing] value chains and redesign[ing] products to use resources in different ways".

Along the same line of reasoning, Soni and Krishnan (2014, p. 36) asserted that "[frugal] innovation is as much about the product, as is about the form and means in which the offering reaches to the hitherto underserved customers". Likewise, Zeschky, Winterhalter and Gassmann (2014, p. 20) argue that the "original motivation, value proposition and value creation mechanisms" are key considerations when developing frugal innovation. In particular, value creation mechanisms refer to the way cross-functional NPDP stages are undertaken and how criteria are chosen by frugal innovators to move forward throughout the NPDP (Zeschky, Winterhalter & Gassmann 2014).

As this book focuses on the concept of frugal innovation from an NPDP angle, the authors argue that achieving frugal innovation NPD as an outcome involves a paradigm shift across all these innovation activities that compose NPD (e.g. marketing, business model, supply chain) (Agarwal et al. 2017; Soni & Krishnan 2014; Winterhalter et al. 2017). In other words, these studies and related perspectives can be supportive materials to inform and shape the NPDP for frugal innovation mapped on the previously consolidated NPDP (see Figure 2.9).

Therefore, the aim of this study is to rationally integrate the frugal innovation literature into the NPDP components to structure the development of new frugal products along the innovation process. To close this gap, this study thus builds on a strong foundation from the consolidated NPDP to explore the NPDP for frugal innovation. In this aim, an extensive review of each NPDP phase, associated stages, tools and techniques has been undertaken in Chapter 3. By mapping out the frugal innovation literature in the consolidated NPDP, the outcome of the next chapter is the development of 15 frugal innovation practices related to the decisions, tools and techniques preferred by frugal innovators.

Notes

1 A preview of this consolidated NPDP is shown in Figure 2.9 in this chapter and a more detailed framework is provided in Chapter 3.
2 Herein onward, the concept of frugal innovation for BOP markets in this study will be related to emerging and developing countries.
3 And more recently researched in developed countries (e.g. Bhatti et al. 2017; Le Bas 2016b; Tiwari, Fischer & Kalogerakis 2016), although the scope of this study is limited to BOP markets in developing countries.
4 While this study used NPDP, different vocabulary such as 'innovation process' was used in the early literature to describe the same phenomenon. Thus, this term can also be understood as NPDP in this section.
5 Chapter 3 will build upon this consolidated framework to reveal frugal innovators' NPDP decisions serving emerging and developing countries.
6 These are leveraged to build the conceptual NPDP framework of this study in Chapter 3.
7 Innovation activities are beyond NPDP activities, encompassing innovation management activities such as NPD strategy, business model or value chain.

References

Abdulsomad, K 2013, 'The transformation of Multinational Corporations (MNCs) from an innovation perspective: Some notes on the theories of MNCs', *AI & Society*, pp. 1–12.

Adams, R, Bessant, J & Phelps, R 2006, 'Innovation management measurement: A review', *International Journal of Management Reviews*, vol. 8, no. 1, pp. 21–47.

Agarwal, N, Grottke, M, Mishra, S & Brem, A 2017, 'A systematic literature review of constraint-based innovations: State of the art and future perspectives', *IEEE Transactions on Engineering Management*, vol. 64, no. 1, pp. 3–15.

Agnihotri, A 2015, 'Low-cost innovation in emerging markets', *Journal of Strategic Marketing*, vol. 23, no. 5, pp. 399–411.

Alkire, S 2002, 'Dimensions of human development', *World Development*, vol. 30, no. 2, pp. 181–205.

Anderson, J & Markides, C 2007, 'Strategic innovation and the base of the pyramid', *MIT Sloan Management Review*, vol. 49, no. 1, pp. 82–88.

Aranda-Jan, CB, Jagtap, S & Moultrie, J 2016, 'Towards a framework for holistic contextual design for low-resource settings', *International Journal of Design*, vol. 10, no. 3, pp. 43–63.

Banerjee, PM & Leirner, A 2013, *Embracing the bottom of the pyramid with frugal innovation*, Brandeis International Business School, Waltham.

Barczak, G, Griffin, A & Kahn, KB 2009, 'Perspective: Trends and drivers of success in NPD practices: Results of the 2003 PDMA best practices study*', *Journal of Product Innovation Management*, vol. 26, no. 1, pp. 3–23.

Basu, RR, Banerjee, PM & Sweeny, EG 2013, 'Frugal innovation: core competencies to address global sustainability', *Journal of Management for Global Sustainability*, vol. 1, no. 2, pp. 63–82.

Belliveau, P, Griffin, A & Somermeyer, S 2004, *The PDMA tool book 1 for new product development*, John Wiley & Sons, Inc., Hoboken, NJ.

Bhatti, YA 2012, 'What is frugal, what is innovation? Towards a theory of frugal innovation', Said Business School Working Paper Series, 1 February, viewed 2 December 2017.

Bhatti, YA, Prime, M, Harris, M, Wadge, H, McQueen, J, Patel, H, Carter, AW, Parston, G & Darzi, A 2017, 'The search for the holy grail: Frugal innovation in healthcare from low-income or middle-income countries for reverse innovation to developed countries', *BMJ Innovations*, pp. bmjinnov-2016-000186.

Bhatti, YA & Ventresca, M 2013, 'How can "frugal innovation" be conceptualized?' Said Business School Working Paper Series, 19 January, viewed 2 December 2017.

Bhuiyan, N 2011, 'A framework for successful new product development', *Journal of Industrial Engineering and Management*, vol. 4, no. 4, pp. 746–770.

Biemans, W, Griffin, A & Moenaert, R 2010, 'In search of the classics: A study of the impact of JPIM papers from 1984 to 2003*', *Journal of Product Innovation Management*, vol. 27, no. 4, pp. 461–484.

Bingham, G, Whitehead, T & Evans, M 2016, 'Design tool for enhanced new product development in low income economies', in P Lloyd and E Bohemia (eds), Proceedings of DRS2016: Design + Research + Society – Future-Focused Thinking, pp. 2241–2256.

Booz Allen Hamilton 1982, *New product development for the 1980s*, Booz Allen Hamilton Consultants, New York.

BOP Innovation Center 2017, *Inclusive business starts here*, viewed 28 November 2017, <www.bopinc.org/>.

Bound, K & Thornton, IW 2012, *Our frugal future: Lessons from India's innovation system*, Nesta, London, viewed 5 January 2018, <www.nesta.org.uk/sites/default/files/our_frugal_future.pdf>.

Brem, A & Voigt, K-I 2009, 'Integration of market pull and technology push in the corporate front end and innovation management – insights from the German software industry', *Technovation*, vol. 29, no. 5, pp. 351–367.

Brem, A & Wolfram, P 2014, 'Research and development from the bottom up – introduction of terminologies for new product development in emerging markets', *Journal of Innovation and Entrepreneurship*, vol. 3, no. 1, p. 9.

Brown, SL & Eisenhardt, KM 1995, 'Product development: Past research, present findings, and future directions', *Academy of Management Review*, vol. 20, no. 2, pp. 343–378.

Cadeddu, S, Donovan, J & Masli, EK 2013, 'Foreign direct investment and economic development: An exploratory study of the internalisation strategy of a technology-intensive multinational', *Journal of International Business and Economy*, vol. 14, no. 1, pp. 1–30.

Cagnazzo, L, Botarelli, M & Taticchi, P 2008, 'Innovation management models: A literature review, a new framework, a case study', *Proceedings of the 3rd European Conference on Entrepreneurship and Innovation*, pp. 55–69.

Calantone, RJ & di Benedetto, CA 1988, 'An integrative model of the new product development process: An empirical validation', *Journal of Product Innovation Management*, vol. 5, no. 3, pp. 201–215.

Campbell, RD, Lewis, PK & Mattson, CA 2011, 'A method for identifying design principles for the developing world', ASME 2011 International Design Engineering Technical Conferences and Computers and Information in Engineering Conference, American Society of Mechanical Engineers, Washington DC, pp. 453–460.

Chen, RR, Ravichandar, R & Proctor, D 2016, 'Managing the transition to the new agile business and product development model: Lessons from Cisco systems', *Business Horizons*, vol. 59, no. 6, pp. 635–644.

Chesbrough, HW 2003, *Open innovation: The new imperative for creating and profiting from technology*, Harvard Business Review Press, Boston, MA.

Chesbrough, HW, Vanhaverbeke, W & West, J (eds), 2006, *Open innovation: Researching a new paradigm*, Oxford University Press, Oxford.

Christensen, C & Raynor, M 2013, *The innovator's solution: Creating and sustaining successful growth*, Harvard Business Review Press.

Collier, P 2008, *The bottom billion: Why the poorest countries are failing and what can be done about it*, Oxford University Press, Oxford.

Cooper, RG 1983, 'A process model for industrial new product development', *IEEE Transactions on Engineering Management*, no. 1, pp. 2–11.

Cooper, RG 1988, 'Predevelopment activities determine new product success', *Industrial Marketing Management*, vol. 17, no. 3, pp. 237–247.

Cooper, RG 1990, *New products: The key factors in success*, American Marketing Association, Chicago, IL.

Cooper, RG 1994, 'Third-generation new product process', *Journal of Product Innovation Management*, vol. 11, no. 1, pp. 3–14.

Cooper, RG 2008, 'Perspective: The stage-gate idea-to-launch process – update, what's new, and NexGen systems', *Journal of Product Innovation Management*, vol. 25, no. 3, pp. 213–232.

Cooper, RG 2010, 'The stage-gate idea to launch system', in *Wiley international encyclopedia of marketing: Part 5: Product innovation and management*, John Wiley & Sons, Inc., New York.

Cooper, RG 2011, *Winning at new products: Creating value through innovation*, Basic Books.

Cooper, RG 2012, 'New products-what separates the winners from the losers and what drives success', *The PDMA Handbook of New Product Development*, vol. 3, pp. 279–301.

Cooper, RG 2013, 'New products: What separates the winners from the losers and what drives success', *PDMA Handbook of New Product Development*, pp. 3–34.

Cooper, RG 2014, 'What's next? After stage-gate', *Research-Technology Management*, vol. 57, no. 1, pp. 20–31.

Cooper, RG 2017, 'Idea-to-launch gating systems: Better, faster, and more agile: Leading firms are rethinking and reinventing their idea-to-launch gating systems, adding elements of agile to traditional stage-gate structures to add flexibility and speed while retaining structure', *Research-Technology Management*, vol. 60, no. 1, pp. 48–52.

Cooper, RG & Kleinschmidt, EJ 1986, 'An investigation into the new product process: Steps, deficiencies, and impact', *Journal of Product Innovation Management*, vol. 3, no. 2, pp. 71–85.

Cooper, RG & Sommer, AF 2016, 'The agile – stage-gate hybrid model: A promising new approach and a new research opportunity', *Journal of Product Innovation Management*, vol. 33, no. 5, pp. 513–526.

Crawford, CM & Di Benedetto, CA 2014, *New products management*, 11th edn., McGraw-Hill Education, New York.

Crossan, MM & Apaydin, M 2010, 'A multi-dimensional framework of organizational innovation: A systematic review of the literature', *Journal of Management Studies*, vol. 47, no. 6, pp. 1154–1191.

Cunha, MPE, Rego, A, Oliveira, P, Rosado, P & Habib, N 2014, 'Product innovation in resource-poor environments: Three research streams', *Journal of Product Innovation Management*, vol. 31, no. 2, pp. 202–210.

Davila, T, Epstein, M & Shelton, R 2012, *Making innovation work: How to manage it, measure it, and profit from it*, FT Press.

de Waal, GA & Knott, P 2010, 'Product development: An integrative tool and activity research framework', *Human Systems Management*, vol. 29, no. 4, 1 January, pp. 253–264.

de Waal, GA & Knott, P 2016, 'Patterns and drivers of NPD tool adoption in small high-technology firms', *IEEE Transactions on Engineering Management*, vol. 63, no. 4, pp. 350–361.

de Waal, GA, Maritz, A, Scheepers, H, McLoughlin, S & Hempel, B 2014, 'A conceptual framework for guiding business transformation and organizational change in innovative ICT projects', *International Journal of Organizational Innovation*, vol. 7, no. 2, pp. 6–17.

Di Benedetto, CA 2013, 'The emergence of product innovation discipline and implications for future research', *The PDMA handbook of new product development*, pp. 416–426.

Dodgson, M, Gann, DM & Phillips, N 2013, 'Perspectives in innovation management', in *The Oxford handbook of innovation management*, Oxford University Press, Oxford.

Ernst, H, Kahle, HN, Dubiel, A, Prabhu, J & Subramaniam, M 2015, 'The antecedents and consequences of affordable value innovations for emerging markets', *Journal of Product Innovation Management*, vol. 32, no. 1, pp. 65–79.

Eyring, MJ, Johnson, MW & Nair, H 2011, 'New business models in emerging markets', *Harvard Business Review*, vol. 89, no. 1/2, pp. 88–95.

Frishammar, J & Florén, H 2008, 'Where new product development begins: Success factors, contingencies and balancing acts in the fuzzy front end', 17th International Conference on Management of Technology, 5–8 April, 47.

Fu, Y 2010, 'New product success among Small and Medium Enterprises (SMEs): An empirical study in Taiwan', *Journal of International Management Studies*, vol. 5, no. 1, pp. 147–153.

Garcia, R & Calantone, R 2002, 'A critical look at technological innovation typology and innovativeness terminology: A literature review', *Journal of Product Innovation Management*, vol. 19, no. 2, pp. 110–132.

Garud, R, Tuertscher, P & Van de Ven, AH 2013, 'Perspectives on innovation processes', *Academy of Management Annals*, vol. 7, no. 1, pp. 773–817.

Gassmann, O, Neumann, L, Knapp, O & Zollenkop, M 2017, 'Frugal: Simply a smart solution', *Roland Berger Focus*, August, Roland Berger GmbH.

Gaubinger, K, Rabl, M, Swan, S & Werani, T 2014, 'Integrated innovation and product management: A process oriented framework', in *Innovation and product management*, Springer, Berlin, Heidelberg, pp. 27–42.

George, G, McGahan, AM & Prabhu, J 2012, 'Innovation for inclusive growth: Towards a theoretical framework and a research agenda', *Journal of Management Studies*, vol. 49, no. 4, pp. 661–683.

Gibbert, M, Hoegl, M & Valikangas, L 2014, 'Introduction to the special issue: Financial resource constraints and innovation', *Journal of Product Innovation Management*, vol. 31, no. 2, pp. 197–201.

Godin, B 2006, 'The linear model of innovation: The historical construction of an analytical framework', *Science, Technology, & Human Values*, vol. 31, no. 6, pp. 639–667.

Gollakota, K, Gupta, V & Bork, JT 2010, 'Reaching customers at the base of the pyramid – a two-stage business strategy', *Thunderbird International Business Review*, vol. 52, no. 5, pp. 355–367.

Govindarajan, V & Ramamurti, R 2011, 'Reverse innovation, emerging markets, and global strategy', *Global Strategy Journal*, vol. 1, no. 3–4, pp. 191–205.

Graner, M & Mißler-Behr, M 2013, 'Key determinants of the successful adoption of new product development methods', *European Journal of Innovation Management*, vol. 16, no. 3, pp. 301–316.

Graner, M & Mißler-Behr, M 2014, 'Method application in new product development and the impact on cross-functional collaboration and new product success', *International Journal of Innovation Management*, vol. 18, no. 1, p. 1450002.

Griffin, A 1997, 'PDMA research on new product development practices: Updating trends and benchmarking best practices', *Journal of Product Innovation Management*, vol. 14, no. 6, pp. 429–458.

Gunday, G, Ulusoy, G, Kilic, K & Alpkan, L 2011, 'Effects of innovation types on firm performance', *International Journal of Production Economics*, vol. 133, no. 2, pp. 662–676.

Hammond, AL, Kramer, WJ, Katz, RS, Tran, JT & Walker, C 2007, *The next 4 billion: Market size and business strategy at the base of the pyramid*, World Resources Institute International Finance Corporation.

Henard, DH & Szymanski, DM 2001, 'Why some new products are more successful than others', *Journal of Marketing Research*, vol. 38, no. 3, pp. 362–375.

Hobday, M 2005, 'Firm-level innovation models: Perspectives on research in developed and developing countries', *Technology Analysis & Strategic Management*, vol. 17, no. 2, pp. 121–146.

Holahan, PJ, Sullivan, ZZ & Markham, SK 2014, 'Product development as core competence: How formal product development practices differ for radical, more innovative, and incremental product innovations', *Journal of Product Innovation Management*, vol. 31, no. 2, pp. 329–345.

IMF 2013, *World economic outlook (April 2013): Hopes, realities, and risks*, World Economic and Financial Surveys, Washington, DC.

Jagtap, S, Larsson, A, Hiort, V, Olander, E, Warell, A & Khadilkar, P 2014, 'How design process for the base of the pyramid differs from that for the top of the pyramid', *Design Studies*, vol. 35, no. 5, pp. 527–558.

Kahle, HN, Dubiel, A & Ernst, H 2013, 'The democratizing effects of frugal innovation', *Journal of Indian Business Research*, vol. 5, no. 4, pp. 230–234.

Kahn, KB, Kay, SE, Slotegraaf, R & Uban, S 2012, *The PDMA handbook of new product development*, 3rd edn., John Wiley & Sons, Inc., Hoboken, NJ.

Karnani, A 2017, 'Marketing and poverty alleviation: The perspective of the poor', *Markets, Globalization & Development Review*, vol. 2, no. 1.

Kawakami, T, Barczak, G & Durmuşoğlu, SS 2015, 'Information technology tools in new product development: The impact of complementary resources', *Journal of Product Innovation Management*, vol. 32, no. 4, pp. 622–635.

Khanna, T & Palepu, KG 2010, *Winning in emerging markets: A road map for strategy and execution*, Harvard Business Review Press, Cambridge, MA.

Kim, J & Wilemon, D 2002, 'Focusing the fuzzy front – end in new product development', *R&D Management*, vol. 32, no. 4, pp. 269–279.

Kline, SJ & Rosenberg, N 1986, 'An overview of innovation', *The Positive Sum Strategy: Harnessing Technology for Economic Growth*, vol. 14, p. 640.

Kochhar, R 2015, *A global middle class is more promise than reality: From 2001 to 2011, nearly 700 million step out of poverty, but most only barely*, Pew Research Centre, viewed 21 September 2018, <www.pewresearch.org/wp-content/uploads/sites/2/2015/08/Global-Middle-Class-Report_8-12-15-final.pdf>.

Koen, PA, Ajamian, GM, Boyce, S, Clamen, A, Fisher, E, Fountoulakis, S, Johnson, A, Puri, P & Seibert, R 2002, 'Fuzzy front end: Effective methods, tools, and techniques', in P Belliveau, A Griffin and S Somermeyer (eds), *The PDMA tool book 1 for new product development*, John Wiley & Sons, Inc., New York, pp. 5–35.

Koen, PA, Bertels, HMJ & Kleinschmidt, EJ 2014, 'Managing the front end of innovation – part II', *Research Technology Management*, vol. 57, no. 3, p. 25.

Kolk, A, Rivera-Santos, M & Rufin, C 2014, 'Reviewing a decade of research on the "Base/Bottom of the Pyramid" (BOP) concept', *Business & Society*, vol. 53, no. 3, pp. 338–377.

Kotelnikov, V 2018, 'Systemic innovation: The new holistic approach for the new knowledge-driven economy', *APCTT*, viewed 6 November 2018, <http://www.1000ventures.com/business_guide/innovation_systemic.html>.

Kotler, P 1997, *Marketing management: Analysis, planning, implementation, and control*, Prentice Hall, Inc., NJ.

Kotler, P 2016, *A framework for marketing management*, 6th edn., Pearson, Boston, MA.

Kotsemir, M & Meissner, D 2013, 'Conceptualizing the innovation process – trends and outlook', *Higher School of Economics Research Paper No. WP BPR*, vol. 10, no. SSRN Electronic Journal.

Krishnan, RT 2010, *From jugaad to systematic innovation: The challenge for India*, Utpreraka Foundation, Bangalore.

Krishnan, V & Loch, CH 2005, 'A retrospective look at production and operations management articles on new product development', *Production and Operations Management*, vol. 14, no. 4, pp. 433–441.

Krishnan, V & Ulrich, KT 2001, 'Product development decisions: A review of the literature', *Management Science*, vol. 47, no. 1, pp. 1–21.

Kumar, N & Puranam, P 2012, 'Frugal engineering: An emerging innovation paradigm', *Ivey Business Journal*, vol. 76, no. 2, pp. 14–16.

Lawson, B 2015, 'New product development process', in *Wiley encyclopedia of management*, John Wiley & Sons, Inc.

Le Bas, C 2016a, 'Frugal innovation, sustainable innovation, reverse innovation: Why do they look alike? Why are they different?' *Journal of Innovation Economics & Management*, vol. 21, no. 3, pp. 9–26.

Le Bas, C 2016b, 'The importance and relevance of frugal innovation to developed markets: Milestones towards the economics of frugal innovation', *Journal of Innovation Economics & Management*, no. 3, pp. 3–8.

Lehner, A-C & Gausemeier, J 2016, 'A pattern-based approach to the development of frugal innovations', *Technology Innovation Management Review*, vol. 6, no. 3, pp. 13–21.

London, T & Hart, SL 2004, 'Reinventing strategies for emerging markets: Beyond the transnational model', *Journal of International Business Studies*, vol. 35, no. 5, pp. 350–370.

London, T & Hart, SL 2010, *Next generation business strategies for the base of the pyramid: New approaches for building mutual value*, Pearson Education, India.

Lutters, E, van Houten, FJAM, Bernard, A, Mermoz, E & Schutte, CSL 2014, 'Tools and techniques for product design', *CIRP Annals – Manufacturing Technology*, vol. 63, no. 2, pp. 607–630.

Mahajan, V & Wind, J 1992, 'New product models: Practice, shortcomings and desired improvements', *The Journal of Product Innovation Management*, vol. 9, no. 2, pp. 128–139.

Marinova, D & Phillimore, J 2003, 'Models of innovation', in LV Shavinina (ed), *The international handbook on innovation*, Elsevier Science, pp. 44–53.

Markham, SK 2013, 'The impact of front-end innovation activities on product performance', *Journal of Product Innovation Management*, vol. 30, pp. 77–92.

Markham, SK & Lee, H 2013, 'Product development and management association's 2012 comparative performance assessment study', *Journal of Product Innovation Management*, vol. 30, no. 3, pp. 408–429.

Maslow, AH 1943, 'A theory of human motivation', *Psychological Review*, vol. 50, pp. 370–396.

Mattson, CA & Wood, AE 2014, 'Nine principles for design for the developing world as derived from the engineering literature', *Journal of Mechanical Design*, vol. 136, no. 12, pp. 121403-1–121403-15.

McCarthy, IP, Tsinopoulos, C, Allen, P & Rose-Anderssen, C 2006, 'New product development as a complex adaptive system of decisions', *Journal of Product Innovation Management*, vol. 23, no. 5, pp. 437–456.

McKinley, W, Latham, S & Braun, M 2014, 'Organizational decline and innovation: Turnarounds and downward spirals', *Academy of Management Review*, vol. 39, no. 1, pp. 88–110.

Millson, MR & Wilemon, D 2006, 'Driving new product success in the electrical equipment manufacturing industry', *Technovation*, vol. 26, no. 11, pp. 1268–1286.

Mukerjee, K 2012, 'Frugal innovation: The key to penetrating emerging markets', *Ivey Business Journal*, viewed 5 February 2018, <www.iveybusinessjournal.com/

uncategorized/frugal-innovation-the-key-to-penetrating-emerging-markets-. VH_3AzGUfzh>.

Murphy, SA & Kumar, V 1997, 'The front end of new product development: A Canadian survey', *R&D Management*, vol. 27, no. 1, pp. 5–15.

Nakata, CC & Berger, E 2011, 'Chapter 18 new product development for the base of the pyramid: A theory-and case-based framework', in C Subhash, D Jain and A Griffith (eds), *Handbook of research in international marketing*, Edward Elgar Publishing, UK, pp. 349–375.

Nakata, CC & Weidner, K 2012, 'Enhancing new product adoption at the base of the pyramid: A contextualized model', *Journal of Product Innovation Management*, vol. 29, no. 1, pp. 21–32.

Nijssen, EJ & Lieshout, KFM 1995, 'Awareness, use and effectiveness of models and methods for new product development', *European Journal of Marketing*, vol. 29, no. 10, pp. 27–44.

Nobelius, D 2004, 'Towards the sixth generation of R&D management', *International Journal of Project Management*, vol. 22, no. 5, pp. 369–375.

Nonaka, I 1990, 'Redundant, overlapping organization: A Japanese approach to managing the innovation process', *California Management Review*, vol. 32, no. 3, pp. 27–38.

OECD 2005, *Oslo manual: Guidelines for collecting and interpreting innovation data*, viewed 10 November 2017, <epp.eurostat.ec.europa.eu/cache/ITY_PUBLIC/OSLO/EN/OSLO-EN.PDF>.

Pansera, M 2013, 'Frugality, grassroots and inclusiveness: New challenges for mainstream innovation theories', *African Journal of Science, Technology, Innovation and Development*, vol. 5, no. 6, pp. 469–478.

Pansera, M & Owen, R 2015, 'Framing resource-constrained innovation at the "bottom of the pyramid": Insights from an ethnographic case study in rural Bangladesh', *Technological Forecasting and Social Change*, vol. 92, pp. 30–311.

Payaud, MA 2014, 'Marketing strategies at the bottom of the pyramid: Examples from Nestlé, Danone, and Procter & Gamble', *Global Business and Organizational Excellence*, vol. 33, no. 2, pp. 51–63.

PDI 2017, *About us*, viewed 5 October 2017, <www.prod-dev.com/aboutus.php>.

PDMA 2017, *About PDMA*, viewed 25th July 2017, <www.pdma.org/members>.

Petrick, IJ 2011, 'Innovation in emerging markets', *Research Technology Management*, vol. 54, no. 4, pp. 8–9.

Pisoni, A, Michelini, L & Martignoni, G 2018, 'Frugal approach to innovation: State of the art and future perspectives', *Journal of Cleaner Production*, vol. 171, no. Supplement C, pp. 107–126.

Poolton, J & Barclay, I 1998, 'New product development from past research to future applications', *Industrial Marketing Management*, vol. 27, no. 3, pp. 197–212.

Prahalad, CK 2005, *The fortune at the bottom of the pyramid: Eradicating poverty through profits*, Wharton School, New Delhi, India.

Prahalad, CK 2009, *The fortune at the bottom of the pyramid, revised and updated 5th anniversary edition: Eradicating poverty through profits*, FT Press.

Prahalad, CK 2012, 'Bottom of the pyramid as a source of breakthrough innovations', *Journal of Product Innovation Management*, vol. 29, no. 1, pp. 6–12.

Radjou, N & Prabhu, J 2015, *Frugal innovation: How to do more with less*, Profile Books, London.

Radjou, N, Prabhu, J & Ahuja, S 2012, *Jugaad innovation: Think frugal, be flexible, generate breakthrough growth*, John Wiley & Sons, Inc.

Rajadurai, S & Parameshwari, C 2014, 'Benchmarking – The first step for frugal engineering', *International Journal of Innovative Science, Engineering & Technology*, vol. 6, no. 1, pp. 282–285.

Ramdorai, A & Herstatt, C 2017, 'Lessons from low-cost healthcare innovations for the base-of the pyramid markets: How incumbents can systematically create disruptive innovations', in C Herstatt and R Tiwari (eds), *Lead market India*, Springer, pp. 119–144.

Rao, BC 2013, 'How disruptive is frugal?' *Technology in Society*, vol. 35, no. 1, pp. 65–73.

Ray, S & Ray, P 2011, 'Product innovation for the people's car in an emerging economy', *Technovation*, vol. 31, no. 5–6, pp. 216–227.

Rosca, E, Arnold, M & Bendul, JC 2017, 'Business models for sustainable innovation – An empirical analysis of frugal products and services', *Journal of Cleaner Production*, vol. 162, no. Supplement, pp. S133–S145.

Rosca, E & Bendul, J 2017, 'Frugal and lean engineering: A critical comparison and implications for logistics processes', in M Freitag, H Kotzab and J Pannek (eds), Dynamics in logistics: Proceedings of the 5th International Conference LDIC, 2016, Springer International Publishing, Bremen, Germany, pp. 335–345.

Rothwell, R 1994, 'Towards the fifth-generation innovation process', *International Marketing Review*, vol. 11, no. 1, pp. 7–31.

Salerno, MS, Gomes, LADV, Silva, DOD, Bagno, RB & Freitas, SLTU 2015, 'Innovation processes: Which process for which project?' *Technovation*, vol. 35, no. 1, pp. 59–70.

Schilling, MA & Hill, CWL 1998, 'Managing the new product development process: Strategic imperatives', *The Academy of Management Executive*, vol. 12, no. 3, pp. 67–81.

Schumpeter, JA 1939, *Business cycles: A theoretical, historical and statistical analysis of the capitalist process*, 1st edn., McGraw-Hill, New York and London.

Sehgal, V, Dehoff, K & Panneer, G 2010, 'The importance of frugal engineering', *Strategy + Business*, Summer 2010, no. 59, pp. 1–4.

Sen, A 1999, *Development as freedom*, Knopf, New York.

Shum, P & Lin, G 2007, 'A world class new product development best practices model', *International Journal of Production Research*, vol. 45, no. 7, pp. 1609–1629.

Šoltés, M, Kappler, D, Koberstaedt, S & Lienkamp, M 2017, 'Flexible, user-and product-centered framework for developing frugal products based on a case study of a vehicle for Sub-Saharan Africa', ASME 2017 International Mechanical Engineering Congress and Exposition, American Society of Mechanical Engineers, pp. V014T07A021-V014T07A021.

Soni, P & Krishnan, R 2014, 'Frugal innovation: Aligning theory, practice, and public policy', *Journal of Indian Business Research*, vol. 6, no. 1, pp. 29–47.

Subramaniam, M, Ernst, H & Dubiel, A 2015, 'From the special issue editors: Innovations for and from emerging markets', *Journal of Product Innovation Management*, vol. 32, no. 1, pp. 5–11.

Takeuchi, H & Nonaka, I 1986, 'The new product development game', *Harvard Business Review*, vol. 64, no. 1, pp. 137–146.

Tao, L, Probert, D & Phaal, R 2010, 'Towards an integrated framework for managing the process of innovation', *R&D Management*, vol. 40, no. 1, pp. 19–30.

Tatikonda, MV & Montoya-Weiss, MM 2001, 'Integrating operations and marketing perspectives of product innovation: The influence of organizational process factors and capabilities on development performance', *Management Science*, vol. 47, no. 1, January, p. 151.

Tidd, J 2001, 'Innovation management in context: Environment, organization and performance', *International Journal of Management Reviews*, vol. 3, no. 3, pp. 169–183.

Tidd, J 2013, *Managing innovation: Integrating technological, market and organizational change*, 5th edn., John Wiley & Sons, Inc., Chichester, West Sussex.

Tidd, J, Bessant, J & Pavitt, K 2005, *Managing innovation – integrating technological, market and organizational change*, 3rd edn., John Wiley and Sons, Inc., Australia.

Tiwari, R, Fischer, L & Kalogerakis, K 2016, 'Frugal innovation in scholarly and social discourse: An assessment of trends and potential societal implications', Joint working paper of Fraunhofer MOEZ Leipzig and Hamburg University of Technology in the BMBF-ITA project, Leipzig, Hamburg.

Tiwari, R & Herstatt, C 2013, '"Too good' to succeed? Why not just try 'good enough'! Some deliberations on the prospects of frugal innovations', Working paper No. 76. Hamburg, Institute for Technology and Innovation Management, Hamburg University of Technology.

Tiwari, R & Herstatt, C 2014, 'Developing countries and innovation', in *Aiming big with small cars*, Springer International Publishing, Switzerland, pp. 19–39.

Tiwari, R, Kalogerakis, K & Herstatt, C 2016, 'Frugal innovations in the mirror of scholarly discourse: Tracing theoretical basis and antecedents', R&D Management Conference, Cambridge.

Trott, P 2012, *Innovation management and new product development*, 5th edn., Financial Times, Prentice Hall, Harlow.

Ulrich, KT 2011, 'Design is everything?' *Journal of Product Innovation Management*, vol. 28, no. 3, pp. 394–398.

Ulrich, KT & Eppinger, SD 2012, *Product design and development*, 5th edn., McGraw-Hill Higher Education, New York.

van den Ende, J, Frederiksen, L & Prencipe, A 2015, 'The front end of innovation: Organizing search for ideas', *Journal of Product Innovation Management*, vol. 32, no. 4, pp. 482–487.

Van Kleef, E, van Trijp, H & Luning, P 2005, 'Consumer research in the early stages of new product development: A critical review of methods and techniques', *Food Quality and Preference*, vol. 16, no. 3, pp. 181–201.

Verworn, B, Herstatt, C & Nagahira, A 2008, 'The fuzzy front end of Japanese new product development projects: Impact on success and differences between incremental and radical projects', *R&D Management*, vol. 38, no. 1, pp. 1–19.

Veryzer, RW 1998, 'Discontinuous innovation and the new product development process', *Journal of Product Innovation Management*, vol. 15, no. 4, pp. 304–321.

Viswanathan, M & Sridharan, S 2012, 'Product development for the BOP: Insights on concept and prototype development from university-based student projects in India', *Journal of Product Innovation Management*, vol. 29, no. 1, pp. 52–69.

Von Stamm, B 2008, *Managing innovation, design and creativity*, 2nd edn., John Wiley & Sons, Inc., Chichester.

Weyrauch, T & Herstatt, C 2017, 'What is frugal innovation? Three defining criteria', *Journal of Frugal Innovation*, vol. 2, no. 1, pp. 1–17.

Whitney, P 2010, 'Reframing design for the base of the pyramid', in T London and SL Hart (eds), *Next generation business strategies for the base of the pyramid: New approaches for building mutual value*, FT Press, Upper Saddle River, NJ, pp. 165–192.

Williamson, PJ 2010, 'Cost innovation: Preparing for a "value-for-money" revolution', *Long Range Planning*, vol. 43, no. 2, pp. 343–353.

Winterhalter, S, Zeschky, MB, Neumann, L & Gassmann, O 2017, 'Business models for frugal innovation in emerging markets: The case of the medical device and laboratory equipment industry', *Technovation*, vol. 66, pp. 3–13.

Wood, AE & Mattson, CA 2016, 'Design for the developing world: Common pitfalls and how to avoid them', *Journal of Mechanical Design*, vol. 138, no. 3, pp. 031101-1–031101-11.

Wooldridge, A 2010, *First break all the rules: The charms of frugal innovation*, viewed 15 October 2017, <www.economist.com/node/15879359>.

World Bank 2015, *Poverty & equity data portal*, viewed 21 September 2018, <http://povertydata.worldbank.org/Poverty/Home>.

Yin, Y, Kaku, I & Liu, C 2012, 'Product architecture, product development process, system integrator and product global performance', *Production Planning & Control*, vol. 25, no. 3, pp. 203–219.

Yunus, M, Moingeon, B & Lehmann-Ortega, L 2010, 'Building social business models: Lessons from the Grameen experience', *Long Range Planning*, vol. 43, no. 2, pp. 308–325.

Zeschky, MB, Widenmayer, B & Gassmann, O 2011, 'Frugal innovation in emerging markets: The case of Mettler Toledo', *Research-Technology Management*, vol. 54, no. 4, pp. 38–45.

Zeschky, MB, Widenmayer, B & Gassmann, O 2014, 'Organising for reverse innovation in Western MNCs: The role of frugal product innovation capabilities', *International Journal of Technology Management*, vol. 64, no. 2, pp. 255–275.

Zeschky, MB, Winterhalter, S & Gassmann, O 2014, 'From cost to frugal and reverse innovation: Mapping the field and implications for global competitiveness', *Research-Technology Management*, vol. 57, no. 4, pp. 20–27.

Zirger, BJ & Maidique, MA 1990, 'A model of new product development: An empirical test', *Management Science*, vol. 36, no. 7, pp. 867–883.

3 Mapping NPDP for frugal innovation

Introduction

This chapter details the NPDP framework for frugal innovation, which is further explored through case studies in Chapter 4 and Chapter 5. To establish this framework, the frugal innovation literature is mapped on the consolidated NPDP developed in Chapter 2 (see Figure 3.1 for a reminder of the four phases and nine corresponding stages). Doing so contextualised the knowledge on which the NPDP framework for frugal innovation is based, leading to the development of 15 frugal innovation management practices.

Each frugal innovation practice highlights the conceptual and practical NPDP approaches related to firms that have developed new frugal products for BOP markets in developing countries worldwide. These are not intended to describe exactly what frugal innovators do, but rather to inform what the literature and case studies have deemed as pivotal to frugal innovators developing new products successfully for BOP markets. These practices and related findings do not refute the existing generic practices of NPDP; instead, they refine them to the context of frugal innovation.

This chapter will first introduce the methodology for the frugal innovation literature review, and the four subsequent sections will illustrate the four phases that form the foundation of the NPDP for frugal innovation. The four phases are divided into the associated stages that align with achieving the goals of each phase. These stages are structured around insights extracted from the NPDP literature for developed countries and related to the key characteristics of decisions taken in this stage. It also includes the most commonly used tools and techniques that facilitate these decisions.

As a final component to exploring each stage, a focused review of the frugal innovation literature is undertaken, including key conceptual and case studies that provide insights into this stage. This part is pivotal, as it establishes the key tenets of NPDP management practices for frugal innovation, which lead to 15 key management practices. The chapter will conclude by explaining the research methods used and the demographics for Prime Cookstoves and Tirta Indonesia Mandiri Foundation as the two case studies of this research.

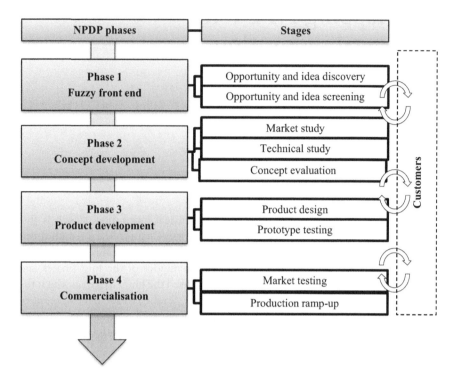

Figure 3.1 Consolidated NPDP: four phases and nine stages

Frugal innovation literature review

To build the framework for this study, the frugal innovation literature review involved identifying right-fit information for the consolidated NPDP foundation. Both academic and non-academic content on both frugal innovation products and frugal innovators' decisions linked to the underlying processes were used. This section explains the methodology of the literature review, including databases, sources, keywords and date search, case studies and software used. These all add validity to the results that established the NPDP framework for frugal innovation.

In this methodology, the choice of databases, sources and keywords was made to search for relevant frugal innovation literature. First, looking at databases and sources, the identification of published articles was carried out via academic databases including ProQuest Central, EBSCOhost, Science Direct and Google Scholar as well as non-academic methods such as the Google search engine to find frugal innovation case studies. This review of frugal innovation literature incorporated academic and non-academic materials, practitioners' articles and information publicly available for triangulation (Yin 2014).

The academic materials consisted of journal articles that are conceptual, based on scientific case studies and/or used as teaching materials (e.g. Macke, Misra & Sharma 2003; Rao 2013; Ray & Ray 2011). These articles were also taken from peer-reviewed journals (e.g. *Journal of Product Innovation Management*), new journals (e.g. *Journal of Frugal Innovation*), books (e.g. Radjou & Prabhu 2015), editor-reviewed publications (e.g. *Harvard Business Review*) and working papers (e.g. Tiwari, Kalogerakis & Herstatt 2014) as well as articles in conference proceedings (e.g. IEEE and ASME conferences) due to their reputable publication status and engineering interest in developing countries.

Non-academic materials were also reviewed, due to the relevance of the other types of publications within the frugal innovation research domain. As Tiwari, Kalogerakis and Herstatt (2016) assert, most of the highly cited publications by scholars originate from non- or semi-academic journals. These include reports such as those published by consulting or government groups (e.g. Bound & Thornton 2012; Gassmann et al. 2017). Non-academic materials, particularly used for case studies, refer to business magazines (e.g. McGregor 2008), firm websites (e.g. Barefoot Power 2017), non-government organisation (NGO) reports (e.g. Business call to action n.d.) and international development organisations (e.g. World Bank 2013).

The search of frugal innovation literature, while not exhaustive, involved juggling and combining four categories of keywords, as shown in Table 3.1, and included all text and titles, abstract, keywords and in-text. The first category is directly linked to frugal innovation and the terms synonymously used in the literature, and the second refers to the topics or variants often associated with frugal

Table 3.1 Categories of keywords for the frugal innovation literature review

Categories	*Examples of key terms or phrases*
Frugal innovation and synonymous terms	Frugal innovation; frugal innovations; frugal engineering; Jugaad innovation; low-cost innovation; cost-innovation; good-enough innovation; Base-of-the-Pyramid (BOP) markets; innovation in developing countries/emerging countries/emerging markets/BOP markets/Bottom-of-the-Pyramid/the poor/low-income markets
Associated topics/ variants	Resource-constrained environment; innovation for development; inclusive innovation; reverse innovation
Innovation process	New product development process; innovation process; product innovation process; new product development; product innovation; product design; product development
Associated phases and/or stages (and synonyms)	Fuzzy front end; concept development; product development; commercialisation; idea and opportunity discovery/generation/screening; market study/research; technical study/specifications; concept generation/evaluation/testing; product design/system design/detailed design; prototype/product testing; market testing; production ramp-up; pilot production

innovation. To restrict the search results of frugal innovation articles around NPDP, the third category is linked to firms' innovation processes and the fourth narrows the focus on the study's consolidated stages and the synonymous terms used within the NPDP literature.

Some articles were filtered out from this keyword search, as they did not match the definition of frugal innovation used in Chapter 2, for example, cost-innovation by Williamson (2010), though they were useful in refining the understanding of the frugal innovation concept. These search results were complemented by snow-balling search, and backward and cross-analysis of references. In addition, articles written in English only were reviewed.

Furthermore, as this study sought to create an NPDP framework based on modern frugal innovation practices, the articles reviewed start from the year 2000. This is because frugal innovation studies have re-emerged in the early 2000s via Prahalad and Hart (2002)[1] and progressed particularly in the last five years (Pisoni, Michelini & Martignoni 2018).

The development of the NPDP framework, including its frugal innovation practices, stems from the review of the conceptual, empirical and case study-based literature. This combination of materials, in particular case study research, enabled refinement of existing theoretical understanding and helped address gaps in frugal innovators' NPDP practices (Siggelkow 2007). The case studies also highlighted frugal innovators' failures and successes experienced throughout the NPDP of their new frugal products.

Moreover, the use of these case studies did not consider whether start-ups, small and medium-sized enterprises, multinationals or social enterprises were the origi-nators of the frugal innovation (Brem & Wolfram 2014; Hossain 2017; Pisoni, Michelini & Martignoni 2018). Additionally, this literature review, including fru-gal innovation case studies where possible, was not intended to be exhaustive or highly technical. Frugal innovation literature and case studies are instead used to illustrate key frugal innovators' management decisions linked to each NPDP stage.

Furthermore, this NPDP framework sourced several case studies of frugal innovation across the four NPDP phases and related stages, in contrast to using one single case study across the whole NPDP. One of the main reasons for this was due to the need for diverse case studies supporting a frugal innovation prac-tice, which enhances the quality criteria of this study. Another key reason was the difficulty of finding information at every decision stage of each case study. Triangulation of findings for each frugal innovation case study was sought across several sources of information to ensure the most refined version of the decisions taken during the NPDP. This search, including backward and forward citation analysis and cross-analysis, ensured a more comprehensive literature review.

While some aspects of the frugal innovation literature were used for a spe-cific stage, there was a possibility of overlap with the rest of the NPDP; how-ever, the most relevant stage was chosen. The primary basis for this study's review was undertaken between 2014 and 2016, although sources that were not identified earlier or those published more recently were added if they were rel-evant (e.g. Numminen & Lund 2017; Ramdorai & Herstatt 2017). Finally, the

NVivo11 qualitative analysis software was used to organise the literature and to gather notes, facilitating the literature review process. Using this software allowed both coding of the literature on the basis of where it fits within the consolidated NPDP as well as retrieving of the information at any time. The next section introduces the first phase of the study's NPDP framework for frugal innovation – the fuzzy front end.

Phase 1: the fuzzy front end and frugal innovation

The fuzzy front end, also often termed the "front end of innovation", is the initial phase of the NPDP when firms[2] instigate the search for innovative new products (Koen, Bertels & Kleinschmidt 2014; Reid & De Brentani 2004). This phase is often viewed as chaotic due to the discovery and screening of new product opportunities where creativity is intertwined with high uncertainties and risks (Kahn et al. 2012a; Smith & Reinertsen 1991).

The literature suggests this is a crucial phase for reducing uncertainties across the NPDP and for the development of 'winning' products, or products that have the potential to be commercialised (e.g. Cooper & Kleinschmidt 1987; Khurana & Rosenthal 1998; Koen, Bertels & Kleinschmidt 2014). This phase also assists managers in investing resources in projects most likely to succeed (Reid & De Brentani 2004; Verworn, Herstatt & Nagahira 2008).

The following subsections discuss the generic fuzzy front end phase of the NPDP, where the main decision-making processes are divided across two overlapping stages: opportunity and idea discovery, and opportunity and idea screening. Building from these stages, frugal innovation literature is utilised in the development of four key frugal innovation practices, highlighting frugal innovators' decisions across these stages' characteristics, tools and techniques.

Opportunity and idea discovery stage

The decisions taken in this stage enable control over both the identification of opportunities and the nurturing of new ideas, resulting in the development of new product opportunities[3] (Cooper 2011). Such opportunities can be defined as "a product description in embryonic form, a newly sensed need, a newly discovered technology, or a rough match between a need and a possible solution" (Ulrich & Eppinger 2012, p. 34). Depending on the innovation strategy, a new product opportunity can respond to an identified opportunity gap in business, market or technology and can widen a firm's new product portfolio, and improve or reduce costs of existing products (Barczak, Griffin & Kahn 2009; Ulrich & Eppinger 2012).

Although decisions made during this stage are deemed to be significant in firms' NPDP (Gassmann & Schweitzer 2014; Langerak, Jan Hultink & Robben 2004), firms still appear inconsistent in choosing what practices suit them best, including the choice over tools and techniques. Looking at the characteristics illustrating the distinctive decisions in this discovery stage, two primary ones identified in the extant literature are discussed ahead, before examining the most common tools and techniques.

Characteristics

The degree of formalisation and the innovation approach chosen by firms describe the two characteristics of this stage. First, the degree of formalisation establishes how much a firm chooses to formalise its processes to discover new product opportunities. The second characteristic includes the technology-push or market-pull discovery of new product opportunity.

The first characteristic describes the actions undertaken to identify or generate new product opportunities, which can be either following formalised procedures or based on informal processes (Cooper 2010; Koen et al. 2002). A formal stage occurs through the decision to implement systematic control over the sources from where new product opportunities appear. In contrast, an informal stage is defined by its unsystematic and unexpected nature, such as from individual creativity or intuition, which enables innovative pathways for new products (Globocnik & Salomo 2015; Koen et al. 2002; Ulrich & Eppinger 2012).

Even though formal procedures are not necessary for NPDP (Koen, Bertels & Kleinschmidt 2014; Rochford 1991), Cooper and Edgett (2008) asserted that having control over the foundations driving the generation of new product opportunities still remains a key advantage for firms. This is especially the case when attempting to "maximize the quality of the *best idea* or the few best ideas" (Girotra, Terwiesch & Ulrich 2010, p. 593). In Cooper's (2011, p. 103) definition of 'discovery stage' or 'ideation stage', his perception of an idea reflects a "feedstock or trigger to the [NPD] process".

The implementation of a formal process enables more systematic events within a firm to "build in a defined, proactive idea-generation and capture system" (Cooper 2011, p. 103). Holahan, Sullivan and Markham (2014) argued that its inclusion as one of the initial stages depends on the nature of the innovation the firm aims to undertake (e.g. incremental versus radical).

Moreover, the innovation approach characteristic mostly relates to where new product opportunities are derived from, such as technology-push and/or market-pull aspects. Driven by the intention of using technological know-how, a firm would undertake a technology-push approach by prioritising methods for further technology development (Whitney 2007). In contrast, the market-pull approach captures methods that enable a firm to be more market-opportunistic; that is, to identify new product opportunities from market gaps (Brem & Voigt 2009).

Both Murphy and Kumar (1997) and Ulrich and Eppinger (2012) argued that seeking market opportunities (i.e. market-pull) can provide valuable inputs into new idea generation. However, looking for new ideas (i.e. technology-push) may also create inputs that reveal opportunities (Börjesson, Dahlsten & Williander 2006; Khurana & Rosenthal 1998).

Even though Brem and Voigt (2009) recommend the combination of both approaches from a long-term perspective, they still need to be separately acknowledged by a firm in a clear way. The innovation approach, undertaken at this stage, is likely to influence how the remaining stages are performed throughout the entire NPDP (Ortt & van der Duin 2008). These characteristics of the opportunity and idea discovery stage are crucial for understanding firms' relevant decisions.

Markham and Lee (2013) also assert the importance of tools and techniques that provide more formal guidance to firms when choosing the sources of new products opportunities. The next section builds from this point, introducing the most common tools and techniques available for firms to undertake this stage more efficiently and effectively.

Tools and techniques

There are various tools and techniques to enhance the effectiveness of discovering new product opportunities. These can provide both internal and external sources of ideas as well as support to control the flow of ideas while remaining within the firm's goals and strategy (Cooper 2011; Kim & Wilemon 2002). The three most common tools and techniques include brainstorming, industry assessments and voice-of-the-customer (VOC) (Baumgartner 2010; Cooper & Edgett 2008; de Waal & Knott 2010; Koen, Bertels & Kleinschmidt 2014; Yeh, Yang & Pai 2010).

Brainstorming is also referred to as a problem-solving technique. TRIZ (Russian acronym) is an example of brainstorming, which aims to trigger a development team's creative and critical thinking (Koen et al. 2002; Trott 2012). In contrast, industry assessments are a set of techniques enabling a firm to analyse its industry environment (Koen et al. 2002). This can include technique such as scenario analysis, which generally offers the most return for value according to the firm's NPD strategy (Crawford & Di Benedetto 2014). Competitive intelligence analysis is another technique, which allows the collection, examination and discussion of strategic competitors information across the market, industry and consumers (Griffin & Somermeyer 2007b; Koen et al. 2002).

Last, VOC refers to customer-driven ideation techniques, such as close interactions between firms and consumers. Cooper and Edgett (2008) and Cooper and Dreher (2010) asserted that these were the most effective techniques for this stage, yet less commonly used compared with the techniques using internally stimulated idea sources. Further examples include consumer visits for in-depth interviews, focus groups and lead-user techniques (Cooper & Edgett 2008; Herstatt & von Hippel 1992) as well as open innovation and social networks (Crawford & Di Benedetto 2011; Markham & Lee 2013).

This understanding of the key characteristics as well as the most common tools and techniques utilised during the opportunity and idea discovery stage frames the review of the frugal innovation literature and the development of two key frugal innovation practices for this stage.

Frugal innovation studies

To discover new ideas and opportunities, the frugal innovation literature suggests two main practices leading to the development of the two initial management frugal innovation Practices 1 and 2. First, frugal innovators tend to manage this stage from a market-pull approach that leverages BOP market constraints. The second is the use of tools and techniques that lean towards external sources of inspiration.

FI PRACTICE 1

With regard to the first practice, frugal innovators often seem to follow a market-pull approach, identifying problems from BOP market constraints (Nakata & Berger 2011; Prahalad 2012). This approach may stem from the uniqueness of consumers' constraints in these markets such as their disposable income (Prahalad 2012) and the resource-poor environment in which they live (Cunha et al. 2014). Examples of this are the M-PESA and the Mitticool fridge.

The M-PESA is an affordable, secure and quick cash transfer operating through text messages, enabling rural, low-income consumers to transfer and deposit money (Hughes & Lonie 2007; World Bank 2013). The M-PESA product originated from Nick Hughes, a Vodafone UK executive[4] who sought to help reduce poverty via the Millennium Development Goals (MDGs) (Hughes & Lonie 2007; United Nations 2016). While the UK Government's Financial Deepening Challenge Fund (FDCF) inspired Hughes' goal to procuring low-income consumers' financial sustainability, he also investigated BOP market constraints related specifically to developing countries. He observed a major impediment to financial transactions for those living within low-income brackets:

> The issue is exactly how money transfer is made to happen in an emerging market where the infrastructure is poorly developed and where very few people have or even want bank accounts.
>
> (Hughes & Lonie 2007, p. 65)

The under-developed banking infrastructure in developing countries was, therefore, determined as a significant barrier. Hughes also realised that local entrepreneurs' capital movements were difficult to conduct in a cheap and safe manner due to this infrastructural barrier (Hughes & Lonie 2007). Versed in telecommunications technology, Hughes envisioned telecommunications networks to enhance the flow of money between entrepreneurs and businesses in developing countries (Hughes & Lonie 2007). This shows how constraints that bound BOP consumers in their current situation may highlight market gaps and problems, leading to new product opportunities for a firm.

Turning to the Mitticool fridge, this affordable cooling system made from clay and operating without electricity conveyed the important role of the inventor's discovery process. He took into consideration low-income Indian people constrained by a region experiencing frequent earthquakes (Earthquaketrack 2018; Institute of Seismological Research 2013; Mitticool 2011). Mansukhbhai Prajapati, a local clay potter and the inventor of this frugal product, saw all his clay pots destroyed in an earthquake that devastated the Gujarat region in India (Mitticool

2011). When local media highlighted that clay pots were the fridge of the poor in India, he questioned how he could assist local communities in recovering from this earthquake and spotted the opportunity to offer more affordable household appliances (Anand 2014; Mitticool 2011). The inventor's consideration for market problems, including this market constrained by the local environment, thus triggered the identification of the need for affordable cooling system for poor people in India, which framed his discovery stage.

These empirical insights highlight the importance of an NPDP grounded in a market-pull approach. This study will, therefore, investigate whether frugal innovators seek out societal problems that factor in the constraints of BOP markets, preferring a market-pull approach to their innovation process. Extending from this, the study will also focus on whether frugal innovators' practices generally remain within the limited scope of BOP market constraints during this stage.

FI PRACTICE 2

The second practice identified reflects the use of tools and techniques to help frugal innovators discover new frugal product opportunities mainly inspired from external sources. That is, frugal innovators appear to first identify new product opportunities by observing and exploring problems in available yet inadequate products for BOP consumers. Such an approach of examining existing product solutions and their associated problems for BOP seems to inspire the development of alternatives to better serve BOP consumers' needs (McManus et al. 2008; Zeschky, Widenmayer & Gassmann 2011). It suggests that such approaches, which focus on existing product offerings, brings to light a need for such a product if an adequately adapted (frugal) version can be produced (Zeschky, Widenmayer & Gassmann 2011). Ahead, several case studies are explored that show the intent of examining existing product solutions during this stage (e.g. the ChotuKool fridge and the Jaipur Foot).

Godrej and Boyce's ChotuKool fridge, an efficient and portable cooling system adapted to rural Indian markets, was developed from identifying the drawbacks in existing fridge solutions (ChotuKool 2014). After participating in a seminar about disruptive innovation, the team questioned the low penetration rate among the Indian BOP population of currently available refrigerators, revealing significant inadequacies in traditional refrigeration units (ChotuKool 2014; Dhanaraj, Suram & Vemuri 2011). Such problems stemmed from the fridges' standardisation to higher-end markets, particularly their high energy consumption and high production and reparability costs as well as inadequate design features such as large size (Eyring, Johnson & Nair 2011).

There are similarities in this approach with the Jaipur Foot, an affordable below-knee prosthetic adapted to Indian BOP patients' lifestyles. This product evolved from the experiences of Dr Sethi and Ram Chandra Sharma observing patients at the Sawai Mansingh Hospital in Jaipur (India). They perceived a low acceptance rate of imported prosthetics among patients fitted with Western design technology (Disability and Development Partners 2013; Macke, Misra &

Sharma 2003). The potential for a new prosthetic or a new fridge opportunity, therefore, came from the design issues of existing products, suggesting that new frugal product opportunities reside in BOP consumers likely to be receptive to a better-designed and tailored product to suit their particular context.

Leveraging these case studies, this research will investigate whether tools and techniques for frugal innovation tend to use external sources of inspiration for their discovery stage to identify new frugal product opportunities like with the Chotu-Kool and the Jaipur Foot cases. For example, it can uncover whether frugal innovators examine the inadequacies of existing product offerings. Tools and techniques using external sources of ideas are thus proposed to be one of the potential practices to direct this stage (as opposed to originating from internally inspired sources).

The next section introduces the opportunity and idea screening stage, which describes the second focus of the fuzzy front end phase. The examination of the frugal innovation literature in the next stage lead to two further key frugal innovation practices.

Opportunity and idea screening stage

The purpose of this stage is to assess new product opportunities discovered in the previous stage and eliminate those not worthy of further investment for both consumers and the firm (Cooper 2011; Ulrich & Eppinger 2012). Such assessment of new product opportunities reveals their compatibility with firms' objectives and competencies, avoiding potential failures (Cooper 2011; Koen, Bertels & Kleinschmidt 2014).

Decisions at the screening stage relate to preliminary appraisals of new product opportunities prior to selecting the 'right' prospects to pursue (Tzokas, Hultink & Hart 2004). Such evaluations can relate to technical, market and/or financial appraisals of a pending NPD project (Martinsuo & Poskela 2011). The main purpose behind this stage is to enable a firm to use a formalised system for better control and increased innovation performance (Cooper 2011). Shaping firms' new product opportunity choices, this stage embeds two key characteristics that define this decision-making stage.

Characteristics

The first characteristic refers to the degree of formalisation structuring this stage, and the second is the type and depth of information that firms use in their evaluation and choice of new product opportunities. Looking first at the degree of formalisation, the decision processes during this stage are influenced by a scale from less to more formal structures. An informal structure provides flexible and adaptive decision-making to select and revise new product opportunities outside a systematic process (Florén & Frishammar 2012). Examples are using intuition or informal discussions to help make decisions (Koen et al. 2002; Koen, Bertels & Kleinschmidt 2014).

In contrast, in a more formal structure there is a variety of systematic ways to help shape decisions, resulting in formal assignments of resources allocated to this process such as time, money and teams (Cooper 2011; Koen et al. 2002). These could also involve decision points where decision-makers explore and prioritise their options (Robben 2010), such as 'screening gates' (Cooper 2011). Conversely, Koen, Bertels and Kleinschmidt (2014) argue that the formal screening processes can happen at any time in the fuzzy front end phase, with a flexibility of occurrence. Tidd (2013, p. 407) describes such systematic selection processes as "a fine balancing act" between the risks of choosing an unsuitable NPD project and rejecting a promising one.

Integrating this screening process before a firm commits to NPD projects increases its ability to both reject the poorer opportunities and to concentrate on the most valuable and innovative ones (Singh & Fleming 2010). A recent study by Markham and Lee (2013), surveying 453 firms among PDMA members from various countries and industries, demonstrated that the rate of new product opportunities that were evaluated and prioritised as part of a formal screening process was significantly higher at 60 per cent as compared with results from older studies like in Cooper and Kleinschmidt (1986). The increase in formalisation during the opportunity and idea selection has been shown to support firms' innovation success.

The second characteristic refers to the types and depth of information reviewed during the assessment and selection of new product opportunities, shaping firms' selection criteria. At this stage, the types of information are generally technical (e.g. legal and technology risks), market (e.g. market attractiveness) and business (e.g. strategic fit, and manufacturing and cost capabilities) (Cooper 2011; Girotra, Terwiesch & Ulrich 2010). These can differ according to a firm's context, including country of origin, product portfolio situation and/or 'newness' of products (Hart et al. 2003; Schmidt, Sarangee & Montoya 2009).

For example, when new products stem from an existing product category, Ulrich and Eppinger (2012) recommended focusing on competitive strategy, market segmentation and/or current product platforms. In contrast, risks and uncertainties increase with completely new products, requiring evaluation of market size and growth, competition, potential for patents and/or existing industry knowledge (Koen et al. 2002; Ulrich & Eppinger 2012).

Occurring early in firms' NPDP, this search of information has generally limited depth in comparison with those occurring in more structured processes at latter stages. Various authors (e.g. Cooper 2011; Koen et al. 2002; Ulrich & Eppinger 2012) have suggested that the search should use 'guessed estimations' and secondary data as a sufficient depth for this stage. For example, one-page overviews of each type of information are suggested to make the screening process time-efficient (Adams, Bessant & Phelps 2006; Koen et al. 2002). The use of a wide range of tools and techniques can positively influence the decisions and outcomes from this stage. The most commonly used during this stage are introduced ahead.

Tools and techniques

There are a variety of tools and techniques that can increase firms' likelihood of choosing the 'right' new product opportunities, although no one method can guarantee successful screening (Cooper 2011; Koen, Bertels & Kleinschmidt 2014). The type of information targeted during this stage usually informs the type of tools and techniques used. The literature reveals the most common tools and techniques are financial measurement, checklist/scoring models, and financial/business models (Koen et al. 2002; Cooper 2011; Pahl, Wallace & Blessing 2007).

Financial measurement enables the screening of new product opportunities based on basic financial metrics as well as their 'newness', and techniques include forecasted sales and profits, discounted cash flow, and net present value (Koen et al. 2002). Checklist tools instead provide a quick prioritising system, using 'must' criteria for strict and rapid elimination of future NPD projects that do not align with firms' key requisites (Cooper 2011; Schmidt, Sarangee & Montoya 2009). The scoring model uses rating scales and weightings with less strict 'should' criteria, opening early discussions about the least promising options (Cooper 2011; Schmidt, Sarangee & Montoya 2009).

Last, financial/business tools can refer to computational models based on inflexible criteria related to new product opportunities and associated economic benefits (e.g. cost/benefit) (Adams, Bessant & Phelps 2006; Cooper 2011). With a clear understanding of the characteristics and the most common tools and techniques utilised, the following section explores frugal innovation studies in line with the opportunity and idea screening stage, leading to the development of two frugal innovation practices.

Frugal innovation studies

At this screening stage, frugal innovators generally undertake in-depth search of market and business information, the basis for the two upcoming frugal innovation Practices 3 and 4. Both types of information are involved in ensuring a sustainable business model for the new frugal product opportunity under study. First, frugal innovators focus on market information, in particular, BOP consumers' unmet needs to evaluate the size of the market and the surrounding problems as well as the long-term necessity for this new product opportunity. The second type of information, business information, refers to identifying internal and external capabilities of frugal innovators such as existing resources and partnerships. This aims to increase frugal innovators' certainties around the technology development and complement these internal capabilities.

FI PRACTICE 3

Frugal innovators' in-depth focus on market information appears as one of the central tenets for screening. As frugal innovators review BOP consumers' unmet needs, they naturally seek to understand why existing products fail and what the value of pursuing an alternative opportunity is (McManus et al. 2008). This translates into a more extensive focus on market-related information to understand such problems and the surrounding scope of unmet needs in the market (McManus et al. 2008; Winter & Govindarajan 2015). Several case studies (e.g. M-PESA and Jaipur Foot) articulate this well at this NPDP stage, illustrating a comprehensive assessment of local consumers' problems with existing products.

For example, Nick Hughes explored the M-PESA project by prioritising the investigation of unmet needs in developing countries over other types of information such as standard financial or technical criteria (Hughes and Lonie 2007). It was noted that the focus on market information was unusual at this screening stage, yet critical – "technology-based companies [like Vodafone] tend to keep R&D focused on the technology rather than the marketplace" (Hughes & Lonie 2007, p. 67). This also stressed the importance of being familiar with BOP markets first, before reviewing the technical aspects of a concept. Prioritising market-driven information showed the importance of assessing this future NPD project based on BOP consumers' unmet needs, which was also in line with the project's association with the MDGs.

Similar to M-PESA, the Jaipur Foot inventors delved into the core problems encountered by local patients. From informally surveying the patients first, instead of seeking a potential technical solution, Sethi and Sharma explored further the 'real reasons' why amputees did not use currently available prosthetic limbs (Disability and Development Partners 2013; Macke, Misra & Sharma 2003). Their observational practices revealed that patients were generally fitted with impractical and expensive prosthetics based on developed countries' standards, which was a significant impediment in their daily lives (Disability and Development Partners 2013). By narrowing their focus on the market problem, they clearly understood the necessity of sourcing an alternative solution to existing products. As the situation with these products did not seem to have improved for many years, the value of developing a new product increased, in particular with such long-term impacts of a new, more adequate frugal product.

On the basis of these insights, this study will explore whether frugal innovators assess their new frugal product opportunity against BOP consumers' unmet needs to identify a meaningful (and profitable) prospect. Frugal innovators tend to undertake more extensive market evaluations to determine the 'meaningfulness' of the new product opportunity for BOP consumers. This study will, therefore, examine whether the opportunity and idea screening stage focuses on market information and, in particular, appraisals of BOP consumers' unmet needs for frugal innovation.

FI PRACTICE 4

With regard to the second frugal innovation practice in the screening stage, frugal innovators appear to assess new frugal product opportunities also based on business information linked to both internal and external capabilities. This could be an attempt to overcome the constraints in the BOP context such as the difficulty of innovating in a potentially unknown environment and of unusual business barriers. In support of a sustainable business model, the following case study, M-PESA, shows that the consideration of external available capabilities is as important as the assessment of matching internal capabilities before choosing new product opportunities for frugal innovation.

The case of M-PESA illustrates that supportive capabilities complemented Vodafone's, which was critical in determining the feasibility to take this new product opportunity forward (Hughes & Lonie 2007; Vodafone 2007). That is, by sourcing Vodafone's technical know-how, Hughes envisioned a telecommunications network that ensured a flow of money between local entrepreneurs, businesses and consumers in developing countries (Hughes & Lonie 2007). While proposing mobile technology as an enabler of financial services for BOP, Hughes determined Vodafone's internal capabilities as limited – "at a practical level, it quickly became clear that we faced a resource issue on the ground" (Hughes & Lonie 2007, p. 67). Due to such limited business capabilities, Hughes sought support in East Africa[5] (Hughes & Lonie 2007).

He engaged with Safaricom,[6] a potential regional partner, to understand how their established operations in Kenya could both fit Vodafone's capabilities and enable further exploration of the M-PESA project (Hughes & Lonie 2007). Susan Lonie, who was part of the project's development team, explained the implication of these early considerations in regard to external capabilities:

> It was critical to understand the systems and capabilities of Safaricom . . . Safaricom would also administer the pilot on the ground, so gaining its commitment was a critical first step.
>
> (Hughes & Lonie 2007, p. 69)

This comprehensive investigation of available capabilities and constraints in the local market allowed the M-PESA project team to envision a sustainable business model through local support. On this basis, this study will investigate whether frugal innovators focus on business information related to internal and external capabilities when screening new frugal product opportunities. Such exploration of relevant capabilities appears to be an important aspect of the screening stage to complement and multiply frugal innovators' capabilities to develop a viable business model.

Phase 1 summary

In summary, the fuzzy front end phase is characterised by two stages: opportunity and idea discovery, and screening (see Figure 3.2). The discovery stage identifies opportunities and generates new product ideas. The review of the frugal innovation literature with regard to this stage uncovered evidence of two key practices for frugal innovators. Frugal innovation Practice 1 suggests that frugal innovators have a market-pull approach delimited within BOP market constraints. This was

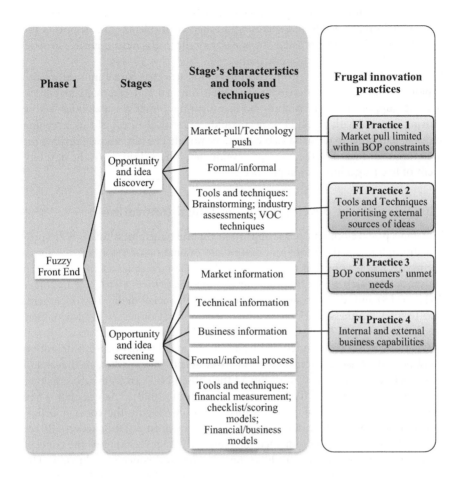

Figure 3.2 Phase 1 summary for frugal innovation

explained by frugal innovators seeking to resolve problems occurring in the BOP context, embracing the constraints these markets impose on them.

Frugal innovation Practice 2 refers to potential tools and techniques that enable the discovery of new frugal product opportunities guided by external sources. The literature review exemplifies this aspect, showing that examining existing products that do not fit BOP consumers' needs but that are still required is one technique to discover new frugal product opportunities.

Furthermore, the screening stage relates to the prioritisation and further investigation of new frugal product opportunities considered likely to become potential NPD projects. Reviewing the frugal innovation literature, another two frugal innovation practices (Practice 3 and Practice 4) were observed and further developed. Practice 3 suggests that once frugal innovators have discovered new product opportunities, their screening approach involves a specific focus on BOP consumers' unmet needs and surrounding market problems. This supports the idea that frugal innovators assess the real size of the problem to evaluate the worthiness of the new product opportunity.

Practice 4 for this fuzzy front end phase indicates that frugal innovators also explore business information related to their internal and external capabilities. Seeking support or collaboration by investigating business capabilities before moving forward with an NPD project could be a critical aspect of this screening stage, in particular to ensure a viable business model. The next section reviews the literature with regard to the concept development phase, leading to the development of five frugal innovation practices.

Phase 2: concept development and frugal innovation

The concept development phase aims to justify the 'worthiness' of an NPD project through detailed exploration, design and evaluation of a concept to deliver the right value proposition to consumers. This phase provides a bridge between "advanced research and technology development activities" (Ulrich & Eppinger 2012, p. 13) and results in the development of a 'concept definition' document, also termed 'business case' or 'product definition' (Cooper 2011; Koen, Bertels & Kleinschmidt 2014; Ulrich & Eppinger 2012).

Often involving cross-functional teams, achieving the final concept definition consists of decreasing uncertainties and risks linked with market, technical and business factors, and boosts feasibility of the chosen NPD projects before further product development occurs (Stockstrom & Herstatt 2008). There is often a fine line between the technical decisions involved in developing the concept definition and the next product development phase (Crawford & Di Benedetto 2014; Trott 2012). This section is divided into three key stages relating to the concept development phase: market study, technical study and concept evaluation. The three stages have guided this study's review of the frugal innovation literature and led to the development of five key frugal innovation practices.

Market study stage

One of the key inputs in developing the right value proposition is the market study stage. This involves the detailed search and analysis of quantitative and qualitative market data to identify consumers' needs, wants and preferences over existing or upcoming products (Cooper 2011; Griffin 2012). These decisions influence in-depth VOC understanding as well as market segments and competitor analysis to establish consumers' requirements and shape the product concept (Otto & Wood 2000; Ulrich & Eppinger 2012).

Decisions taken here help reduce market uncertainties and risks in regard to the NPD project before full product development (Markham & Lee 2013; Verworn, Herstatt & Nagahira 2008). Markham and Lee (2013) emphasised that a detailed market study is a significant moderating factor in the success of

NPD projects. These requirements are also vital to NPD projects as they guide the development team from understanding the target market to establishing the engineering specifications of the product (Veryzer 2010). The team's perceptions of consumer needs influence how these needs are further translated into technical and design characteristics (i.e. product attributes) (Griffin 2012; Veryzer 2010). A detailed market study stage is characterised by a search of different market data, as explained ahead.

Characteristics

This stage is characterised by the collection of market data based on consumers' needs, market segment and competitor analysis to define what the target market is attracted to in a product (Cooper 2011). The type of information collected is generally guided by the firm's mission statement (or design brief), where the targeted market segment and prerequisite constraints developed from the fuzzy front end phase help build the boundaries of the NPD project (Koen et al. 2002; Ulrich & Eppinger 2012). The subjective nature of consumers' needs, as well as the information stemming from market segment and competitor analysis on which firms' NPD decisions are grounded, are described ahead (Ulrich & Eppinger 2012; Zirger & Maidique 1990).

The first type of information a firm might investigate when preparing an NPD project relates to consumers' needs, wants and preferences, and the nuances that exist between them. Consumers' needs are defined as "[p]roblems to be solved" (Kahn et al. 2012b, p. 445), "problems that a product . . . solves and the functions it performs" (Griffin 2012, p. 216) or "any attribute of a potential product that is desired by the customer" (Ulrich & Eppinger 2012, p. 75). Such definitions highlight the clear link between these needs and their impact on technical aspects of product design.

Furthermore, the problems identified by the consumers usually enable the identification of distinct latent (or tacit), unmet or unarticulated preferences, wants or needs. The latter are generally translated into matching product attributes such as functions, features and benefits (Hauser & Dahan 2007; Ulrich & Eppinger 2012). For example, during the course of consumers' purchasing decisions, consumers could describe aspects of a product, which, once analysed, illuminate what is preferable or crucial to them (Ulwick 2005). Markham and Lee's (2013) study emphasised that their sampled 'best' firms actively sought diverse consumers' needs during this stage, and also connected the types of information sought during this phase to the level of NPD project success. Extant literature recommends working with lead users who are usually ahead of the trends, to enhance familiarity between new consumers and new products to be introduced into the market (Cooper & Edgett 2008; Herstatt & von Hippel 1992).

Additional market data essential to this stage relate to the targeted market segment and competitor analysis. These can incorporate the analysis of consumers' opinions, market size, growth and segments, and competitors' products (Cooper 2011; Hauser & Dahan 2007). For example, studies of target costing, determining in advance a target cost and a profit margin from a competitor's product, can deliver key information such as what competitors do and what consumers are willing to pay (Cooper 2011). This enables firms to more efficiently manage their own cost targets through the remainder of the NPDP (Gaubinger et al. 2015b).

Such information can also stem from consumers' stated problems linked with existing or future solutions they are familiar with, as this could help in prioritising specific product requirements (Cooper 2011; Griffin 2012; Veryzer 2010). The type of information to search and the way to handle these data also generally influence the product acceptance and the firm's innovation performance (Ulrich & Eppinger 2012; Verworn, Herstatt & Nagahira 2008). Tools and techniques to support these NPD decisions also impact on firms' decisions at this stage (Griffin 2012; Ulrich & Eppinger 2012), and the three most common tools and techniques are discussed ahead.

Tools and techniques

Various market research tools and techniques facilitate the integration of VOC, market segment and competitor analysis into a firm's NPDP (Cooper, Edgett & Kleinschmidt 2004). However, getting the right information can be challenging for development teams, as consumers may not clearly identify what is problematic about existing products or the proposed product (Griffin 2012; Trott 2012). In the literature, the three most common tools and techniques addressing such issue are focus groups, interviews and consumer visit/observations (Cooper 2011; Ulrich & Eppinger 2012; Urban & Hauser 1993).

The focus group technique consists of in-depth discussions about the use of a potential product, generally occurring in a room of fewer than 15 participants (Crawford & Di Benedetto 2011; Ulrich & Eppinger 2012). One-to-one interviews – one of the cheapest methods – can also provide insights into consumers' needs in their environment (Ulrich & Eppinger 2012); however, interviewed consumers may not individually articulate the subtle nuances from latent needs (Griffin 2012). The use of observation provides an understanding of consumers' purchasing behaviours, needs and wants while watching them during home visits such as with ethnography, an intrinsic technique for a specific product usage, yet expensive (Babin & Zikmund 2015; de Waal & Knott 2010; Griffin 2012).

Building from this point, the following section explores the related frugal innovation literature and highlights specific practices undertaken during this market study stage, leading to the development of frugal innovation Practice 5 and Practice 6.

Frugal innovation studies

In the frugal innovation literature, the collection of market data appears undoubtedly critical for developing frugal products, with two practices particularly evident at this stage. These frugal innovation practices are the identification of specific

BOP consumers' needs (FI Practice 5), and the tools and techniques used for this, which encourage greater engagement and closeness with consumers than generic tools and techniques allow (FI Practice 6).

FI PRACTICE 5

Practice 5 relates to the prioritisation of specific BOP consumers' needs as a starting point for firms' concept development phase (Prahalad 2012). Frugal innovators lean towards understanding the problems from the consumer perspective, as opposed to superficially initiating this stage by anticipating technical solutions (Whitney 2010). The literature indicates three main types of market information is explored here: meaning of affordability, integration of complementary needs (i.e. aspirational, latent) and contextual information such as where the potential product is to be used (McManus et al. 2008; Mukerjee 2012; Pitta, Subrahmanyan & Tomas Gomez-Arias 2008; Viswanathan & Sridharan 2012; Weyrauch & Herstatt 2017).

With respect to affordability, Mukerjee (2012, p. 1) suggests that firms should understand "what customers feel is an affordable price". Many scholars (e.g. Anderson & Markides 2007; Bingham, Whitehead & Evans 2016; Lim, Han & Ito 2013; Weyrauch & Herstatt 2017) have pointed out that price is extremely impactful on product acceptance. While frugal innovation implies the need to be cheaper than premium versions due to BOP consumers' low disposable income, it is also important to delve into the meaning of affordability during this stage. Affordability goes beyond the frugal product price, including additional cost-effective advantage such as low-cost of ownership (Ramdorai & Herstatt 2017). In addition, seeking what BOP consumers perceive as affordable helps identifying a price-point ratio based on consumers' views instead of basing it on firms' financial objective (Prahalad 2012; Weyrauch & Herstatt 2017).

The ChotuKool fridge is an excellent example of the importance to understand affordability based on BOP consumers' needs and perceptions. This led to the ChotuKool being sold at half the price of the cheapest standard refrigerators (Dhanaraj, Suram & Vemuri 2011). At this time, the price range for standard refrigerators was around 7,000 IDR (approximately 97 USD, 7 September 2018). The development team realised that BOP consumers perceived standard fridges as not fitting with what they needed by comparing its price and the functionality these fridges offered. For example, standard fridges had too much storage and integrated a freezer, two functionalities that were costly for the development team and not desired by BOP consumers.

Within this context, the lightweight ChotuKool alternative had a critical advantage in functionality for its price when compared with standard fridges, as consumers could move the ChotuKool around the house according to their needs. They could also sell drinks on the side of the road to generate additional household income, an unusual perspective to consider in determining a price-point ratio. One of the meanings of affordability in this case was intertwined with BOP consumers purchasing the ChotuKool with the possibility of choosing where to place it at home, and being entrepreneurs and/or having additional income streams (Whitney 2010).

Looking at the second type of market information, the exploration of complementary needs reflect the issues with some existing products. Not only do these relate to inadequacy and impracticality with how BOP consumers live, they also do not often integrate other essential and aspirational needs (Viswanathan & Sridharan 2012). Some of these available products do not resonate with why BOP consumers would use them. For example, BOP consumers living in austere environments with low disposable income clearly consider whether it will be a long-term investment when making purchase decisions (Viswanathan & Sridharan 2012).

Furthermore, a cheap-looking product may not fit BOP consumers' long-term investment needs or their lifestyle aspirations, as these consumers also often seek recognition via quality belongings (Jagtap et al. 2015; Pitta, Subrahmanyan & Tomas Gomez-Arias 2008; Prahalad 2012). This is often reflected in the demand by BOP consumers for more quality, adequate and robust products, contrasting with current product offerings such as cheap existing alternatives or de-featured Western products (Viswanathan & Sridharan 2012; Whitney 2010).

A key empirical example is the Prahalad's (2012) biomass cookstove, a 20 USD energy-efficient and clean product, targeting rural Indian BOP consumers. Developed by Professor Prahalad and his team,[7] the investigation of BOP consumers' life aspirations such as self-esteem was essential in the stove design (Prahalad 2012). Price and functionality were not the only key determinants that needed to be considered; potential biomass stove users not only desired a functional product, but also wanted a stylish one (Prahalad 2012). This highlights the importance of understanding BOP consumers' complementary needs such as aspirational and emotional desires in relation to owning an appealing product (Pitta, Subrahmanyan & Tomas Gomez-Arias 2008; Prahalad 2012).

Finally looking at the contextual information, particular aspects of the context in which consumers live can become impediments for firms when trying to understand BOP consumers (Mattson & Wood 2014). Subtle nuances may stem from their heterogenic cultures (e.g. different perceptions of what is important), dispersed locations (e.g. urban, rural, mountains), and/or the resource-poor environment in which they often live (e.g. unreliable energy, under-developed infrastructure) (Prahalad 2012; Whitney 2010).

The case of the Jaipur Foot is a good example of the importance of adding contextual usage needs as part of the concept development phase, a vital consideration in ensuring product acceptance (Gollakota, Gupta & Bork 2010). Amputees were willing to try the Jaipur Foot, as this new prosthetic addressed their unmet needs with this design adapted to their lifestyle (Gollakota, Gupta & Bork 2010). That is, amputees could not walk comfortably with former prosthetic products because of the rugged environment they lived in, making them self-conscious around friends and in their home village. The Indian tradition of sitting cross-legged and squatting as well as frequent rice farming activities also needed to be considered (Macke, Misra & Sharma 2003).

A critical motivator to be fitted with the Jaipur Foot was that patients could work again and provide food, security, support and education to their family (Gollakota, Gupta & Bork 2010; Prahalad 2009). The Jaipur Foot not only addressed aspirational needs (e.g. self-esteem and pride to walk again), it also integrated additional product usage contexts (e.g. in villages and common work). In addition to targeting the need to sit cross-legged and squatting, the product factored in the context of consumers' working environments (e.g. agricultural fields) (Gollakota, Gupta & Bork 2010). Failing to consider this contextual information would have meant some key market requirements in the conceptualisation of the Jaipur Foot would have been neglected.

Inspired by these case study examples, this study will investigate whether frugal innovators seek specific consumer information during this stage. This study will explore whether the meaning of affordability, integration of complementary needs and product usage context in the market study stage are important practices.

FI PRACTICE 6

With regard to the second practice, Practice 6, the frugal innovation literature suggests tools and techniques that encourage greater engagement and relationship development as a basis for understanding consumers' routines (Aranda Jan, Jagtap & Moultrie 2016; Prahalad 2012; Wood & Mattson 2014). To better understand consumers' problems and preferences, scholars such as Prahalad (2012), Whitney (2010) and Wood and Mattson (2014) recommend addressing the lack of available market data regarding BOP consumers with more practical (field-based) investigations during this stage.

Frugal innovation literature indicates the immersion of the development teams at various levels in BOP consumers' environments as one of the most effective techniques (Wood & Mattson 2014). In line with this, Sehgal, Dehoff and Panneer (2010, p. 3) recommended spending "time in people's homes and watching how they actually use products, rather than relying on focus groups or other secondary or tertiary research". This technique may involve being locally present in the product context, interacting with BOP consumers, or simulating BOP consumers' context (Mattson & Wood 2014; Viswanathan & Sridharan 2012).

Hughes and Lonie (2007, p. 80) also emphasise that an NPD project in BOP markets should focus time "on the ground assessing customers' needs well ahead of designing the functional specification of any technology-based solution". Viswanathan, Yassine and Clarke (2011, p. 567) supported this by asserting:

> Most important perhaps, when compared to product development in relatively resource-rich contexts that managers can relate to, is the need for deep listening and understanding of customer needs.

This way of investigating consumers' needs via their routine offers several advantages to a firm, such as getting deeper insights into the real problems consumers face based on the environment surrounding them (Kashyap 2012, 2017; Viswanathan & Sridharan 2012). Firms would also increase local responsiveness and their understanding of the targeted consumers, and develop stronger connections with local communities (Simanis & Hart 2009; Viswanathan & Sridharan 2012). Such immersion may also enable early identification of critical consumers' information, which could reduce uncertainties about the future product success as well as early funding of in-depth market research (Ramdorai & Herstatt 2017). Case studies (i.e. Prahalad's biomass stove case and the ChotuKool fridge) clearly show that this local understanding, which derived from deeper engagement with local communities, is vital in the concept development phase.

As a result of his own experience, Prahalad (2012) used a four-step process for the concept development of the biomass cookstove project, with two steps specifically consumer-related: 'immersion in their life and work styles', and integrating 'consumers insights' (p. 8). Physical immersion and analytical research techniques were also part of this step and provided this project with clearer insights into Indian families' lifestyles and needs. Prahalad (2012, p. 7) highlighted how video-ethnography, in conjunction with content analysis of the ethnographic results "led to a deep immersion into a consumer's life", which opened doors to observing women's 'decision processes' and variances of stove usage between southern and northern Indian families. The whole cooking context, including decisions made before and after, was thus considered when determining how the stove would be used (Prahalad 2012).

This practice-based fieldwork was also evident in the ChotuKool fridge example. That is, by observing, videotaping and interviewing BOP consumers, instead of simply relying only on interviews or other 'self-documentary' techniques (Whitney 2010), the team discovered essential Indian BOP consumer preferences. Such information included the context in which they live, the way they use fridges, their food consumption patterns, and how some overcame the absence of a cooling system (Eyring, Johnson & Nair 2011; Whitney 2010). Other critical information included the routine of buying food on a daily basis and preserving leftovers, meaning that the size of the cooling system mattered (as seen in Practice 5) (Whitney 2010).

On the basis of these empirical insights, this study will investigate whether frugal innovators use tools and techniques that provide them with deeper insights into consumers' lives. The frugal innovation literature also highlighted the value in developing connections, spending time and immersing firms' development team in the local settings (Prahalad 2012; Simanis & Hart 2009). Hence, the tools and techniques of the market study stage may focus on a firm's immersion with targeted consumers for deeper insights, which establish the sixth proposed frugal innovation practice.

Technical study stage

During the technical stage, firms make decisions about product performance, technological/product specifications, and feasibility of concepts (Cooper 2011;

Murthy, Rausand & Østerås 2008). The form that the concept will take is generally derived from both market and technical requirements, and the technology that will be used is developed as a firm decomposes problems and generates a multitude of alternative functional designs (Trott 2012). These tentative conceptual designs mainly originate from the exploration of three key product attributes: functions, features and benefits (Krishnan & Ulrich 2001; Pahl, Wallace & Blessing 2007; Ulrich & Eppinger 2012).

The primary goal of the technical study stage is to reduce the technical uncertainties of an NPD project, by strengthening firms' choice of new concepts, diverse product attributes and concept opportunities (Crawford & Di Benedetto 2011; Liu, Chakrabarti & Bligh 2003). As Krishnan and Bhattacharya (2002) argue, this is a critical stage where the development of feasible product specifications occurs before going to full product development. Recent literature has suggested flexibility when establishing such specifications, as consumers' preferences tend to change quickly, like agile development principles suggest (Cooper 2017). To establish these technical aspects, three primary characteristics define the technical study stage of an NPD project and are introduced ahead.

Characteristics

Product *functions, features* and *benefits*[8] are the three main characteristics that describe this stage. The first relates to the targeted specifications that will translate into the desired performance the product should reach in order to satisfy customers, the product *function*. The second refers to the generation of functional designs based on technological principles, the product *features*. The third and final characteristic concerns the potential form and augmented features of the concept, the product *benefits*.

First, target performance stems from the translation of consumers requirements into a technical language, the product specifications, which informs 'what' the product should do in a measurable way. The establishment of these metrics – or specifications – for the desired performance sets the targeted product *functions* (Crawford & Di Benedetto 2014; Ulrich & Eppinger 2012). The development of target performance does not answer 'how' the product will address market and technical specifications but provides details on the required functional performance that the future product should target (Otto & Wood 2000). Such target performance also sets the position of the future product in the market (Cooper 2011).

This technical language regarding the target performance – also termed 'design requirements' (Trott 2012) – provides the foundation of the targets and constraints imposed on subsequent design solutions (Ulrich & Eppinger 2012). In particular, target performance creates "functional nuances . . . that . . . dictate the [product] engineering trade-offs" (Griffin 2012, p. 216). In other words, there are uncertainties that this targeted performance is technically feasible, which often leads development teams to search for the most suitable engineering trade-offs.

With regard to the second characteristic, this is when development teams explore 'how' to respond to these *functions* by seeking alternative technological principles for the generation of technical design. These are the product *features* on which each of the targeted functions can rely and which are used to shape the functional design of the concept (Cooper 2011; Ulrich & Eppinger 2012). After exploring the feasibility of each technological principle, each can be developed through creating outlines of product architecture, systems, subsystems and components (Yin, Kaku & Liu 2012).

Such outlining enables firms to explore "component technology that offers the product its ability to perform at the level set in its specifications" (Krishnan & Bhattacharya 2002, p. 314). Firms can, therefore, determine a range of technical combinations for each function that the product has to serve, forming the basic arrangement and interactions of key components within the product (Krishnan & Ulrich 2001; Osteras, Murthy & Rausand 2006).

Looking at the final characteristic, this is where development teams solidify the conceptual design of a new product by giving it a concrete form and augmented features, the product *benefits* (Crawford & Di Benedetto 2014). Consideration of the form of the product involves the development of further *benefits* to help satisfy consumers' needs. The type of innovation undertaken by the firm will influence the form of the product and the tasks involved. For example, the specific role of industrial design is to satisfy the ergonomic and aesthetic aspects, a critical trait for user-driven innovation (Gemser & Leenders 2001). Although necessary for the translation of the written idea into graphics, industrial design is less important for technology-driven innovations (Ulrich & Eppinger 2012).

Facilitating the ideation for each of these characteristics, a variety of tools and techniques can help fulfil such technical specifications (Chakrabarti, Morgenstern & Knaab 2004). The next section introduces the most commonly used tools and techniques identified in previous research.

Tools and techniques

Bounded by a firm's objectives as well as market and technical requirements, a variety of tools and techniques can offer systematic structure to the technical research of concepts (Kahn 2010b; Pahl, Wallace & Blessing 2007; Ulrich & Eppinger 2012). For example, combining qualitative and quantitative methods (Crawford & Di Benedetto 2014) can increase the probability of obtaining a larger range of design ideas to respond to market and technical specifications (Hauser & Dahan 2007). The most common tools and techniques include Quality Function Deployment (QFD) (Crawford & Di Benedetto 2014; Whipple, Adler & McCurdy 2008), ideation (Pahl, Wallace & Blessing 2007; Ulrich & Eppinger 2012) and trade-off analysis (Crawford & Di Benedetto 2014; Whipple, Adler & McCurdy 2008).

With regard to QFD, this tool embeds problem-solving processes such as the House of Quality. This is where a firm prioritises specific aspects of the problem, such as prioritising consumers' needs, so they can be reflected in the design of the concept (Hauser & Dahan 2007; Otto & Wood 2000; Wheelwright &

Clark 1992). In contrast, ideation techniques such as brainstorming or morphological analysis are problem-solving methods used by development teams to decompose the set of product functions without prioritising a specific problem (Ulrich & Eppinger 2012). Such techniques reframe the understanding of multidimensional problems and generate possible solutions for each function and sub-function into an integral solution (Ulrich & Eppinger 2012). Trade-off analysis such as dimensional/relationship analysis relates to the trading off of all product functions and features in accordance with consumer needs (Whipple, Adler & McCurdy 2008). These results trigger ideation for new concepts based on the relationships made between functions and features (Crawford & Di Benedetto 2014).

The importance of the technical study stage in reducing technical uncertainties, including considering these three characteristics and tools and techniques, builds a strong background to review frugal innovators' practices. The frugal innovation literature discussed ahead emphasises two practices linked to the target performance and tools and techniques to develop frugal products.

Frugal innovation studies

Two key frugal innovation practices are evident from this literature. The first, FI Practice 7, is focusing on primary product functionality and business model specifications. This helps frugal innovators to reduce their focus on secondary (non-functional and non-essential) specifications and to integrate early business model design. The use of tools and techniques by frugal innovators on the basis of comparing existing technologies/products is the second practice, FI Practice 8. This technique is aimed at identifying products that address similar functions with basic technologies or trade-offs in architectural structures of existing technological platforms.

FI PRACTICE 7

With regard to primary product functionality and business model specifications, this emphasis narrows firms' focus on essential functionality while seeing a frugal innovation as addressing business model issues. The former helps to intensify focus on broader performance requirements that are linked to primary functionality of the product (Prahalad 2012; Weyrauch & Herstatt 2017; Zeschky, Winterhalter & Gassmann 2014). In line with this, Rao (2013) recommended development teams to focus on 'must have' functions and features as a minimum threshold while keeping in mind cost reduction across the NPDP.

This may help frugal innovators prioritise performance requirements critical for BOP consumers and avoid striving for the optimisation of each targeted performance that are not important for these consumers (Rao 2013). In a relevant study, Weyrauch and Herstatt (2017, p. 11) further elaborated on this by suggesting that technical characteristics attributed to frugal products are linked to "substantial cost reduction, concentration on core functionalities, and optimised performance level". Focusing on the core essentials does not, however, mean a reduction of the performance levels, but rather an increased focus on targeted performance that builds around the core functionality of the concept (Rao 2013; Weyrauch & Herstatt 2017; Whitney 2010).

Furthermore, the inclusion of business model requirements suggests that frugal concepts are often designed considering how to reach BOP consumers (e.g. downstream service, pricing) and how to overcome local constraints (e.g. infrastructure, education or energy needs) (Gassmann et al. 2017; Lehner & Gausemeier 2016; Simanis 2011). Thus, addressing business model specifications early in the design process is vital to address BOP consumers' expectations with the right product design (Petrick & Juntiwasarakij 2011; Viswanathan, Yassine & Clarke 2011).

For example, a product may not be as affordable if its downstream services (e.g. convenient access to repair or maintenance) are not aligned with the value proposition, as it could result in higher costs (Tiwari & Herstatt 2013; Viswanathan, Yassine & Clarke 2011). Key cases of a team's focus on primary functional and business model requirements are the biomass stove of Prahalad (2012) and the Leveraged Freedom Chair (LFC) wheelchair.

While iterations were needed in the biomass cookstove, the technical study had a focus on essential functions and features such as a smoke-free and energy-efficient stove. Key product attributes were worked on in order to "focus on [the] total delivery of value" (Prahalad 2012, p. 6). For Prahalad (2012), the total product value relied on the 'innovation sandbox', delimiting the development team's focus to fewer business model and product-centric requirements. Such requirements included (1) ease-of-use and aspirational needs, (2) safe-to-use in accordance with global standards, (3) scalability and (4) affordability (Prahalad 2012, p. 8). Looking specifically at the ease-of-use to exemplify the focus on primary functionality and business model specifications, this aspect related to both the product (helping consumers understand how the stove functions) and the business model (ensuring a convenient supply of wood and pellet to the stove). It included thinking about downstream services, such as taking into account of shops that would supply the fuel to consumers.

Similarly, the LFC wheelchair, a low-cost, all-terrain, lever-powered wheelchair, also relied on four primary targeted performances based on the development team's understanding of BOP consumers' needs. The team established an affordability performance, the possibility of mobility both indoor and outdoor, an effectiveness performance based on distance range and road types (e.g. muddy roads) and an easy maintenance performance (Winter 2013; Winter & Govindarajan 2015). These targeted performances did not express 'how' the product will function and what it will look like, but they ensured that the development team did not "miss [. . .] one of them, . . . [otherwise] it probably would have failed" (Winter & Govindarajan 2015).

On the basis of these insights, this study will explore whether the technical study stage for frugal innovators focuses on primary product functionality and business model specifications. This is a departure from the technical study stage for developed countries, which searches for optimal performance across a higher number of specifications to generate the best solution, which ultimately exceeds consumers' needs. This study will, therefore, investigate whether frugal innovators focuses on primary product functionality and business model specifications with optimised performances linked to BOP consumers' needs.

FI PRACTICE 8

Looking at Practice 8, the frugal innovation literature highlights techniques that enable the exploration of existing technologies or products as a benchmark for the technical study of frugal products. Most frugal innovators may seek simpler technological principles and/or architectural structure of products that deliver similar functional and cost outputs to those they seek to develop. This suggests two possible techniques to the technical study stage: searching for more basic technological principles on which functions are based and/or for an architectural structure including components of the product.

The first technique encourages the development team to "use existing technology in imaginative new ways" (Wooldridge 2010) and adapt the new concept around it. Some studies have also highlighted that these technological principles should be less complex and more functional when responding to targeted performance (Rao 2013; Ray & Ray 2011). In line with this, Prahalad (2012) suggests that the technology used in frugal products should not be too costly or too sophisticated – at least during its initial introduction. As frugal products often have distinct functionalities and features from premium alternatives, seeking basic technology could also enable the prioritisation of primary functions and reduced costs (Prahalad 2012).

In addition to seeking basic technological principles, the underlying architectural structure and components of existing products and technologies may also offer the development team adapted functional outputs for their new concepts. In this context, frugal innovators would determine what structures or components are involved in providing comparable functions to those they seek, especially to achieve both reduced costs and complexity (Lim, Han & Ito 2013; Rao 2013; Zeschky, Winterhalter & Gassmann 2014). For example, Viswanathan, Yassine and Clarke (2011) suggest the incorporation of a modular architecture where several product functionalities rely on a lower number of components than new products usually do. Thus, depending on the level of product complexity, frugal innovators may focus on existing technology or products, creatively exploring these to generate new concepts (Cunha et al. 2014; Viswanathan, Yassine & Clarke 2011).

Empirical studies emphasise the important role that basic technologies and/ or the exploration of product's architecture and components have on the development of frugal products. For example, the M-PESA and Siemens Fetal Heart Monitor reflect the re-use of resources and simple technologies that are locally available or are already operating in the BOP markets context. Furthermore, the Tata Nano car shows how seeking architectural structure in other products can address a team's targeted performance.

The first example of using 'imaginative' approaches to basic technological principles in existing products is the M-PESA case. Seeking to address the primary
functionality – giving financial access to 'the unbanked' – the development team
leveraged simpler, local and already accessible mobile technology for their technical study stage (Hughes & Lonie 2007; Nakata & Berger 2011). Rather than
striving for breakthrough technological outcomes, they instead looked for basic
technologies (e.g. mobile technology) that were already applicable in East Africa
and how these could be re-used and re-applied in different ways (Hughes &
Lonie 2007). Hughes and Lonie (2007) reflected:

> Even at the early concept stage we expected to use a very basic applica-
> tion of mobile communication, called SMS (or text messaging). . . . This
> wasn't about new technology, it was about a new application of existing
> technology.
>
> (p. 66)

In this NPD project, they integrated text-messaging technology as the foundation for their frugal product. The idea was to find a technology that could be
extensively used among BOP consumers, as opposed to one based on a smart-
phone, for example, with which they were unfamiliar and which the existing
infrastructure did not support. Following a feasibility study, text-messaging technology was adapted to the primary functions required while responding to cost
and local constraints. This technology clearly addressed geographical banking
accessibility at low cost.

Similarly, Siemens developed a 'Fetal Heart Monitor', avoiding using breakthrough technology like the traditional ultrasound technology used in heart
monitor (Agnihotri 2015; Radjou & Prabhu 2013). The development team
ensured that the new functions instead relied on simple features, which microphone technology principles addressed (Agnihotri 2015). The advantage to using
basic, less-expensive technology like that in microphones was the simplicity of its
use; for example, it did not require experts to manipulate it, unlike a device relying on ultrasound technology (Löscher 2011).

An example of exploring existing products, and the underlying architecture
and components is the Tata Nano car, often cited as the world's cheapest car
and priced at 2,500 USD. This car targeted Indian BOP consumers who could
not afford a conventional one (Ray & Ray 2011). The studies by Ray and Ray
(2011) and Lim, Han and Ito (2013) highlighted the development teams' exploration of existing alternatives as a creative 'benchmark' for further technical and
cost exploration. In particular, one point of reference denoted a cost-reduced car
model, the Maruti 800, developed by a foreign firm decades ago and considered
as the formally cheapest car in India (Ray & Ray 2011).

By focusing on this existing technological platform, the development team
sought to create "an altered performance package through architectural innovation" (Ray & Ray 2011, p. 218). They extracted the technological principles
behind the Maruti motor engine and worked around this model for the Tata

Nano (two cylinders instead of the standard three of the Maruti) (Lim, Han & Ito 2013; Ray & Ray 2011).

Building from these empirical insights, this study will, therefore, examine whether frugal innovators seek simpler technology, and/or explore other products and their underlying architecture and components, as a basis for the technical study. Such techniques include the search of existing concepts, drawing on pre-existing technologies, platforms and architectures, rather than focusing purely on seeking breakthrough technology and/or developing new functional products. Thus, the tools and techniques of the technical study stage may involve practices related to the search of basic technological principles, and/or architecture and components from existing products.

The concept development phase also relies on the concept evaluation stage before entering the product development phase. This is the final stage within the concept development phase, and this study highlights one specific practice undertaken by frugal innovators.

Concept evaluation stage

The concept evaluation stage involves both screening and selection decisions required in refining concepts and choosing the most viable one. To justify an NPD project, firms first assess concepts by exploring various types of evaluating criteria derived from previous marketing and technical studies and from the management of broader project portfolios (Cooper 2011; Murphy & Kumar 1996). Evaluating criteria entails the assessment of technical performance (e.g. technology and manufacturing feasibility) established throughout the concept development phase as well as the project relevance to the firm (e.g. financial aspects), and the benefits to the market (e.g. market value) (Cooper 1988; Crawford & Di Benedetto 2014).

Moving into further development without appropriate evaluation could incur higher costs related to wasted time and financial resources allocated to NPD projects, such as unavailability of human resources for other projects, and/or ineffective commercialisation efforts of a failed product (Krishnan & Ulrich 2001; Tidd & Bodley 2002). This evaluation stage finalises the concept definition and justifies the NPD project before further product development. It supports the firm in its investment decision-making, including prioritisation of the most commercially viable solutions (Crawford & Di Benedetto 2014; Schmidt, Sarangee & Montoya 2009). The concept evaluation stage is composed of interrelated characteristics intrinsic to these investment decisions, as discussed ahead.

Characteristics

There are three key characteristics that define how the most viable concepts are assessed and chosen. The first relates to marketing assessments, focused on evaluating the appeal of the concept(s) to the market to reduce the chance of product failure (Crawford & Di Benedetto 2014). The second integrates business and economic information so that firms can evaluate whether a project is in line with its strategic and financial objectives (Martinsuo & Poskela 2011). The third characteristic relates to the use of technical information in evaluating concepts (Cooper 2011; Pahl, Wallace & Blessing 2007; Takai, Jikar & Ragsdell 2011).

Assessments at the market level enable the evaluation of selected concepts' positioning and benefits as well as sales targets (Cooper 2011; Crawford & Di Benedetto 2014). They also facilitate the development and refinement of the attributes offered by the potential concept under evaluation. These include the final design of the product, the advantages offered to the users and the potential technologies on which each function will rely (Crawford & Di Benedetto 2014; Pahl, Wallace & Blessing 2007; Ulrich & Eppinger 2012). The aims of this marketing characteristic are to increase the likelihood of product acceptance, to reduce expenditure in later NPDP phases and to eliminate concepts with lower chances of success (Crawford & Di Benedetto 2014).

With regard to undertaking business and financial analysis, the aim is to evaluate the strategic, financial and resource-fit of the proposed product, reducing investment uncertainties before it moves forward (Cooper 2011; Crawford & Di Benedetto 2014). Such output can include quantitative and qualitative components of firms' business and economic analysis such as sales forecasts, profit margins, and cost and capital estimates (Cooper 2011). Relevant quantitative analysis can be performed by exploring estimations of revenue as well as costs for development, capital and manufacturing, estimated throughout the NPDP via various tools and techniques (Crawford & Di Benedetto 2014; Ulrich & Eppinger 2012). The qualitative results add further understanding of how the NPD project interacts with the firm's market and its competitive contexts (Ulrich & Eppinger 2012).

When firms evaluate concepts on the basis of technical factors, they seek to refine technical and manufacturing feasibility in accordance with their resources and objectives. The development team narrows and widens the alternative concepts on the basis of technical as well as strategic, business and financial objectives. For example, they can do so by trading off between product attributes (i.e. function, features, benefits) and firms' resources (i.e. manufacturing, IP, legal), enabling technical iteration on the concept (Cooper 2011; Pugh 1991).

This occurs until the development of final product specifications is aligned with the diverse sets of constraints established by the firm, influencing how a firm evaluates the value of a NPD project (Pahl, Wallace & Blessing 2007). It has recently been recommended that firms decrease their focus on finalising product specifications and instead move forward with a flexible and less complete set of performance requirements in line with agile development (Cooper 2017). Assessed iteratively across the concept development phase and the NPDP, the three characteristics discussed imply that firms use different tools and techniques according to their goal when evaluating NPD projects. The gathering of market, business and technical factors is often influenced by the use of various tools and techniques, and the three most common are discussed ahead.

Tools and techniques

Numerous tools and techniques exist to assist firms with better screening and selection decisions. These help evaluate the most appropriate concepts, while considering what the market expects, what is technically feasible and the financial implications (Crawford & Di Benedetto 2014). Such evaluative tools and techniques are best used in combination, along with subjective judgments, as all of them have drawbacks if used independently (Cooper 2011; Lin & Chen 2004). The three most common ones are concept testing (Cooper & Sommer 2016; Crawford & Di Benedetto 2014), benefit measurement techniques (Cooper 2011; Crawford & Di Benedetto 2014; Gaubinger et al. 2015b) and financial/economic models (Barczak, Griffin & Kahn 2009; Cooper 2011; Markham & Lee 2013).

Concept testing techniques allow the assessment of consumers' responses on the product, which refine firms' evaluations of each concept on the basis of their market appeal (Crawford & Di Benedetto 2014; Kahn 2010a). Depending on firms' objectives, techniques like storyboards or mail surveys are recommended by scholars and practitioners; more contemporary virtual and physical forms of the product like 'protocepts' are also suitable for sale or for achieving technical milestone such as proof-of-concept (Cooper & Sommer 2016; Koen & Bertels 2010).

Benefit measurement techniques such as scoring models or the Analytical Hierarchy Process involve the selection of concepts on the basis of business and economic criteria (Cooper 2001; Ulrich & Eppinger 2012). The scoring technique focuses less on financial measurement and more on business advantage, using a weighting system that integrates criteria set by firms' priorities for each NPD project (Cooper 2011).

The use of financial/economic models reduces and offsets some uncertainties related to the economic and financial risks of potential NPD projects (Adams, Bessant & Phelps 2006). These include cost-benefit analysis (Pahl, Wallace & Blessing 2007), sensitivity analysis for cost analysis, Net Present Value, discounted cash profit and amortisation, break-even analysis, payback period and/or return on investment (ROI) (Cooper 2011; Thamhain 2014). Building from this point, the next section introduces the approaches adopted by frugal innovators for the concept evaluation of their NPDP, leading to the development of one key frugal innovation practice.

Frugal innovation studies

When evaluating their concepts, frugal innovators appear to address specific criteria and/or to test an early version of the concept with BOP consumers as potential tools and techniques for this NPDP stage (FI Practice 9). The introduction of the concept to BOP consumers helps getting a sense of what product attributes these consumers may prefer and then refine the concept under development.

FI PRACTICE 9

Looking first at criteria, their integration into this NPDP stage could help frugal innovators to identify and address the key priorities of targeted BOP consumers. Bingham, Whitehead and Evans (2016) suggest the development of tools and techniques that allow a comprehensive assessment of the concepts under development using eight design criteria. Frugal products are assessed based on affinity, desirability, reparability, durability, functionality, affordability, usability and sustainability. Such criteria along with others including criteria related to the whole NPD project (i.e. funding, quality, convenience) could help recognise the suitability of each proposed product (Bingham, Whitehead & Evans 2016).

Second, while the development team can assess these criteria both internally and with consumers, these can also be answered by testing the concept using the local environment as a 'laboratory'. This term 'laboratory' stems from the more realistic settings and the potential to uncover additional consumer insights and market understanding when the concept is presented to BOP consumers (Mattson & Wood 2014). This is because consumers may become familiar with the product and related attributes, and show preferences that will eventually reframe the concept under evaluation (Prahalad 2012; Simanis & Duke 2014).

In line with this, Mattson and Wood (2014, p. 121403–2) introduced the concept of co-design, highlighting that:

> [c]o-design can be implemented to varying degrees . . . designers must involve resource-poor individuals in the concept generation, concept selection and other important phases of product development.

According to Radjou, Prabhu and Ahuja (2012, p. 192), assessing concepts by being locally present enables the product to be "quickly rolled out and tested using immediate customer feedback", providing a measure of potential product success. While such a physical version may require more time and money investment earlier in the process, engaging with consumers this way could lessen the risks and uncertainties about product acceptance.

On the basis of their often unusual needs, low literacy and the resource-constrained context, BOP consumers' first impression of the product could, in fact, significantly affect the results of this testing, especially if a physical version is not presented earlier (Simanis 2009, 2011). While Simanis (2011) does not consider this laboratory approach as a formal prototype testing approach, Simanis (2011, p. 119) nevertheless suggests the conceptualisation of a product offering based on consumers' feedback and "co-develop[ed] by the company and community team through events conducted with close friends and family of the community team".

The concept in this development phase is not designed to be at its optimal version, as supported by how frugal innovators focus their technical study on addressing essential specifications (as detailed in Practice 7). Testing a value proposition that remains broad increases the possibility for potential customers to adapt, familiarise and embed the physical concept in their lives, creating new markets for the new product (Simanis 2011; Simanis & Duke 2014). Wood and Mattson (2014) suggest the presence of a validation stage that requires to be iterative with other stages in the concept development phases to improve the development team's understanding of consumers' needs.

It is, therefore, argued in this study that spending more time with consumers during the concept development phase decreases "time, effort and money on the more structured, measurable back end of the innovation process [the product development and commercialisation phases in this study]" (Radjou & Prabhu 2015, p. 34). Empirical studies (i.e. General Electric (GE) Healthymagination, Kanchan Arsenic Filter (KAF) water filter, and ChotuKool fridge) suggest both the development of criteria helps validate innovations for BOP consumers as well as the use of 'co-design/creation' which emphasises the benefits of evaluating the product in the context of use via an early physical version.

Healthymagination is a validation process developed by GE, which includes three key criteria to assess the validity of concepts developed for BOP consumers (GE Healthcare 2017). Such concept evaluation and selection are based on the value proposition of the intended product, ascertaining whether it provides cheaper, better and accessible healthcare as compared with existing alternatives (Ramdorai & Herstatt 2017). Before implementing this formal evaluation process, GE also decreased its focus on financial criteria to test out frugal innovation projects such as its electrocardiogram (ECG) Mac 400 (Singh 2011).

The KAF is another example that illustrates the role of criteria and the use of early prototypes in the evaluation of concepts. Here, the development team sought to involve consumers throughout the development of their new water filter for Nepalese arsenic-tainted water. They undertook this project by "set[ting] out to co-design an arsenic remediation technology for villages in the Terai (Southern) Nepal" (Murcott 2007, p. 138). Out of 50 potential technological principles, eight technologies including the KAF were deemed most appropriate to address water issues in Southern Nepal, which led to further testing (Murcott 2007). These technologies were first screened by technical, financial and social design criteria such as meeting World Health Organization (WHO) standards, technology usability acceptance, and affordability for BOP consumers on less than 1 USD a day (Murcott 2007).

Real-life testing was also essential, as it boosted the team's understanding of the local cultural, geographical and environmental settings and their influences on the design (Murcott 2007). These eight technologies chosen out of the 50 potential designs were also tested in a laboratory as well as within a consumer context, a testing ground for iteration (Ngai et al. 2007). To keep costs low, these prototypes were developed locally. That is how they discovered the supply of local chemicals for the filtering system of some of the concepts, such as chlorine, could not be easily found locally (or at all). The budget structure for the price-point of affordability was going to suffer from additional costs if chlorine was used, which influenced the way the team approached further evaluation and selection of these technologies, integrating "local supply chains, costs, and availability" criteria (Murcott 2007, p. 139).

The ChotuKool fridge is another illustration of the role of consumers' feedback in the evaluation and selection of concepts. The innovator Godrej developed several prototypes of the concept based on co-creation, and from "a series of prototypes for feedback . . . [o]ver time, a consensus set of features emerged . . . [and] came the ChotuKool" (Innosight 2017, p. 2). This shows that the development team did not seek to develop an optimal solution at first; instead, the innovation leader insisted that the team dedicated time to undertake "systematic exploration and experimentation" (cited in Dhanaraj, Suram and Vemuri 2011, p. 4) of simple versions of potential concepts.

While developing physical versions can increase costs, Godrej's team offset these with the advantages that co-creation events offer. Such events multiplied the breadth and scope of feedback for product acceptance across the concept and product development phases (Innosight 2017; Whitney 2010). This continuous learning from direct and steady contact between the physical concept, the development team and consumers influenced effective iterations on the final concept (Whitney 2010).

These empirical insights have emphasised the difference with the traditional approach to concept testing, which tends to "ask [. . .] customers to validate an existing product idea, rather than discover unmet needs for a potential product" (Radjou & Prabhu 2012, p. 33). Introducing a concept in BOP consumers' lifestyle for testing opens opportunities for firms to learn and co-design with them. This study will, therefore, investigate whether frugal innovators use specific criteria and/or a physical version of their concepts to allow iteration on the product via testing the concept acceptance.

Phase 2 summary

In summary, the key role of the concept development phase is to justify the worthiness of selected NPD project(s) and associated value proposition, via the exploration, design and evaluation of a concept. Three stages shape the innovation decisions occurring during the concept development phase: the market study, technical study and concept evaluation (see Figure 3.3).

First, the market study stage helps firms understand how consumers perceive value proposition, directing the development team to establish needs and wants that are later translated into technical and design characteristics. The review of the frugal innovation literature during this phase led to the establishment of key frugal innovation Practice 5 and Practice 6.

Practice 5 specifically refers to a firm's primary focus on BOP consumer information. The corresponding literature shows that frugal innovators often factor in the meaning of affordability, complementary (e.g. aspirational and critical) needs and product usage contexts. Practice 6 relates to tools and techniques used by frugal innovators to engage with the context where BOP consumers live, to obtain deeper insights into and understanding of their unmet needs.

Looking at the second stage, the technical study is recognised as the translation of consumer needs into a technical language, and generally leads to the

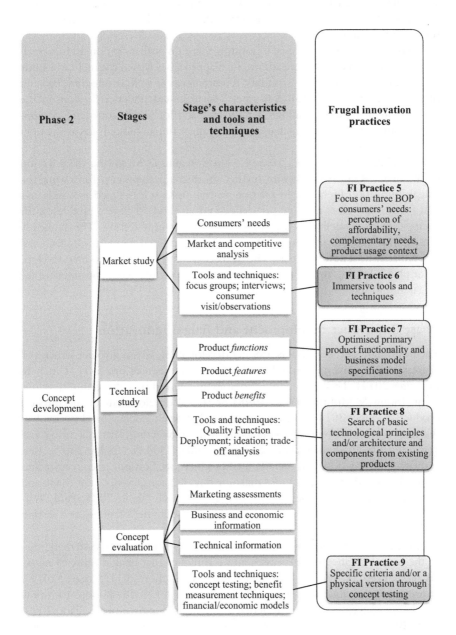

Figure 3.3 Phase 2 summary for frugal innovation

development of functional design and the establishment of technical feasibility. The review of the frugal innovation literature led to the development of frugal innovation Practice 7 and Practice 8, across the technical study characteristics and tools and techniques.

Practice 7 suggests that frugal innovators focus on primary product functionality and business model specifications. Such approaches within the technical study stage reduce the focus on secondary requirements as well as integrate broader requirements linked to BOP consumers' environment. Practice 8 discusses the exploration of basic technological principles and/or architecture and components from existing products that can offer similar functional outputs as the ones they seek to develop.

Regarding the third stage, concept evaluation aims at narrowing the selection of the final NPD project before further product development. Reviewing the frugal innovation literature in relation to this third stage, Practice 9 indicates that frugal innovators may use pre-defined criteria and/or have a preference for a simple physical version of a product for early concept testing. This is mostly due to firms' unfamiliarity with BOP consumers' preferences and the consumers' unfamiliarity with new products. The next section moves to the product development phase, leading to the development of three key management practices for frugal innovation.

Phase 3: product development and frugal innovation

The next phase of the NPDP is product development, which involves structured processes that convert accepted concepts into commercial products (Ulrich & Eppinger 2012). This phase is also commonly referred to as 'technical development' (Song & Montoya-Weiss 1998) or 'actual development of the physical product' (Cooper 2011). The process of developing a complete product involves the translation of chosen concepts along with engineering, manufacturing and marketing development (Rainey & Rainey 2005; Tidd & Bodley 2002). Relevant engineering decisions include final product specifications, architecture and materials; manufacturing includes make-or-buy decisions, component shape and interface, logistics and assembly factors (Krishnan & Ulrich 2001; Pahl, Wallace & Blessing 2007). Marketing encompasses packaging, branding and testing (Krishnan & Ulrich 2001).

In contrast with earlier phases, product development is more systematic due to the use of engineering processes and techniques that enable firms to measure, anticipate and commit time and resources (Bhuiyan 2011; Cooper 2011). However, the iterative nature of NPDP still allows for feedback loops to review the chosen concepts while in the actual product development phase (Tidd 2009; Vivek 2013). This flexibility has been defined as agile development using a 'build-test-feedback-revise' approach (Cooper 2010; Cooper & Sommer 2016).

The principal outputs from this phase are a performing product as well as a process plan documenting drawings, bills of materials and a model of assembly and production (Ulrich & Eppinger 2012). The following subsections discuss the two main stages of this product development phase: product design and prototype testing. The corresponding review of the frugal innovation literature leads to the development of three important frugal innovation Practices 10, 11 and 12, emphasising specific practices across the characteristics, tools and techniques of both NPDP stages.

Product design stage

When concepts are selected for further development, this stage instigates the technical advancement of engineering design parameters, drawing on the technical output from previous stages. It involves decisions regarding the development of "a solution principle by determining the general arrangement and preliminary shapes and materials of all components" of the product (Pahl, Wallace & Blessing 2007, p. 5). In addition to general design layouts, shapes and materials, development teams further investigate those design parameters by establishing components geometry, surface properties, tolerances, supply chain management and manufacturing costs and processes (Pahl, Wallace & Blessing 2007; Ulrich 1995; Ulrich & Eppinger 2012).

This stage finalises physical design parameters by linking with the other stage of this NPDP phase, the prototype testing stage, and deciding on production processes (Ulrich & Eppinger 2012). These concurrent decisions help reduce product development costs, in alignment with the formerly planned fixed budget. Bounded by previously established technical, market and economic constraints, this stage generally encompasses the most important decisions, and influences on the product, production and supply chain performance and their associated costs (Pahl, Wallace & Blessing 2007; Ulrich 1995). The product design stage mainly relies on two characteristics that underline firms' decisions regarding the engineering design of a product and are discussed ahead.

Characteristics

There are two primary characteristics that define the key decisions of this NPD stage: system design and detailed design. First, the product system design involves choosing the most appropriate architecture, set of systems and subsystems (Ulrich & Eppinger 2012). The second detailed design characteristic relates to the evaluation and implementation of product design, and associated systems of production and supply chain requirements (Krishnan & Ulrich 2001; Pahl, Wallace & Blessing 2007).

First, firms determine the product system design, also termed 'embodiment design', by initiating decisions around the architectures of the product, particularly those that govern the placement and proportion of components (Osteras, Murthy & Rausand 2006; Pahl & Beitz 2013; Ulrich & Eppinger 2012). Such product architecture can be integral or modular, which mean that these can differ by the amount of functional elements assigned across a number of building blocks (Stone, Wood & Crawford 2000; Ulrich & Eppinger 2012). Exploring a product's architecture relates to finding "how the functional elements are assigned to the chunks [or building blocks] and how the chunks are interrelated" (Crawford & Di Benedetto 2014, p. 331).

Establishing the system design is a fundamental part of firms' NPD strategy, as a number of aspects will be significantly influenced by the way product components interface and integrate with each other. Such aspects include the product size, form and performance; marketing strategies; and associated manufacturing decisions (e.g. production methods and assembly costs) (Crawford & Di Benedetto 2014; Pahl, Wallace & Blessing 2007; Ulrich & Eppinger 2012; Wheelwright & Clark 1992). System design decisions also establish the new product's life cycle, including upgrades, add-ons, re-use and flexibility, which is key in the alignment with a firm's NPD strategy (Ulrich & Eppinger 2012; Vivek 2013).

Complementing the system design are decisions on the detailed design, the second characteristic. These decisions involve definitive layouts of the product architecture and systems to optimise final details (Pahl & Beitz 2013; Ulrich & Eppinger 2012). The final details of a product refer both to the individual components such as interfaces, surface properties, materials, tolerances and the choice of suppliers, and to production, assembly, tooling and operational costs (Pahl, Wallace & Blessing 2007; Ulrich & Eppinger 2012). When deciding on product detailed design characteristics, a firm searches for the "maximum utilisation of the most suitable materials . . . at cost-effectiveness and at ease of production, with due attention being paid to standards" (Pahl, Wallace & Blessing 2007, p. 437). Exploration of the detailed design is accountable not only for the associated manufacturing costs, assembly planning and supply chain decisions, but also the reliability and performance of the product (Osteras, Murthy & Rausand 2006).

As the output of the product design stage relies on firms' capabilities, including their cost and manufacturing restraints, a variety of tools and techniques is available to achieve product design goals (Crawford & Di Benedetto 2014). Three of the most common tools and techniques are discussed ahead.

Tools and techniques

Tools and techniques enable more effective and efficient use of resources, time and decision-making in the product development stage, with some being easier, cheaper and faster to use, such as 3D printing (Graner & Mißler-Behr 2012; Luchs, Swan & Creusen 2016; Macdonald et al. 2014). Often used in combination (Yeh, Yang & Pai 2010), the most commonly used tools and techniques according to the literature include Design for Manufacturing (DfM) and Design for Assembly (DfA) (Graner & Mißler-Behr 2013; Ulrich & Eppinger 2012), computer-aided design/engineering (CAD/CAE) (Graner & Mißler-Behr 2013; Lutters et al. 2014; Pahl, Wallace & Blessing 2007) and failure mode experiment analysis (FMEA) (Barczak, Griffin & Kahn 2009; Graner & Mißler-Behr 2013).

The DfM technique helps firms minimise manufacturing costs via assessing materials and other resources while optimising quality and controlling ROI (Ulrich & Eppinger 2012). DfA focuses on developing easy-to-assemble products, facilitating the development of simpler product systems (Crawford & Di Benedetto 2011; Yeh, Yang & Pai 2010). CAD/CAE enables the translation of product design ideas into visual supports using software tools (Ulrich & Eppinger 2012). Although expensive, this tool's advantages include time- and cost-efficiencies in helping development teams make the 'right' design decisions (Thomke 2006) and is often considered as positively influencing NPDP performance (Yeh, Yang & Pai 2010). The FMEA technique helps manage risks and attempts to remove potential defects in the final product (Graner & Mißler-Behr 2013). It enables a firm to assess product design performance before it engages in developing the final version of the product (Barczak, Griffin & Kahn 2009).

The role of the design stage and associated tools and techniques involves important decisions that can influence the outcomes of the NPDP. To better understand this stage in the context of frugal innovation, the corresponding frugal innovation literature discussed ahead highlights two distinct practices associated with frugal innovation.

Frugal innovation studies

Frugal innovation literature mainly focuses on two practices related to the product design stage characteristics, tools and techniques. The first practice, FI Practice 10, relates to the key product design characteristics; frugal innovators appear to seek the use of minimal resources and prioritise local sourcing such as available materials, suppliers, labour and/or components (Tiwari & Herstatt 2012). However, while such sourcing has advantages, FI Practice also states that frugal innovators may balance this decision between the costs and performance of the local resource used (Rao 2013). The second practice, FI Practice 11, reflects the use of Design for X (DfX) techniques, where X is replaced by design strategies pertaining to frugal innovation, such as Design for Multiple Purposes (Viswanathan & Sridharan 2012) or Design for Modularity (Ray & Ray 2010) (more DfX are discussed ahead).

FI PRACTICE 10

With respect to the first practice of the product development phase, frugal innovators appear to balance minimal resources' use via locally available existing components, suppliers, labours and/or materials with both performance and costs (Rao 2013; Tiwari & Herstatt 2012). Such priority avoids unnecessary optimal and expensive resources while still guaranteeing quality outputs. Some of these resources can happen to be too expensive and/or not available locally, which would require them to be sourced internationally. Thus, while costs and quality are two important factors in frugal innovation, frugal innovators may balance between local make-or-buy decisions to ensure the right level of performance and costs in relation to the product functionality they seek to obtain in the frugal product design (Rao 2013; Weyrauch & Herstatt 2017).

Targeting existing local resources can help simplifying the original design of the product components. Doing so can lead to the standardisation of manufacturing processes such as through the cost-efficient re-use of local factories (Numminen & Lund 2017; Ray & Ray 2011). Furthermore, using local suppliers often makes product maintenance easier, particularly product servicing and repairs, which BOP consumers find more convenient and more acceptable (Agarwal, Brem & Grottke 2018; Bingham, Whitehead & Evans 2016; Weidner, Rosa & Viswanathan 2010). With these different benefits, empirical studies (i.e. GE ECG Mac 400 and the LFC wheelchair) illustrate the search for local resources while also considering cost against performance needs in the product design of frugal innovation.

The first example is the affordable, portable and easy-to-use ECG Mac 400. Developed by the GE Healthcare team in Bangalore, they combined the use of local labours and resources into the development of the ECG design. First, the development team involved in this NPD project worked in a locally based GE subsidiary in India, where local Indian engineers were employed. This enhanced affordability of the product on the basis of low labour costs. Another cost reduction via using local resources stemmed from the specific knowledge of the GE team aligning the product system and detailed design to fit with locally available or existing components to simplify sourcing (Bound & Thornton 2012; Ramdorai & Herstatt 2017). On the basis of their knowledge of locally available 'off-the-shelf' components, the team chose locally sourced, 'ready-made' parts, rather than designing new ones for the GE's ECG (McGregor 2008; Ramdorai & Herstatt 2017).

For example, the printer that was a feature designed to allow rural doctors to diagnose patients on the spot was an existing printer used for bus ticket, and had clear advantages linked with cost and design features for the ECG product (McGregor 2008; Ramdorai & Herstatt 2017; Singh 2011). As the printer had originally been designed and manufactured for India's public transport system, it was already engineered to sustain the humid and dusty Indian environment. According to Ishrak, the CEO of GE Healthcare's clinical systems unit, this was a successful time and cost performance aspect that might not have been attained if it was newly or proprietary designed by GE (Omar Ishrak, cited in McGregor 2008). The ECG design was not only about finding the cheapest development option, it also involved adapting what was locally available by pondering the right performance-cost ratio. This printer added value to the overall quality of the ECG Mac 400, it was cheaper, robust and allowed diagnosing rural patients on the spot.

The second example is the LFC wheelchair, made of locally sourced bicycle components (Winter 2013). Created by Winter Amos, an assistant professor in the Department of Mechanical Engineering at Massachusetts Institute of Technology (MIT), the wheelchair was developed and trialled in East Africa, Guatemala and India (Winter & Govindarajan 2015). The design decisions were clearly balanced between inexpensive local bicycle parts with the overall cost and performance of the product. For example, integrating local bicycle components into the LFC drivetrain design assisted in the simplification and cost reduction of its manufacturing due to localised sourcing (i.e. local welding tools for bike tubes, local labour) (Core Jr 2011; Winter & Govindarajan 2015). Not only were the costs of manufacturing reduced due to the abundance and cheapness of local bicycle parts, but also the presence of local repair shops facilitated efficient repair of the wheelchair for patients (Winter 2013; Winter et al. 2010).

The advantages of these local resources delivered significant value for BOP consumers in the creation and performance of an easy-to-maintain and low-cost wheelchair (Bingham, Whitehead & Evans 2016; Winter & Govindarajan 2015). Originating from earlier decisions to simplify the technological principles and system of the product, the development team also simplified the product architecture of the gear that underpinned the product functionality, leading to a more efficient single gear chain available locally (Winter et al. 2012). In addition, simplifying other parts of the product design reduced complexity of the sub-level aspects of the components and increased adaptability to locally available components, allowing balance between the product's overall quality, costs and design (Winter 2013).

On the basis of these examples, this study will explore whether frugal innovators consider the use of locally available components in balance with the cost and performance of the overall product design. While it appears evident that some local resources may not reach firms' quality standards, frugal innovation literature indicates a search for substitution of constituent local parts that do not negatively affect the product performance. Therefore, this study will investigate whether the product design stage involves prioritising local outsourcing with a consideration of costs and performance of the product.

FI PRACTICE 11

A recent rising trend in frugal innovation literature is Design for X (DfX) techniques, where X provides the strategic design guidelines to the development team on how resources will be used in the product design stage (Eastman 2012; Kuo, Huang & Zhang 2001). Each guideline provides a set of associated methods to reach the X strategy design, which the frugal innovation literature highlights with X strategies in product design that respond specifically to BOP markets.

Examples of this are "Design for Development" (Oosterlaken 2009), "Design for the BOP" (Jagtap et al. 2015; Whitney 2010), "Design for Micro-Enterprises" (Austin-Breneman & Yang 2013), "Design for the Developing World" (Mattson & Wood 2014) and "Design for Low-Income Settings" (Aranda-Jan, Jagtap & Moultrie 2016). These extended interpretations of DfX embrace holistic strategies, often discussing various decisions across a firm's NPDP such as at the technical study, design, testing, consumers' integration and/or product distribution level, thus overlapping with other NPDP phases.

Such design strategies can also be disaggregated into objectives that are more specific to the product development phase including decisions for the product design stage. Several examples of DfX linked to the product design stage are

Designs for Postponement (Radjou & Prabhu 2015), for Multiple Purposes, for Customisation, for Low Literate Users and for Local Sustainability (Viswanathan & Sridharan 2012), and Design for Modularity (Ray & Ray 2011). Following are two studies, one from Viswanathan and Sridharan (2012) and one from Austin-Breneman and Yang (2013), which discuss the implications of these DfX techniques.

The study of Viswanathan and Sridharan (2012) elaborated on a variety of critical DfX strategies established from 13 frugal innovation NPD projects for the Indian BOP undertook by university students in business (MBA), engineering and industrial design. For example, this study suggested the incorporation of Design for Multiple Purposes, implying a product "being multifunctional and contextually malleable" (p. 62), which meant more modularity in the product architecture. A modular system design integrates architecture, interfaces and components of the product that can adjust to incremental modifications of the original product design, which explains the role of Design for Multiple Purposes (Ray & Ray 2011; Ulrich & Eppinger 2012).

Modular architecture suggests that development teams can thus learn, iterate and gradually refine the final product quickly and cheaply to suit consumers' preferences due to its flexible construction (Prahalad 2012; Viswanathan & Sridharan 2012; Viswanathan, Yassine & Clarke 2011). This is in response to most of the Indian BOP consumers using new products in an unpredictable way, adapting their usage of the product according to their situation (Prahalad 2012; Viswanathan & Sridharan 2012).

Furthermore, the study of Austin-Breneman and Yang (2013) provides examples of frugal design strategies embedded in what they referred to as "Design for Micro-Enterprises". This technique aims to design products to support end users in becoming 'micro-entrepreneurs', including generating extra income from on-selling the product. In order to design frugal products that empower micro-entrepreneurs, these authors explored several case studies and subsequently developed guidelines to apply throughout the NPDP. These include Designs for Entrepreneurial Business Plan, for Reliable Brand Identity and for Multifunctionality.

With regard to product design, the guidelines included Design for Reliability to help develop a robust product, Design for Maintainability to guarantee easy repair and others like Design for Upgradeability, which resembles Viswanathan and Sridharan's (2012) Design for Multiple Purposes. The case studies clearly articulated the importance of incorporating such strategies when undertaking product design, in particular to avoid BOP markets failure and ensure BOP consumers entrepreneurial outcomes.

Based on these empirical studies, this study will explore whether frugal innovators use specific design strategies during the product design stage of frugal innovation. While more generic techniques focus on the firms' manufacturing and assembly aspects of the product (e.g. DfM and DfA), DfX techniques in the design of frugal products appear to widen the focus on aspects that BOP consumers value. Hence, the tools and techniques of the product design stage may include DfX techniques specifically aimed at frugal design strategies.

The product development phase also relies on the testing and refinement of prototypes, which validates the quality and performance of a chosen product design and the entire NPD project. The prototype testing stage, the third and concluding stage of the product development stage will be explored in the following section, including the development of one key decision by frugal innovators, establishing the 12th frugal innovation Practice.

Prototype testing stage

The prototype testing stage relates to the testing, refinement and validation of the product to ensure desired benefits and performance expectations are met as part of the feasibility of the project (Cooper 2011; Di Benedetto 2010). This stage can be also referred to as 'product use testing' (e.g. Crawford & Di Benedetto 2011) and 'development testing' (e.g. Bhuiyan 2011). The prototype testing stage is critical in addressing both design and marketing issues, from testing the product performance and its functionality, the technicalities as well as the consumer acceptance (Crawford & Di Benedetto 2014; Krishnan & Ulrich 2001). The outcomes of this stage have been shown to significantly affect market success or failure, prior to the commercialisation phase.

Generally within a controlled environment, this stage involves the use of a prototype that has been defined as an "approximation of the product along one or more dimensions of interest" (Ulrich & Eppinger 2012, p. 291). While the development of prototypes for testing does not involve the definitive production processes, the production processes are also reviewed and refined throughout this stage (Vivek 2013). This stage critically influences how the development team achieves an accurate, flawlessness and functional product that matches the expected target performance requirements (Cooper 2011). The testing and refinement of these prototypes are often guided by decisions characterised by criteria and form, as discussed ahead.

Characteristics

Two key characteristics are associated with the prototype testing stage: the different types of information (or criteria) sought based on firms' goals (Cooper 2011) and the form the prototype takes when a firm tests a particular aspect of it (e.g. visual, crude, physical models) (Crawford & Di Benedetto 2014; Ulrich & Eppinger 2012). The first characteristic reflects criteria in relation to the intended goal of the development team during this testing stage. Various technical and marketing criteria are used to develop, refine and validate product acceptance, marketing strategy, alternative designs, engineering parameters such as robustness and usability and the overall performance of the product (Cooper 2011; Gaubinger et al. 2014). These intertwined criteria enable a firm to trade off and refine various aspects of the product to find the right balance of performance, before moving to the next NPDP phase (Di Benedetto 2010).

To ensure the product meets market expectations, both comprehensive technical testing and consumer-oriented testing may occur (Gaubinger et al. 2014). The goal of each testing effort is to collect qualitative and/or quantitative data to refine and optimise the final product (Crawford & Di Benedetto 2014). According to Ulrich and Eppinger (2012), such testing can relate to multiple goals (i.e. learning, communicating, integrating or demonstrating milestones), depending on a firm's objectives and criteria. Many scholars support the importance of early prototyping, which allows testing and feedback (Cooper 2017; Crawford & Di Benedetto 2014; Ulrich & Eppinger 2012).

The second characteristic reflects the prototype form chosen for the testing, helping development teams and/or consumers to see and/or physically manipulate the product. The form of the product depends on the function the development team is testing during this stage (Crawford & Di Benedetto 2014). These decisions are largely guided by timelines, budgets and costs, benefits, as well as what firms want to reveal to the targeted market segment and competitors at the time of testing (Krishnan & Ulrich 2001). The prototype used at this stage should be cautiously selected, as it may influence time-to-market delays, consumers' and competitors' reactions, corresponding costs and other aspects jeopardising the success of NPDP efforts (Cooper 2011; Crawford & Di Benedetto 2014; Garcia 2014).

For technical testing, software tools and 3D printing enable development teams to focus their resources on specific product aspects (Di Benedetto 2010; Macdonald et al. 2014). Ulrich and Eppinger (2012) interpreted the development of prototypes as the construction of physical and/or analytical versions of the product, to be used via a focused or comprehensive approach. For example, a comprehensive prototype is a "fully operational version" (p. 247) of the final product before moving into further production (Ulrich & Eppinger 2012). Based on a firm's goals and criteria, some prototypes can also use a focused form that concentrates on one or several attributes of the final product, narrowed down to satisfy consumer needs (Di Benedetto 2010; Ulrich & Eppinger 2012). Tools and techniques can facilitate the intended goals of a firm and the choice over the prototype form, and the three most commonly used tools and techniques are introduced ahead.

Tools and techniques

There are a range of tools and techniques that can be employed to test prototypes, delivering different types of quantitative and qualitative data. The choice of such testing is generally associated with a firm's goals, product complexity and outcomes from earlier testing efforts (Crawford & Di Benedetto 2014). The three most common tools and techniques employed at this stage are in-house testing (Cooper 2011), beta testing (Gaubinger et al. 2014; Markham & Lee 2013) and gamma testing (Markham & Lee 2013; Tidd & Bodley 2002).

In-house testing (or alpha testing) facilitates the testing of the product in controlled settings such as in a laboratory or internal to the firm via firms' employees or with controlled variables and moderators (Cooper 2011; Garcia 2014). This testing gauges whether a product is working in line with the specifications, which can reveal potential product deficiencies (Crawford & Di Benedetto 2014; Griffin & Somermeyer 2007a). In contrast, beta testing usually refers to guided user and real consumers testing, meaning a short check on all the product functions in the usage context, to measure consumers' behaviours and reactions to the product (Cooper 1990; Garcia 2014; Gorchels 2006). Gamma testing is a more advanced form of testing, involving the detailed construction and assessment of pre-production prototypes to finalise the product specifications (Tidd & Bodley 2002; Ulrich & Eppinger 2012). This testing is generally a final verification of the product characteristics before more production investment is made (Ulrich & Eppinger 2012).

With these most common tools and techniques and the understanding of the key characteristics for prototype testing, the next part discusses the corresponding frugal innovation literature. The 12th frugal innovation Practice is developed, which relates to the importance of early field-testing as part of the prototype testing stage for frugal innovation.

Frugal innovation studies

The frugal innovation literature highlights the use of early field-testing techniques, including product fits within distinct social, environmental and political contexts (FI Practice 12). The socio-economic environment in which BOP consumers live is often challenging to reproduce in a laboratory, reflecting the importance of early field-testing during product development (Donaldson 2006; Mattson & Wood 2014).

FI PRACTICE 12

Field-testing is defined as "[prototype testing] with users from the target market in the actual context in which the product will be used" (Griffin & Somermeyer 2007a, p. 480). For frugal innovation, field-testing techniques may enable realistic results regarding BOP consumers' preferences as they distinguish between what the product achieves (its functions) and what it provides to consumers in their environment (Mattson & Wood 2014). In line with this, Wood and Mattson (2016) reinforced how testing prototypes in the field among local communities ensures that firms refine their understanding of consumers' expectations and product usage context. Viswanathan, Yassine and Clarke (2011, p. 567) referred to this as "contextual product testing".

This technique could also strengthen specific product dimensions related to frugal innovation. Those could refer to boundaries of affordability, accessibility, availability and awareness (Prahalad 2012) and be related to price, reachability, appearance and/or usability (Ngai et al. 2007). For example, Nakata and Weidner (2012) highlighted that one of the key aspects of successful frugal products is consumers' perception of the product, including its core functionality. This is because the intended value proposition of the proposed frugal product could be hindered by consumers' 'visual comprehension', or "how readily a product is understood through visual cues" (Nakata & Weidner 2012, p. 23).

As observed in previous stages across the concept and product development phases, continual contact with BOP consumers often prevails in frugal innovators' NPDP, emphasising the use of co-designing/creating, partnering and inclusive approaches (Mattson & Wood 2014; Murcott 2007). The importance of these approaches stem from the constant changes in consumers' needs, which can affect the design of various product attributes and related specifications (Radjou & Prabhu 2015). Relevant empirical studies (e.g. Barefoot Power Go Lamp and the KAF) have signalled the importance of testing prototypes early in the field.

A particularly good illustration of a frugal product benefitting from the field-testing technique is the Barefoot Power Go Lamp (or 'firefly'). This is an affordable, solar rechargeable and portable light that provides illumination from 6 to 20 hours to rural BOP consumers (Barefoot Power 2017; Business call to action n.d.). This product underwent extensive field-testing in BOP markets of various developing countries to understand and adapt to the specific criteria of local consumers (Business call to action n.d.; de Gooijer 2013). This translated into incremental modifications of the lamp's design aspects in line with how potential consumers would use it.

A key field-testing example was in Kenya and Uganda, where it was realised that local consumers who trialled the solar lamp also used it for charging phones. This led to modifications of the solar panel power performance from 1 to 1.5 watts, which allowed local phones to be charged easier and faster (Da Silva & Sloet 2012). This field-testing clearly demonstrates that this usage preference of BOP consumers could have been difficult to reproduce in laboratory settings, especially when customisation to such local context is required.

Another study that exemplifies the application of early field-testing in the product development phase is the KAF for the Nepalese BOP market (Murcott 2007). Combined with technical testing in laboratory, the development team undertook field-testing of three water filters, including the KAF, and took almost one year to confirm that the KAF was the most suitable and accepted product for Nepalese BOP market (Mattson & Wood 2014; Murcott 2007). For example, local consumers preferred the KAF because it provided faster water output and required less maintenance than the other filters being tested (Murcott 2007). Such feedback was highly valuable and illustrated the importance of field-testing as opposed to laboratory trials, as other water filters were also performing equally in laboratory. This example also showed the importance of longer term testing as opposed to short checks with consumers.

Based on these insights, this study will explore whether frugal innovators integrate early field-testing in their prototype testing efforts. While generic prototype testing suggests firms adapt the choice of the testing in accordance with their time, budget and benefits, field-testing practices for frugal products appears vital in the development of successful NPD. The main reason is that social, economic and political characteristics of the BOP markets environment influence how these consumers both shape their preferences and identify product benefits. Thus, this study will examine whether the tools and techniques of the prototype testing stage include early field-testing as a key frugal innovation practice, which may include the idea of co-design/creation.

Phase 3 summary

During the product development phase, firms convert concepts into working and functional products to become sellable versions. Two stages occur during this phase, including the product design and prototype testing stages (see Figure 3.4). The former stage is the technical advancement of the concept's engineering design drawing on technical output from previous stages. The review of the corresponding frugal innovation literature led to the development of frugal innovation Practice 10 and Practice 11.

Practice 10 relates to prioritising minimal resource use through local outsourcing, traded off with the cost and performance of the overall product design. Seeking available local resources is shown as beneficial both for the firms (performance,

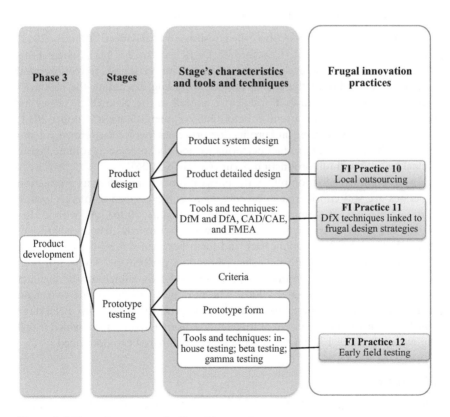

Figure 3.4 Phase 3 summary for frugal innovation

time and costs) and BOP consumers (convenience and affordability). On the other hand, frugal innovators ensure that these local resources are up to the performance needs that the frugal product should achieve. Frugal innovation Practice 11 reflects specific tools and techniques that frugal innovators use, including DfX techniques such as Design for BOP and Design for the Developing World and more NPDP specific such as Design for Multiple Purposes.

Moving to the second stage, the prototype testing stage involves the testing, refinement and validation of the product to ensure desired benefits and performance expectations are met as part of the feasibility of the project. With regard to the frugal innovation literature, the frugal innovation Practice 12 is informed through the use of early field-testing by frugal innovators in their prototype testing stage. It appears to be an essential aspect where their prototype is tested in the field as early as possible to refine different aspects of the product on the basis of BOP consumers' preferences. Moving forward, the following section explores the final phase of the NPDP for frugal innovation – the commercialisation phase. This leads to the development of three key practices for frugal innovation across the market testing and production ramp-up stages.

Phase 4: commercialisation and frugal innovation

The commercialisation phase, also called 'testing and validation' (Bhuiyan 2011; Cooper 2011) or 'launch' (Crawford & Di Benedetto 2014), is where firms bring the product from development to market. This phase aims to reinforce and finalise the feasibility of the overall project, including examining the product's economic viability and market acceptance as well as the planned processes for product manufacture and assembly before full commercialisation (Cooper 2011; Gorchels 2006). Marketing and production processes involve the refinement and testing of both the final product performance and the increase in volume before formal roll-out and full production occur (Gorchels 2006).

At this commercialisation phase, the physical product as well as its production processes are still considered as prototypes to achieve speed-to-market before high-volume output commences (Carrillo & Franza 2006). As with earlier phases, this phase is also iterative in nature, where a firm may change the product or production details by going back and forth between stages (Cooper 2011). When a firm is satisfied with the achieved product performance levels, it is then ready for scaling up its production processes and fully launching the product (Osteras, Murthy & Rausand 2006). The next parts introduce the two main stages involved in this phase: market testing and production ramp-up. Each stage concludes with an investigation of frugal innovation literature, from which frugal innovation Practice 13, Practice 14 and Practice 15 have been developed.

Market testing stage

This stage assists in the final testing and validation through real-life conditions of the product associated with its marketing plan (Cooper 2011; Griffin &

Somermeyer 2007a; Ozer 1999). Real-life conditions involve testing the product among different segments of the targeted consumers, offering a firm with a variety of marketing benefits (Osteras, Murthy & Rausand 2006) such as innovation diffusion through awareness and adoption (Olson 2007). The more market testing there is, the more likely there is a faster rate of adoption (if the product is accepted) (Crawford & Di Benedetto 2014).

At this market testing stage, the product under consideration can prove it has achieved its performance requirements by being accepted under the conditions tested in the product development phase (Crawford & Di Benedetto 2014). This testing stage also provides valuable insights into final design refinement, plus greater certainty to a firm's investment before the full product launch (Cooper 2011). However, some firms may not undertake this stage, determining it as more of a 'nice to have', such as based on time and cost pressures or aligned with their objectives, investment risks and the industry (Kotler 2016). Two key characteristics of this stage are introduced ahead.

Characteristics

The primary goal of market testing is to facilitate the evaluation and validation of the product and its associated marketing strategy, with two key characteristics linked to this stage. The first characteristic involves the implementation and testing of firms' marketing strategy before full commercialisation of the new product. The second is the collection of forecasting data, including quantitative data based on consumers' purchase intent.

The marketing strategy starts with assessing the validity of the plans associated with the new product (Cooper 2011; Ozer 1999). During the previous phases of the NPDP, a firm will have accumulated knowledge on its marketing strategy combining early management decisions, which is often tested and refined through a broader group of consumers at this stage (Kotler 2016; Ulrich & Eppinger 2012).

In particular, firms focus on testing several aspects of their marketing mix strategies (e.g. place, promotion, price, product) before full commercialisation (Awa 2010; Kotler 2016). Such aspects include finding the best way to reach consumers – distribution and sales force, and to raise awareness of the new product – advertising and promotion, including pricing and additional downstream services (Cooper 2011; Kotler 2016). This is where firms pursue combinations of marketing strategies to assess how these elements interact (Cooper 2011). The main purposes of these marketing objectives are to encourage consumers to purchase the new product, to refine each element of the marketing strategy, and to enable prediction data for consumers' purchase intent (Gaubinger et al. 2015a).

The second characteristic is where firms forecast the potential success of a new product via quantitative data from targeted markets (Cooper 2011). This is where a firm collects data to identify how much of the market they can capture, the volume of future sales and how much cash will be received from the purchases (Crawford & Di Benedetto 2014). These data outline the validity of the product and associated marketing strategy (in parallel with the production ramp-up stage), generally deriving from consumer reactions to the product and associated marketing approaches. These data also inform a firm about whether the market testing results have met its financial expectations (Cooper 2011; Gaubinger et al. 2015a). Crawford and Di Benedetto (2014) suggest that penetration rates and ROI are generally the traditional data sought when a firm undertakes this market testing stage.

If the results are not satisfactory, the firm can adjust and refine aspects of the product or its associated marketing strategies prior to commercialisation (Cooper 2011; Ozer 1999). The key outcome of market testing is to effectively evaluate and validate the full launch planning by the development team (Crawford & Di Benedetto 2014). At this stage, there is a variety of tools and techniques that can help firms obtain valuable data from consumers and determine the overall project's worthiness. The three most common are discussed ahead.

Tools and techniques

There is a variety of tools and techniques that can be used alone or in combination at this market testing stage (Crawford & Di Benedetto 2014; Dahan & Hauser 2002). These are generally in accordance with previous testing outcomes, the firm's industry and the type of quantitative data collected to assess estimated profits, sales/revenues and/or ROI. The three most common tools and techniques are simulated test marketing (Cooper 2011; Kotler 2016), test marketing (Crawford & Di Benedetto 2014; Kotler 2016) and limited roll-out (Crawford & Di Benedetto 2014).

Simulated test marketing is an inexpensive tool that evaluates marketing strategy by stimulating consumers to purchase a product in an environment controlled by the firm (or a consulting, or market research firm) (Cooper 2010; Dahan & Hauser 2002). Such false buying situations provide laboratory/statistical models that lead to the collection of sales forecast and market share data (Crawford & Di Benedetto 2014; Nijssen & Frambach 2000). In contrast, test marketing is where the product and the entire marketing package are introduced to diverse cities and/or specific market segments, which generally already represent the final targeted market (Crawford & Di Benedetto 2014; Ozer 1999). Although an expensive and time-consuming technique, this assessment of the firm's marketing strategy and launch plans provides thorough sales forecasts (including usage, price and competitor activity) (Cooper 2011; Crawford & Di Benedetto 2014; Gorchels 2006).

The more contemporary 'limited roll-out' technique involves introducing the new product at a limited scale, targeting the 'right' consumer segments irrespective of their geographical environment (Crawford & Di Benedetto 2014; Nijssen & Frambach 2000). This technique gradually stretches out the product roll-out while refining its marketing strategy to increase adoption rates (Crawford & Di Benedetto 2014). Incorporating these most common tools and techniques and characteristics of the market testing stage, the next section examines the frugal innovation literature associated with this stage. Many of the frugal innovator practices relate to the marketing strategy implemented at this stage, which, in turn, leads to the development of two frugal innovation practices.

Frugal innovation studies

Two key practices were identified in the literature in relation to how frugal innovators approach the market testing stage. First, some frugal innovators test their product and marketing strategy through local trusted networks including word-of-mouth (WOM) (FI Practice 13). The second practice relates to their NPD promotion approach, including consumer engagement via physical demonstration and training (FI Practice 14). Such engagement helps ensure the product and its benefits are comprehensively understood to increase consumer adoption.

FI PRACTICE 13

With regard to the practice of leveraging local trusted networks, such engagement involves market testing via an existing social infrastructure that include WOM practices (Weidner, Rosa & Viswanathan 2010). The literature also shows that it is critical for frugal innovators to leverage local networks when promoting and testing their new product, including through informal groups within local communities as well as local NGOs and/or government partnerships. One of the main reasons for considering local networks during market testing is the local constraints attributed to under-developed physical distribution and promotion channels that are generally available for high-income markets (Sharma & Iyer 2012). BOP consumers' purchasing decisions often rely on local trusted distributors and vendor networks (Furr & Dyer 2015; Radjou & Prabhu 2015). BOP consumers tend to build such social infrastructure as alternative methods to access product necessities and leapfrog local under-developed physical infrastructure (Radjou & Prabhu 2015; Viswanathan & Sridharan 2012).

Purchasing from local trusted sources also highlights a 'community mindset' where BOP consumers appreciate long-term relationships and are loyal to their communities (Jain 2011; Radjou & Prabhu 2015). This mindset often frames the conditions of the market testing stage in BOP markets, pushing it into strategic community testing that helps form long-term relationships with consumers as well as local agents promoting to their acquaintances (Simanis 2011). Initiating market testing in BOP markets and/or local villages where the concept and the prototype have been tested earlier also allows firms to access more consumers by widening market testing to other villages and regions (Whitney 2010).

Furthermore, many NGOs have been operating in local settings for extended periods. They are familiar with BOP consumers' behaviours and preferences and the need for a low-cost business approach and adapted marketing techniques to reach local communities (Brugmann & Prahalad 2007). As NGOs' experience and networks give in-depth knowledge of consumers and potential distribution and promotion channels adapted to the local BOP, frugal innovators often benefit from working with local NGOs. Moreover, local government partnerships can also help firms obtain a foothold in the targeted market. For example, firms could join government programs that support local projects and issues (Mattson & Wood 2014). Mattson and Wood (2014) recommend using local government parties to reach targeted BOP consumers to increase positive perceptions about the product (e.g. trust), facilitating higher adoption rates and testing outputs.

Testing within local community networks can thus lead to rapid sharing of product knowledge across local communities, enabling firms to leapfrog local constraints, refine products characteristics and bolster certainties in relation to the scalability of the project. Case studies (e.g. Prahalad's (2012) biomass cook stove and the ChotuKool fridge) highlight how beneficial it is to collaborate with local networks to market test new frugal products.

With the biomass cookstove, the development team collaborated with an NGO at the market testing stage, which simplified the process of spreading new product awareness among local consumers (Prahalad 2012). The collaboration elicited familiarity with consumers and leveraged the NGO's previous initiatives in local villages. In particular, an NGO redirected the development team towards local entrepreneurs, such as female networks, as potential partners in the distribution network. According to Prahalad (2012, p. 9), entrepreneurial women networks were "an indispensable part of the logistics system for making stoves accessible and fuel available all the time". This aligns with the idea that local networks can be an effective technique for the market testing stage.

For the ChotuKool fridge, local networks, including WOM, sales agents and NGOs, were the main drivers behind distribution and promotion testing of the fridge (Singh, Gambhir & Dasgupta 2011). Due to earlier testing, the fridge was promoted via WOM across various Indian regions, without spending significant money on marketing campaigns (Whitney 2010). Furr and Dyer (2015) described Godrej's approach as "business model experiments", where village gatherings organised by local groups were leveraged through NGOs' knowledge, including with more than 600 women. The focus on local network for market testing this fridge also included working with existing postal shops for distribution as well as local agents present in the communities for promotion and sales (Innosight 2017). Godrej succeeded in getting closer to intended consumers as well as developing long-term relationships through locally trusted sources such as postal shops (Furr & Dyer 2015).

Spurred on by these empirical cases, this study will examine whether local networks are a critical aspect of frugal innovators' marketing strategies to engage BOP consumers during the market testing stage. The use of local networks by frugal innovators is a shift from the more traditional market testing stage where firms that target higher-income markets generally engage in well-established distribution and promotion channels. Hence, this study will explore whether the market testing stage involve testing distribution and promotion of the new product through existing local networks for frugal innovation.

FI PRACTICE 14

The second practice observed in the literature relates to frugal innovators' promotional methods, supporting greater engagement with local BOP consumers through product demonstration and training (Chikweche & Fletcher 2012). As BOP consumers are often characterised by a lack of technology and lower levels of literacy, this may inhibit knowledge dissemination about new products, technology, firms and brands (Nakata & Weidner 2012; Radjou & Prabhu 2015). This method of promotion through demonstration and training, therefore, encourages, demonstrates and teaches local consumers about the product and its associated benefits (Weidner, Rosa & Viswanathan 2010).

Through local networks, frugal innovators may engage in promotional techniques that include demonstration and product training for the promotional images and branding of the frugal product. As part of training consumers, training local agents is also often critical for establishing learning mechanisms for local consumers (Hart, Sharma & Halme 2016), through extensively engaging with the local community. It also involves developing and strengthening relationships to ensure that local consumers and/or agents can evolve via the firm's business model (Hart, Sharma & Halme 2016; Simanis & Hart 2009).

Local agents and consumers are subsequently included in the local economy by being involved in firms' distribution network, thereby promoting inclusive growth and potential positive social change (Whitney 2010). Case studies, including M-PESA, biomass cookstove and the Barefoot Power Go Lamp, show the benefits of putting a substantial amount of time, engagement and education dedicated to local agents and potential consumers for new products.

The M-PESA highlights the challenges that can be encountered when introducing a product to new BOP consumers. The development team implemented 'familiarisation' training with employers and consumers (Hughes & Lonie 2007, p. 74). To avoid consumer misunderstanding regarding the product benefits, M-PESA's local employees were trained so they could support local consumers and agents on a long-term basis. This training was first aimed at getting the sales team comfortable with the concept that was completely new in the local context (Nakata & Berger 2011). Various issues stemming from consumers' product usage challenged the development team, leading them to implement additional consumer training and fine-tuning of the product (Hughes & Lonie 2007). This included educating consumers not familiar with using a mobile phone as well as finding an appropriate location to undergo training. Consumer training was beneficial, as it also helped revealing the impractical number of tasks involved in the financial transactions supported by M-PESA, which led the development team to simplify M-PESA transactions process before its full launch (Hughes & Lonie 2007).

With regard to the case of the biomass cookstove and the Barefoot lamp, Prahalad (2012) illustrated the importance of intensive training for women involved in the door-to-door distribution of the product. This was based on the positive impact on women's income growth and knowledge about the product technology. Similarly, the development team at Barefoot sought to promote the Barefoot solar lamp through engaging with local communities via training (Business call to action n.d.). While this training included workshops about selling strategies, the development team also delved further into product technicalities for repairs and servicing, installation and customer service (Business call to action n.d.).

Building from these empirical cases, this study will, therefore, explore whether frugal innovators engage further with their consumers during their market testing stage. While this approach does not exclude traditional marketing promotion such as brochures and social media marketing, frugal innovators are, however, often physically engaged with their consumers (end users and/or distribution agents). Instead of using marketing campaigns over several months, most frugal innovators focus on providing local marketing support via demonstration and training. Many frugal innovators integrate these types of inclusive strategies both for the product to be sold and to positively influence the local community. Thus, this study will investigate whether the market testing stage for frugal innovation include product demonstration and training as key promotional strategy.

The final stage of the commercialisation phase is the production ramp-up stage, which refers to piloting and validating the product, the production processes and the related quality standards before full launch. An examination of corresponding frugal innovation literature is also presented, which led to the development of a final frugal innovation practice, Practice 15.

Production ramp-up stage

The production ramp-up stage, or production planning (Glock, Jaber & Zolfaghari 2012), refers to the organisation and finalisation of assembly, fabrication and quality in both the production processes and the desired product performance before full-scale launch (Murthy, Rausand & Østerås 2008; Ulrich & Eppinger 2012). This stage involves several runs/series of production outputs to produce the final product with intended production processes (Almgren 2000). This is where firms slowly increase production while introducing the product to the market, influencing the operation and supply chain management of the production process (Surbier, Alpan & Blanco 2014; Terwiesch & E. Bohn 2001).

Due to the increase in production volume, trialling the manufacturing and assembly processes also allows firms to integrate continuous learning and training processes while moving towards full high-volume capacity (Almgren 2000). Effective management during the production ramp-up stage is critical. It enables firms to control variables related to possible losses in quantity, manufacturing costs and delay in time-to-market while maximising quality across the product and production (Almgren 2000; Brauner et al. 2016).

The production ramp-up stage, therefore, acts as a production testing platform before full production, providing beneficial inputs into assessing the whole project validity, particularly the production levels that include quality, volume and costs (Surbier, Alpan & Blanco 2014). There are two key characteristics in relation to decision-making during this production ramp-up stage, discussed ahead.

Characteristics

With the production ramp-up stage providing various benefits to the whole NPD project, production strategy and quality standards are the two most relevant characteristics. The first is in relation to firms planning for their production strategies such as timelines and volume level, to guide their decisions in preparing and releasing first product outputs for market launch. The second relates to quality standards via Quality Assurance (QA)/Quality Control (QC), including human factors controlled through the training of the production workforce.

With regard to the first characteristic, there is a variety of production strategies that are generally aligned with a firm's industry, goals and production complexity (Almgren 2000). These strategies reflect the firm's approach with regard to timelines and product outputs when testing production processes (Surbier, Alpan & Blanco 2014). This is critical characteristic, as the targeted production outputs may affect timelines in relation to the desired product performance and the efficiency of production processes (Surbier, Alpan & Blanco 2014).

Winkler, Heins and Nyhuis (2007) suggested a two-step process to ensure firms can adhere to product delivery and production quality timelines. In their first step, the 'preparation step', the focus is on the production volume and the implementation of the production plants including the capacity of manufacturing tools and equipment. The second step, the 'run-up step', starts when the first product output can be replicated and suitable to consumers, with focus on the production workforce training as well as the supply chain and organisational management (Winkler, Heins & Nyhuis 2007). A firm can thus undertake small-scale runs of product outputs at low-volume production (Almgren 2000; Ulrich & Eppinger 2012).

However, small-scale runs generally provide less quality and quantity product output, and requires more resources such as time, labour and materials (Winkler, Heins & Nyhuis 2007). While firms can adequately comprehend the environment where the production is undertaken, firms should have a strategic schedule while testing the production process through releasing low-volume levels of the final product and speed up process towards full production (Almgren 2000; Brauner et al. 2016). Generally, accelerating the production ramp-up stage provides firms with better and faster investment performance for their time-to-market, product development and production efforts (Li et al. 2014).

The second characteristic consists of establishing control over the quality standards during production ramp-up stage including QA/QC and human factors. QA refers to a "[p]art of quality management focused on providing confidence [to the firm] that quality requirements will be fulfilled" (ISO 9000, cited in Dale et al. 2016, p. 19), whereas QC is a "[p]art of quality management focused on fulfilling quality requirements" (ISO 9000, cited in Dale et al. 2016, p. 16). Controlling these variables is important due to their moderating effect on the final performance of the production output, including validating the whole NPD project. As the development team better understands the variables influencing production and product performance, they can fine-tune the production system and associated outputs (Juerging & Milling 2005; Ulrich & Eppinger 2012).

In fact, the management of human factors is a critical variable during the production ramp-up stage, especially with the difficulty of finding skilled and experienced workforce in more modern production processes (Brauner et al. 2016). An important controlling aspect is training the production workforce with a particular focus on the learning curve of these employees (Glock, Jaber & Zolfaghari 2012; Osteras, Murthy & Rausand 2006; Terwiesch & E. Bohn 2001). The level of learning will, however, differ on the basis of the firm's industry. For example, in the automotive sector, production processes are often automated, requiring less intensity in training employees (Surbier, Alpan & Blanco 2014). In addition to continuous learning and refinement, safety and legislative aspects are also examined in this stage.

Overall consideration of these aspects helps to control those variables that could negatively impact on product performance and production outputs during the production ramp-up stage (Surbier, Alpan & Blanco 2014; Ulrich & Eppinger 2012). A variety of tools and techniques can support a firm's production strategy, and enable an efficient and effective production ramp-up, with the three main ones discussed ahead.

Tools and techniques

As one of the final NPDP stages before full commercialisation, tools and techniques can assist firms in making decisions in regard to the development of appropriate production processes, product output timing and workforce training before full commercialisation (Leffakis 2016; Ulrich & Eppinger 2012). Three of the most common tools and techniques in this context are flexible manufacturing systems (FMS) (Carrillo & Franza 2006), computer-aided manufacturing (CAM) (Carrillo & Franza 2006) and FMEA (Dudek-Burlikowska 2011; Thia et al. 2005).

FMS tools shorten the time spent testing and adapting products prior to full production due to the flexibility of production processes (Carrillo & Franza 2006). Such tools allow faster learning and product entry to market, as firms can more efficiently test different product versions and associated production processes (Carrillo & Franza 2006). CAM is an expensive software tool focusing on the management of resources before and during production ramp-up stage (Carrillo & Franza 2006). Despite its high costs, this computer-aided tool can be beneficial, as it enables the planning of the production processes along with scheduling, monitoring and controlling operations and associated product and production quality (Groover & Zimmers 1983).

FMEA enables the management of risks particularly when a firm seeks to implement changes and/or improvements in production processes (Dudek-Burlikowska 2011). The aim of applying this tool at the production ramp-up stage is to spot potential failures and their frequency of occurrence to anticipate their effect on the production outputs (Scipioni et al. 2002). Moving from the characteristics, tools and techniques of this stage, the next part examines how frugal innovators tend to undertake the production ramp-up stage.

Frugal innovation studies

Within the sparse frugal innovation literature focused on the production ramp-up stage, few authors claim that generic production systems targeting high-income markets require some changes for frugal innovation (Ahuja 2014; Gassmann et al. 2017). Frugal innovators generally seem to adhere to running small-scale production as well as enforcing strict quality standards over a long-term strategy in their production ramp-up stage (FI Practice 15). Limiting production output to smaller quantities – instead of aiming for a rapid scale-up as suggested in the NPDP literature – may stem from several factors at the product and production levels.

FI PRACTICE 15

In the context of frugal innovation, firms may consider two aspects to plan their production strategy, including anticipating ongoing product refinements and taking time to adapt their production operations. First at the product level, the preference for low-volume production can relate to the ongoing requirement for product refinements adapted to meet consumer demands. This is because in the context of BOP markets, a new product reaches consumers early and they are often recognised for their diverse purchasing behaviours and preferences, generally depending on their geographical environment (Viswanathan, Yassine & Clarke 2011; Whitney 2010).

Due to the diversity of BOP consumers, frugal innovators are more likely to be more aware of the need to introduce product variants at the micro-level and across international BOP markets. Hence, low-volume production may help in minimising investment risks, as frugal products can still adapt and evolve alongside consumers' preferences. Donaldson (2006) gives an insight into this with Kenyan innovators preferring small-scale production due to less investment risks including the possibility to be more adaptable to consumer demand and local manufacturing processes.

Second, engaging in longer time period, small-scale production in the targeted market can also lead to initiating production ramp-up using local small factories for testing. Firms can then start their production earlier, using associated expertise labour and local equipment in the design and production processes of frugal products (Ray & Ray 2011; Seghal, Dehoff & Panneer 2010). Local production may ensure simple and cheap resources, which can also lower commercialisation costs (Gollakota, Gupta & Bork 2010; Ray & Ray 2011). In line with this, Gassmann et al. (2017) advocate simplifying firms' production strategy goals through avoiding automated equipment and preferring re-using existing ones to reach firms' desired production outputs faster.

Such use of local resources including factories and associated labour means that optimising the quality standards of new products is a requirement, including via QA/QC and employee training. Possibly due to the lack of local regulations in BOP markets (Khanna & Palepu 2010), like in the study of Donaldson (2006) in Kenya, minimum quality standards might not be guided by local regulations. To overcome this issue, an important aspect of quality standards emphasised in the NPDP literature is optimising production workforce's training around the manufacturing process (Glock, Jaber & Zolfaghari 2012; Winkler, Heins & Nyhuis 2007). As suggested by Surbier, Alpan and Blanco (2014), labour intensive and less automated production often requires additional workforce training. To ensure strict quality standards due to working with local labour, comprehensive training of the workforce may then become a significant feature of frugal innovators' production ramp-up.

This can impact on QA/QC, as an important aspect of strict quality standards on frugal product quality is to meet consumers' expectations (Gassmann et al. 2017). To ensure high-quality output, frugal innovators may, therefore, need time to ensure strict quality standards such as QA/QC and employee training across production processes. This helps adjusting to the local production environment, which small-scale production allows.

Furthermore, in the context of BOP, small-scale production often entails abundant local 'skilled artisans' with inexpensive wages to compensate extensive training, lower costs of operations and flexible time for adaptation (Gollakota, Gupta & Bork 2010, p. 361). It is often the case that local artisans in the BOP markets context have intensively worked in the same industry for many years, enabling faster adaptation by firms to local factories and vice versa.

Despite the lack of research on frugal innovators' practices in relation to production ramp-up, it appears that frugal innovators may concentrate on small-scale production for longer periods. Frugal innovators tend to reduce investment risks by fine-tuning their production processes with more time spent on quality standards via quality product and labour training. Hence, this study will explore whether the production ramp-up stage factor in low-volume production timelines for longer periods, which benefits quality standards such as QA/QC and workforce training.

Phase 4 summary

In summary, the commercialisation phase involves testing and validating the product, and associated marketing strategy including market acceptance and the planned production processes involved in the manufacture and assembly. Two stages occur during the commercialisation phase, including market testing and production ramp-up stages (see Figure 3.5).

The market testing stage first involves decisions in relation to the final testing and validation of the product, and its associated marketing plan in real-life conditions. The review of the corresponding frugal innovation literature identified two key practices, Practice 13 and Practice 14. The use of local networks (e.g. NGOs,

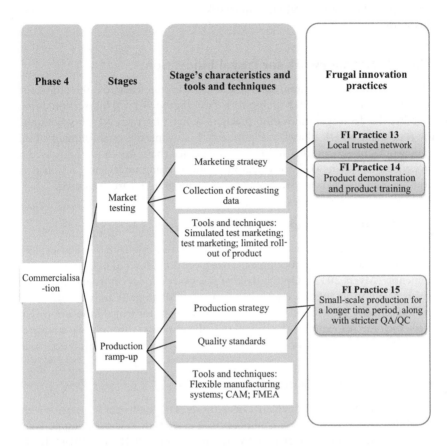

Figure 3.5 Phase 4 summary for frugal innovation

government and/or local informal groups) when testing the distribution and promotion of new products was observed as pivotal in frugal innovators' market testing, establishing frugal innovation Practice 13. With regard to Practice 14, the literature highlighted the role of product demonstration and training as key promotional methods for frugal innovators. As opposed to using marketing campaigns over several months, frugal innovators appear to physically engage with their consumers to provide marketing support.

The second stage of commercialisation, in relation to production ramp-up, is the finalisation of assembly, fabrication and quality in both the firms' production processes and the desired product performance. Stemming from the frugal innovation literature, the final Practice 15 suggests that frugal innovators consider low-volume production timelines for longer periods, allowing firms to enforce stricter quality standards via QA/QC and intensive training. The next section will summarise these four phases, nine stages and 15 frugal innovation

Practices to illustrate the NPDP framework for frugal innovation that underpins this study.

The NPDP framework for frugal innovation

The review of the frugal innovation literature was mapped across the nine stages of the consolidated NPDP framework (see Figure 3.1). This section brings together the 15 frugal innovation practices derived for each NPDP stage under the four main NPDP phases in Figure 3.6. Following the establishment of this framework, the section that follows will introduce the research methods used to investigate this framework for frugal innovation. Using interviews and observations techniques, two case studies and their demographics are presented.

Research methods and data collection

This study of frugal innovation practices is based on a qualitative and exploratory enquiry, an appropriate approach to explore complex and understudied phenomenon (Myers 2013). On the basis of this study's focus on frugal innovation, which is still in its infancy especially from a NPDP angle (Cunha et al. 2014), this exploratory study developed a NPDP framework for frugal innovation. This study then further explores the Indonesian phenomenon through two strategies: the establishment of a consolidated NPDP framework and a case study approach.

Framework guiding the study

To build a conceptual framework (here the NPDP for frugal innovation), the initial development of theory is important in case study research, despite being time-consuming and cumbersome (Merriam & Tisdell 2015; Yin 2014). In this study, the research design approaches the literature through the review of a well-established theory (the NPDP literature for developed countries), supplemented by the use of a nascent theory (frugal innovation literature).

Doing so directed the development of 15 key frugal innovation practices, which underlines the NPDP framework for frugal innovation, and has also guided the data collection and analysis processes. This approach aligned with Maxwell's (2013, p. 49) conviction that "[a] useful high-level theory gives you a framework for making sense of what you see" and that using theory via a conceptual framework "draws your attention to particular events or phenomena, and sheds light on relationships that might otherwise go unnoticed or misunderstood" (pp. 49–50).

Case study strategy

Subsequently to this strategy, two Indonesian case studies were investigated. A case study is a research strategy often used in social science, business and management research due to the unique information and angle it can provide

NPDP (Four phases and nine stages)

Phase 1: Fuzzy front end

Opportunity and idea discovery
FI Practice 1: The opportunity and idea discovery stage has a market-pull approach that is limited within the scope of BOP markets constraints.
FI Practice 2: The tools and techniques in the opportunity and idea discovery stage allow external idea sources.

Opportunity and idea screening
FI Practice 3: The opportunity and idea screening stage focuses on market information, in particular appraisals of BOP consumers' unmet needs.
FI Practice 4: The opportunity and idea screening stage focuses on business information linked with internal and external capabilities.

Phase 2: Concept development

Market study
FI Practice 5: The market study stage has a focus on BOP consumer information related to affordability, additional needs and product usage context.
FI Practice 6: The tools and techniques in the market study stage focus on a firm's immersion with targeted consumers for deeper insights.

Technical study
FI Practice 7: The technical study stage focuses on primary product functionality and business model specifications.
FI Practice 8: The tools and techniques used in the technical study stage involve seeking basic technological principles and/or architecture and components from existing products.

Concept evaluation
FI Practice 9: The tools and techniques in the concept evaluation stage integrate a set of criteria and/or simple physical version to test concept acceptance.

Phase 3: Product development

Product design
FI Practice 10: The product design stage prioritises local outsourcing weighted off with costs and performance.
FI Practice 11: The tools and techniques in the product design stage include DfX techniques specifically aimed at frugal design strategies.

Prototype testing
FI Practice 12: The tools and techniques in the prototype testing stage include early field-testing.

Phase 4: Commercialisation

Market testing
FI Practice 13: The market testing stage involves testing distribution and promotion of the new product through existing local networks.
FI Practice 14: The market testing stage includes product demonstration and training as key promotional strategy.

Production ramp
FI Practice 15: The production ramp-up stage factors in low-volume production timelines for longer periods, which benefit intensive learning, training, and quality standards.

Figure 3.6 Summary of 15 frugal innovation practices

(Eisenhardt & Graebner 2007; Yin 2014). The case study strategy is particularly helpful for research related to NPD, as it allows asking 'why' and 'how' questions regarding firms' managerial decisions (e.g. Brem & Voigt 2009; Rahim & Baksh 2003; Tao, Probert & Phaal 2010). With the paucity of studies regarding the NPDP for frugal innovation, the case study design allowed to gain frugal innovators' insights within the contextual settings of their NPDP.

The unit of analysis for this study's data collection is the frugal innovators' NPDP. In particular, this unit of analysis refers to the NPDP of two Indonesian start-ups, which have executed a frugal innovation NPD project that has reached Indonesian BOP consumers. This unit of analysis allowed a deeper understanding of the decisions and priorities of key actors involved across the four phases of the NPDP for frugal innovation.

Interview and observation techniques

As qualitative enquiry through a case study strategy enables the combination of research methods (Eisenhardt 1989), techniques such as semi-structured interviews, observations and secondary data were chosen for this study's data collection. These techniques are often used when studying NPDP decision-making in developed countries (e.g. Brem & Voigt 2009; Veryzer 1998) and have also been used to help advance academic- and practice-based frugal innovation literature (e.g. Anderson & Billou 2007; Anderson & Markides 2007; Donaldson 2006; Zeschky, Widenmayer & Gassmann 2011). The use of these techniques that include direct interactions captured key decision-makers' perceptions, opinions and experiences in regard to the NPDP of frugal innovation.

Observation via field visits was adopted as a research technique to complement interviews. It helped in capturing and further examining "participant/s in their own environment, or in the environment being studied" (National Health and Medical Research Council 2015, p. 24) and was utilised in this study through the use of field notes and photography. The integration of this technique was important to this study, as firms' NPDP is often managed in accordance with its context (e.g. size, country, industry, corporate culture) (Henard & Szymanski 2001). Research was undertaken through being physically present in the firms sites, increasing credibility and dependability of this study's findings (Saunders, Lewis & Thornhill 2009).

Combined with observations and interviews, secondary data were also obtained for triangulation of sources and findings, improving the credibility of this qualitative study across the research process, including data collection and analysis (Golafshani 2003; Stake 1995). While the data collection process is often separate from the data analysis, the generation of findings is frequently intertwined with this analysis, which is discussed ahead.

Thematic data analysis

The interviews were transcribed from an audio recording device, and the data were organised by NPDP phases and stages using NVivo11, a qualitative data analysis software. This was the first step to initiate the transcription process, data cleaning and thematic analysis process. The organisation of data follows the six key steps of thematic analysis, one of the most relevant techniques for qualitative study (Braun & Clarke 2006), such as for this exploratory study.

Thematic analysis enables the exploration of data patterns (themes) that are most relevant to this study's objectives (Braun & Clarke 2006; Guest 2012). In this study, the conceptual NPDP framework, including derived practices of frugal innovators' NPDP, not only helped during the data collection to guide interview questions, it also guided the thematic coding.

Furthermore, this study focused on Indonesia. As the frugal innovation literature has mostly concentrated on geographical areas such as India and China (Agarwal et al. 2017), studying frugal innovation in other developing countries such as Indonesia adds knowledge to the field. The focus on Indonesia means much of the study's research outcomes are unique, with the following part describing the demographics of the two case studies chosen in this study.

Indonesian sample

Developing countries such as Indonesia offer new BOP market opportunities for firms. They are also often observed as innovation hubs where new products are developed to be affordable and adapted to local needs like what frugal innovation proposes to achieve (Agarwal et al. 2017; Lee et al. 2011; Prahalad 2012). Such markets are also often deemed as heterogeneous due to differing institutional environments, restricting the generalisation of research to one geographical region (Bhatti & Ventresca 2013; Sheth 2011). In line with this, this study delimits its geographical boundary within the Association of Southeast Asian Nations (ASEAN) and focuses on the growing economy of Indonesia. Two start-ups were selected in Indonesia, and 13 interviews and six observational visits were conducted across Java Island. This information is further detailed in the two next parts.

Prime Cookstoves

Between the beginnings of October 2015 to December 2015, nine interviews were conducted in English with Prime Cookstoves (Prime[9]), made up of seven face-to-face and two Skype interviews (see Table 3.2). These were complemented by four observational visits (see Table 3.3). First looking at interviewees, all participants were involved in different phases of the NPDP, from the initial idea for the Prime cookstove product until the later stage of development where the product was introduced to the market.

Participant 1 (Prime former BDM) was initially in charge of developing Prime's business operations. The former business developer manager (BDM) previously worked with a local NGO, which had a major role in the commercialisation phase of the Prime cookstove product.[10] He then decided to get involved in Prime's marketing function to support market expansion, including the promotion, distribution and sale of the Prime cookstove through managing Ditana, the subsidiary distributor of Prime.

Table 3.2 Prime interviewees' details

Interviewees	Interviewee positions	Time (minutes)	Date (2015)	Location
Participant 1	Former business developer manager (BDM)	189	18 October	Jakarta
Participant 2	Inventor and founder	303	11 & 16 November	Malang (East Java)
Participant 3	Logistics manager (including quality control)	116	10 & 11 November	Surabaya (East Java)
Participant 4	Production manager (production partner)	53	11 November	Sidoarjo (East Java)
Participant 5	Sales manager 1 (including marketing)	119	12, 13 & 14 November	Semarang (Central Java)
Participant 6	Sales manager 2 (including marketing)			
Participant 7	Agent (distributor of Prime Cookstoves)	60	14 November	Semarang (Central Java)
Participant 8	Local NGO program officer & manager of tech kiosk	121	2 December	Ubud (Bali)
Participant 9	Local NGO program leader (distribution and training of products)			

Table 3.3 Prime observation sites

Site no.	Type of site	Date observed (2015)	Location of site
1	Warehouse	11 October	Sidoarjo, East Java
2	Production facility and partner's production site	11 October	Sidoarjo, East Java
3	Small factory	16 October	Malang, East Java
4	Ditana head office	12, 13 & 14 October	Semarang, Central Java

Participant 2 (Prime Inventor) invented the product. He was involved in the initial development of the Prime cookstove from its discovery when he identified the need for new cooking methods for Indonesian BOP consumers, through to its production, promotion and sale. At the time of the interview, the inventor oversaw decisions in relation to the development and refinement of the Prime cookstove initially sold through Prime in Sidoarjo (East Java) and Prime's more recent production partner. In 2017, the inventor could undertake product testing, as he had acquired his workshop but this information was not considered in this case study. The inventor has also been a committee member of the Indonesian

Clean Cookstove Programme for the Indonesian Ministry of Energy and Mineral Resources since 2011 (Primestoves 2017).

Participant 3 (Logistics Manager) was involved in the development of the Prime cookstove's production, QC and supply chain. The logistics manager coordinated production outputs, including the QC process that involved robustness testing of the Prime cookstove. He was in charge of the repair, recycling, stocking, organisation and supervision of the downstream supply chain from inventory of the stove to delivery to the consumers.

Participant 4 (Production Manager) was Prime's production partner, with which Prime worked to scale-up the Prime cookstove. Prime had recently partnered with this new production firm in the development and ramp-up production of the stove at the time of the visit in Indonesia in 2015. Both the production and logistics managers supervised the entire production process of the stove, including manufacturing and assembly. The production manager and his team, along with the inventor's approval and the logistics manager's supervision, would suggest refinements of the product as well as test processes according to Prime's goals.

Participant 5 (Prime Sales Manager 1) and Participant 6 (Prime Sales Manager 2) had the same role in promotion and sales, managing different areas around Semarang (Central Java region). They had direct contact with local consumers in low-income, urban and rural communities in the Semarang area. Employed by Ditana, the sales team undertook demonstrations, training and sales for distribution to local agents and local consumers. They were generally the main employees planning meetings with local communities for demonstration of the stove. They also arranged the meeting and training of agents for distribution, giving more insightful information to this study's data due to leveraging the local presence for observational visits.

Participant 7 (Prime Agent) was one of several agents who distributed the Prime cookstove, buying stoves from Ditana to sell across the communities. This agent also informed local communities of the existence of Prime Cookstoves and the possibility of becoming a sub-agent. Ditana provided agents with relevant training, including how to use and maintain the stove as well as other business and marketing techniques.

Participant 8 (Local NGO Program Office and Manager) and Participant 9 (Local NGO Program Leader) were both involved in the downstream distribution of the Prime cookstove. These roles were linked to the local NGO program, through which the Prime cookstove was sold. These two participants shared insights into their intermediary role between Prime and end users. In particular, Participant 8 was in charge of listening to end users' product wants and needs as well as undertaking due diligence on frugal innovators and other type of firms that could address such demands. She was also involved in managing the 'technology fair' in Ubud (Bali, Indonesia), where she and her team presented various frugal and other innovations to local communities. While Participant 9 assisted Participant 8, he was in charge of the training of agents interested in distributing the Prime cookstove.

Moving to the second primary data technique, interviews were complemented with four observational visits at Prime's facilities, including Prime's warehouse, two production sites and Ditana's head office (see Table 3.3). By being locally present and using the observation technique, a rich set of information was derived, such as a sense of the innovation process context and the opportunity to take photography and additional field notes. As Patton (2005) suggests, these notes included descriptions of the workplace structure and operations as well as the NPDP including how some of the employees undertook their relevant role.

Regarding the observation sites, the first warehouse site was under the responsibility of the logistics manager and included the quality control, disassembly/assembly, repair, recycling, stocking, preparation and distribution of the Prime cookstove orders. Observation was undertaken on how the warehouse operated, including how the process between these diverse activities ran. Several staff members were available to answer questions about their role in the process that included testing the Prime cookstove, and to explain the product functions and answer other queries.

The second and third observation sites were the two production facilities, including a small factory and the production manager's facility. The small factory where the inventor worked was the first used for the manufacturing and assembly of the Prime cookstove in Malang. This small factory was previously manufacturing kerosene stoves, and the inventor was happy to explain how he adjusted the kerosene stove factory infrastructure for the Prime cookstove. He described the whole manufacturing process while also introducing local labourers. During the visit, observation was undertaken on the customised manufacturing stamping tools and moulds, and the creation of different components as well as the rest of the production process.

The other production facility was the future new production site in Sidoarjo, which was overseen by the production manager in coordination with the logistics manager and inventor. Prime outsourced the production to their partner, which had a production site with higher capabilities than the smaller factory including mass production capacity. However, while the production was intended to be outsourced to this partner, the product development at this new production remained under the control of the inventor and logistics manager. This site visit enabled a closer look at the production equipment as well as the production processes of the Prime cookstove, such as the raw materials and stamping tools used in the creation of its components.

A fourth site visit was undertaken, which was related to Ditana's head office in Semarang, where Prime's former BDM was in charge of operations. This office is focused on product sales, training and demonstrations both on site and in the field. Here, participation occurred in meetings with the sales staff before joining them in the field where, as part of Ditana's sales strategy, they publicly demonstrated the stove to villagers including at community gatherings. Local demonstrations were also observed, which was an insightful and rich activity to monitor discussions with local consumers including questions to the sales teams before and after the demonstrations. With a more contextual understanding of the Prime Cookstoves case study, the next section introduces the second case study, Tirta Indonesia Mandiri Foundation (Tirta[11]).

Tirta Indonesia Mandiri Foundation

Across October 2015 and December 2015, four face-to-face interviews were conducted in English at Tirta (see Table 3.4), which were complemented by two observational visits (see Table 3.5). The data were collected using semi-structured interviews and involved a small team of key respondents, all involved in the key NPD processes. The interviews were undertaken with four participants involved in the marketing, design and development, product testing and production of the product Tirta CupuManik (TCM) water filter.[12] The interviewees were all Indonesians and based in Java, one of the main Indonesian Islands.

Participant 1 (Inventor) is behind the creation of the product. He was in charge of the entire development of the TCM water filter from the discovery of the new product opportunity for water filter to the introduction of this product to the market. His focus was related to the financial, technical and marketing aspects of the TCM water filter, including generating new ideas, concept development, product design, prototype testing and productions as well as decisions related to its market such as promotion and distribution.

Participant 2 (Marketing Manager), in collaboration with the inventor, had the important role of promoting and developing the distribution and demonstration of the TCM water filter. This role was critical for its success, as Tirta relied on the marketing manager's connections with local people, including rural communities and members of local associations as well as friends and neighbours. The role of the marketing manager also allowed iteration on products as she transferred feedback heard from local people to the inventor for further refinements.

Table 3.4 Tirta interviewees' details

Interviewees	Interviewee positions	Time (minutes)	Date (2015)	Location
Participant 1	Inventor and founder	108	9 October	Jakarta, West Java
Participant 2	Marketing manager	77	9 October	Jakarta, West Java
Participant 3	Production manager	36	14 October	Purwakarta, West Java
Participant 4	Product testing manager	61	14 October	Purwakarta, West Java

Table 3.5 Tirta observation sites

Site no.	Type of site	Date observed (2015)	Location of site
1	Headquarters	9 October	Jakarta, West Java
2	Production facility	14 October	Purwakarta, West Java

Participant 3 (Production Manager) looked after the manufacturing of the ceramic pot filter, which is the core technology of the TCM water filter. He was also involved in the purchase of the raw materials as well as the components that made up TCM water filter. While he worked in collaboration with the inventor, the production manager was on-site continuously, thus managing and overseeing the production and testing of the TCM water filter for QC concerns.

Finally, Participant 4 (Product Testing Manager) managed all the processes involved in testing the ceramic pot filters throughout their manufacturing processes. With his specific expertise in ceramic products, he was in charge of utilising traditional testing methods and discarding faulty ceramic pots. As part of his role, he was also involved in the manufacturing of the ceramic pots, including formulating the final ingredients for the ceramic component of the TCM water filter. His involvement consisted of several steps, such as preparing the right quantity of raw materials, timing the mixing of ingredients, shaping, drying, stamping and cooking the ceramic pots, which are all critical steps in the performance of the final product.

In addition to interviews, an observation technique was also utilised as part of this study to contextualise and triangulate the interviews and secondary data. For this case study, the observations were undertaken at two sites (see Table 3.5). Each visit is described ahead and explains the role and advantage of these visits in building the context of the interviews for this case study.

The first observational site visit occurred at the headquarters in Jakarta, where the inventor and the marketing manager were located. The main role of the headquarters site was to store and market the final prototype of each TCM water filters for sales, including previous prototypes and newer versions. The main stakeholders would also meet and make decisions towards next steps for Tirta. This site allowed insights into the previous versions of the TCM water filter, the documents related to the inventor's publications in the field of water sanitation and the brochures developed for promoting the TCM water filter.

The second observation site was the production site, where all the processes involved in producing the TCM water filter are established in Purwakarta (West Java Province). The main people in charge were the production manager and the product testing manager. This includes the manufacturing of the ceramic pot (mixing ingredients and pot shape moulds), the burning, storage and testing area of the ceramic pots, the soaking in nitrate silver solution, and the assembly of plastic container and pots to form the final product.

Moving from this point, this study now turns to the in-depth discussion of each case in the subsequent chapters. It draws together the primary and secondary data described earlier for each case study. It is also framed around the NPDP framework for frugal innovation, focusing on exploring the key management practices that have been identified from existing literature on frugal innovation.

Notes

1 This notion first emerged in the 1970s via the 'appropriate technology' movement and the publication *Small is beautiful* of Schumacher (1973) (Kaplinsky 2011).

2 Hereafter, 'firm(s)' is used interchangeably with 'development team', both denoting the key actors involved in the NPDP stages.
3 The term 'new product opportunity' encompasses new opportunities and ideas.
4 Nick Hughes was operating on behalf of Vodafone and was the key person who identified and explored M-PESA as a potential opportunity. This study discusses the capabilities of Vodafone in the M-PESA project, of which Nick is the initiator.
5 Geographical zone targeted by UK Government's FDCF.
6 A fast-growing mobile network service based in East Africa, previously fully owned by Telkom Kenya and now part of Vodafone Group, and often described as the innovator of M-PESA (Safaricom 2017).
7 This project was undertaken in collaboration with British Petroleum (BP).
8 Italic font has been added to these three attributes from here for readers' convenience.
9 For simplification, Prime Cookstoves is shortened to Prime from here.
10 See Chapter 4 for further details about Prime Cookstoves' background and the Prime cookstove product.
11 For simplification, Tirta Indonesia Mandiri Foundation is shortened to Tirta from here.
12 See Chapter 5 for further details about Tirta's background and TCM water filter product.

References

Adams, R, Bessant, J & Phelps, R 2006, 'Innovation management measurement: A review', *International Journal of Management Reviews*, vol. 8, no. 1, pp. 21–47.

Agarwal, N, Brem, A & Grottke, M 2018, 'Towards a higher socio-economic impact through shared understanding of product requirements in emerging markets: The case of the Indian healthcare innovations', *Technological Forecasting and Social Change*, vol. 135, pp. 91–98.

Agarwal, N, Grottke, M, Mishra, S & Brem, A 2017, 'A systematic literature review of constraint-based innovations: State of the art and future perspectives', *IEEE Transactions on Engineering Management*, vol. 64, no. 1, pp. 3–15.

Agnihotri, A 2015, 'Low-cost innovation in emerging markets', *Journal of Strategic Marketing*, vol. 23, no. 5, pp. 399–411.

Ahuja, S 2014, 'Cost vs. value + empathy: A new formula for frugal science', *Design Management Review*, vol. 25, no. 2, pp. 52–55.

Almgren, H 2000, 'Pilot production and manufacturing start-up: The case of Volvo S80', *International Journal of Production Research*, vol. 38, no. 17, pp. 4577–4588.

Anand, R 2014, *When an earthquake hit Gujarat, he invented "Mitticool", A clay fridge that runs without electricity*, viewed 3 January 2018, <www.thebetterindia.com/14711/mitticool-rural-innovation-nif-mansukhbhai/>.

Anderson, J & Billou, N 2007, 'Serving the world's poor: Innovation at the base of the economic pyramid', *Journal of Business Strategy*, vol. 28, no. 2, pp. 14–21.

Anderson, J & Markides, C 2007, 'Strategic innovation and the base of the pyramid', *MIT Sloan Management Review*, vol. 49, no. 1, pp. 82–88.

Aranda-Jan, CB, Jagtap, S & Moultrie, J 2016, 'Towards a framework for holistic contextual design for low-resource settings', *International Journal of Design*, vol. 10, no. 3, pp. 43–63.

Austin-Breneman, J & Yang, M 2013, 'Design for micro-enterprise: An approach to product design for emerging markets', ASME 2013 International Design Engineering

Technical Conferences and Computers and Information in Engineering Conference, American Society of Mechanical Engineers, p. 1–11.

Awa, HO 2010, 'Democratizing the new product development process: A new dimension of value creation and marketing concept', *International Business Research*, vol. 3, no. 2, p. 49.

Babin, BJ & Zikmund, WG 2015, *Exploring marketing research*, Cengage Learning.

Barczak, G, Griffin, A & Kahn, KB 2009, 'Perspective: Trends and drivers of success in NPD practices: Results of the 2003 PDMA best practices study*', *Journal of Product Innovation Management*, vol. 26, no. 1, pp. 3–23.

Barefoot Power 2017, *Barefoot go portable solar light*, viewed 18 January 2018, <www.barefootpower.com/products/solar-portable.html>.

Baumgartner, J 2010, 'Idea management', in *Wiley international encyclopedia of marketing*, John Wiley & Sons, Inc.

Bhatti, YA & Ventresca, M 2013, 'How can "frugal innovation" be conceptualized?' Said Business School Working Paper Series, 19 January, viewed 2 December 2017.

Bhuiyan, N 2011, 'A framework for successful new product development', *Journal of Industrial Engineering and Management*, vol. 4, no. 4, pp. 746–770.

Bingham, G, Whitehead, T & Evans, M 2016, 'Design tool for enhanced new product development in low income economies', *Proceedings of DRS2016: Design + Research + Society – Future-Focused Thinking*, pp. 2241–2256.

Börjesson, S, Dahlsten, F & Williander, M 2006, 'Innovative scanning experiences from an idea generation project at Volvo cars', *Technovation*, vol. 26, no. 7, pp. 775–783.

Bound, K & Thornton, IW 2012, *Our frugal future: Lessons from India's innovation system*, Nesta London, viewed 5 January 2018, <www.nesta.org.uk/sites/default/files/our_frugal_future.pdf>.

Braun, V & Clarke, V 2006, 'Using thematic analysis in psychology', *Qualitative Research in Psychology*, vol. 3, no. 2, pp. 77–101.

Brauner, P, Philipsen, R, Fels, A, Fuhrmann, M, Ngo, QH, Stiller, S, Schmitt, R & Ziefle, M 2016, 'A game-based approach to raise quality awareness in ramp-up processes', *The Quality Management Journal*, vol. 23, no. 1, p. 55.

Brem, A & Voigt, K-I 2009, 'Integration of market pull and technology push in the corporate front end and innovation management – insights from the German software industry', *Technovation*, vol. 29, no. 5, pp. 351–367.

Brem, A & Wolfram, P 2014, 'Research and development from the bottom up – introduction of terminologies for new product development in emerging markets', *Journal of Innovation and Entrepreneurship*, vol. 3, no. 1, p. 9.

Brugmann, J & Prahalad, CK 2007, 'Cocreating business's new social compact', *Harvard Business Review*, vol. 85, no. 2, pp. 80–90.

Business call to action n.d., *Barefoot power: Generating safe, affordable energy while reducing the carbon footprint*, viewed 12 January 2018, <www.businesscalltoaction.org/sites/default/files/resources/barefoot.pdf>.

Carrillo, JE & Franza, RM 2006, 'Investing in product development and production capabilities: The crucial linkage between time-to-market and ramp-up time', *European Journal of Operational Research*, vol. 171, no. 2, pp. 536–556.

Chakrabarti, A, Morgenstern, S & Knaab, H 2004, 'Identification and application of requirements and their impact on the design process: A protocol study', *Research in Engineering Design*, vol. 15, no. 1, pp. 22–39.

Chikweche, T & Fletcher, R 2012, 'Revisiting the marketing mix at the Bottom of Pyramid (BOP): From theoretical considerations to practical realities', *Journal of Consumer Marketing*, vol. 29, no. 7, pp. 507–520.

ChotuKool 2014, *Evolution of ChotuKool*, viewed 10 November 2018, <http://chotu kool.com/evolution_chotuKool.aspx>.

Cooper, RG 1988, 'Predevelopment activities determine new product success', *Industrial Marketing Management*, vol. 17, no. 3, pp. 237–247.

Cooper, RG 1990, 'Stage-gate systems: A new tool for managing new products', *Business Horizons*, vol. 33, no. 3, pp. 44–54.

Cooper, RG 2001, *Winning at new products: Accelerating the process from idea to launch*, Perseus Pub, Cambridge, MA.

Cooper, RG 2010, 'The stage-gate idea to launch system', in *Wiley international encyclopedia of marketing: Part 5: Product innovation and management*, John Wiley & Sons, Inc., New York.

Cooper, RG 2011, *Winning at new products: Creating value through innovation*, Basic Books.

Cooper, RG 2017, 'Idea-to-launch gating systems: Better, faster, and more agile: Leading firms are rethinking and reinventing their idea-to-launch gating systems, adding elements of agile to traditional stage-gate structures to add flexibility and speed while retaining structure', *Research-Technology Management*, vol. 60, no. 1, pp. 48–52.

Cooper, RG & Dreher, A 2010, 'Voice-of-customer methods', *Marketing Management*, vol. 19, no. 4, pp. 38–43.

Cooper, RG & Edgett, SJ 2008, 'Ideation for product innovation: What are the best methods', *PDMA Visions Magazine*, vol. 1, no. 1, pp. 12–17.

Cooper, RG, Edgett, SJ & Kleinschmidt, EJ 2004, 'Benchmarking best NPD practices-III', *Research Technology Management*, vol. 47, no. 6, pp. 43–55.

Cooper, RG & Kleinschmidt, EJ 1986, 'An investigation into the new product process: Steps, deficiencies, and impact', *Journal of Product Innovation Management*, vol. 3, no. 2, pp. 71–85.

Cooper, RG & Kleinschmidt, EJ 1987, 'New products: What separates winners from losers?' *The Journal of Product Innovation Management*, vol. 4, no. 3, pp. 169–184.

Cooper, RG & Sommer, AF 2016, 'The agile – stage-gate hybrid model: A promising new approach and a new research opportunity', *Journal of Product Innovation Management*, vol. 33, no. 5, pp. 513–526.

Core Jr 2011, *Case study: Leveraged freedom chair, by Amos Winter, Jake Childs and Jung Tak: Enabling freedom for the disabled in developing countries*, viewed 15 January 2018, <www.core77.com/posts/18507/case-study-leveraged-freedom-chair-by-amos-winter-jake-childs-and-jung-takenabling-freedom-for-the-disabled-in-developing-countries-18507>.

Crawford, CM & Di Benedetto, CA 2011, *New products management*, 10th edn., McGraw-Hill Irwin, Boston.

Crawford, CM & Di Benedetto, CA 2014, *New products management*, 11th edn., McGraw-Hill Education, New York.

Cunha, MPE, Rego, A, Oliveira, P, Rosado, P & Habib, N 2014, 'Product innovation in resource-poor environments: Three research streams', *Journal of Product Innovation Management*, vol. 31, no. 2, pp. 202–210.

Da Silva, IP & Sloet, B 2012, *Barefoot power lights up rural Africa*, viewed 8 December 2017, <www.mercatornet.com/articles/view/barefoot_power_lights_up_rural_africa>.

Dahan, E & Hauser, JR 2002, *Product development: Managing a dispersed process*, Sage Publications Inc.

Dale, BG, Papalexi, M, Bamford, D & van der Wiele, A 2016, 'TQM: An overview and the role of management', in *Managing quality 6e: An essential guide and resource gateway*, John Wiley & Sons, Inc., Chichester, pp. 3–35.

de Gooijer, H 2013, *Field test solar – LED lanterns*, viewed 8 December 2017, <http://picosol.org/phocadownload/Rapporten/fieldtest-solar-lights-cambodia.pdf>.

de Waal, GA & Knott, P 2010, 'Product development: An integrative tool and activity research framework', *Human Systems Management*, vol. 29, no. 4, 1 January, pp. 253–264.

Dhanaraj, C, Suram, B & Vemuri, P 2011, 'Godrej Chotukool: A cooling solution for mass markets', *Richard Ivey School of Business*, University Western Ontario, p. #W11498.

Di Benedetto, CA 2010, 'Product testing', in *Wiley international encyclopedia of marketing*, John Wiley & Sons, Inc.

Disability and Development Partners 2013, *Dr Pramod Karan Sethi: The Jaipur foot – history and controversy*, viewed 15 January 2018, <http://ddpuk.org/drsethi.html>.

Donaldson, K 2006, 'Product design in less industrialized economies: Constraints and opportunities in Kenya', *Research in Engineering Design*, vol. 17, no. 3, pp. 135–155.

Dudek-Burlikowska, M 2011, 'Application of FMEA method in enterprise focused on quality', *Journal of Achievements in Materials and Manufacturing Engineering*, vol. 45, no. 1, pp. 89–102.

Earthquaketrack 2018, *Recent earthquakes Near Gujarat, India*, viewed 2 February 2018, <https://earthquaketrack.com/p/india/gujarat/recent>.

Eastman, CM 2012, *Design for X: Concurrent engineering imperatives*, Springer Science & Business Media.

Eisenhardt, KM 1989, 'Building theories from case study research', *Academy of Management Review*, vol. 14, no. 4, pp. 532–550.

Eisenhardt, KM & Graebner, ME 2007, 'Theory building from cases: Opportunities and challenges', *Academy of Management Journal*, vol. 50, no. 1, pp. 25–32.

Eyring, MJ, Johnson, MW & Nair, H 2011, 'New business models in emerging markets', *Engineering Management Review, IEEE*, vol. 42, no. 2, pp. 19–26.

Florén, H & Frishammar, J 2012, 'From preliminary ideas to corroborated product definitions: Managing the front end of new product development', *California Management Review*, vol. 50, no. 4, pp. 20–43.

Furr, N & Dyer, J 2015, *How Godrej became an innovation star*, viewed 18 January 2018, <www.forbes.com/sites/innovatorsdna/2015/05/13/how-godrej-became-an-innovation-star/#34835f77fd3d>.

Garcia, R 2014, *Creating and marketing new products and services*, CRC Press.

Gassmann, O, Neumann, L, Knapp, O & Zollenkop, M 2017, 'Frugal: Simply a smart solution', *Roland Berger Focus*, August 2017, Roland Berger GmbH.

Gassmann, O & Schweitzer, F 2014, 'Managing the unmanageable: The fuzzy front end of innovation', in O Gassmann and F Schweitzer (eds), *Management of the fuzzy front end of innovation*, Springer International Publishing, Cham, pp. 3–14.

Gaubinger, K, Rabl, M, Swan, S & Werani, T 2014, 'Integrated innovation and product management: A process oriented framework', in *Innovation and product management*, Springer, Berlin Heidelberg, pp. 27–42.

Gaubinger, K, Rabl, M, Swan, S & Werani, T 2015a, 'The new product development', in *Innovation and product management*, Springer, Berlin, Heidelberg, pp. 175–206.

Gaubinger, K, Rabl, M, Swan, S & Werani, T 2015b, 'Product concept', in *Innovation and product management*, Springer, Berlin, Heidelberg, pp. 135–173.

GE Healthcare 2017, *Making healthymagination a reality*, viewed 5 December 2017, <healthymagination.gehealthcare.com/en/process>.

Gemser, G & Leenders, MAAM 2001, 'How integrating industrial design in the product development process impacts on company performance', *Journal of Product Innovation Management*, vol. 18, no. 1, pp. 28–38.

Girotra, K, Terwiesch, C & Ulrich, KT 2010, 'Idea generation and the quality of the best idea', *Management Science*, vol. 56, no. 4, pp. 591–605.

Globocnik, D & Salomo, S 2015, 'Do formal management practices impact the emergence of bootlegging behavior?' *Journal of Product Innovation Management*, vol. 32, no. 4, pp. 505–521.

Glock, CH, Jaber, MY & Zolfaghari, S 2012, 'Production planning for a ramp-up process with learning in production and growth in demand', *International Journal of Production Research*, vol. 50, no. 20, pp. 5707–5718.

Golafshani, N 2003, 'Understanding reliability and validity in qualitative research', *The Qualitative Report*, vol. 8, no. 4, pp. 597–606.

Gollakota, K, Gupta, V & Bork, JT 2010, 'Reaching customers at the base of the pyramid – a two-stage business strategy', *Thunderbird International Business Review*, vol. 52, no. 5, pp. 355–367.

Gorchels, L 2006, *The product manager's handbook*, 3rd edn., McGraw-Hill, New York.

Graner, M & Mißler-Behr, M 2012, 'The use of methods in new product development – a review of empirical literature', *International Journal of Product Development*, vol. 16, no. 2, pp. 158–184.

Graner, M & Mißler-Behr, M 2013, 'Key determinants of the successful adoption of new product development methods', *European Journal of Innovation Management*, vol. 16, no. 3, pp. 301–316.

Griffin, A 2012, 'Obtaining customer needs for product development', in *The PDMA handbook of new product development*, John Wiley & Sons, Inc., pp. 211–230.

Griffin, A & Somermeyer, S 2007a, 'Appendix II: The PDMA glossary for new product development', in *The PDMA tool book 3 for new product development*, John Wiley & Sons, Inc., Hoboken, NJ, pp. 465–508.

Griffin, A & Somermeyer, S 2007b, *The PDMA toolbook 3 for new product development*, John Wiley & Sons, Inc., Hoboken, NJ.

Groover, M & Zimmers, E 1983, *CAD/CAM: Computer-aided design and manufacturing*, Pearson Education.

Guest, G 2012, *Applied thematic analysis*, Sage Publications, LA.

Hart, S, Jan Hultink, E, Tzokas, N & Commandeur, HR 2003, 'Industrial companies' evaluation criteria in new product development gates', *Journal of Product Innovation Management*, vol. 20, no. 1, pp. 22–36.

Hart, S, Sharma, S & Halme, M 2016, 'Poverty, business strategy, and sustainable development', *Organization & Environment*, vol. 29, no. 4, pp. 401–415.

Hauser, J & Dahan, E 2007, *Chapter 8: New product development*, McGraw Hill, Columbus, OH.

Henard, DH & Szymanski, DM 2001, 'Why some new products are more successful than others', *Journal of Marketing Research*, vol. 38, no. 3, pp. 362–375.

Herstatt, C & von Hippel, E 1992, 'From experience: Developing new product concepts via the lead user method: A case study in a "low-tech" field', *Journal of Product Innovation Management*, vol. 9, no. 3, pp. 213–221.

Holahan, PJ, Sullivan, ZZ & Markham, SK 2014, 'Product development as core competence: How formal product development practices differ for radical, more innovative, and incremental product innovations', *Journal of Product Innovation Management*, vol. 31, no. 2, pp. 329–345.

Hossain, M 2017, 'Mapping the frugal innovation phenomenon', *Technology in Society*, vol. 51, pp. 199–208.

Hughes, N & Lonie, S 2007, 'M-PESA: Mobile money for the "unbanked" turning cellphones into 24-hour tellers in Kenya', *Innovations*, vol. 2, no. 1–2, pp. 63–81.

Innosight 2017, *Godrej – Co-creating with rural consumers helps achieve inclusive growth*, viewed 18 October 2017, <www.innosight.com/wp-content/uploads/2016/01/Client-Impact-Story-PDF-Godrej.pdf>.

Institute of Seismological Research 2013, *Catalogue of earthquakes in Gujarat region from earliest time to Dec 2013*, viewed 2 February 2018, <https://isr.gujarat.gov.in/sites/default/files/eq_catalogue_gujarat.pdf>.

Jagtap, S, Larsson, A, Warell, A, Santhanakrishnan, D & Jagtap, S 2015, 'Design for the BOP and the TOP: Requirements handling behaviour of designers', in A Chakrabarti (ed), *ICoRD'15 – research into design across boundaries Volume 2*, vol. 35, Springer, India, pp. 191–200.

Jain, SC 2011, 'Chapter 19: Bottom of the pyramid market: Theory and practice', in *Handbook of research in international marketing*, 2nd edn., Edward Elgar Publishing, UK, pp. 376–390.

Juerging, J & Milling, PM 2005, 'Interdependencies of product development decisions and the production ramp-up', The 23rd International Conference of the System Dynamics Society, Boston, MA, Citeseer.

Kahn, KB 2010a, 'Concept testing', in *Wiley international encyclopedia of marketing*, John Wiley & Sons, Inc., New-York.

Kahn, KB 2010b, 'New-product forecasting', in *Wiley international encyclopedia of marketing*, John Wiley & Sons, Inc., New York.

Kahn, KB, Barczak, G, Nicholas, J, Ledwith, A & Perks, H 2012a, 'An examination of new product development best practice', *Journal of Product Innovation Management*, vol. 29, no. 2, pp. 180–192.

Kahn, KB, Kay, SE, Slotegraaf, RJ & Uban, S 2012b, 'New product development glossary', in KB Kahn, SE Kay, SU Rebecca & J Slotegraaf (eds), *The PDMA handbook of new product development*, John Wiley & Sons, Inc., pp. 435–476.

Kaplinsky, R 2011, 'Schumacher meets Schumpeter: Appropriate technology below the radar', *Research Policy*, vol. 40, no. 2, pp. 193–203.

Kashyap, P 2012, *Rural marketing*, Pearson Education, India.

Kashyap, P 2017, *The future Lies entirely in rural markets*, viewed 18 October 2017, <http://businessworld.in/article/The-Future-Lies-Entirely-In-Rural-Markets/17-04-2017-116446/>.

Khanna, T & Palepu, KG 2010, *Winning in emerging markets: A road map for strategy and execution*, Harvard Business Review Press, Cambridge, MA.

Khurana, A & Rosenthal, SR 1998, 'Towards holistic "Front Ends" in new product development', *Journal of Product Innovation Management*, vol. 15, no. 1, pp. 57–74.

Kim, J & Wilemon, D 2002, 'Focusing the fuzzy front – end in new product development', *R&D Management*, vol. 32, no. 4, pp. 269–279.

Koen, PA, Ajamian, GM, Boyce, S, Clamen, A, Fisher, E, Fountoulakis, S, Johnson, A, Puri, P & Seibert, R 2002, 'Fuzzy front end: Effective methods, tools, and techniques', in P Belliveau, A Griffin and S Somermeyer (eds), *The PDMA toolBook 1 for new product development*, John Wiley & Sons, Inc., New York, pp. 5–35.

Koen, PA & Bertels, HMJ 2010, 'Front end of innovation', in *Wiley international encyclopedia of marketing*, John Wiley & Sons, Inc., New-York.

Koen, PA, Bertels, HMJ & Kleinschmidt, EJ 2014, 'Managing the front end of innovation – Part II', *Research Technology Management*, vol. 57, no. 3, pp. 25–35.

Kotler, P 2016, *A framework for marketing management*, 6th edn., Pearson, Boston, MA.

Krishnan, V & Bhattacharya, S 2002, 'Technology selection and commitment in new product development: The role of uncertainty and design flexibility', *Management Science*, vol. 48, no. 3, pp. 313–327.

Krishnan, V & Ulrich, KT 2001, 'Product development decisions: A review of the literature', *Management Science*, vol. 47, no. 1, pp. 1–21.

Kuo, T-C, Huang, SH & Zhang, H-C 2001, 'Design for manufacture and design for "X": Concepts, applications, and perspectives', *Computers & Industrial Engineering*, vol. 41, no. 3, pp. 241–260.

Langerak, F, Jan Hultink, E & Robben, HSJ 2004, 'The role of predevelopment activities in the relationship between market orientation and performance', *R&D Management*, vol. 34, no. 3, pp. 295–309.

Lee, Y, Lin, BW, Wong, YY & Calantone, RJ 2011, 'Understanding and managing international product launch: A comparison between developed and emerging markets', *Journal of Product Innovation Management*, vol. 28, no. s1, pp. 104–120.

Leffakis, ZM 2016, 'A framework to identify best quality management practices and techniques for diverse production ramp-up environments: Propositions for future research', *Quality Management Journal*, vol. 23, no. 1, pp. 20–44.

Lehner, A-C & Gausemeier, J 2016, 'A pattern-based approach to the development of frugal innovations', *Technology Innovation Management Review*, vol. 6, no. 3, pp. 13–21.

Li, H-HJ, Shi, YJ, Gregory, M & Tan, KH 2014, 'Rapid production ramp-up capability: A collaborative supply network perspective', *International Journal of Production Research*, vol. 52, no. 10, pp. 2999–3013.

Lim, C, Han, S & Ito, H 2013, 'Capability building through innovation for unserved lower end mega markets', *Technovation*, vol. 33, no. 12, pp. 391–404.

Lin, C-T & Chen, C-T 2004, 'New product go/no-go evaluation at the front end: A fuzzy linguistic approach', *IEEE Transactions on Engineering Management*, vol. 51, no. 2, pp. 197–207.

Liu, YC, Chakrabarti, A & Bligh, T 2003, 'Towards an "ideal" approach for concept generation', *Design Studies*, vol. 24, no. 4, pp. 341–355.

Löscher, P 2011, 'Less is more', *The Economist*, viewed 2 December 2017, <www.economist.com/node/21537984>.

Luchs, MG, Swan, KS & Creusen, ME 2016, 'Perspective: A review of marketing research on product design with directions for future research', *Journal of Product Innovation Management*, vol. 33, no. 3, pp. 320–341.

Lutters, E, van Houten, FJAM, Bernard, A, Mermoz, E & Schutte, CSL 2014, 'Tools and techniques for product design', *CIRP Annals – Manufacturing Technology*, vol. 63, no. 2, pp. 607–630.

Macdonald, E, Salas, R, Espalin, D, Perez, M, Aguilera, E, Muse, D & Wicker, RB 2014, '3D printing for the rapid prototyping of structural electronics', *IEEE Access*, vol. 2, pp. 234–242.

Macke, S, Misra, R & Sharma, A 2003, *Jaipur foot: Challenging convention*, Case Study Series, University Michigan Business School Case, Ann Arbor, MI.

Markham, SK & Lee, H 2013, 'Product development and management association's 2012 comparative performance assessment study', *Journal of Product Innovation Management*, vol. 30, no. 3, pp. 408–429.

Martinsuo, M & Poskela, J 2011, 'Use of evaluation criteria and innovation performance in the front end of innovation*', *Journal of Product Innovation Management*, vol. 28, no. 6, pp. 896–914.

Mattson, CA & Wood, AE 2014, 'Nine principles for design for the developing world as derived from the engineering literature', *Journal of Mechanical Design*, vol. 136, no. 12, pp. 121403-1–121403-15.

Maxwell, J 2013, 'Chapter 3: Conceptual framework: What do you think is going on', in *Qualitative research design: An interactive approach*, 3rd edn., SAGE, Thousand Oaks, CA.

McGregor, J 2008, *GE: Reinventing tech for the emerging world*, viewed 31 January 2018, <www.bloomberg.com/bw/stories/2008-04-16/ge-reinventing-tech-for-the-emerging-world>.

McManus, T, Holtzman, Y, Lazarus, H, Chandra, M & Neelankavil, JP 2008, 'Product development and innovation for developing countries: Potential and challenges', *Journal of Management Development*, vol. 27, no. 10, pp. 1017–1025.

Merriam, SB & Tisdell, EJ 2015, *Qualitative research: A guide to design and implementation*, John Wiley & Sons, Inc.

Mitticool 2011, *The Mitticool story*, viewed 15 December, <http://mitticool.com/owner-profile/>.

Mukerjee, K 2012, 'Frugal innovation: The key to penetrating emerging markets', *Ivey Business Journal*, viewed 5 February 2018, <www.iveybusinessjournal.com/uncategorized/frugal-innovation-the-key-to-penetrating-emerging-markets#.VH_3AzGUfzh>.

Murcott, S 2007, 'Co-evolutionary design for development: Influences shaping engineering design and implementation in Nepal and the global village', *Journal of International Development*, vol. 19, no. 1, pp. 123–144.

Murphy, SA & Kumar, V 1996, 'The role of predevelopment activities and firm attributes in new product success', *Technovation*, vol. 16, no. 8, pp. 431–449.

Murphy, SA & Kumar, V 1997, 'The front end of new product development: A Canadian survey', *R&D Management*, vol. 27, no. 1, pp. 5–15.

Murthy, DP, Rausand, M & Østerås, T 2008, *Product reliability: Specification and performance*, Springer Science & Business Media.

Myers, MD 2013, *Qualitative research in business and management*, Sage Publications.

Nakata, CC & Berger, E 2011, 'Chapter 18 new product development for the base of the pyramid: A theory-and case-based framework', in *Handbook of research in international marketing*, 2nd edn., Edward Elgar Publishing, UK, pp. 349–375.

Nakata, CC & Weidner, K 2012, 'Enhancing new product adoption at the base of the pyramid: A contextualized model', *Journal of Product Innovation Management*, vol. 29, no. 1, pp. 21–32.

National Health and Medical Research Council 2015, *National statement on ethical conduct in human research*, viewed 18 January 2018, <www.nhmrc.gov.au/

_files_nhmrc/publications/attachments/e72_national_statement_may_2015_150
514_a.pdf>.

Ngai, T, Shrestha, R, Dangol, B, Maharjan, M & Murcott, S 2007, 'Design for sustainable development – household drinking water filter for arsenic and pathogen treatment in Nepal', *Journal of Environmental Science and Health – Part A Toxic/Hazardous Substances Environmental Engineering*, vol. 42, no. 12, pp. 1879–1888.

Nijssen, EJ & Frambach, RT 2000, 'Determinants of the adoption of new product development tools by industrial firms', *Industrial Marketing Management*, vol. 29, no. 2, March, pp. 121–131.

Numminen, S & Lund, PD 2017, 'Frugal energy innovations for developing countries – A framework', *Global Challenges*, vol. 1, no. 1, pp. 9–19.

Olson, DW 2007, 'Market testing and postlaunch evaluation for consumer goods', in *The PDMA handbook of new product development*, John Wiley & Sons, Inc., pp. 479–496.

Oosterlaken, I 2009, 'Design for development: A capability approach', *Design Issues*, vol. 25, no. 4, pp. 91–102.

Ortt, JR & van der Duin, PA 2008, 'The evolution of innovation management towards contextual innovation', *European Journal of Innovation Management*, vol. 11, no. 4, pp. 522–538.

Osteras, T, Murthy, DNP & Rausand, M 2006, 'Product performance and specification in new product development', *Journal of Engineering Design*, vol. 17, no. 2, pp. 177–192.

Otto, KN & Wood, KL 2000, *Product design: Techniques in reverse engineering and new product development*, Prentice Hall, Pearson College.

Ozer, M 1999, 'A survey of new product evaluation models', *Journal of Product Innovation Management*, vol. 16, no. 1, pp. 77–94.

Pahl, G & Beitz, W 2013, *Engineering design: A systematic approach*, Springer Science & Business Media.

Pahl, G, Wallace, K & Blessing, L 2007, *Engineering design: A systematic approach*, 3rd edn., Springer, London.

Patton, MQ 2005, 'Qualitative research', in *Encyclopedia of statistics in behavioral science*, John Wiley & Sons, Inc.

Petrick, IJ & Juntiwasarakij, S 2011, 'The rise of the rest: Hotbeds of innovation in emerging markets', *Research Technology Management*, vol. 54, no. 4, pp. 24–29.

Pisoni, A, Michelini, L & Martignoni, G 2018, 'Frugal approach to innovation: State of the art and future perspectives', *Journal of Cleaner Production*, vol. 171, no. Supplement C, pp. 107–126.

Pitta, D, Subrahmanyan, S & Tomas Gomez-Arias, J 2008, 'Integrated approach to understanding consumer behavior at bottom of pyramid', *Journal of Consumer Marketing*, vol. 25, no. 7, pp. 402–412.

Prahalad, CK 2009, *The fortune at the bottom of the pyramid, revised and updated 5th anniversary edition: Eradicating poverty through profits*, FT Press.

Prahalad, CK 2012, 'Bottom of the pyramid as a source of breakthrough innovations', *Journal of Product Innovation Management*, vol. 29, no. 1, pp. 6–12.

Prahalad, CK & Hart, S 2002, 'The fortune at the bottom of the pyramid', *Strategy+ Business*, vol. 26, pp. 2–14.

Primestoves 2017, *Meet our teams – Prof. Dr. M. Nurhuda*, viewed 5 November 2017, <www.primestoves.com/>.

Pugh, S 1991, *Total design: Integrated methods for successful product engineering*, Addison-Wesley, Wokingham.

Radjou, N & Prabhu, J 2015, *Frugal innovation: How to do more with less*, Profile Books, London.

Radjou, N & Prabhu, J 2013, *Frugal innovation: A new business paradigm*, viewed 5 October 2017, <knowledge.insead.edu/innovation/frugal-innovation-a-new-business-paradigm-2375>.

Radjou, N, Prabhu, J & Ahuja, S 2012, *Jugaad innovation: Think frugal, be flexible, generate breakthrough growth*, John Wiley & Sons, Inc., Jossey-Bass, USA.

Rahim, RA & Baksh, MSN 2003, 'Case study method for new product development in engineer-to-order organizations', *Work Study*, vol. 52, no. 1, pp. 25–36.

Rainey, D & Rainey, DL 2005, *Product innovation: Leading change through integrated product development*, Cambridge University Press, New York.

Ramdorai, A & Herstatt, C 2017, 'Lessons from low-cost healthcare innovations for the base-of the pyramid markets: How incumbents can systematically create disruptive innovations', in C Herstatt and R Tiwari (eds), *Lead market India*, Springer, pp. 119–144.

Rao, BC 2013, 'How disruptive is frugal?' *Technology in Society*, vol. 35, no. 1, pp. 65–73.

Ray, P & Ray, S 2010, 'Resource-constrained innovation for emerging economies: The case of the Indian telecommunications industry', *IEEE Transaction on Engineering Management*, vol. 57, no. 1, pp. 144–156.

Ray, S & Ray, P 2011, 'Product innovation for the people's car in an emerging economy', *Technovation*, vol. 31, no. 5–6, pp. 216–227.

Reid, SE & De Brentani, U 2004, 'The fuzzy front end of new product development for discontinuous innovations: A theoretical model', *Journal of Product Innovation Management*, vol. 21, no. 3, pp. 170–184.

Robben, H 2010, 'Opportunity identification', in *Wiley international encyclopedia of marketing*, John Wiley & Sons, Inc.

Rochford, L 1991, 'Generating and screening new products ideas', *Industrial Marketing Management*, vol. 20, no. 4, pp. 287–296.

Safaricom 2017, *Safaricom annual report and financial statements 2017*, viewed 5 January 2018, https://www.safaricom.co.ke/images/Downloads/Resources_Downloads/Safaricom_2017_Annual_Report.pdf.

Saunders, M, Lewis, P & Thornhill, A 2009, *Research methods for business students*, 5th edn., FT Press, Prentice Hall, Harlow, New York.

Schmidt, JB, Sarangee, KR & Montoya, MM 2009, 'Exploring new product development project review practices*', *Journal of Product Innovation Management*, vol. 26, no. 5, pp. 520–535.

Schumacher, EF 1973, *Small is beautiful: A study of economics as if people mattered*, Blond & Briggs, London.

Scipioni, A, Saccarola, G, Centazzo, A & Arena, F 2002, 'FMEA methodology design, implementation and integration with HACCP system in a food company', *Food Control*, vol. 13, no. 8, pp. 495–501.

Sehgal, V, Dehoff, K & Panneer, G 2010, 'The importance of frugal engineering', *Strategy + Business*, Summer 2010, no. 59, pp. 1–4.

Sharma, A & Iyer, GR 2012, 'Resource-constrained product development: Implications for green marketing and green supply chains', *Industrial Marketing Management*, vol. 41, no. 4, pp. 599–608.

Sheth, JN 2011, 'Impact of emerging markets on marketing: Rethinking existing perspectives and practices', *Journal of Marketing*, vol. 75, no. 4, pp. 166–182.

Siggelkow, N 2007, 'Persuasion with case studies', *Academy of Management Journal*, vol. 50, no. 1, pp. 20–24.

Simanis, E 2009, *At the base of the pyramid, when selling to poor consumers, companies need to begin by doing something basic: They need to create the market*, viewed 31 November 2017, <www.wsj.com/articles/SB10001424052970203946904574301802684947732>.

Simanis, E 2011, 'Needs, needs, everywhere, but not a BoP market to tap', *Next Generation Business Strategies for the Base of the Pyramid*, pp. 103–126.

Simanis, E & Duke, D 2014, 'Profits at the bottom of the pyramid: A tool for assessing your opportunities', *Harvard Business Review*, vol. 92, no. 10, pp. 87–93.

Simanis, E & Hart, S 2009, 'Innovation from the inside out', *MIT Sloan Management Review*, vol. 50, no. 4, pp. 77–86.

Singh, J 2011, 'GE healthcare: Innovating for emerging markets', INSEAD Case Study.

Singh, J & Fleming, L 2010, 'Lone inventors as sources of breakthroughs: Myth or reality?' *Management Science*, vol. 56, no. 1, pp. 41–56.

Singh, MG, Gambhir, A & Dasgupta, J 2011, 'Innovation in India: Affordable innovations', *The Global Innovation Index*, pp. 77–86.

Smith, PG & Reinertsen, DG 1991, *Developing products in half the time*, Van Nostrand Reinhold, New York.

Song, XM & Montoya-Weiss, MM 1998, 'Critical development activities for really new versus incremental products', *Journal of Product Innovation Management*, vol. 15, no. 2, pp. 124–135.

Stake, RE 1995, *The art of case study research*, Sage, Thousand Oaks, CA.

Stockstrom, C & Herstatt, C 2008, 'Planning and uncertainty in new product development', *R&D Management*, vol. 38, no. 5, pp. 480–490.

Stone, RB, Wood, KL & Crawford, RH 2000, 'A heuristic method for identifying modules for product architectures', *Design Studies*, vol. 21, no. 1, pp. 5–31.

Surbier, L, Alpan, G & Blanco, E 2014, 'A comparative study on production ramp-up: State-of-the-art and new challenges', *Production Planning & Control*, vol. 25, no. 15, pp. 1264–1286.

Takai, S, Jikar, VK & Ragsdell, KM 2011, 'An approach toward integrating top-down and bottom-up product concept and design selection', *Journal of Mechanical Design*, vol. 133, no. 7, pp. 071007-1–071007-10.

Tao, L, Probert, D & Phaal, R 2010, 'Towards an integrated framework for managing the process of innovation', *R&D Management*, vol. 40, no. 1, pp. 19–30.

Terwiesch, C & Bohn, RE 2001, 'Learning and process improvement during production ramp-up', *International Journal of Production Economics*, vol. 70, no. 1, pp. 1–19.

Thamhain, HJ 2014, 'Assessing the effectiveness of quantitative and qualitative methods for R&D project proposal evaluations', *Engineering Management Journal*, vol. 26, no. 3, pp. 3–12.

Thia, CW, Chai, KH, Bauly, J & Xin, Y 2005, 'An exploratory study of the use of quality tools and techniques in product development', *The TQM Magazine*, vol. 17, no. 5, pp. 406–424.

Thomke, SH 2006, 'Capturing the real value of innovation tools', *MIT Sloan Management Review*, vol. 47, no. 2, Winter, pp. 24–32.

Tidd, J 2009, *Managing innovation: Integrating technological, market and organizational change*, 4th edn., John Wiley & Sons, Inc, Chichester.

Tidd, J 2013, *Managing innovation: Integrating technological, market and organizational change*, 5th edn., John Wiley & Sons, Inc., Chichester, West Sussex.

Tidd, J & Bodley, K 2002, 'The influence of project novelty on the new product development process', *R&D Management*, vol. 32, no. 2, pp. 127–138.

Tiwari, R & Herstatt, C 2012, 'Assessing India's lead market potential for cost-effective innovations', *Journal of Indian Business Research*, vol. 4, no. 2, pp. 97–115.

Tiwari, R & Herstatt, C 2013, '"Too Good' to Succeed? Why Not Just Try' Good Enough!" Some deliberations on the prospects of frugal innovations', Working paper No. 76. Hamburg Institute for Technology and Innovation Management (TIM), Hamburg University of Technology (TUHH), Hamburg.

Tiwari, R, Kalogerakis, K & Herstatt, C 2014, 'Frugal innovation and analogies: Some propositions for product development in emerging economies', Working Paper, Technologie-und Innovationsmanagement, Technische Universität Hamburg-Harburg.

Tiwari, R, Kalogerakis, K & Herstatt, C 2016, 'Frugal innovations in the mirror of scholarly discourse: Tracing theoretical basis and antecedents', R&D Management Conference, Cambridge.

Trott, P 2012, *Innovation management and new product development*, 5th edn., Financial Times, Prentice Hall, Harlow.

Tzokas, N, Hultink, EJ & Hart, S 2004, 'Navigating the new product development process', *Industrial Marketing Management*, vol. 33, no. 7, pp. 619–626.

Ulrich, KT 1995, 'The role of product architecture in the manufacturing firm', *Research Policy*, vol. 24, no. 3, pp. 419–440.

Ulrich, KT & Eppinger, SD 2012, *Product design and development*, 5th edn., McGraw-Hill Higher Education, New York.

Ulwick, A 2005, *What customers want: Using outcome-driven innovation to create breakthrough products and services*, Harvard Business School Press, Harvard.

United Nations 2016, *The millennium development goals and beyond 2015*, viewed <www.un.org/millenniumgoals/>.

Urban, GL & Hauser, JR 1993, *Design and marketing of new products*, 2nd edn., Prentice Hall, Englewood Cliffs, NJ.

Verworn, B, Herstatt, C & Nagahira, A 2008, 'The fuzzy front end of Japanese new product development projects: Impact on success and differences between incremental and radical projects', *R&D Management*, vol. 38, no. 1, pp. 1–19.

Veryzer, RW 1998, 'Discontinuous innovation and the new product development process', *Journal of Product Innovation Management*, vol. 15, no. 4, pp. 304–321.

Veryzer, RW 2010, *Wiley international encyclopedia of marketing*, John Wiley & Sons, Inc.

Viswanathan, M & Sridharan, S 2012, 'Product development for the BoP: Insights on concept and prototype development from university-based student projects in India', *Journal of Product Innovation Management*, vol. 29, no. 1, pp. 52–69.

Viswanathan, M, Yassine, A & Clarke, J 2011, 'Sustainable product and market development for subsistence marketplaces: Creating educational initiatives in radically different contexts*', *Journal of Product Innovation Management*, vol. 28, no. 4, pp. 558–569.

Vivek, B 2013, 'Introduction to products, processes, and product development', in *Designing complex products with systems engineering processes and techniques*, CRC Press, pp. 3–22.

Vodafone 2007, *Safaricom and Vodafone launch M-PESA, a new mobile payment service*, viewed 25 January 2018, <www.vodafone.com/content/index/media/voda fone-group-releases/2007/safaricom_and_vodafone.html>.

Weidner, KL, Rosa, JA & Viswanathan, M 2010, 'Marketing to subsistence consumers: Lessons from practice', *Journal of Business Research*, vol. 63, no. 6, pp. 559–569.

Weyrauch, T & Herstatt, C 2017, 'What is frugal innovation? Three defining criteria', *Journal of Frugal Innovation*, vol. 2, no. 1, pp. 1–17.

Wheelwright, SC & Clark, KB 1992, *Revolutionizing product development: Quantum leaps in speed, efficiency, and quality*, Free Press.

Whipple, N, Adler, T & McCurdy, S 2008, 'Applying trade-off analysis to get the most from customer needs', in *The PDMA toolBook 3 for new product development*, John Wiley & Sons, Inc., pp. 75–105.

Whitney, DE 2007, 'Assemble a technology development toolkit', *Research Technology Management*, vol. 50, no. 5, pp. 52–58.

Whitney, P 2010, 'Reframing design for the base of the pyramid', in T London and SL Hart (eds), *Next generation business strategies for the base of the pyramid: New approaches for building mutual value*, FT Press, Upper Saddle River, NJ, pp. 165–192.

Williamson, PJ 2010, 'Cost innovation: Preparing for a "value-for-money" revolution', *Long Range Planning*, vol. 43, no. 2, pp. 343–353.

Winkler, H, Heins, M & Nyhuis, P 2007, 'A controlling system based on cause – effect relationships for the ramp-up of production systems', *Production Engineering*, vol. 1, no. 1, pp. 103–111.

Winter, AG 2013, 'Helping the disabled get off-road and on with their lives (Case study)', *Mechanical Engineering-CIME*, vol. 135, no. 11, p. S18.

Winter, AG, Bollini, MA, DeLatte, DH, Judge, BM, O'Hanley, HF, Pearlman, JL & Scolnik, NK 2010, 'The design, fabrication, and performance of the east african trial leveraged freedom chair', ASME 2010 International Design Engineering Technical Conferences and Computers and Information in Engineering Conference, pp. 753–760.

Winter, AG, Bollini, MA, Judge, BM, Scolnik, NK, O'Hanley, HF, Dorsch, DS, Mukherjee, S & Frey, DD 2012, 'Stakeholder-driven design evolution of the leveraged freedom chair developing world wheelchair', ASME 2012 International Mechanical Engineering Congress and Exposition, American Society of Mechanical Engineers, pp. 361–368.

Winter, AG & Govindarajan, V 2015, 'Engineering reverse innovations: Principles for creating successful products for emerging markets', *Harvard Business Review*, vol. 93, no. 7–8, pp. 80–89.

Wood, AE & Mattson, CA 2014, 'A method for determining customer needs in the developing world', ASME 2014 International Design Engineering Technical Conferences and Computers and Information in Engineering Conference, American Society of Mechanical Engineers, pp. V02AT03A047-V02AT03A047.

Wood, AE & Mattson, CA 2016, 'Design for the developing world: Common pitfalls and how to avoid them', *Journal of Mechanical Design*, vol. 138, no. 3, p. 031101.

Wooldridge, A 2010, *First break all the rules: The charms of frugal innovation*, viewed 15 October 2017, <www.economist.com/node/15879359>.

World Bank 2013, *Mobile payments go viral: M-PESA in Kenya*, viewed 23 January 2018, <http://go.worldbank.org/XSGEPAIMO0>.

Yeh, T, Yang, C & Pai, F 2010, 'Performance improvement in new product development with effective tools and techniques adoption for high-tech industries', *Quality and Quantity*, vol. 44, no. 1, pp. 131–152.

Yin, RK 2014, *Case study research: Design and methods*, 5th edn., Sage Publications, Los Angeles, CA.

Yin, Y, Kaku, I & Liu, C 2012, 'Product architecture, product development process, system integrator and product global performance', *Production Planning & Control*, vol. 25, no. 3, pp. 203–219.

Zeschky, MB, Widenmayer, B & Gassmann, O 2011, 'Frugal innovation in emerging markets: The case of Mettler Toledo', *Research-Technology Management*, vol. 54, no. 4, pp. 38–45.

Zeschky, MB, Winterhalter, S & Gassmann, O 2014, 'From cost to frugal and reverse innovation: Mapping the field and implications for global competitiveness', *Research-Technology Management*, vol. 57, no. 4, pp. 20–27.

Zirger, BJ & Maidique, MA 1990, 'A model of new product development: An empirical test', *Management Science*, vol. 36, no. 7, pp. 867–883.

4 Prime Cookstoves

Cooking with frugal innovation

Introduction

Presenting a significant global challenge, our first case study explores the development of an Indonesian solution to traditional cooking methods. Globally, traditional methods for cooking and heating are used by over three billion people in middle and low-income countries around the world (WHO 2018). Insights from the World Health Organization (WHO) suggest that this accounts for approximately *four million premature deaths annually* – due to highly toxic burning of solid fuels (WHO 2018). In Indonesia, these stark numbers are also reflected with some 24 million households continuing to use traditional cookstoves, leading to premature deaths in approximately 165,000 Indonesians each year (World Bank 2014a).

As Rodrigo Chaves, World Bank Country Director for Indonesia, reflects, the introduction of cleaner cooking solutions will present "better health for millions of Indonesians [and] will reduce their health-care costs and their risks of falling into poverty" (World Bank 2014b). This presents a massive development challenge for Indonesia and is mirrored by the broader global challenge to move low-income families away from traditional methods of cooking and heating. Matching this challenge is the significant opportunity offered for frugal innovation to present a suitable solution that is within reach of BOP consumers. Prime Cookstoves (Prime) is an organisation that has engaged specifically with this opportunity, developing a biomass cookstove – the Prime fuelwood cookstove[1] – tailored to meet the needs not only of Indonesian BOP consumers, but also of other low-income countries in Asia and globally.

The chapter explores how Prime managed the NPDP of its Prime cookstove. Beginning with a broader context about Prime, this chapter explores the development of Prime and Prime cookstove from its introduction in 2013. The subsequent section provides a narrative analysis structured around the four NPDP phases and associated 15 key frugal innovation practices, providing insights from Prime and its activities to develop and introduce the Prime cookstove. This is built around primary and secondary data, including in-depth interviews with the Prime cookstove inventor and key development team members.

Prime Cookstoves overview

Established in 2013, Prime develops, manufactures and distributes clean, fuel-efficient and affordable biomass cookstoves. The key target markets of Prime are Indonesian Base-of-the-Pyramid (BOP) consumers (low-income and rural consumers) as well as international BOP consumers such as in Asian, South and Central American and African countries (*The Jakarta Post* 2015). Headquartered in Norway, Prime operates in Indonesia with manufacturing and distribution sites located across Java Island.

Prime was established through the partnership between Kreasi Daya Mandiri (KDM) and Differ Group. KDM was the company under which the first three stove prototypes were invented and formerly manufactured under the name UB Kompor biomass – UB-01, UB-02 and UB-03. Professor Muhammad Nurhuda is the founder of KDM and inventor of the Prime cookstove. He earned a PhD in theoretical atomic and nonlinear optical physics and then became a researcher and lecturer in renewable energy and energy efficiency at the University of Brawijaya (in Malang, one of the main cities of Java Island).

Differ Group, who invested in firms developing renewable energy and energy-efficient products, aimed to support the full-scale development of small low-carbon projects such as KDM's cookstoves (Differ 2015). After positive test results, Differ recognised Nurhuda's invention as one of the leading technologies globally, which led to the establishment of Differ Cookstoves under which Prime and Ditana Energy Solutions (Ditana) subsidiaries were created in 2013. Each of these firms had an important role in the R&D and commercialisation of the Prime cookstove.

Prime was established to develop and commercialise the different Prime cookstove products for international distribution. Prime first relied on the production of stoves from KDM, and focused on expanding international markets and developing supportive activities for local and international "marketing strategy and materials" (Prime former BDM). Prime recently established a partnership with a local automated production as part of scaling up its production output (Logistics Manager). At the time of these interviews, Nurhuda's factory still produced early versions (UB-02) of the Prime cookstove.

Ditana was also established in Indonesia as an independent subsidiary to distribute Prime cookstove products to the Indonesian market. Its core aim was to understand consumer demand across a variety of geographical locations in Indonesia while seeking both individual and groups of agents for local distribution. Ditana has played a significant role in increasing Prime cookstove demand and sales, having sold more than 10,000 units (Ditana Group 2016).

Together, KDM and Prime have sold more than 30,000 Prime cookstoves and exported to more than 20 countries in Asia and Africa (personal communications from the CEO of Prime 2018). Building from this point, the next section provides further details on the Prime cookstove, including its frugal characteristics.

Product overview: Prime cookstove

Prime sells two cookstoves – Prime fuelwood and Prime granular. The focus of this study is, however, only on the Prime cookstove fuelwood (also named UB-03) as seen in Figure 4.1. The choice of the Prime fuelwood over the Prime granular is based on the comprehensive NPD activities Prime undertook throughout the entire NPDP for this stove, in particular as it was the first developed and the main product that has been introduced to the market.

The Prime cookstove is a clean and energy-efficient biomass cookstove with low CO_2 emissions, operating on top-lit updraft (TLUD) technology that uses "preheating, counter-flow and co-firing burning mechanism" (Primestoves 2017b). It can be fuelled with a wide variety of wood biomass such as coconut shell, wood sticks and agricultural by-products. This frugal product has specific characteristics that qualify it as a frugal innovation, as seen in Table 4.1.

Figure 4.1 Prime cookstove fuelwood (UB-03)

Credit: Prime Cookstoves AS

Table 4.1 Frugal characteristics of the Prime cookstove

Frugal characteristics	Description
Market	BOP consumers (low-income and rural consumers)
Affordability	25 USD wholesale
Core functionality	– Heat water/food – Generate fertiliser (recovery of charcoal ash) – Customised flame size and duration – Firepower up to 6kW – Consumes 60% less fuelwood than traditional stone fire – Smoke-free during cooking; less toxic than traditional stone fire – Uses diverse biomass (fuelwood, woodchips, briquettes, coconut husks, corncobs, other bulky biomass)
Durability	– 2 years' lifetime – Can support over 100kg – Can be used indoor and outdoor – Warranty: 6 months for burning chamber and 10 months for stove body
Usability	– Easy-to-use – Local staff training for end user assistance and end users' training – Portable: 3.5kg of weight – No electricity required; natural airflow – No need for refuelling (0.5–2 hours burn time depending on fuel type) – Customer-tailored product (colour, size and fuel)

With this contextual understanding of Prime and the Prime cookstove, the next section explores the key frugal practices implemented by Prime when developing the Prime cookstove.

Phase 1: the fuzzy front end for frugal innovation

As noted earlier, the fuzzy front end is the initial phase of the NPDP and revolves around the search for innovative new products. For frugal innovation, this revolves around four distinct practices directing the identification and screening stages for the opportunity or key idea. Frugal innovators tend to undertake this first stage embedding a market-pull approach limited within BOP constraints, and with a focus on tools and techniques favouring external sources of stimulation. The third and fourth practices highlight the criteria to which frugal innovators tend to focus such as BOP consumers' needs, and internal and external business capabilities. The next sections introduce these four key practices, exploring how Prime has implemented this phase in line with their development of the Prime cookstove.

FI Practice 1: the opportunity and idea discovery stage has a market-pull approach that is limited within the scope of BOP markets constraints

Before identifying the problem with cooking devices, the inventor's innovation approach had a clear social orientation, searching for problems to solve within the scope of the local BOP population as well as Indonesian market constraints. The inventor considered addressing the lack of technology innovations that specifically tackled Indonesian BOP consumers' problems, which directed him towards potential opportunity and idea for frugal products.

The inventor's willingness to examine everyday problems of Indonesian BOP was inspired by research projects done within his professional career. This included cutting-edge laser technology projects and academic jobs in developed countries. Bounded by the goal to improve poor Indonesian consumers' lives, he reflected how the projects he had worked on in developed countries prompted his search for potential new product opportunities in Indonesia:

> I was a theoretical physicist . . . doing research on laser technology . . . but why not in Indonesia . . . I always thought what I could do for the people in Indonesia . . . after I stopped doing research on laser, I started to look at research that had a direct relation to the people in Indonesia.
>
> (Prime Inventor)

Aware of the benefits of cutting-edge technologies that had advanced developed countries, the inventor leveraged and adapted this experience and expertise to solve problems occurring in Indonesia. By considering problems encountered by BOP consumers in Indonesia, the discovery stage of the Prime cookstove was clearly defined by a social and market-pull approach.

In addition to discovering new product opportunities for specific market problems, the inventor had personal frustrations about the lack of technology innovations developed in the Indonesian context, a major constraint for Indonesian BOP consumers. Lacking access to adapted products, the inventor concentrated on resolving a perceived gap in technological innovation specific to the BOP consumers of Indonesia, guiding his discovery stage:

> Why we did not develop our own [Indonesian] technology that has direct impact with people here in Indonesia? That was a question that came to my mind; then we started to find problems that we can solve, and the stove is one of the problems.
>
> (Prime Inventor)

On the basis of his technological background, the inventor focused on solving issues created by the lack of technological solutions addressing Indonesian BOP consumers' needs, which revealed issues with current cooking methods. The development of the Prime cookstove emerged from the inventor's intent to develop innovative solutions for Indonesian BOP consumers, conveying a market-driven approach narrowed to the local constraints existing in Indonesia.

FI Practice 2: the tools and techniques of the opportunity and idea discovery stage allow external idea sources

The discovery of the Prime cookstove opportunity stemmed from the identification of specific problems encountered by Indonesian BOP consumers with existing liquefied petroleum gas (LPG) stoves. By seeking problems experienced specifically at the local low-income level, the inventor identified a 'call-to-action' by the Indonesian Government due to LPG explosion issues, perceiving this as a new product opportunity for an alternative solution.

With an ambition to solve local technological problems, the inventor discovered the LPG conversion program that had been introduced to substitute kerosene with LPG stoves. This program, however, led to new 'calls to action' to address the issue of LPG explosions. As the inventor aimed to address local consumption problems – "problems that [he and his team] could solve" (Prime Inventor) – the Government's need to find alternatives to LPG stoves explosions matched his innovative intentions. The focus was particularly on addressing the fatalities from consumers' stove misuse and from the LPG bottle leaks (Afrida 2010). The inventor sought an opportunity to find safer alternatives to this inadequate product offering:

> I saw there was a program by the government to consult in order to replace kerosene [stoves] with LPG [stoves]; and then every day, there were explosions because of the LPG misuse; that was terrible so the government wanted to replace LPG and find alternatives.
>
> (Prime Inventor)

The recurring explosions indicated that LPG stoves were inadequate for local BOP consumers who often lacked education about its usage and were not familiar with this type of product. The significant portion of the Indonesian population using LPG stoves, and the deadly outcomes that were occurring from explosions, motivated the inventor to resolve this urgent technical problem.

FI Practice 3: the opportunity and idea screening stage focuses on market information, in particular appraisals of BOP consumers' unmet needs

Three types of market information were considered as critical in pursuing the Prime cookstove project, in particular those related to three BOP consumer issues with LPG stoves. First, the urgency of addressing the LPG stove problems; second, the many drawbacks of LPG stoves such as local consumers' dependency on this fuel; third, the Indonesian Government expenditure on LPG subsidies, which, in the inventor's opinion, would not have been sustainable over time.

First, one of the main motivations for the inventor to start his research on the Prime cookstove project was the high frequency of LPG stove explosions, a pressing issue reinforcing the need for an alternative solution to LPG stoves: "I started in 2008 because there were very frequent LPG explosions, the users were afraid of being the next victim" (Prime Inventor). This market situation, pivotal to the inventor's decision to progress with this project, indicated the importance of understanding the level of necessity for a new product opportunity. This project was also inspired by the inventor's primary motivation of using his expertise to have a positive impact on local people's lives.

Furthermore, the inventor also believed that LPG fuel – as a main source of energy for cooking – was unsustainable, expensive and hard to access geographically (particularly in rural locations). While the Indonesian Government had initiated the kerosene-to-LPG conversion program, this solution was not adequate for the cooking needs of the majority of Indonesian BOP consumers living in rural areas. In some regions of Indonesia, LPG remained an inaccessible and expensive cooking fuel for rural and BOP people (World Bank 2014b). At the initial stage of the program, subsidised LPG bottles were not extended outside the major areas of Java Island (Pertamina & WLPGA 2015), causing an uneven distribution of subsidised LPG spread across Indonesia:

> The Government had already started the LPG conversion program, but only in Jakarta and surrounding areas, but not in East Java [where the inventor lives]. There was LPG in East Java, but only in 12kg cylinder bottles, which is not subsidised.
>
> (Prime Inventor)

Not only was LPG fuel inaccessible to rural communities, but also the "subsidised LPG . . . in 3kg cylinder" (Prime Inventor) was also unavailable in suburbs surrounding the inventor's location. This information about the geographic unavailability of subsidised LPG and the potential high costs of unsubsidised LPG was decisive for the inventor in exploring the alternative stove opportunity.

The former BDM concurred, highlighting the primary goal of the inventor was not necessarily about making profit, but rather to help Indonesian BOP consumers to avoid such fuel dependency:

> I think, what he [the inventor] wanted was for Indonesian people, poor people, to be able to be self-sustaining in terms of energy. I think it was his goal; [he developed the stove] not only for business.
>
> (Prime former BDM)

In addition to the inventor's socially oriented goal, he was also willing to address Indonesian BOP consumers' reliance on products that were not necessarily adequate for their situation. The inventor was aware of the lack of available options for Indonesian BOP consumers, as the former BDM reflects:

> He [the inventor] also knows many people outside of Malang and other people in the villages who need this [a biomass stove], because there is no . . . existing product that can replace the [traditional] three-stones fire.
>
> (Prime former BDM)

In other words, those who did not have access to the government's LPG program had to either accommodate the high price of unsubsidised LPG or continue using existing cooking methods (including inefficient biomass stoves, three-stone fires or kerosene stoves) and then suffer from their negative effects (including smoke toxicity).

Finally, the Indonesian Government, which had already been experiencing issues with significant expenditures in subsidising previous kerosene programs, was likely to incur similar problems with the kerosene-to-LPG program. According to the inventor, while the LPG fuel was more affordable for local consumers due to government subsidies, this still remained a huge expense for the Government. He perceived that the government's budget for LPG subsidies would be reconsidered over time – which ended up occurring (IEA 2015). This influenced his decision to move forward with the Prime cookstove project:

> We have [developed] an alternative solution because LPG has been subsidised by government for more than around US \$4.5 billion, so it's a lot of money. Now the Indonesian Government tries to provide another alternative and is slowly cutting subsidy for LPG.
>
> (Prime Inventor)

For the inventor, the very real possibility of the subsidy being removed for LPG fuel increased the potential need for an alternative cooking product. This was particularly the case when considering that LPG would become unaffordable without these subsidies for low-income consumers.

FI Practice 4: the opportunity and idea screening stage focuses on business information linked with internal and external capabilities

During the screening stage for this opportunity, the inventor focused on available resources including his own expertise and cheap local manufacturing sites that could enable quick experiments on different product concepts. The inventor consciously leveraged his own expertise from an extensive career in laser physics before committing to the stove opportunity. In addition to his personal expertise, the inventor was knowledgeable about local and cheap 'workshops' (small factories), which was also valuable in the decision to commence the stove project.

The inventor trusted his own expertise and capabilities in laser physics to be a sufficient technical basis for the development of the cookstove opportunity.

On top of his extensive expertise in advanced technologies, the inventor also had developed technologies for Indonesia that did not rely on fossil fuels. With this in mind, his primary aim was to use his knowledge in physics and science to develop an environmentally friendly product that positively affected the lives of Indonesians. This technical and research expertise was evident in his reflection on his professional background:

> Research in the area of laser physics only affects so-called developed countries such as Japan, Germany, not Indonesia. So then, I started to develop technology for renewable energy.
>
> (Prime Inventor)

He clearly understood the potential benefits of sustainable energy innovations, particularly when applied within a socio-economic context of developing countries including Indonesia. With his experience working in advanced physics and laser technology, the inventor was confident in focusing on renewable energy technologies, including "solar cooker, solar water heater, [and] . . . biodiesel stove" (Prime Inventor) with "11 patented energy solutions" (Primestoves 2017a). These projects clearly underpinned his confidence to pursue the Prime cookstove project.

Furthermore, another basis in deciding to pursue the cookstove opportunity was his prior development of local sustainable products, which included cooperating with low-cost manufacturing sites (workshops) in Malang. His access to local manufacturing sites meant access to cheaper workspaces for experimentation and quick prototyping, reducing R&D costs. This was critical as there were limited finances for this project – "most of my projects on stoves were self-financed" (Prime Inventor) – so knowledge of cheap local factories progressed the product's development and manufacturing. The inventor reflected on his experience with these manufacturing sites:

> Normally I go to workshops. There are many in Malang. It would depend on the device. For the stove, I came to the workshop and contacted the technician directly. After that, we tested the product with our feeling; if it is good then we continue, otherwise we withdraw the concept.
>
> (Prime Inventor)

This knowledge about the availability of technical workspaces in the inventor's own area guaranteed a rapid and inexpensive way to undertake R&D. This also set a very clear context for understanding the feasibility and sustainability of the stove project.

Phase 2: concept development for frugal innovation

Turning now to the concept development phase for frugal innovation, as noted earlier, this progresses the ideas and opportunities explored into a more tangible and detailed evaluation of a potential concept. From the context of frugal innovation, this includes five key practices to direct the NPDP. This begins with Practice 5 that brings a focus on three specific information linked to BOP consumer, directing the market study undertaken on the concept. Tools and techniques for this NPDP stage represents Practice 6 and relies on frugal innovators' immersed approach to the market study stage.

As part of the technical study stage, Practice 7 focuses on primary functionalities and business model specifications. On the other hand, Practice 8 recommends tools and techniques leading firms to leverage basic technological principles and/or architecture and components from existing products to undertake the technical study stage. The final practice of the concept development phase, Practice 9, facilitates the conceptual evaluation stage, highlighting the importance for concept testing using criteria and/or simple physical version to test concept acceptance.

FI Practice 5: the market study stage has a focus on BOP consumer information related to affordability, complementary needs and product usage context

When developing the Prime cookstove, the inventor had a clear focus on two key types of consumer information to inform his market study: affordability and product usage context. First, it was clear to the inventor that there was a need for the stove to be affordable, to allow cost-effective utilisation by consumers. This was more than simply a purchase price-point, but also understanding the ongoing use of the product. Second, the inventor also clearly focused the market study on considering product usage including cultural preferences in cooking methods, which provided critical product requirements for the development of the Prime cookstove.

When looking at consumer information around affordability, it was clear that the inventor wanted to develop an affordable product for BOP consumers. His understanding of affordability for consumers went however beyond the product price by including affordability in the product use. The need for an affordable price was clearly important, as the Prime cookstove was targeted at the Indonesian "people with low income, the low-income families" (Prime Inventor). But the inventor noticed that BOP consumers prioritised affordable products that are also inexpensive to use.

For example, the inventor was eager to develop stoves where fuels were available at low or no cost for consumers to be more economical. This was reflected on by the inventor when examining richer people's preference for convenience in cooking products, which a LPG stove offered compared to biomass fuel. A product relying on biomass had a less convenient, yet economical use for the cookstove. As he perceived the cost of LPG would become more expensive over time, he understood BOP consumers' preference for cost-effective products and compared the use and price of LPG fuel over biomass fuel (including biomass pellets, another form of fuelwood):

Poor people normally think what is more economical, but rich people only think what things are much more convenient for them . . . So I think if LPG is not subsidised anymore, then for the same energy that [they] will get, people will pay much higher for LPG compared to even biomass pellet.

(Prime Inventor)

Contrasting with higher-income consumers who generally prioritise convenience over cost-effectiveness, the inventor understood the difference with BOP consumers' preference for a product that rather had an economical use. Although both high- and low-income consumers in Indonesia had comparable cooking necessities, the way the product was used was the key difference when assessing their perceptions of affordability.

The perception of affordability also relied on BOP consumers' comparison of price and the advantages with other cookstoves. A Prime sales manager elaborated on this, suggesting that BOP consumers tended to compare the price of the Prime cookstove with existing products: "They say [Prime cookstove's] too expensive, because most of them often compare it with LPG stove" (Prime Sales Manager 1). The fact that consumers compared the Prime cookstove with existing products emphasised the need for the product to have additional cost advantages. This consumer information about the broader product affordability informed the development of the Prime cookstove, which offered a high-efficiency combustion technology and the possibility to re-use the used charcoal for agricultural purposes.

When looking at the product usage context, the inventor evaluated a range of global competitors' products used by Indonesian consumers, which revealed usage problems. By reviewing core problems in existing failed products, the inventor concluded that a user-friendly product (not too difficult to operate for BOP consumers) was essential. By investigating both affordable and more expensive products, he could understand why some existing products were considered impractical by Indonesian BOP consumers:

So I looked at what stoves have been developed by other people around the world: what are the advantages and disadvantages, what is good and what is not good from the stoves . . . Yes, even the expensive one.

(Prime Inventor)

One example of an expensive product the inventor shared was a launched German stove, which Indonesian consumers had initially been interested in. Despite its high cooking efficiency, consumers quickly experienced issues with this product, which halted their purchase and use of it. In investigating this further, the inventor identified important impractical aspects of the product during its use within the Indonesian context:

[This] German brand . . . is expensive, very efficient in fuel, but my question was "why people [no longer] use the stove?" . . . because it's not practical . . .

every one or two minutes we need to insert more wood sticks in the burning chamber . . . [b]ut people in Indonesia, they also work on other jobs during cooking, . . . it is VERY [emphasised by the inventor] important.

(Prime Inventor)

In the context of Indonesian BOP consumers, the need for extended flame duration was critical in the development of the Prime cookstove to avoid continual addition of fuel to the stove. Such insights provided the inventor with a set of detailed criteria for product usage, helping him identify critical Indonesian market needs about practicality.

By examining a range of global brands that had failed to be accepted by Indonesian consumers, the inventor also explored why a stove less premium than the German one was also perceived as impractical: "Technically, he [provider of competing product] made a very good stove . . . but it is too complicated . . . it's not practical . . . for the people. Nobody used this stove" (Prime Inventor). This focus on other stoves that had failed revealed constructive information about how the product usage context was critical in the development of a new cooking device.

FI Practice 6: the tools and techniques of the market study stage focus on a firm's immersion with targeted consumers for deeper insights

While a lack of funding prevented the inventor from pursuing formal market research, his Indonesian background and local presence enabled the observation and leveraging of his personal understanding of local consumer preferences and needs. This included his personal knowledge of Indonesian BOP consumers' routines and behaviours. In addition, the inventor was physically immersed in the local environment for many decades, which provided sufficient information to start the project and was an advantage compared with competitors' development team (such as with the German product).

This reliance on the inventor's long-term and personal knowledge of Indonesian BOP consumers was one of the cheapest methods for obtaining market information. As an Indonesian-born citizen, the inventor had been embedded in the local context for decades. Thus, when asked how he came up with the main performance requirements of the Prime cookstove, he highlighted the importance of observing people around him as the key technique: "We observed actually" (Prime Inventor). His affiliation with the targeted consumers, including witnessing cookstove use through his daily life in Malang, facilitated his understanding of their needs, as he further explained:

Most of my projects on stove were self-financed. So we just observed here "Oh" because we think about what other people normally think about stoves. Remember, I come from a village in Java here, so I know how a stove works, and understand what people want from a stove.

(Prime Inventor)

Due to his limited budget, the inventor leveraged this experience with BOP consumers to refine his understanding of consumer expectations for a potential new cooking device. This local proximity clearly enabled more market certainty to refine the most adequate cooking methods for these consumers. In contrast with the inventor's lived experiences with stove users, the German development team (discussed earlier) lacked consideration of specific Indonesian BOP consumers' needs. According to the inventor, this was particularly true in their perceptions on the notion of time and work activities: "So possibly, designers of the German stove think that people or women who use the stove were allocating their time only for cooking, not for other jobs" (Prime Inventor).

The inventor questioned the experience and methods of competitors' development teams in identifying BOP information. In observing and comprehending end users and their everyday activities, the inventor had built a broader understanding of how cooking activities were undertaken in Indonesia, such as the notion of time during cooking. The inventor had the advantage of living with potential consumers and observing their daily routines to translate critical needs as close to reality as possible. However, it is important to highlight some limitations in the inventor's initial interpretation of these BOP consumers' needs. For example, the inventor did not consider aesthetic needs[2] in his first product concepts for the Prime cookstove, which impacted upon initial product acceptance.

FI Practice 7: the technical study stage focuses on primary product functionality and business model specifications

When considering the technical study stage, the inventor considered two key types of target performance: the business model specifications and primary product functionality. During this stage, the inventor factored in the broader Indonesian context into both the Prime cookstove concept and the corresponding business model. This included supply chain decisions, such as the need for a high-quantity fuel supply. The inventor also prioritised primary functionality within the product concept, including the efficiency of the stove such as the flame stability and smoke emissions, leaving the stove aesthetics as a secondary consideration.

Looking first at business model specifications, these were factored into targeted performance, including the availability and quantity of fuel supplies in Indonesia. This meant product acceptance was determined not only by the product performance, but also the facilitation of cheap and accessible fuel supplies for consumers. Fuel quantities from naturally abundant resources were also factored in to avoid fuel shortage constraints. In an interview with an Indonesian newspaper, the inventor revealed his conviction that Indonesian communities did not need to use fossil fuel energy with its many drawbacks. He recognised that natural resources in Indonesia could be used as an alternative fuel for new products: "[There are] many things on earth that we can use as a fuel" (Prime Inventor, cited in Irawati 2011).

Furthermore, based on the issues encountered with LPG across Indonesia, another key objective was to deliver a product that did not require costly and hard-to-access fuel. The inventor first sought to adapt the concept to operate on naturally abundant resources, such as Jatropha oil. However, by considering business model specifications, the inventor subsequently determined that a Jatropha plant-based product did not match well with the Indonesian context. This is because the abundance of Jatropha oil was not natural, but rather originated from industrial plantations:

> I thought it would be better if the stove was fuelled with biomass instead of Jatropha Curcas . . . Jatropha is difficult to plant and find here, but we can find wood everywhere.
>
> (Prime Inventor)

It was clear that the inventor realised the importance of fuel supply for Indonesian BOP consumers. He subsequently generated a biomass stove concept, taking account of specifications beyond the product and incorporated business model specifications related to the fuel supply. As opposed to a stove fed with Jatropha, he focused on a stove that had widely available and accessible fuel sources (e.g. biomass), which meant a better value proposition for Indonesian BOP consumers.

With regard to primary product functionality, two aspects related to technology efficiency were prioritised ahead of the aesthetics of the product. The inventor concentrated on performance related to flame stability to ensure longer flame duration and less smoke emission during cooking for comfort and for reducing health-related issues.[3] The flame had to remain stable from the time wood started burning until it turned into black charcoal, requiring a combustion technology:

> The stability means the stove can provide a very stable fire . . . there's a transition from wood burning to charcoal burning. In most designs that I have developed, there was always a problem when the charcoal started to burn, then there was a lot of smoke. It was not stable.
>
> (Prime Inventor)

As the primary functionality of the stove was to provide a stable flame for duration, it was important that the burning technology met this important requirement. This illustrated a clear focus from the inventor on primary functionality that the stove had to achieve during the technical study stage.

The other primary functionality aspect was to ensure minimal smoke during the cooking process. Here, the inventor examined how much smoke was emitted during cooking, rather than the more common and extended focus after the flame had been turned off. This directed the development of the stove technology, with a clear focus on performance in relation to smoke-free functionality:

> The second [focus] is about emission. If the flame is too smoky with too much sulphate, it's not accepted by the people. During [cooking], the stove always emits smoke, but if we can reduce the amount of smoke during, not after the flame dies, it would be a very good thing.
>
> (Prime Inventor)

While existing products provided a clean, smoke-free flame from the beginning of the cooking process to the end, such as the LPG stove, the inventor did not focus on this performance. Rather, he focused on establishing target performance aimed at reducing smoke emission specifically during the cooking process. He prioritised the emission performance during cooking, without seeking to reduce the smoke emission throughout the entire burning process. A simple solution was developed for stopping smoke emissions after using the Prime cookstove through putting a lid on top of the stove.

A clear distinction was made between the inventor's priorities, including allocating the external design as a secondary requirement: "At first, I didn't think about how the stove would look like, only how it works" (Prime Inventor). The main reason for this was that if the technology did not provide the right performance expected by consumers, the trade-off to the outside design would make it unlikely that consumers would use the product. The inventor reflected on this:

> What we have to develop is . . . the performance of the combustion technology [Prime cookstove technology]. Even if the stove looks very good, but if the technology does not work, then people will leave the stove . . . how the stove looks like is secondary.
>
> (Prime Inventor)

The inventor narrowed his focus to addressing technology efficiency adapted to Indonesian BOP consumers' needs, which did not integrate targeted performance related to the stove's external design. The primary purpose was to avoid creating a new design and instead identify a practical external design that BOP consumers could quickly relate to.

The inventor, therefore, chose an external design based on the popularity and commonality of a round stove: "Normally the stoves we found in Africa, or even the prototype made by [provider of competing product] . . . and most biomass stoves were cylindrical" (Prime Inventor). His reason for choosing a cylindrical shape originated from international popularity. The fact that the inventor did not spend extra time at this stage on what he considered a secondary product functionality showed his focus on primary product functionality.

However, the external design of the Prime cookstove was gradually altered on the basis of Indonesian BOP consumers' feedback, which resulted in higher product acceptance. The external design ended up being an important aspect of the concept development.

FI Practice 8: the tools and techniques of the technical study stage involve seeking basic technological principles and/or architecture and components from existing products

Underpinning the technical stage and addressing the required product performance, the inventor searched for potential designs through technological principles in other similar products. The initial focus was to attain simple technological principles that included proven efficient technology that could be adopted. An example of this was the benefits stemming from gasification technology, which relied on basic physics principles and enabled longer flame duration due to natural airflow.

The inventor reflected on this process: "I tried to adopt existing technologies that can be used easily and [that are] environmentally friendly" (Prime Inventor, cited in Irawati 2011). The aim was to ensure that the technology used relied on basic, but proven, technology principles. Within this context, the inventor first sought to experiment and learn from the gasification technology invented by "the champion of the stoves [provider of competing product]" (Prime Inventor), from which he then enhanced the stove performance over time. As the inventor reflected:

> [the first prototype] was an imitation from what I learnt from the internet initially, [about] how the basic principles of . . . the gasification stove work . . . made by [provider of competing product] . . . After we did experiments, we got a conclusion that his stove should be improved . . . Then we went ahead with our own concept. And our concept was not used for other technology [*he meant for other stoves*].
>
> (Prime Inventor)

As the gasification technology was outside the inventor's core competencies, he experimented with the gasification technology and used the results of his own work as a basis for further adaptation of this technology for Indonesian consumers. The gasification technology was subsequently fine-tuned into a patented technological system for the Prime cookstove (Nurhuda 2012). The inventor appreciated this type of technology for its efficiency and simplicity, which were derived from the basic science principles on which it was based:

> We have to learn a lot from the physics, from the thermodynamics, the aerodynamics . . . the character of heat purifications and so on. It is very important. From physics, we know how the nature works, it is not magic . . . everything [is] explained by physics.
>
> (Prime Inventor)

Choosing the gasification technology was a significant decision, as it meant that the stove would rely on basic principles involving physics and science theories based on 'nature', such as thermodynamic principles with heat purification. By choosing to integrate these basic technological principles into the stove, it was in fact easier to control the variables of the technological principles, which were based on physics (or natural) theories.

Another advantage of basic technological principles included the performance of natural airflow used in the Prime cookstove mechanisms. The first design of the UB-01 stove included an electrical fan aimed at longer flame duration, which was a primary functionality in the stove. Due to BOP consumers' negative feedback, the inventor subsequently explored natural airflow as a more adapted technology to address this primary functionality. The inventor ended up replacing the electric blower with simpler technological principles based on natural airflow, using 'simpler' physics principles:

> I think the simple stove is more efficient for us than the stove that uses electricity . . . its [functioning] is caused by blower, . . . the second one is caused by natural draft . . . without electrical power [for UB-02].
>
> (Prime Inventor)

Natural airflow was more relevant, as it still offered the same functional performance as the technology based on electricity. Such identification of other ways of creatively using existing technological principles led to more BOP consumers' acceptance due to delivering the right product performance.

FI Practice 9: the tools and techniques of the concept evaluation stage integrate a set of criteria and/or simple physical version to test concept acceptance

The inventor did not directly evaluate his concepts with his potential consumers. He instead assessed their technical feasibility through experiments with a simple version based on three key criteria for toxicity, safety and comfort. The first prototype UB-01 moved towards the development stage without consumers evaluating this concept, which proved to be an unsuccessful practice. The inventor had to revert to the technical study stage to rework the technology underlying the functioning of the concept, from electric blower to natural draft, as consumers did not accept this product. In the second UB-02 version, the testing involved self-utilisation of the stove to ensure the technology fit with toxicity, safety and comfort criteria.

In concept UB-01, which moved to product development stage without any concept testing with consumers, the inventor's first intuitive action was to develop five UB-01 stoves with an electric blower. Known as 'forced draft' (Saloop et al. 2016), this is a common feature added by stove developers, according to the inventor: "Many people have developed stoves, which . . . used electricity . . . Initially we developed a stove that uses electricity to power the blower" (Prime Inventor). The inventor believed the past popularity of a stove with an electrical fan would lead to general consumer acceptance. However, this first prototype received negative feedback when it was introduced to the market:

> At first, I didn't think about the market, but after I had been able to develop five of the first stove [UB-01] . . . with electrical power . . . after I got the prototype, I tried to demonstrate it to society . . . the society couldn't accept the stove. . . . [They] thought that it is not effective because it still used electricity connected to the grid. . . . So I started to develop a stove . . . without electrical power.
>
> (Prime Inventor)

The inventor found out only after introducing five stoves that consumers did not accept the use of an electric fan in the stove. This meant that the inventor had to change the technological principles (as per frugal innovation Practice 8) on which the stove relied upon. On the basis of this failure, the inventor experimented with another technology for UB-02, along with three essential criteria when developing his stove: safety (stable stove), toxicity (flame and smoke emission) and comfort (less smoky):

> Firstly . . . when we had been able to develop a new stove with a new concept . . . I tried it [the UB-02] by myself. . . . There are at least three minimum factors that we have to keep in mind when we develop . . . this stove: first the stability, the emission, and three the comfort.
>
> (Prime Inventor)

After developing a concept that was not forced draft like the electric fan, a stove based on natural draft [UB-02] was tested, to assess whether this technology would fit the criteria. Testing through the criteria imposed on the design, on which the technology was based, led to an experimental prototype that was meeting sufficient outcomes sought by the inventor.

Phase 3: product development

Progressing past the concept development phase, the next phase relates to the product development and aims to convert concepts into a commercial product. Three key frugal innovation practices frame this phase, with the first practice, frugal innovation Practice 10, focusing on product design and the importance of local outsourcing balancing performance and costs. Frugal innovation Practice 11 brings frugal innovators' attention to DfX techniques that are specifically in line with frugal design strategies. The last practice of the product development phase, Practice 12, is reflected in the prototype testing stage where early field-testing is recommended, including the concept of co-design.

FI Practice 10: the product design stage prioritises local outsourcing weighted off with costs and performance

The design of the Prime cookstove involved prioritising local resources as well as trade-off decisions between performance requirements at the product design level and product development costs. First, the development of the components was guided by the availability of local equipment and labour in an existing local factory, which reduced product development, and production time and costs. Second, while the inventor first integrated local recycled materials into the stove components, he later decided to weigh-off the costs of more expensive materials in some components for longer durability.

The inventor identified an opportunity to leverage local factories, which included outsourcing components and design characteristics of the Prime cookstove. The shift in government policy on the LPG conversion program which led to discontinuing subsidies for kerosene fuel and stoves meant that many of these local manufacturers went bankrupt. This was an opportunity for the inventor to re-use their manufacturing equipment:

> After the transition of the use of kerosene to LPG, some stove manufacturers went bankrupt and they left some unused dies [manufacturing tool for stamping] and big machines.
>
> (Prime Inventor)

These locally available resources provided already designed components. The inventor determined that this machinery produced adequate performance and cost-effective components:

> We were self-financing during the development . . . I think it [the design of the kerosene stove] is okay, even if it is not very good; because by using existing dies, we don't need to buy new ones.
>
> (Prime Inventor)

It provided both a time- and cost-effective advantage in comparison with buying or designing new equipment:

> If we didn't use the existing dies, for every stove design that we had to develop, probably if very new, we probably needed more than 30,000 USD. That's a lot of money for us. But if we use already existing dies, with some modification, we probably will spend only 3,000 to 5,000 USD.
>
> (Prime Inventor)

Inspired by financial constraints, the inventor opted for local existing sites that enabled time and cost savings on decisions for machineries and stamping tools. For example, the Prime cookstove table was designed by re-using the stamping tools from kerosene stove tables:

> We modified the stove table from previous kerosene stove table. We re-used the dies . . . from which I made some modification to fit with our needs, for my stove's needs.
>
> (Prime Inventor)

Such re-use of local manufacturing factories provided time and cost efficiency in coordinating components and modifying or making equipment to produce the stove, enabling flexibility in manufacturing requirements. Similar to the stove table, local manufacturing resources and consumers' feedback directed final decisions in regard to the square body shape of the UB-03. Indonesian consumers preferred the square shape due to their familiarity with this form of existing kerosene stoves, which benefitted the inventor in saving further costs by adapting his design and manufacturing needs to existing resources.

The former BDM pointed out that both consumer feedback and the potential to re-use available manufacturing resources were primary reasons for choosing the final square-shaped stove design:

> I think another reason for him [the inventor], other than making it similar [or familiar] to what people were used to, is that he wanted to use the existing factories . . . [they are] quite similar as they use same kind of materials, same kind of equipment.
>
> (Prime Former BDM)

Re-using existing resources had evident advantages, including lowering the costs of development through the re-use of local equipment. However, the components that had proprietary design, such as those shaping the technological principles on which the stove operated (like the combustion chamber), were designed in-house by the inventor:

> [For] the combustion chamber, we cannot use the concept of the kerosene stove. Only the over part, the stove table, the stove leg, the stove tank, but for the internal combustion chamber, we must think and develop ourselves.
>
> (Prime Inventor)

While the stove legs and table components were re-used from the kerosene stove, the components linked to the combustion chamber were designed in-house. This meant that the inventor could modify the shape of some components by leveraging the original stamping tools and making some changes on these in a time-efficient manner.

Additional advantages of local factories included low-cost local labour: "You know the labour in Indonesia is quite cheap, compared to other countries" (Prime Inventor). Leveraging the employment of local skilled labourers was also cost-advantageous in terms of human resource training and management. These factories had 'know-how' (Prime former BDM), and by working closely with them from the beginning, the inventor could exchange his ideas in a faster and simpler way with local technicians:

> So I draw with . . . my pencil . . . I asked the technicians . . . I brought the picture . . . we just met last night with the technicians and we talked . . . At 5 o'clock [on the interview day], that prototype was ready, very quick.
>
> (Prime Inventor)

Collaborating on the drawings of components was clearly enough for the inventor and the technicians to develop prototypes, reducing time for coordinating functional teams around the development of the product design. The access to local capabilities as well as re-use of local factory equipment were, therefore, important parts of the inventor's final design decision. Local factories offered cost advantages and influenced design decisions on the basis of locally available equipment and labourers who were used to local manufacturing processes.

Some of the materials were later weighed-off with the costs of more expensive materials that ensured better durability, as the inventor integrated local recycled materials into the stove components. The inventor initially designed the stove through recycled materials for the first two prototypes: UB-01 and UB-02. However, the use of cheap materials for some of the stove components needed to be changed for stronger ones, which were more expensive. As reflected by the inventor, a non-robust stove would have jeopardised the brand:

> Back then [before 2012] when we used cheap materials . . . the shape [and] materials as normally used by kerosene stove . . . the stove could only work for two months . . . that's dangerous for us . . . then I thought it would be good if the stove price could be rather higher, but with a longer lifetime.
>
> (Prime Inventor)

This experience with low-quality materials revealed that it was more important to increase the stove lifespan through more expensive and durable parts. The inventor's understanding of how cheap materials could damage product acceptance by Indonesian BOP consumers made him redesign some of the components with more reliable materials: "I sought what materials we can use, but keeping the cost affordable for the people" (Prime Inventor). Still keeping the price relatively affordable, the inventor clearly differentiated between those components that needed more expensive materials and those that did not.

For example, more expensive materials were necessary to ensure the thickness of the metal and the anti-corrosive coatings (Fulland 2016). It was important that the combustion chamber and stove table were designed with stainless steel, as these components had to withstand the heat of the stove and the humid weather conditions. Yet the stove tank did not require such strong materials, which was a decision that helped keep the Prime cookstove affordable for Indonesian BOP consumers:

> The combustion chamber and the stove table must be strong enough to resist the heat, as well as the corrosion. But . . . pre-heating tool, or . . . stove tank . . . [were] not important to be replaced [if we wanted] to keep the price low, because if we replace all materials with stainless steel materials, then the price will be higher and the people can't afford to buy the stove. That's why we chose only selective materials to be replaced with good materials.
>
> (Prime Inventor)

Thus, while local sourcing of materials was beneficial during the design stage, the performance of some components could not be traded-off with their price, as it could have jeopardised the primary functionality of the stove.

FI Practice 11: the tools and techniques of the product design stage include DfX techniques specifically aimed at frugal design strategies

Although DfX techniques were not formally utilised, a design that required easy maintenance was needed. This included guidelines driving the Prime cookstove design to incorporate a removable component – the combustion chamber of the stove, a part frequently damaged. As this part was also an expensive stove element, the stove was required to be designed for easy maintenance and/or replacement in case of damage, resulting in a cost-effective benefit for Prime and the consumers.

As part of the development of a product that was cost-effective for both Prime and the targeted consumers, the ability to replace the most expensive part removed the need to pay for an entire brand-new stove: "Usually, the first thing that will break is the burning chamber, and this is replaceable, so they [the consumers] can buy the burning chamber [when it is broken]" (Prime former BDM). The inventor developed the burning chamber, the part of the stove where wood combustion occurred, with the aim to be manufactured as a removable component. The combustion chamber was thus part of the primary functionality of the Prime cookstove, with performance likely to diminish over time.

Enabling the replacement of key components was also advantageous due to the unforeseen usage of the stove by Indonesian BOP consumers. Feedback from the NGO's observation of the Prime cookstove usage in the field showed it might be misused, leading to quicker damage to its mechanism. The logistics manager pointed out this stove misuse by consumers: "Perhaps when in the field, we never know . . . when we see that the cookstove is already damaged, [we think] people may have used it for other things" (Prime Logistics Manager). For example, the former BDM shared his experience of consumers misusing the stove due to their limited knowledge about maintaining it:

> In Lombok . . . [m]any people misused the stove because they didn't know how to maintain the stove; when they wanted to turn off the flame, they used water, which . . . would break the stove as a consequence of rust.
>
> (Prime Former BDM)

In this example, the main component of the stove that was damaged was the combustion chamber with the wood-burning mechanism. Thus, designing a replaceable combustion chamber was critical, as it was a part of the stove that was often misused by these consumers. Enabling this replacement of the combustion chamber also allowed low-cost and fast maintenance and replacement of it.

FI Practice 12: the tools and techniques of the prototype testing stage include early field-testing

UB-01 and UB-02 were developed in small amounts and tested with friends, relatives and other consumers, without undertaking early field-testing. After the

UB-01 failed to be accepted by consumers, the concept was changed to UB-02, from which the inventor sold more than 1,000 stoves. This sale however led to critical feedback and modification of product design and performance, highlighting the essential role that early field-testing among local communities could have had on the Prime cookstove if it had been undertaken before further sales occurred.

The first initiative involved the introduction of five UB-01 working models, to obtain reactions from a small number of Indonesian BOP consumers. The inventor learnt that these consumers were not necessarily attracted by how the stove worked. For example, a stove with a fan fuelled by electricity proved less successful than a stove providing the same performance without electricity. This verified that testing the stove's technology in the early stages was beneficial to avoid engaging in more complete development of a less appealing product.

The resulting combustion technology that did not use electricity (UB-02) was also shared among close friends, family and other people in the inventor's neighbourhood to collect further feedback on what could be improved on the stove: "I give for free to some people around me, around here, or to my mother. I asked them to try the stove . . . [t]o get the feedback [about] what should be improved" (Prime Inventor). The inventor improved the stove on the basis of past negative feedback and the opinions of those people who were closely connected to him. When testing both prototypes, he was aware of the importance of sharing a few working models with potential users to enable refinements before full-scale manufacture, which could not be derived from laboratory testing.

However, although this proved beneficial to the final product, piloting the Prime cookstove among broader Indonesian communities earlier could have had clear advantages to its development (as field-testing did not occur during product development, this example overlaps with the market testing stage). After testing the UB-02 with friends and relatives, the inventor promoted and sold stoves himself, secured a contract with the Indonesian Ministry of Research and Technology which bought 1,000 stoves and also sold them to a local NGO.

The inventor reflected on this contract with the Indonesian government: "The government subsidised the stove to test the response from the people . . . I had sold to government around 1,000 stoves" (Prime Inventor). Although the government helped introduce this stove to Indonesian BOP consumers, there were drawbacks to this approach. For example, the roll-out of this quantity of stoves through a third party meant high-volume production with no direct contact with the consumers, removing the ability to effectively test and refine the usability and/or robustness of the stove.

The former BDM confirmed this lack of direct contact with consumers: "He [the inventor] did not really deal with the users . . . government has no contact, as they just give it away [the stoves to BOP consumers]" (Prime former BDM). Thus, while the inventor was able to sell 1,000 stoves, he did not get as much feedback from these consumers as he would have liked. The inventor instead followed up separately with these and other consumers, as reflected on here:

> We wanted to get responses by phone, feedback and other things . . . I contacted them to ask whether they are satisfied with this stove . . . I asked them to take some photograph and send via email.
>
> (Prime Inventor)

This follow-up facilitated to understand BOP consumers' preferences and opinions on the stove. In addition to the government purchase of 1,000 stoves, a local NGO also bought several hundred UB-02. The initial Prime cookstove received feedback showing that BOP consumers did not accept the stove due "to its short duration of combustion and the firewood required for combustion" (Nawilis 2011). The inventor received key insights, which led to a redesign of the stove:

> I had sold around 1,000 stoves and I got the feedback from the people about the casing, the durability of the flame . . . to be longer than 30 or 40 minutes . . . from the feedback, then we improved.
>
> (Prime Inventor)

The technology involved in the UB-03 better matched consumer preferences, particularly in relation to flame duration:

> People normally spend every time between one to two hours for cooking in average, and I tested the stove, the UB-03, it can provide flame for one until two hours. So I think it's good if we can fulfil what people want. So after that, we made the stove.
>
> (Prime Inventor)

On the basis of previous feedback on the UB-02, the inventor "developed UB-03, with a new concept of combustion" (Prime Inventor). Such continuous engagement with consumers helped the inventor to incrementally and iteratively add criteria across the stove experimentation stage: "I learnt . . . from the fact, by experiments" (Prime Inventor). However, the characteristics of the product design could have been refined during this prototype testing stage before the production of more than 1,000 UB-02 stoves.

Another example of critical feedback received after the product was used in the field was that the stove could be damaged within a few months. This feedback was crucial, as it provided direction on which materials should be used in the Prime cookstove design:

> The material that we used was material used in kerosene stove . . . that was until 2011. . . And with our partner [local NGO] . . . [a]fter the stove was received by the user . . . what the users' response, after two months, was that

the stove was damaged . . . We observed what was mostly broken. First, the firing chamber because it holds very strong heat, [and second] . . . the stove table was totally corroded, so we realised it was not good to use these materials. We [then] tended to use more expensive materials.

(Prime Inventor)

As the inventor did not yet know all the different ways consumers would use the stove, this feedback enabled him to refine design decisions on materials used in the components. This led to the design of a stove with a longer product lifespan, adapted to the specific needs of Indonesian BOP communities. When choosing the original materials for the stove, as the inventor did not know how consumers would use it, he opted for recycled materials that could later be upgraded according to their feedback: "We still did not know how the stove will be used by the people, and we still did not have any evidence that the stove will sustain until one year" (Prime Inventor).

This learning of common consumer usage proved the importance of testing prototypes out in the field, as opposed to laboratory or prototype testing with only a few consumers. An additional example supporting the importance of field-testing was the casing (the external square or round design), which reflected two key preferences related to consumer familiarity and safety. With regard to familiarity, the inventor realised that consumers did not emotionally connect with the round shape of the stove, as they were used to the square shape of kerosene and LPG stoves. Consumers also believed that that round shape was not safe, as it was not stable on the floor:

The [square shape of] kerosene stove came to us [as a feedback] . . . Instead of cylinder stove, they said they want to have square stove like kerosene stove . . . square stove is much safer compared to cylinder stove.

(Prime Inventor)

This reinforced that testing in the field would have been beneficial in ensuring the right design characteristics of the stove. Thus, on the basis of this feedback, there were two types of stoves available at this point: round and square shapes. The former BDM reflected on why some innovators had failed in entering the Indonesian BOP market and why it was important to test the stove in field during the development phase to refine some important design characteristics of the product:

Many technologies [*by technologies, he meant products*] . . . like cook stoves, were designed by developed countries, and tested in expensive and modern laboratories, and the results were always good; but the problem is, when it comes to developing countries, sometimes people just cannot accept the technology [*product*], it's very different from what they [*communities*] used to use, for example cook stove for cooking.

(Prime former BDM)

The former BDM emphasised how essential it was to test prototypes with consumers. This stemmed from his observation of significant differences between laboratory settings and the actual context of use. Thus, through being put in the context of usage, consumers increasingly accepted the Prime cookstove. The introduction of the stove later in the market testing stage showed the benefits of testing new products with consumers to evaluate whether it fit with their contextual situation and preferences.

Phase 4: commercialisation

Once the product has been developed, the final phase is to move into the commercialisation phase. Here, more active market testing is undertaken and the production is ramped up. Three final frugal innovation practices are evident within this phase, beginning with the market testing stage where frugal innovation Practice 13 focuses on local distribution through local trusted networks. Frugal innovation Practice 14 looks at promotional methods relying on product demonstration and training. The final frugal innovation practice, Practice 15, relates to the production ramp-up stage and emphasises frugal innovators' tendency to run small-scale production for longer periods. This strategy allows stronger control over production variables and quality standards.

FI Practice 13: the market testing stage involves testing distribution and promotion of the new product through existing local networks

The promotion and distribution of the Prime cookstove occurred through traditional channels as well as local distributors, government and local NGO networks. These all significantly increased consumer awareness and sales of this new cookstove. The inventor first promoted his stove through local media, which led to engagement with several distributors across Indonesia as well as the Indonesian Ministry of Research and Technology. Local NGOs also widened the distribution and selling of the Prime cookstove, benefitting from their familiarity with networks of local consumers and from their local business manners.

Looking first at local media promotion, the inventor's first marketing initiative involved the promotion of the UB-02 through media coverage, reaching Indonesian distributors and the Indonesian Ministry of Research and Technology. Ensuring later financial stability, this was also initially aimed at increasing Indonesian consumers' awareness of the cookstove:

> When I had been able to develop a prototype [of UB-02] . . . I invited some friends . . . journalists to see my stove . . . That was the factor that increased . . . our stove [to be] well-known . . . then our stove was covered by newspaper and in online version.
>
> (Prime Inventor)

As part of these traditional marketing techniques, Ditana also later engaged in newspaper advertisements to sell the Prime cookstove to local consumers and to find distribution agents: "This [newspaper advertisement] is to recruit agents here" (Prime former BDM). The inventor also sold many cookstoves through distributors who had reacted positively to his traditional promotions:

> We need users, so we use any means . . . to sell my stove . . . In the case of distributors like in Toraja, Sulawesi, they [distributors] redistribute again the stoves . . . they get 200 stoves from me, and then 50 are sent to distributors A, B and C, and so on . . . I think the distributor in Toraja has sold more than 2,000 stoves.
>
> (Prime Inventor)

In addition to the sale of stoves through Indonesian distributors, the Indonesian Ministry of Research and Technology purchased 1,000 stoves "to test the response from the people" (Prime Inventor). However, this meant a lack of direct contact with consumers, which was deemed a less appropriate approach to sell the product, as the former BDM reflected:

> At the time, [the Indonesian] Government . . . bought 1,000 cookstoves from him to be distributed somewhere in rural areas, but . . . the Government just give it away for free and people would not be trained and would not . . . complain because it's for free.
>
> (Prime former BDM)

The disadvantage of free cookstove distribution occurred when households getting appliances for free neither used them as frequently, nor valued them as much as they would have had they bought them. There was, therefore, a lack of feedback from consumers using the product. However, this channel still instigated the low-volume production and distribution of the Prime cookstove, which ensured the financial stability in the short term.

When the inventor first collaborated with this NGO in 2010, the introduction of Prime product through a local NGO alleviated complaints about the UB-02 flame duration and provided several benefits to the inventor. This local NGO had a solid local network and knowledge about consumer preferences, payment strategy and consumers' training as well as a system for collecting their feedback, which was highly beneficial to the market testing of the Prime cookstove.

Leveraging from this NGO's collaboration, the UB-03 stove was developed and reached a wider range of communities across Indonesia. Feedback was considered essential in the stove redesign and marketing strategy (Nawilis 2011; Prime Inventor). This local NGO was "one of the biggest customers of [the inventor]" (Prime former BDM), a primary source of ongoing sales and feedback.

The benefits of collaborating with this NGO's networks first provided proximity with formal and informal groups such as fishermen or sewing groups. For example, as the key target markets were communities spread across different regions of Indonesia, the NGO helped Prime overcome a lack of access to remote groups that were not always known or easily reachable:

> That's why we work with local partners; local NGOs already have an established network of people; for example, they work with farmers' groups, women groups, sewing group, fisherman groups.
>
> (Prime former BDM)

The substantial benefit of presenting the Prime cookstove to informal groups via the NGO was access to a broad network of villagers in remote communities. In fact, these remote groups gave access to an extensive number of consumers, sometimes reaching several hundred:

> Many of these local partners are organisations [or groups] [that are] formal or informal . . . On Alor island located in remote areas, there was an informal group, a savings loan group . . . A lot of villagers, almost 500 households, almost all of them were part of this savings loan group.
>
> (Prime former BDM)

With the existence of remote groups, it was evident that leveraging existing formal and informal groups was an effective approach to access more consumers in a shorter amount of time. In addition to their networks, collaborating with this local NGO also meant access to in-depth knowledge about local consumers and how to do business locally. This local, well-established NGO assisted newly established firms such as KDM or Prime with the initial steps of entering the market:

> [This local NGO] . . . knows that there are many good technologies, frugal innovations, out there, but they are not reaching the people because the companies don't have knowledge, resources, budget; so their role is . . . to connect the companies to the poor people.
>
> (Prime former BDM)

Many innovations did not reach Indonesian BOP consumers due to a knowledge gap existing between innovators and consumers. Another advantage of working with this local NGO was the testing of pricing strategy including instalment payments for BOP consumers: "They [the NGO] can develop systems that will enable them [the consumers] to buy technology like stove" (Prime former BDM). One of the main roles of the NGO was to buy stoves on behalf of a community member, such as a distributor agent, which helped consumers pay for the stove in accordance with their disposable income. Adapting payments this way let agents sell the stoves via an instalment system that maintained profit margins while reimbursing the NGO loan.

The effectiveness of this method resided in two aspects, including community empowerment, when buying the stove. Such empowerment included willingly providing feedback, as compared with when consumers received free stoves from the government:

> It empowers the community . . . they have a sense of ownership because they buy . . . the stoves. So if something goes wrong, they will talk about it: "oh this is not good; I don't know how to use it, teach me".
>
> (Prime former BDM)

This sense of ownership meant that consumers felt they had the right to comment on the stove, either asking questions or sharing what they did not like about the cookstove. The second aspect was the influence of this consumer feedback on refining the stove design. Not only did this enable the NGO to collect data across a period of time, but also there was a systematic process for collecting consumers' reactions to the product. Their approach to gathering data facilitated valuable feedback for the Prime inventor:

> [This local NGO] . . . also collected feedback and conducted impact assessments, and from it, they also came up with some [design] suggestions and feedback to Prof. Nurhuda [the inventor].
>
> (Prime former BDM)

Such feedback derived from working with this local NGO offered critical insights from consumers, which led the Prime cookstove design to receive final refinements. This stemmed from the advantages of having feedback from diverse communities in different living contexts: "It's not that easy either because feedback from one community is also different to other communities" (Prime former BDM). For example, adding legs to the base of the stove was inspired by key feedback that highlighted the different types of floor in consumers' houses. The conclusion was that a cookstove without legs was inadequate for wooden houses:

> Prof. Nurhuda came up with a . . . cylindrical [stove that] doesn't have legs. . . . Then . . . [this local NGO] tried to introduce this on Mentawai Islands but they have a style of house . . . where the floor is wood. . . . [T] hey also usually cook on the house floor . . . we only found out later when cooking for two hours . . . it burns the floor . . . it creates black marks because of the heat.
>
> (Prime former BDM)

Reaching out to diverse communities facilitated the realisation that the Prime cookstove was not suitable for all types of houses in Indonesia. This might not have become evident if the inventor had limited himself to selling the stoves in his own network, instead of collaborating with this local NGO. The collaboration with this local NGO clearly allowed Prime to capitalise on the NGO's knowledge while also minimising indirect costs for introducing the Prime cookstove across different Indonesian communities.

FI Practice 14: the market testing stage includes product demonstration and training as key promotional strategy

As highlighted earlier, engaging with local consumers was essential in promoting the Prime cookstove. In order to do this, Prime development team utilised brochures and product demonstrations, and provided extensive training. These were further extended with the establishment of Ditana's local sales team and a supportive funding for testing pricing strategy. Simple brochures were developed with instructions for operation and maintenance of the Prime cookstove. Demonstrations were also used to increase product awareness and acceptance among (potential) users and distribution agents. Local users and distribution agents' training on stove usage and maintenance was provided through the collaboration with the local NGO. Furthermore, Prime established a strong local presence with Ditana's localised sales team to leverage employee knowledge about local communities. Through Ditana, a global financial institution was recruited to support this effort, providing funding for testing pricing strategy related to the stove.

To ensure BOP consumers' understanding of the functioning of the product, brochures and other materials were developed and given when the Prime cookstove was introduced. The inventor explained this: "We accompany our stove with just one brochure, which explains how to use the stove correctly and I also put a video of a stove use on YouTube that helped very much" (Prime Inventor). The use of brochures was important for BOP consumers to remember the important operational and maintenance instructions to consider.

This promotional strategy was, however, complemented further by a more engaged approach with consumers, including product demonstration and training. The importance of stove demonstrations came from the insights by the former BDM, who had acquired years of experience in working with Indonesian BOP consumers. Direct demonstrations of how the product operated in real life increased awareness and adoption of the Prime cookstove (which Ditana implemented later), a critical strategy to achieve cookstove acceptance:

> From all the experiences I got since 2011, nobody would buy cookstove until they see how it works . . . even if they see nice pictures and explanations, they would be like "Okay, but show me how it works"; they have to see the flame . . . that's the challenge, so they [firms] have to do stove demonstrations.
>
> (Prime former BDM)

As the former BDM reflected, the consumers made purchasing decisions on the basis of what they understood and felt about the Prime cookstove functionality. In contrast with one-on-one promotional methods, demonstrating the product to a wider market was more effective:

> Thanks to [the local NGO] that has local partners, formal or informal organisations, it was much easier than going door to door as you work with these

multi-groups . . . [W]hen there are many people and groups, that's when you do stove demonstration; otherwise if one-on-one it takes time and energy to do stove demonstration, so you would never reach sales target.

(Prime former BDM)

Demonstrations were, therefore, a key method in the marketing strategy of Prime to create wider awareness and to increase the adoption rate of the Prime cookstove among Indonesian BOP communities. Demonstrations were also crucial to ensure local consumers appropriately perceived the value proposition of the Prime cookstove. Moreover, several promotional benefits stemmed from the collaboration with the local NGO. They included educational training for targeted consumers, such as how to use and maintain the product. The former BDM discussed this further, stating:

They [the NGO] not only sell the product, they give consignment [see note⁴] . . . and training to women to train the customers as well. They are not only doing the training on how to use it, but also how to maintain the stoves.

(Prime former BDM)

The local NGO's training ensured agents and other targeted consumers knew how to use and look after the product, which could ensure they understood all the advantages of the product (Napitupulu 2014). This also minimised potential misuse of the stove, such as breaking the combustion chamber or not maintaining the stove correctly, which could affect product durability. The former BDM, who initially worked with this local NGO, detailed how this training led to better usage of the Prime cookstove:

It was successful, many people after up to two years still use the stove. That's because the local NGO provided training, training and training; they train the salesperson, the users, so they still could use the stove.

(Prime former BDM)

Using product training as a promotional and selling technique was a vital part of the market testing stage and is still essential, as the cookstove requires ongoing behavioural change (e.g. top-loading fuel). Prime clearly benefitted from working at the local level, optimising its local presence and pushing its marketing strategy.

Further effort to develop a strong local presence involved Prime creating its own distribution channel, Ditana. Ditana stemmed from the creation of a local team and the integration of local business methods including distribution, promotion and advertising methods adapted to the Indonesian context. This was reinforced through direct contact with consumers through local sales teams in the Central Java region, as well as in East Nusa Tenggara and North Sumatra.

The creation of these local teams under the responsibility of the former BDM empowered Ditana to build a strong distribution and promotion strategy around the Prime cookstove in Indonesia. In a discussion with the former BDM, it was made clear that integrating local staff in Ditana's decision-making and promotional works was critical in refining the approach to reach local markets:

> Usually when we want to decide [about promotion] . . . we ask our local staffs because they are from there . . . "What do you think? Which one makes you want to buy more? Is this important? . . . Okay, come back tomorrow with any ideas, any thoughts".
>
> (Prime former BDM)

The potential for local staff to be involved in such decisions revealed the flexibility of the local subsidiary in adapting its marketing approach. Corresponding advantages included the ability for the local sale teams, with relevant knowledge of the local environment, to work faster and more inclusively and more independently from the local NGO.

Finally, independence also increased from the assistance from a global financial institution, which provided financial support for the distribution and promotion of stoves in some strategic remote areas throughout Indonesia. This support enabled the testing of pricing strategy, such as through payment instalments (Bolton 2014). This responded to some of the problems encountered with consumers who purchased the stove on the basis of seven separate instalment payments, which was not a successful pricing strategy. This resulted in the giving away of many stoves, which were never fully paid for by consumers. It showed that market testing involved the use of important resources (e.g. time and financial investment), which was more feasible via the support of this global financial institution as well as the local NGO.

FI Practice 15: the production ramp-up stage factors in low-volume production timelines for longer periods, which benefit intensive learning, training and quality standards

As a final key practice, the production ramp-up was much smaller scale for the first five years. This allowed tighter control on quality standards, employee training and flexibility in decision-making. The choice to start with a small local factory and small-scale production was based on the inventor's early decision to re-use a local manufacturing site. Moving to bigger production facilities several years after, it enabled production of the Prime cookstove via cost-effective and systematic manufacturing and assembly processes. Slowing down the upscale process guaranteed that strict quality standards were enforced via QA/QC across both the small factory and the larger manufacturer as well as via training of employees. Prime was also able to experience gradual learning by allowing flexibility across the production processes during production ramp-up stage, enhancing faster decision-making.

Looking first at the choice to start with a small local factory, the inventor began operations through a small-scale production in a local 'home' factory, which previously produced kerosene stoves. The inventor leveraged existing machinery, know-how and labour by adapting to his manufacturing and assembling needs in accordance with his intended sales to the Indonesian Government and the local NGO partner. The former BDM explained the advantages of using this smaller factory:

> He [the inventor] used a small . . . "home industry factory" in Malang . . . [he] used one of them to produce his stoves, because they know how to do, they have equipment and machineries.
>
> (Prime former BDM)

The inventor manufactured at this small scale, leveraging former kerosene stove factory resources. The capacity of this small-scale factory was sufficient in meeting the initial demand and in delivering low-cost production: "I started to manufacture it with a little bigger amount, and then started to sell it" (Prime Inventor). This started with small-scale sales to consumers with: "200 to 500 units sold per year . . . in a lot of different areas, but it stays small scale" (Prime former BDM).

Five years later, Prime's goal was to scale-up its production capacities through collaborating with a larger local production partner. The major differences between the two production facilities were in relation to the capacity of the machinery as well as the experts using them. The small factory did not have the capacity to support business development (both nationally and internationally): "This was 'home industry', local manufacturing, so it has very limited resources" (Prime former BDM).

Some of the local factory's processes involved in production, such as at the production site in Malang, were still manual: "In Malang, we'd register each product per unit manually" (Prime Logistics Manager). While the local home factory favoured local employment, Prime's intention to scale-up stemmed from their goal for larger, more effective and more standardised manufacturing in accordance with the growing consumer demand for the Prime cookstove.

The advantages of a larger production partner at this time included bigger and more cost-effective capacities with more modern and faster equipment, such as certain automated machineries using more controlled and systematic methods: "The difference is only that we have machines that Malang [factory] doesn't have . . . here, we also have experiences in developing kerosene stoves and LPG stoves" (Prime Production Manager). Furthermore, the production partner used techniques that did not depend on highly expensive tools:

> You know, a modern bigger factory perhaps has software, but we don't have it here because it's too expensive, so we do trial-and-error . . . We use the experience of our people.
>
> (Prime Production Manager)

Highly experienced staff also enabled the production partner to compensate for the absence of sophisticated tools such as software by solving problems through a trial-and-error approach. Although it often took longer to address production problems with trial-and-error, the experience, expertise and know-how acquired by these staff without any computer software allowed learning and mastering of stove manufacturing while maintaining affordable production cost for Prime.

Looking at quality standards, strict QA/QC was implemented in both the small local factory and the newer production partner's facilities. At the initial factory in Malang (where the inventor lived), one of the benefits obtained was the ability to closely monitor production processes and output. The inventor explained how this local monitoring enabled thorough QA/QC throughout the production process:

> We want to make sure that the [stoves] we sent are perfect, according to my concept. Amongst 1,000 stoves that we sent, normally there is one or two that are not very well. The criteria, for example . . . [i]f the welding is not good, then we have to solve it. We have to put attention on . . . such small criteria.
>
> (Prime Inventor)

It is evident here that the inventor placed significant importance on QC, including finer detail like welding. His physical presence at the production site allowed greater supervision and tighter control over the product detail flaws. Such attention to detail remained when Prime established a warehouse in Sidoarjo in Eastern Java and initiated the collaboration with the production partner's bigger production facility. At the time of the interview, Prime was in the process of outsourcing the production. To ensure strict QA/QC was established, Prime's development team in Sidoarjo first learnt via manual assembly and disassembly and also used this to control the production partner's trialled outputs:

> From Malang to here [in Sidoarjo], there were many learning steps including . . . for quality control, we opened and unscrewed it [the stove] manually for quality control, and now we have machines to make sure about quality control.
>
> (Prime Logistics Manager)

By involving the local staff at the warehouse in such disassembly and assembly processes, their understanding of QA/QC standards became more refined. Although the production partner had more automated machinery, which generally allows stricter QA/QC, Prime's development team still disassembled and re-assembled the production partner's outputs. Auditing QC on the trial samples included ensuring that various product aspects were at high-quality standards:

That's why we must reject [the production output] even if they [the production partner] did the quality control [there]. We must do it again with the same steps as what they [production partner] did.

(Prime Logistics Manager)

As part of its auditing process, Prime took the time required for QC during this production ramp-up stage, as strict QC was a priority in the development of the Prime cookstove. This was clearly confirmed by Prime's strict QC on the production partner:

We shall have 25 units of sample [from the production partner], and we will check everything. If everything is okay, then we will make an order for the first 500 units and then check it again. The first 500 need to be checked also by us, and then we'll continue with them for regular order at a local factory.

(Prime Logistics Manager)

This double-checking on the product manufactured and assembled by the production partner clearly revealed strict QC implementation over the Prime cookstove. Furthermore, to ensure quality standards, Prime supported training of employees including with its production partner. Slowing down the scale-up process gave the development team time to learn and implement strict QA/QC with the production partner: "That's why we chose to do it step by step. We didn't know their human resources and the source of the machinery [of the production partner]" (Prime Logistics Manager). The priority during this stage was to go 'step by step', to assess and ensure that the production outputs were up to Prime's quality standards, such as QC and training.

Prime was willing to provide training to local employees, as operators generally lacked comprehensive understanding of the Prime cookstove: "It's much easier for them to understand if I show something, rather than only read and explain about our program" (Prime Logistics Manager). By working closely with Prime's partners, as well as with the production partner's workers, the integration of this training enabled tighter control over the quality standards, including the end product (QC). It also created a functional team that was knowledgeable and experienced. Prime's partner NGO agreed that the stoves developed by Prime "are a clear market leader in terms of fuel efficiency, portability, value for money, and quality assurance" (Primestoves 2017b). The Prime cookstove has indeed also showed its quality attributes on the basis of consumer acceptance.

In addition, allowing time for ongoing learning has also enabled flexibility in the production processes to better understand all the variables that could affect the product quality. Changing the production from the 'home' factory in Malang to the new location in Surabaya allowed for gradual learning and adaption to product modifications and production changes with the production partner. The production manager supported this gradual learning approach of going "step by step. After we understand the steps, it's easier and faster for the next improvement" (Prime Production Manager).

Working locally and in a close relationship with the production partner allowed for product modifications, which was helpful for Prime, as the design of the product was more likely to endure slight transformations from testing:

> They [production partner] are very open to discussions when we need to change some design. They have the capacity to change the dies [stamping tools], and then also price, they are still in line with our budget.
>
> (Prime Logistics Manager)

The proximity to their production partner also simplified decision-making during this production ramp-up stage and enabled flexibility over production changes. In addition, the logistics manager was located close to the production partner (around 5km from Prime warehouse to the factory in Sidoarjo), which enhanced the local partnership, including more flexibility, and faster and more effective decision-making.

Prime Cookstoves summary

In summary, the majority of the NPDP frugal innovation practices was identified, clarified and exemplified by Prime's NPDP management. These observations confirm that this book's NPDP framework for frugal innovation is relevant to Indonesian start-ups dealing with Indonesian BOP consumers' problems. An overview of the four NPDP phases discussed earlier are summarised in Table 4.2.

Table 4.2 Prime NPDP summary

NPDP stages	Prime's NPDP management
Opportunity and idea discovery	*FI Practice 1: The opportunity and idea discovery stage has a market-pull approach that is limited within the scope of BOP market constraints.* ■ **Market-pull:** Sought to address sustainability problems encountered by Indonesian BOP consumers ■ **BOP constraints:** Aware of the lack of local technological innovations *FI Practice 2: The tools and techniques of the opportunity and idea discovery stage allow external idea sources.* ■ **External sources such as querying problems with existing product:** Indonesian Government call to action highlighted problems with existing LPG stoves including recurring explosions
Opportunity and idea screening	*FI Practice 3: The opportunity and idea screening stage focuses on market information, in particular appraisals of BOP consumers' unmet needs.*

NPDP stages	Prime's NPDP management
	■ **Consumer safety:** Emergency of situation due to LPG stove explosions ■ **Consumer lack of alternative solutions:** Inaccessible and unaffordable LPG fuel for rural BOP consumers and toxic kerosene stoves ■ **Consumer unaffordability for future cooking devices:** Unsustainable government's LPG subsidies leading to potential future government expenditure decrease *FI Practice 4: The opportunity and idea screening stage focuses on business information linked with internal and external capabilities.* ■ **Internal expertise:** Personal knowledge and experience in basic physics and previous NPD ■ **External available resources:** Awareness of local small technical workspaces for rapid and cheap R&D on the stove project + Sought financial viability of the NPD project due to limited budget
Market study	*FI Practice 5: The market study stage has a focus on BOP consumer information related to affordability, additional needs and product usage context.* ■ **Meaning of affordability:** Consideration of affordability beyond the product price, including of cost-effectiveness when using the stove (e.g. via high efficiency of biomass fuel and charcoal re-use for agricultural purpose) ■ **Product usage context:** Fuel required to be accessible for BOP consumers and cost-effective in its production ■ **Additional needs**: Did not consider aesthetic needs, though it was later recognised as an important BOP consumers' need *FI Practice 6: The tools and techniques of the market study stage focus on a firm's immersion with targeted consumers for deeper insights.* ■ **No formal tools and techniques** ■ **Informal involvement with consumers:** Informal observation and living locally ■ **Assess competitors' failure** + No formal tools and techniques due to lack of funding and NPDP guidance
Technical study	*FI Practice 7: The technical study stage focuses on primary product functionality and business model specifications.* ■ **Primary product functionality:** – Focus on core performance linked to a part of the cooking process – Smoke efficiency including flame stability and smoke emission (exclusive of aesthetic needs) ■ **Business model specifications:** Ensured accessible and affordable fuel supply based on naturally abundant resources

(*Continued*)

Table 4.2 (Continued)

NPDP stages	Prime's NPDP management
	FI Practice 8: The tools and techniques of the technical study stage involve seeking basic technological principles and/or architecture and components from existing products. ■ **Basic technology:** Sought basic science principles in using gasification technology and natural airflow + **Benefits:** Led to simpler, more practical, more efficient and more accepted product; better control over variables
Concept evaluation	*FI Practice 9: The tools and techniques of the concept evaluation stage integrate a set of criteria and/or simple physical version to test concept acceptance.* ■ **No concept testing:** Unsuccessful stove received negative feedback from BOP consumers, which led to reverting to the technical study stage to modify the technology of the second prototype (UB-02) + Possibly due to restrained budget
Product design stage	*FI Practice 10: The product design stage prioritises local outsourcing weighted off with costs and performance.* ■ **Prioritised local resources:** Adapting the Prime cookstove to local factories (available equipment and labour, easy cross-communication), local components (standardised) and use of local materials + **Benefits:** Cost-effective ■ **Performance-cost ratio:** Change from recycled materials to more expensive stainless components for some parts of the stove + **Benefits:** Time-efficient decision-making + **Coping with costs increase:** Analysis of components requiring stainless steel and not requiring stainless steel *FI Practice 11: The tools and techniques of the product design stage include DfX techniques specifically aimed at frugal design strategies.* ■ No formal DfX techniques ■ **Pattern of strategic design (design for easy maintenance):** – Designed combustion chamber component to be removable (ease of maintenance) allowing maintenance/repair in case of damage – Allowing easy cleaning and recovery of charcoal ash
Prototype testing	*FI Practice 12: The tools and techniques of the prototype testing stage include early field-testing.* ■ **No formal testing:** Shared few working models with friends and family ■ **Failure to field-test:** Sold more than 1,000 stoves which led to critical changes in the Prime cookstove; early field-testing could have enabled these changes earlier before further sale + Required quick ROI to support further R&D

NPDP stages	Prime's NPDP management

Market testing	*FI Practice 13: The market testing stage involves testing distribution and promotion of the new product through existing local networks.*
	
	■ **Traditional promotion:** Newspaper to consumers and agents of distribution; social media
	■ **Locally trusted network:** Partnership with Indonesian Ministry of Research and Technology and a local NGO to reach high number of consumers
	+ **Benefits:** Access to knowledge about how to do business locally; testing of marketing strategy in relation to distribution, sales and promotion; lower risks and costs of investment
	+ **Benefits of selling to NGOs:** Allowed to connect Prime to diverse communities of consumers and faster
	
	FI Practice 14: The market testing stage includes product demonstration and training as key promotional strategy.
	
	■ **Product demonstration:** Via the local NGO partner as well as via establishing a local sale team for scale up (Ditana)
	+ **Benefits:** BOP consumers' appropriate perception of the stove's value proposition and brand
	■ **Product training:**
	  – Extensive training with local distribution agents and local users to avoid misuse and educate how to maintain the stoves
	  – Implementation of Ditana's local sale teams with great knowledge of local communities
	+ As pricing strategy via instalments was risky, searching for funding assistance (e.g. global financial institution) was critically helpful

Production ramp-up	*FI Practice 15: The production ramp-up stage factors in low-volume production timelines for longer periods, which benefits quality standards such as QA/QC and workforce training.*
	
	■ **Low-volume for longer periods:**
	  – Small-scale production for 5 years (2010–2015) adapted to consumer demand as well to implement strict QC
	  – Outsourced via re-using equipment, local labour and know-how of a small local factory
	  – Manual assembling process
	  – Reduction of time-to-market and production costs
	■ **Quality standards:** Strict QA/QC enforced at small factory via local supervision and control on product details (e.g. welding) and at production partner's site, via local supervision and double QC via disassembly/reassembly
	+ Faster and more-effective decision-making
	+ Flexibility for ongoing learning, product and production modifications

Notes

1 Hereafter, this study refers to the 'Prime fuelwood cookstove' as the 'Prime cookstove'.
2 As detailed in frugal innovation Practice 9 and Practice 12.
3 The carbon monoxide and particulate matter in the smoke may contribute to pulmonary diseases.
4 The action of "sending stoves to local partners with an agreement that payment will occur as sales start picking up" (Fulland 2017, p. 27).

References

Afrida, N 2010, 'Recall pressure mounts as more injured in LPG explosions', *The Jakarta Post*, viewed 4 December 2016, <www.thejakartapost.com/news/2010/07/03/recall-pressure-mounts-more-injured-lpg-explosions.html>.
Bolton, S 2014, *Starting up clean cookstove sales in North Sumatra*, viewed 16 January 2018, <https://kopernik.info/update/starting-up-clean-cookstove-sales-in-north-sumatra>.
Differ 2015, *What we do*, viewed 5 January 2018, <www.differgroup.com/about/>.
Ditana Group 2016, *Ditana energy solutions*, viewed 8 September 2016, <www.ditanagroup.com/en/>.
Fulland, C 2016, *Partner spotlight: Prime cookstoves*, viewed 15 November 2017, <http://cleancookstoves.org/about/news/07-20-2016-partner-spotlight-prime-cookstoves.html>.
Fulland, C 2017, 'Enablers to cookstoves: Enabling distributor financing for a demand-driven market for clean cookstoves', *Boiling Point*, no. 69, pp. 26–29.
IEA 2015, *Energy and climate change*, International Energy Agency, viewed 5 October 2017, <www.iea.org/publications/freepublications/publication/WEO2015SpecialReportonEnergyandClimateChange.pdf>.
Irawati, D 2011, *Kemandirian Energi Lewat Kompor/Energy independence through stove*, viewed 18 January 2018, <http://health.kompas.com/read/2011/11/01/02360027/kemandirian.energi.lewat.kompor>.
The Jakarta Post 2015, *World-class Indonesian stove lost in local market due to subsidy*, viewed 15 January 2018, <www.thejakartapost.com/news/2015/10/23/world-class-indonesian-stove-lost-local-market-due-subsidy.html>.
Napitupulu, M 2014, *Life lessons from a clean cookstove agent*, viewed 18 January 2018, <https://kopernik.info/update/life-lessons-from-a-clean-cookstove-agent>.
Nawilis, C 2011, *Muhammad Nurhuda, biomass stove UB.03–1*, viewed 18 January 2018, <https://kopernik.info/update/muhammad-nurhuda-biomass-stove-ub03-1>.
Nurhuda, M 2012, *Biomass stoves from Indonesia*, viewed 2 February 2018, <http://stoves.bioenergylists.org/taxonomy/term/1931>.
Pertamina & WLPGA 2015, *Kerosene to LP gas conversion programme in Indonesia: A case study of domestic energy*, viewed 7 February 2018, <www.wlpga.org/wp-content/uploads/2015/09/kerosene-to-lp-gas-conversion-programme-in-indonesia.pdf>.
Primestoves 2017a, *Meet our teams – Prof. Dr. M. Nurhuda*, viewed 5 November 2017, <www.primestoves.com/>.
Primestoves 2017b, *Prime Cookstoves, highly efficient, ultra clean biomass cookstoves: Product specifications*, viewed 10 November 2018, <www.primestoves.com/img/docs/product%20spec%20sheet_2.2_low.pdf>.

Saloop, T, Krishnan, RG, Mohan, VM, Thomas, I & Kumar, S 2016, 'A study on the biomass cook stoves used in Kerala and to develop a theoretical design of T-Lud natural draft gasifier stove as an option for Kerala's cooking culture', *International Journal of Innovative Research and Development*, vol. 5, no. 6.

WHO 2018, *Health and sustainable development – cleaner cookstoves*, viewed 21 July 2018, <www.who.int/sustainable-development/housing/strategies/cleaner-cook stoves/en/>.

World Bank 2014a, *Cleaner cook stoves for a healthier Indonesia*, viewed 28 April 2018, <www.worldbank.org/en/news/feature/2014/11/03/cleaner-cook-stoves-for-a-healthier-indonesia>.

World Bank 2014b, *Indonesia: Government will provide universal access to clean cooking practices*, viewed 21 July 2018, <www.worldbank.org/en/news/press-release/2014/08/14/indonesia-government-will-provide-universal-access-to-clean-cooking-practices>.

5 Tirta Indonesia Mandiri Foundation

Drinking with frugal innovation

Introduction

The case study in this chapter, Tirta Indonesia Mandiri Foundation (Tirta), addresses another pressing world issue related to the 6th United Nations' Sustainable Development Goal: providing worldwide access to safe drinking water. Exploring Tirta's NPDP sheds light on the development of a water filter device created for this challenge and more specifically for Indonesian BOP consumers. This type of product is especially needed, with the World Health Organization (WHO) showing that in 2015, safe basic water services such as piped water on premises were available only to 22 per cent of the world population (WHO/UNICEF 2015). Some three in ten people, or 2.1 billion people do not have access to a water free of contamination and "readily available . . . at home" (WHO/UNICEF 2017).

Without this basic water service, 263 million people worldwide require more than 30 minutes outside their home to fetch water from safe sources and 159 million still drink untreated water from wells or other unsafe sources (WHO/ UNICEF 2017). Almost two million people worldwide drink water that is soiled with faeces (Bain et al. 2014), a problem globally known as causing deadly diseases such as diarrhoea, typhoid and polio. According to the WHO, *half a million people die from diarrhoea each year* due to contaminated water (WHO 2018).

With a population of nearly 264 million (World Bank 2017), Indonesia has some 27 million people who are unable to access basic water services (WHO/ UNICEF Joint Monitoring Programme for Water Supply and Sanitation 2017). Water quality was assessed by a joint Government and UNICEF program in the special region of Yogyakarta. Results showed that "2 out of 3 drinking water samples [were] contaminated with faecal bacteria" (UNICEF 2014). This is not surprising, as 150,000 children who are 5 years old or younger die each year in Indonesia due to diseases caused by unsafe water and bad sanitation (UNICEF 2014).

Despite the urgency of this problem, millions of low-income Indonesian people cannot afford better water services (Water.org 2018). Without even considering the size and scope of the problem in Indonesia, this problem most broadly opens up huge opportunities for frugal innovators worldwide to develop NPD for this type of global challenge. Tirta is a not-for-profit organisation that has engaged with developing such NPD, in particular for providing continuous access to clean drinking water for low-income consumers in Indonesia. In this endeavour, Tirta has developed the Tirta CupuManik (TCM) water filter, an NPD tailored to the Indonesian BOP consumers, providing access to clean drinking water across the diverse Indonesian islands.

This chapter presents an overview of how Tirta managed the NPDP of TCM water filter. It will first present Tirta's background and then the TCM NPD project, setting the broader context for this case study. Subsequently, each NPDP phase and stage will be explored for the development of the TCM water filter. This will provide insights into the frugal innovation practices that have been implemented by Tirta as part of this NPD project.

Tirta Indonesia Mandiri Foundation overview

Founded in 2009, Tirta is a not-for-profit organisation that manufactures afford-able household ceramic water filters, including the TCM water filter. These ceramic' filters provide drinkable water from almost any sources such as piped water, wells or swamped water. Tirta was established from a partnership of seven founders: Risyana Sukarma, Alizar Anwar, Hening Darpito, Rizafsyah Taufik, (the late) Christina Budhi Setyani, Sugiono Sugiri and Poppy Wijaya. The purpose of the Foundation's product was to ensure Indonesian BOP consumers meet their basic water needs, in particular helping urban and rural low-income consumers avoiding fatal water borne diseases (tcm-filter 2018b). Today, Tirta has three permanent employees, which can increase in accordance with the TCM water filter's demand (from three to seven employees).

The inventor[1] of the TCM water filter (and CEO of the Foundation) gradu-ated from the Bandung Institute of Technology (Bandung, Indonesia) in 1974 and the IHE Delft Institute for Water Education (Delft, The Netherlands) in 1980. After taking an early retirement as a government official, the inventor and chair of the Foundation, Risyana Sukarma, worked for the World Bank address-ing Water Sanitation and Hygiene (WASH) problems in Indonesia.

Since his retirement from the World Bank in 2007, Sukarma did various con-sulting jobs for water and sanitation issues in Indonesia and started undertaking research with the aim of addressing water issues in Indonesia. Later, he focused on the development of new products under the Foundation. Being intimately aware of water problems in Indonesia through his entire career, he chose the name for his not-for-profit business to stand for: "Tirta is water. Cupu is recep-tacle. Manik means treasure. So it's like 'water treasure in a receptacle'" (Tirta Inventor).

The next section provides details about Tirta's NPD project, elaborating on the key characteristics of the TCM water filter and in particular those related to its frugal characteristics.

Project overview: TCM water filter

The TCM water filter is a ceramic pot-type water treatment providing drinkable water at home; producing 99.88 per cent bacteria-free water. While it can also filter metal particles like manganese and iron to some extent, the TCM water filter cannot filter salty water, water with heavy metals or severely polluted water before the water has undergone other forms of treatment.

The TCM water filter consists of a ceramic filter pot and a plastic container/receptacle,[2] which can come in three different shapes (as shown in Figure 5.1) as well as in different colours (upon request). Customisable from three available options, BOP consumers can buy a standard version (the simplest and cheapest), the Lion Star brand or the Green Leaf brands. These three options have a ceramic pot inside the container, which is made out of clay and combustible materials (such as rice husks). The pot is coated with silver nitrate to eliminate bacteria and viruses, forming the micro-pores engendering the filtration of water. All options come with a tap and a lid.

Table 5.1 provides a more detailed breakdown on the key characteristics of the TCM water filter and its related frugal attributes.

With this broader understanding of the background on Tirta and the TCM water filter, the following sections introduce the results from the case study on the development of the TCM water filter structured around the four NPDP phases and the associated frugal innovation practices.

Phase 1: the fuzzy front end for frugal innovation

As discussed in Chapter 3, the fuzzy front end phase instigates the firms' NPDP with the emergence and selection of new product ideas and opportunities. With

Figure 5.1 Simple and cheapest TCM water filter (left); TCM Lion Star water filter (middle); and TCM Green Leaf water filter (right)

Credit: Risyana Sukarma

Table 5.1 Frugal characteristics of the TCM water filter

Frugal characteristics	Description
Market	Indonesian urban and rural low-income markets
Affordability	20–50 USD
Core functionality	– Household water treatment – Filter out 99.88% of bacteria and some metals – Filtration rate between 1.5L and 3.5L/hours; average flow rate per day: 10–35L customer-tailored product (colour and brand of the container)
Durability	– Approximately 2 to 3 years' lifetime depending on water sources – Easy maintenance, using water and scrub – Replaceable ceramic pot and tap
Usability	– No electricity required: self-sufficient (water sits by itself) – Portable: 3.5kg (weight) – Almost every source of water (except saline water, heavily polluted water and water heavy metals) – Dirty water capacity: 9L – Clean water storage capacity: approximately 6L

regard to frugal innovation, four key frugal innovation practices have emerged from the literature, which highlight the NPDP preferences of frugal innovators across the two key stages of the fuzzy front end phase, the discovery and screening of opportunities and ideas.

The two first frugal innovation practices emphasise the importance to take a market-pull approach limited by BOP constraints during the discovery stage, with techniques stimulating the development teams' ideas based upon external sources of inspiration. The frugal innovation Practices 3 and 4 focus on criteria prioritised by frugal innovators during the screening stage, including those linked to BOP consumers' unmet needs and internal and external business capabilities.

FI Practice 1: frugal innovators will have a market-pull approach that is limited within the scope of the BOP market constraints

The development of the TCM water filter emerged from the inventor's knowledge of the limitations within the Indonesian water infrastructure for BOP consumers and the associated societal problems. This is indicative of a market-pull approach being adopted by the inventor. The first distinct limitation resided within the Indonesian water utilities, not often well connected to BOP consumers' home premises, considerably reducing their access to clean water. Second, and highlighting the inventor's market-pull approach, was the identification of market problems with the water supply across various regional areas in Indonesia, leaving people with expensive, unhealthy and unsustainable options to access water.

First of all, the inventor had spent a career employed in the public sector working with "water sanitation" (Tirta Inventor) issues in Indonesia and was well aware of the water constraints experienced by the local consumers. The low level of performance of many water facilities across the main islands of Indonesia prevented access to clean, drinkable water for a wider part of the Indonesian population. The inventor reflected on the extent to which poor water quality and access occurred across Indonesia:

> As you know, Indonesia is still having problems with water supply . . . We have still limited access to water from utility. Most people still rely on field sources like wells and especially in Jakarta, [there is] 50 to 60% . . . pipes of water supply . . . As well as other cities, so in total, there is 50%, even less [people] than that [who are not supplied].
>
> (Tirta Inventor)

Supporting the inventor's data, a report in 2013 conducted on households in Daerah Khusus Ibukota (DKI) Jakarta Metropolitan area (the Special Capital Region which consists of Jakarta and five surrounding regencies) illustrated that more than 40 per cent of Jakarta had a problem with the quality of the water supplied (Asian Development Bank 2016). This report emphasised that water quality problems could also occur even through water utilities.

In this report, clean water was defined as the access of 'improved water',[3] which included piped water, tap, bottled water, tube well, dug well and rainwater tank (WHO/UNICEF 2017). In contrast, 'unimproved' water is defined as water that can be sourced from unprotected dug wells and tank trucks (WHO/ UNICEF 2017). By identifying important constraints in the Indonesian water supply quality, the inventor looked further at problems from the market level. It became quickly apparent to the inventor these market constraints were the main impediments leading to poor access to clean water for the Indonesian population.

A second aspect highlighted the market-pull approach adopted by the inventor. There was a distinct focus on identifying gaps existing at the Indonesian market level, including tackling the lack of existing solutions to accessing clean water. This unaddressed market problem went beyond the limited access to clean water: while most of the urban population in Indonesia did not have access to clean water, the rural population did not necessarily have access to neither clean nor unclean water at all.

With this in mind, the inventor dedicated his efforts towards providing solutions for Indonesian people who had scarce access to clean water:

> After I retired, I was thinking I should do something else, trying to do some product that can fill the gap. Some of the people in the villages . . . relying on irrigation water . . . that cannot be drank directly . . . it is polluted but there is some sort of small treatments, simple treatments to make the water become potable. People . . . in urban areas had problems because they don't have enough choice for water.
>
> (Tirta Inventor)

The inventor was clear about these two problems – the rural population not having easy access to water and the urban population having access to water with limited treatment options. These underlying problems with water supply for both rural and urban areas clearly triggered the inventor to investigate solutions to this water access problem, reinforcing the idea that water supply and water quality was a problem to be addressed.

FI Practice 2: the tools and techniques of the opportunity and idea discovery stage allow external idea sources

As part of the opportunity and idea discovery, the inventor, through his local presence and his field of work in water sanitation, noticed BOP consumers' lack of access to clean drinking water. He had continued to be involved with his previous work after retiring, which reinforced his understanding of the ongoing problems. While his local knowledge was largely tied to having lived and worked in Jakarta, he also did extensive fieldwork in both rural and urban locations. This really supported his further investigation of a possible new product opportunity in this space.

Looking first at the fact that the inventor lived and worked in Indonesia, including working in the water sanitation field, this had a critical role in framing the identification of local problems with water utilities and access to clean water. With his local presence in Jakarta, he could personally observe people encountering problems with water access and water quality, including himself.

The inventor had been a governmental official for the Ministry of Public Works "for 19 years . . . [addressing] human settlement (housing, building, water sanitation, drainage, urban housing)" (Tirta Inventor). As the inventor was "in charge of reviewing the water supply facilities in the country and all the cities" (Tirta Inventor), he was intimately aware of water problems in Indonesia, and in particular with the quality and access of water for both urban and rural populations.

After the inventor retired, he remained involved part-time in water issues through his work outside the government, as he reflects: "I retired earlier to work for the World Bank" (Tirta Inventor). The inventor's observation of current problems with existing water infrastructure was leveraged from examining the environment in which he was embedded. These insights led his focus to narrow down on finding solutions to Indonesian water supply issues.

FI Practice 3: the opportunity and idea screening stage focuses on market information, in particular appraisals of BOP consumers' unmet needs

Before moving forward on the water filter idea, the inventor examined further market information related to how three types of 'improved water' sources did not meet the needs of low-income consumers. This includes piped water, bottled water and refilled water, which the inventor further investigated looking specifically at their high prices, low-quality levels and difficult access for Indonesian consumers. These particular unmet needs triggered the inventor in looking further into a more appropriate water treatment device.

The inventor first looked at how existing products were not meeting market needs and addressing water access problem, with a specific focus on three key products: piped water, bottled water and refilled water. The first, piped water, the inventor emphasised as not being able to produce good quality water. According to the inventor, this was due to being re-contaminated from deteriorated pipe conditions and leading to a situation where it potentially required further treatment before being fit for consumption and use. Piped water was further limited, because it was not a common type of water source across all of Indonesia, with distinct limitations in the existing infrastructure.

The two other ways to access water in Indonesia referred to as 'improved' source of water are bottled water (small bottles, both premium and low-cost brands) and refilled water (large containers being refilled at refilling water stations). However, the inventor believed that both of these options were too expensive for low-income consumers, limiting their potential options to piped water, which, in itself, was also severely constrained through infrastructure problems. The extent of this issue is evident, with approximately 50 million low-income consumers in Indonesia not having access to 'improved' sources and piped water, according to the inventor and the Asian Development Bank (2016).

The inventor detailed this further on his reflections on available solutions for water supply and highlighted the key issues around the low quality and high prices of these options:

> In urban [areas], there is still a problem . . . it's very polluted and many of the piped water are not always able to produce good quality water. So all the people start to buy . . . bottle of water, but bottled water is very expensive, especially the one with brands. People have another choice, like . . . refilled water. . . . This is also expensive but of course they don't buy it in bulk but they buy by the bottle. In bottle, you don't feel that it is expensive. It's like 1,000 IDR (0.069 USD, 9 August 2018) per refilled bottle, so no problem. If you accumulate per month, the expenses become very high. Compared with piped water for example the price is 6,000 IDR (0.41 USD, 9 August 2018) for cubic meter (for 1,000L) and water bottle is 4,000 IDR for 1L (0.27 USD, 9 August 2018).
>
> (Tirta Inventor)

The inability to build trusted piped water sources often led Indonesian people to use bottled water and, as one of the only options to access clean water, bottled water was expensive. This created real barriers for BOP consumers within Indonesia. The possibility to use refilled water had similar affordability issues for BOP consumers, pushing them to purchase new water bottles and incurring the cost if they wished to have clean water.

The issues with price, accessibility and water quality all influenced the inventor towards creating an inexpensive and accessible option for low-income consumers within Indonesia:

Based on that fact, I was thinking of producing something that can be useful to people, and not very expensive, they can afford it and it can help them in accessing water much easier, so that's how I started.

(Tirta Inventor)

The investigation of these unmet needs influenced the inventor to develop a more affordable and easier way to access better quality water than the current available options. In line with this, the inventor emphasised the importance of helping with market problems and that this was not only around a profit-oriented goal: "It's not only because we are trying to get some profit, we are here to recover the cost of course, but also we want to help people" (Tirta Inventor). It was clear that before moving forward with the TCM water filter, market information was more important than financial information at this NPDP stage.

FI Practice 4: the opportunity and idea screening stage focuses on business information linked with internal and external capabilities

A key basis in driving forward the opportunity and idea screening stage was the personal knowledge of the inventor in water and sanitation. At the early stages of exploring solutions, the inventor did not seek collaboration with external partners. The main reason was because the TCM project was a side project and he did not want to utilise the local networks he had acquired throughout the years of working with the Government. Second, the personal knowledge and background of the inventor positively affected his decision to move forward with the TCM, in particular with his water education diploma from IHE Delft, in the Netherlands.

Looking first at the lack of engagement with external sources, the inventor made it clear that the TCM project emerged as a side project to his main work, which was the underlying reason for not seeking external collaboration. The inventor expressed throughout the interview that he did not initially invest 100 per cent of his time on this project; it was more of a 'hobby': "Out of my hobby at home, I started to do some research and trials-and-error on this physical product" (Tirta Inventor). The inventor did not seem interested in formally approaching external partners as part of screening process for the TCM project.

Another reason for not reaching out for external collaboration was his personal values and beliefs that actually led him to avoid utilising his personal network throughout the whole TCM development. It appeared that asking for help from colleagues was not perceived as something positive for the inventor:

Sometimes they [the Government department with whom he used to work] approach me, they try to buy [his product] . . . but I don't want to try because they are my ex-colleagues so I don't want to use this network.

(Tirta Inventor)

The inventor did not want, or see, the necessity to ask his former colleagues for collaboration, as the TCM project was a side project. This limited the inventor's business capabilities at the start of the TCM project.

Second, the inventor had a personal background and knowledge about water and sanitation in Indonesia, which seemed to have positively impacted upon his decision to explore further the TCM project, as detailed in frugal innovation Practice 3. The inventor graduated and worked with the Ministry of Public Works in the field of water and environmental sanitation for the last two decades:

> Since I already worked in water supply, since I graduated, I started to work with Public Works, . . . I started to do some research . . . technology is okay for me I can handle it.
>
> (Tirta Inventor)

So there was clearly an opportunity to leverage the inventor's external knowledge about water problems in Indonesia, which he had acquired since his graduation. His confidence to explore the TCM project further clearly stemmed from his professional and personal knowledge of the water issues in Indonesia and translated into his self-confidence to become an innovator and entrepreneur in the same area.

Phase 2: concept development for frugal innovation

Following the discovery and screening of new product opportunities and ideas, development teams undertake further market and technical study, and evaluation as part of the concept development phase. With regard to frugal innovation, five key frugal innovation practices have emerged from the literature. Frugal innovation Practice 5 and Practice 6 highlight the exploration of three primary BOP consumers' information as part of the market study stage, along with the use of more immersive techniques.

In the technical study stage, the frugal innovation literature highlights a focus on primary functionalities and business model specifications, translating into the key frugal innovation Practice 7. In this same NPDP stage, frugal innovation Practice 8 suggests the use of techniques leveraging basic technologies and/or existing product architecture/components in the technical conceptualisation of the NPD project.

In the final concept evaluation stage of the concept development phase, the frugal innovation literature emphasises the importance for using specific criteria and a simple physical version of the concept as an approach to concept testing. In the next sections, the underpinning decision-making of Tirta will be studied structured around these five key frugal innovation practices.

FI Practice 5: the market study stage has a focus on BOP consumer information related to affordability, complementary needs and product usage context

Building from unaffordable, unreliable and inaccessible water due to inadequate existing solutions, the inventor explored various types of BOP consumer information to build in the TCM water filter design. This includes first, problems around affordability with the current sources of water available to BOP consumers. The inventor went beyond the product price and took into consideration the cost of the unreliable quality of the piped and refilled water, restricting the options for BOP consumers to expensive products. Second, the inventor also considered needs that were key for the survival of Indonesian consumers and looked at filling low-income consumers' daily water needs

First looking at the product affordability, the inventor targeted an affordable product and also looked beyond the product price, taking account of the quality of the water supplied by existing solutions. The aim of the inventor was to develop an affordable new product: "My first intuition was to sell it in an affordable way" (Tirta Inventor). In line with this, the inventor conducted a worldwide investigation into water filters to establish a price-point accepted for BOP consumer and identified the price range of 300,000 IDR (nearly 21 USD, 9 August 2018): "For this, we have international kind of range. 20 USD, 30 USD maximum" (Tirta Inventor). Looking locally, the inventor identified that one of the key solutions that was available was over 50 USD (e.g. 550,000 IDR), which he considered as being 'too pricy' for local consumers, particularly for BOP consumers:

> [Local brand] was, 5 years ago . . . 550,000 IDR but . . . [this price] is [for] the basic type. If you add electricity and hot water, you have to add . . . another 35 USD. . . . Rich people can buy, but I'm thinking about the one who are in need of water and they can't afford to buy. They have to spend a lot of money just to get water for drinking . . . I'm comparing with the people who also buy . . . from refilled water, they buy water like 3,000 IDR per gallons [approximately 4L]. . . . So I compared with that. I came up with the price.
>
> (Tirta Inventor)

On the basis of the price of available solutions for the low-income consumers, the inventor realised that there were very few options available to access clean water in an affordable manner. While this was influential in setting the price-point for the inventor, he also emphasised that setting a price-point that was too 'cheap' could lead to negative connotations for BOP consumers, which could then undermine the product acceptance – "I try to make it cheaper as possible so people can afford it. But cheap is not always a good strategy either because if you talk cheap then people think it is not good" (Tirta Inventor). Understanding the price range was important, as it gave the inventor a cost bracket for further consideration, particularly when making it as cheap as possible would not have necessarily led to product success.

Moreover, it was also important to go beyond the product price, as piped water was extremely affordable; however, the quality of the water led to more costs for consumers. The inventor noted that piped water provided cheap access to water as compared with bottled water or refilled water. Comparing piped water price (0.0004 USD for 1L) with other options, refilled water price (0.07 USD for 1L) was approximately 170 times more expensive and water bottle (0.28 USD for 1L) was 700 times more expensive than piped water. Regardless of the cheap price of piped water, this affordability was nevertheless undermined by the quality of the water supplied across Indonesia (both within cities and within the country-side) and the lack of facilities enabling piped water access:

> In the beginning, I was trying to bridge between the quality that they [the pipes] can produce and the water quality that people will drink. Because in most cases, even they [the pipes] are already very good, construction-wise, we are not sure whether this is potable water only they distribute to the people. [For example] . . . in the region, it is not as good as in the city, so . . . [every solution] is [providing water of] somewhat below standard.
>
> (Tirta Inventor)

So even though piped water was the cheapest available water, this solution was not of sufficient quality to allow consumers to drink this directly. Even with access to piped water, this quality issue often resulted in consumers going back to using bottled water or boiling water, and contributing to a cycle of spiralling costs and continued inefficiencies in the system.

The inventor emphasised how cost ineffective boiling water was, including waiting for the water to cool down and buying associated fuel to cook the water:

> Even if they [consumers] subscribe to piped water in their city or their village, they still have to buy bottle water for drinking. Or boiling it. Boiling also means buying kerosene or gas, to boil the water. And boiled water is warm. You have to make it cool first to be able to drink it instantly, except for making coffee or tea.
>
> (Tirta Inventor)

So while piped water appeared affordable at face value, the affordability was not isolated to piped water. Another possibility with piped water was by buying the water from those who have access to piped water. Doing so had advantages to save money and time (as compared with fetching groundwater or have a membership with water utility company), but it still did not necessarily allow consumers to drink safe water directly from the source. So despite the availability of piped water, consumers still required an alternate solution to access drinkable water with less probability for contaminated water. The real costs behind piped water involved time inefficiency and additional costs for fuel (for boiling water or buying bottles of water for drinking).

A similar issue emerged when considering refilled water, as this was also subject to issues related to water quality. This was investigated by the Ministry of Health, who identified issues with the water quality failing to meet health requirements that the Indonesian Government had established:

> For refilled water . . . [t]here are businesses here, people get the water from the ground, and they put some ozone to kill bacteria in the water. This is

unbranded basically, and sometimes it is not really regulated. So many people . . . including some research made by the Minister of Health says that businesses produce water that does not comply with the health requirements.

(Tirta Inventor)

The inventor of the TCM filter clearly emphasised his concerns about the water quality provided by refilled water suppliers. As a result, the cost and quality aspects were underpinning the inventor's concept of affordability within the Indonesian context, extending beyond just the product price to a consideration of extended issues in achieving quality levels to allow consumption by Indonesian consumers.

Turning now to look at the inventor's consideration of Indonesian consumers' survival, while this sounds somewhat dramatic, the inventor took into account their basic health needs required to survive, including drinking approximately two litres of water a day. By willing to provide affordable clean water to BOP consumers, the inventor also considered this as a complementary need, reflecting that:

Quality-wise as well, the water cannot be consumed directly from the tap like in some other areas. Here [in Jakarta] you cannot for example. It is the bridge between that limitation and people's need to drink water. . . . While for daily needs, you need at least 2 litres of water per day to keep your body healthy, they'll rely on drinking the only accessible water.

(Tirta Inventor)

The inventor was clear that integrating a basic health need was a priority in the further TCM design. This approach translated into developing a product that could empower people to drink water from any sources, to meet their basic needs for survival without having issues linked with the quality and available access of this water.

FI Practice 6: the tools and techniques of the market study stage focus on a firm's immersion with targeted consumers for deeper insights

While there were no use of formal immersive tools and techniques to understand consumers' needs, the way the inventor acquired knowledge was by being locally embedded. The reason for the lack of formal tools and techniques was also his part-time involvement in this project and the shortage of marketing expertise during the development of the TCM water filter.

While the inventor did not use any formal marketing tools and techniques, he was nevertheless locally embedded throughout the development process, as seen in the earlier NPDP stages. With his local presence, the inventor could both observe local people and understand their particular preferences and needs, which provided important information about the targeted consumer groups. While locally embedded, the inventor did, however, acknowledge the constraints related to his lack of time and marketing efforts in the development of the TCM water filter.

The first reason for this was at the time of the interview, the inventor started this NPD project while working part-time with the World Bank: "I still do some work as a consultant so I cannot give 100 per cent of my time for this" (Tirta Inventor). With the time commitment to his other job, the inventor simply did not have enough time to become fully involved in the TCM water filter project. This may have led him to be less aware of the efforts needed at this stage of the NPDP. The inventor reflected on the insufficient time dedicated to the marketing function: "I did not do as much as marketing efforts as I should have done . . . I don't have any facility to do so yet; I don't have people who are experts in marketing" (Tirta Inventor). The inventor's lack of information and time had a substantial impact on the way the market study stage of the TCM project was undertaken. This included the lack of use in formal techniques such as immersion in the targeted consumer groups.

FI Practice 7: the technical study stage focuses on primary product functionalities and business model specifications

For the technical study stage, the inventor focused on both the performance requirements linked to primary product functionalities and business model specifications relating to the technology production. The inventor narrowed down his technical study to guarantee high water quality, implying developing an efficient filtering process that removed the bacteria that cause diseases. Another key primary functionality was linked to the speed/rate of filtration, an important factor found to influence product acceptance and adoption. Finally looking at technology production, the ease of the ceramic technology production was an important business model specification for the inventor to consider during this NPDP stage.

Looking first at one of the primary functionalities of the product, the inventor focused on the efficiency of the filtering process, guaranteeing clean water at any time. He prioritised performance requirements related to the removal of bacteria causing infectious diseases, leading his technical study to concentrate on this function: "Quality is the first thing. I don't compromise quality . . . [p]otable water" (Tirta Inventor). While it was obvious that drinkable water is the core goal of a water filter, this nevertheless shows the inventor left out secondary performance requirements at this stage of development:

> After two-three years, I have developed this and found this is quite highly acceptable in terms of quality and then I tested it at the laboratory and it was ok . . . the tests were based on eliminating the bacteria. These . . . bacteria can cause diarrhoea, gastro-enteritis and all those stomach-aches.
>
> (Tirta Inventor)

With this narrow focus, the inventor sought to reach a sufficient level of filtration required to make the water drinkable (removing bacteria) as opposed to seeking optimisation of the performance requirements going beyond this aspect.

The inventor sought optimal performance of the filtering process on a primary functionality, with further refinement in later phases.

An additional primary functionality that was intertwined with the quality of the filtering concerned the speed of the filtration rate. This was also an influential factor affecting the water quality performance and a factor influencing the product acceptance. Reaching a certain filtration speed was essential because consumers gave particular importance to the waiting time in getting drinkable water. However, the inventor faced the challenge that depending on the speed of the water being filtered, the filtration rate could also affect the quality of the filtration function. The speed of filtration mostly relying on the ingredients underpinning the composition of the ceramic, which are also involved in the filtration efficiency, as the inventor reflected:

> My priority in the beginning was to put the proper composition, which sieves potable water. . . . The filter can sip and eliminate bacteria and other substances in water. . . . In the beginning, when you have different mix, either it's going too fast in the flow rate or too slow. Too fast means that you have risk for bacteria to go through and passing the water; too slow, people would not want to wait for water for days just to get one glass of water.
>
> (Tirta Inventor)

The ingredients utilised in the composition of the ceramic pot filter were the key moderating factors for water quality and speed of water filtration rate. This was one of the most important aspects in the conceptualisation of the TCM design specifications. Moreover, the filtration rate functionality was explored further, with the targeted performance requirements also enabling the possibility of consuming water instantly faster rather than using boiled water. This aspect established the boundaries of the inventor's targeted performance requirements towards 'speed' functionality: "So people don't have to boil water. They just put it here . . . and they just regularly fill it and take it from here. That's what I had in mind" (Tirta Inventor). The inventor's aim was to make water access easier than existing solutions, accelerating the speed of water consumption between the point of access and the point of drinking the water.

When exploring the business model specifications of the TCM water filter, the inventor considered ceramic as a potential technology to filter water. According to the inventor, one of the key business model specifications related to the ceramic technology was the ease and low cost of finding the ingredients for manufacturing the ceramic. While the primary product functionality was to focus on removing bacteria from the water, the technology used in removing these bacteria aimed to rely on a technology that could be found locally and with lower costs involved. The inventor explained how the composition of the ceramic ingredients was suitable in the context of BOP consumers: "The key in this is the combination of rice husk and clay, it's abundant and cheap, you can take it for free basically" (Tirta Inventor). The inventor considered the ease and cost-effective aspects of the ingredients as being key in underpinning the filtering properties of the ceramic technology.

Embedded in the business model specifications of the TCM water filter design, another advantage of the ceramic technology was its flexible composition. The ceramic technology was also efficient when clay was combined with other types of combustible materials, like rice husk, sawdust and coffee husks (MIT 2008). The inventor aimed to ensure that the technology could be adapted to the local context (such as incorporating easily found rice husks), taking account of business model specifications during this technical study stage.

FI Practice 8: the tools and techniques of the technical study stage involve seeking basic technological principles and/or architecture and components from existing products

In the technical study of the TCM water filter, the inventor sought a technology that was simple, functional and adapted to the performance requirements established in the Indonesian context. The inventor instigated this NPDP stage first through seeking simple technologies capable of filtering water. He identified an old ceramic technology, which was proven as effective in other Asian countries by a globally recognised institution. In addition, choosing this ceramic technology as the underlying technical principles for the TCM water filter offered three critical benefits linked to its simplicity and suitability. First, the technology relied on only two possible ceramic structures. Second, it had the advantage of avoiding an additional mechanism for water pressure, relying instead on 'gravity'. Third, ceramic offered a micro-filtration capacity, which was an optimal performance when compared to other too advanced filtrating properties like Nano-filtration.

Looking more closely into the different types of technologies, the inventor explored a range of different filtration technologies during the technical study. His goal was to use a simple filtration technology that could fit the expected primary functionality he established (getting clean water almost instantly). He dug further into an old ceramic technology: "I read this article, a book I received when I was looking for this kind of technology" (Tirta Inventor). The inventor detailed this research process further, including ceramic technologies suitability in addressing the filtration performance requirements:

> This [ceramic] is an old technology. . . . The concept was developed years ago in London when London's Thames river was heavily polluted in the 1800s, some of the pottery [factories] made [filtering] tests [using ceramic] and they found that this is quite effective to remove bacteria. . . . I start to believe, this is nice and interesting. Why I don't start to produce it?
> (Tirta Inventor)

Searching for filtering technologies, ceramic technologies appeared as a simple solution that was suitable for effectively removing bacteria. The inventor reflected that this was an "appropriate, low-cost technology" (Tirta Inventor), which was in line with his goal of a new product relying on a "simple, yet functioning and affordable" technology (Tirta Inventor).

Moreover, the inventor identified that the ceramic technology functionality was particularly adapted for the Indonesian context, as its utilisation in other Asian countries had already been demonstrated. Previous studies undertaken by the World Bank in Cambodia showed how suitable and simple the ceramic technology was in addressing the local issues. This influenced the inventor's decision to adapt and work with the ceramic technology in Indonesia:

> Out of my hobby at home, I started to do some research and trials-and-error on this physical product but then finally I found a publication, . . . cross published by the World Bank under one [research] division called Water and Sanitation Program . . . they have some research in Cambodia. I found that they produce ceramic filter, so this is not my genuine finding or innovation; I just copy from them, the principles of the concept.
>
> (Tirta Inventor)

Willing to re-use an existing effective and basic technology, the inventor explored where and how the ceramic technology was utilised worldwide with the aim of adapting it to Indonesia. This helped identifying the potential of the ceramic filtering properties to respond to the inventor's targeted performance requirements and Indonesian problems. Furthermore, the inventor identified three key benefits using this ceramic technology. First, the underlying bases for the simplicity of the ceramic technological principles were its two possible structures: pot type and candle type. These structures could shape the ceramic technology, which showed how straightforward ceramic filtering operated. The inventor explained:

> This is a very simple design, you don't have many choices, this technology you have only two types of filter, one is the pot type, the pot type is coming from inside to outside; the candle type is from outside to inside.
>
> (Tirta Inventor)

The technological principles chosen for the TCM water filter were based on a simple design, which highlighted the inventor's interest for basic technologies. A second advantage of this technology was the possibility to use 'gravity', an optimal way to accelerate the filtration rate, instead of additional mechanism, which adequately fit market requirements.

Indeed, as discussed in frugal innovation Practice 7, if the filtration system screened the water too quickly, the filtration capabilities could have become less effective. The inventor discussed how the ceramic technology achieved the targeted requirements for filtration rate without compromising the quality of the water filtered and without utilising an additional pressuring system:

> [Getting running water] is difficult, but this is [about] gravity . . . you put water, it allows to sit on its own, without any pressure. If you put pressure, you have risk to have higher filtration rate . . . You are gaining filtration rate

but you have the risk to not qualify to the quality of water; maybe bacteria would pass through because of pressure; this is the limitation . . . My strategy is to change the composition [of the ceramic], to make more clay and fewer husks; so it's denser, it's less porous.

(Tirta Inventor)

The filtration properties of the ceramic allowed an appropriate sieving of the water for an appropriate filtration speed. This performance requirement was achievable by the simplicity of how the ceramic technology operated, which offered an optimal performance.

Finally, the ceramic properties offered a degree of micro-filtration that had important local advantages when compared with higher performing filtration process like Nano-filtration. The inventor highlighted that Nano-filtration had limitations in the Indonesian context, particularly around the high cost of using the technology and the unsuitability to operate this locally:

The beauty of this [i.e. micro-filtration] is that common people can do it, with some training even my people can do it with some instructions but nano-filtration is advanced technology . . . it needs a big factory, that's why I don't go with nano, . . . you need a lot of money to make it, or you have to buy from them [technology developers].

(Tirta Inventor)

By choosing the ceramic technology, the inventor explained that its performance was adequate to address the core functionalities of the TCM water filter concept. Not only was it sufficient for meeting the targeted performance requirements, it was particularly adapted to the local context avoiding extra costs and lack of experienced labour.

FI Practice 9: the tools and techniques in the concept evaluation stage integrate a set of criteria and/or simple physical version to test concept acceptance

The inventor did not develop a physical version of the product to test with consumers as part of the concept evaluation stage, relying rather on reaching two key criteria: water access and affordability. He, however, admitted the importance of developing a working product so that consumers could see it be functioning and understand whether they were interested. Although the inventor did not show the TCM concept with a physical version, the inventor developed key quality criteria such as ensuring potable water is reachable and that it is affordable to do so.

At first, the inventor did not develop a physical version of the concept before moving forward to the product development phase; however, he had technical criteria in mind that had to be reached. The inventor was clear that he was not concerned about the marketing side at this stage of development: "No, I haven't done it yet [to ask users if they like it or not]" (Tirta Inventor). The inventor did not seek direct consumers' feedback mainly because his first intention was to ensure that the technical aspects of the concept could address the various requirements set previously. The inventor focused on reaching quality criteria:

> This is quite highly acceptable in terms of quality and then I tested it at the laboratory and it was ok. . . . Once it's produced, then . . . there is a big challenge. Bigger challenge than the technical facts, the marketing here is still an issue for this product.
>
> (Tirta Inventor)

While the inventor focused on the technical aspect of the product, he also did not realise the importance of considering further marketing as part of the concept evaluation stage, thus undermining the role of developing a physical version. While the inventor did not engage in formal testing, the product still had to meet key quality criteria related to its reachability and affordability. The inventor's focus for the quality of the product was related to its price and its access from which the targeted performance requirements were developed:

> My basic concept is to have more people . . . [accessing water for] themselves. Again, the intention is not from the business point of view but the social point of view, more people will have access to good water, potable and affordable price.
>
> (Tirta Inventor)

The result that mattered for the inventor was to provide drinkable water at an affordable price as well as making consumers less dependent on water service providers by giving access to clean water whatever the supplying source. It was important to note that the inventor was later aware that new products required to be operated in front of consumers to know whether they would be interested.

When asked how consumers could provide feedback about their possible interest in the product, the inventor emphasised the importance to demonstrate a working product: "We have to introduce it. There is no [other] way. So you have to make the [product] . . . I have to introduce it to them" (Tirta Inventor). The importance of showing the product to potential consumers was emphasised by the inventor, as he explained that the introduction of a new product was a big challenge. However, his approach to evaluate the TCM water filter concept at the concept development phase did not include testing with consumers.

Phase 3: product development for frugal innovation

Moving from the concept development phase where the NPD project becomes more feasible technically, financially and marketing wise, the product development phase leads to the physical design of the product. This phase is associated with two NPDP stages including the product design and prototype testing. Regarding the three frugal innovation practices related to this NPDP phase, the first one, frugal innovation Practice 10, recommends that local outsourcing be considered against the costs and performances of the local resources during the product design stage.

During this stage, Design for X (DfX) is also highlighted as an important technique to be used by frugal innovators, and in particular when X relates to a frugal design strategy (frugal innovation Practice 11). Frugal innovation Practice 12 relates to the preference for early field-testing as part of the prototype testing stage.

FI Practice 10: the product design stage prioritises local outsourcing weighted off with costs and performance

Looking first at considerations related to outsourcing, the inventor clearly adapted the product design of the TCM water filter taking into account locally available resources. The inventor initially used a locally designed ceramic container for his first prototype, until he realised that these did not satisfy his quality standards. Learning from this failure, the inventor designed his own ceramic pot filter – the core aspect of TCM water filter, leveraging on local workshops and potters' equipment. Investigating other components of the TCM water filter, the inventor modified the composition of the ceramic technology to be based on a locally abundant raw material. Finally, another component that the inventor ensured of local availability was the 'tap', which was easy to find locally, allowing easier repair.

The inventor's first decision about the ceramic components of the TCM water filter focused on using already-made components. For the first TCM prototype, the inventor chose a ceramic container made by local potters. He initially explored ceramic containers manufactured on Java Island, from the potteries in Plered (approximately 110km from Jakarta) and Kasongan, Yogyakarta (located approximately 530km from Jakarta). In exploring various pottery factories, the aim of the inventor was to prioritise existing design and to avoid re-creating the 'wheel': "This prototype is from Yogyakarta, Kasongan. This one is from Plered. I didn't ask them to make a design, they make their own design" (Tirta Inventor). Initiating the product design stage through this approach allowed the inventor to utilise existing designed containers for the TCM water filter, removing the need to design and manufacture this component.

The performance of these ceramic containers, however, did not satisfy his quality standards. When the inventor bought 20 pots, most of them did not meet the performance requirements set by the inventor. With continuous leaking, he reflected on the importance of not compromising on the performance of the container:

> We purchased 20 units altogether . . . I tested one by one. So only very few were really good, the rest was not good . . . I couldn't sell this to people. Otherwise, there were complaints.
>
> (Tirta Inventor)

When the container's design quality did not reach the standards of performance sought after testing, the inventor reconsidered his decisions regarding the choice of a ceramic container and replaced this with a plastic container. However, more recently, the inventor found another place in Klaten, Central Java, where they produce ceramic containers that do not leak. This led the inventor to add a product option with a ceramic container that he did not make and instead rely on a locally made ceramic container.

Learning from this process, the inventor decided to design his own ceramic pot filter – the core mechanism of TCM water filter, an important component in the effective functioning of the TCM product. The inventor still made use of locally available resources to reduce logistics and product development costs. To create his own design for the ceramic pot filter, the inventor believed in combining local and global knowledge including increasing local resource use – "global knowledge but used locally can be used with local materials with some sort of changes and you can do it" (Tirta Inventor). Willing to leverage global expertise and local resources, the inventor made use of a local "ex-car repair workshop" in Purwakarta, West Java, and worked with local potteries in Plered ('workshop', in this context, is defined as a small production, hands-on factory). Plered and Purwakarta cities were two of the key ceramic suppliers providing local, cheap and superior raw materials on Java Island.

The sourcing of raw materials and equipment decreased logistic and product development costs. Costs were important aspect of this NPDP stage, as the inventor had to overcome his low capital while designing a quality product:

> It's expensive to make [things] on your own. If I have a lot of money, I can have my own design, my own package, with my ornament, ceramic, or plastic, but I don't have money that much. . . . We buy [components] from distributors because we can't buy easily from the market now.
>
> (Tirta Inventor)

Outsourcing from local suppliers was cost-effective for the inventor, which drove him to trade-off various components of the product. Purwakarta is located 20km from a centre of pottery in Plered; thus, the inventor had easy sourcing of raw materials such as clay and rice husks for the ceramic, as well as local equipment. For example, the inventor was "using [a] kiln belonging to a potter in Plered" (Tirta Inventor). Working closely in these two cities provided the inventor with cheap and functional equipment and raw materials, as he reflects:

> Near Purwakarta, there is a small town called Plered. It is the centre of ceramics, so I don't have problems with sources of ceramics. They have plenty there and it's very cheap. . . . At the beginning, I had to go to the factory to do firing [with the furnace] but now I have my own oven to fire the ceramics.
>
> (Tirta Inventor)

The inventor leveraged the presence of local potteries for the components of the TCM water filter, which included the sourcing of ceramics as well as their furnace system. In addition to working with local potters and accessing raw materials like clay, other ingredients were needed to make the ceramic, including sawdust and rice husks. As Indonesia has an abundance of rice fields, the inventor integrated rice husks in his ceramic composition, ensuring local materials were integrated in the TCM water filter: "The choice of the combustion material was rice husk, something that is locally available" (Tirta Inventor).

When looking at the way the inventor approached the design of the TCM water filter, the inventor also utilised components that were easily found in local shops in case repair was necessary. This decision was beneficial for consumers, as it avoided high costs of maintenance and difficulties in getting their product repaired. For example, the plastic tap utilised in the design of the TCM water filter was purposely chosen to enable consumers to buy it from shops or repair it themselves:

> You can buy it easily. [It was] . . . on purpose, because you can buy it near here, I buy it from a better and cheaper one but you can buy it from producer market. It is easy to get. [When] people call me, [I tell them] you can buy from shop or can repair by yourself, and then they did and they say, "it's working now".
>
> (Tirta Inventor)

The choice of local components for the TCM water filter, such as the tap, was more advantageous for consumers, as they could repair the product easier. The inventor even factored into the decision process the rural areas where potential suppliers were located, instead of looking more broadly:

> I bought it in Cengkareng, West Jakarta. Somewhere . . . in a very remote place, very slum area. If you buy from the market, it is 7,000 IDR (approximately 0.47 USD, 11 November 2018). From there, it is 2,500 IDR to 3,000 IDR (0.17 to 0.20 USD, 11 November 2018). It's cheaper and better.
>
> (Tirta Inventor)

This process of local sourcing was an essential part in lowering the product price as well as for getting components that were readily accessible to consumers. The inventor expressed the advantages of a component that could be found locally, as consumers could go to local shops: "If they say it's broken, 'check the tap first, it is the first step and buy from shop', it's not very difficult" (Tirta Inventor). Instead of people having to send the product back to the inventor, the inventor made the decision to empower consumers to repair the TCM water filter by going to their local shops.

While the inventor went with locally available resources, he did not overlook the quality of these components. The main reason was that some components could reduce the TCM water filter quality. For example, the TCM water filter 'tap' could have downgraded the overall quality of the filtrated water due to water having to run through it. Hence, the inventor sought a superior tap component, trading-off between its performance and its costs:

> The tap [that the inventor chose] basically has had no problem in three years . . . The bad one has a lot of variety of quality, sometimes only within two weeks it is broken. There are some springs, and some rings in the tap; and sometimes the ring doesn't work. Sometimes the spring doesn't work. Sometimes it is just broken. It is very easily broken if it is not in a good quality. So it has to be a good quality.
>
> (Tirta Inventor)

Sourcing locally could certainly involve the supply of bad quality components such as easily broken 'tap' for ceramic filter; however, the inventor did not compromise the quality of the components that he chose to integrate in the design of TCM water filter. It became important to weigh-off the performance and the cost of the resources outsourced with local resources, as local outsourcing had cost and time benefits, while being careful with quality.

FI Practice 11: the tools and techniques of the product design stage include DfX techniques specifically aimed at frugal design strategies

While no formal DfX techniques were applied, the inventor followed three design strategies to ensure the TCM water filter was easy to maintain, replaceable and customisable. First, out of the two possible structures that the ceramic technology required (pot type or candle type), the inventor chose the one that was easily maintained by BOP consumers. Furthermore, the inventor decided to make the repair of the ceramic filter pot easier when arriving at the end of its life cycle or in case of breakage. Finally, the TCM water filter could be customisable in accordance to consumers' preferences and disposable income

To choose between the two filter structures (the pot filter and candle type filter), the inventor took into account the way consumers would use the product. With his knowledge of the Indonesian BOP consumers, the inventor chose the 'pot filter' structure: "From the beginning I decided to go with pot filter" (Tirta Inventor). Considered more practical, the probability of water leakage when consumers would clean the pot filter was lower than when cleaning the candle type:

> I wasn't in favour of candle type [because] it has a risk of leaking due to a screw so if people don't care about the screwing, it's leaking and you have no use of the filter because the water is going through the leaks and not through the filter.
>
> (Tirta Inventor)

Because of the risk that maintenance would not be done properly, the inventor preferred using the pot filter structure. This was because it was less likely to cause problems with leaking and damaging water quality, and it relied on a simple structure for cleaning (as compared with the candle type screwing). Moreover, the inventor made sure that the ceramic pot filter would be easy to replace when it was less efficient or broken to allow for cheaper repair. While the ceramic pot had a life cycle of three years, it was designed to be removable when needed, as it was essential to avoid replacing the entire product. The tap and the ceramic pot filter were both replaceable components overcoming the need to pay for the whole product when broken. The inventor explained this idea for the pot filter:

> This filter only lasts three years at the most. You have to replace the pot after three years . . . passing this period, consumers come back to me and they say "do you still have pots"? "yes I still have pots", so I can send it to them . . . they have to pay for the pot. . . . The most expensive part is the container.
>
> (Tirta Inventor)

As the container of the TCM water filter was the most expensive part, the inventor designed the product so that people could pay only for the ceramic pot. Thus, the TCM water filter design stage was led by design guidelines allowing consumers to own a product that was easy and cheap to repair.

Finally, exploring the customisation of the TCM water filter, the inventor decided to make the plastic container customisable on the basis of BOP consumers' preferences. The inventor first developed two types of containers, ceramic and plastic (before realising the drawbacks of a ceramic container) and then moved on with a simple plastic container. Despite receiving little feedback from the users, the inventor and the marketing manager realised that consumers did not necessarily want the cheapest water filter option. As different people would have different income levels, the inventor decided to provide two types of external design possible:

> For example, I have two designs now, one is a very simple bucket, . . . people think it's a bucket for paint. They don't like it . . . they still don't trust it. . . . [The second one] . . . is from the local brand Lion Star, the brand for household plastic and they like it; it was more expensive, even village people, "I want this", "this is more expensive", but they still want it, better than the other one which was a simple one.
>
> (Tirta Inventor)

As the inventor realised that consumers were ready to pay more to get an aesthetically 'better' product (while remaining under their budget), this led the inventor to have a customisable design of the TCM water filter. As "[t]he container is the one that makes it expensive" (Tirta Inventor), a good-looking container could have thus been too expensive for some consumers. Having several options enabled consumers to make a choice in accordance to aesthetic preferences and their affordability between a simple and cheaper version of the

TCM water filter, and a 'fancier' and more expensive version with a local brand (Lion Star):

> You have to serve all the level of people. That's why I make two types, so it can serve both. It's up to them. If they want to buy . . . the simple white one or the coloured one Lion Star.
>
> (Tirta Inventor)

Ensuring the desire of consumers was taken into account in the product design was important, as the inventor identified different type of BOP consumers. In conclusion, these specific goals of easy maintenance, replacement and customisation illustrated the design strategies that the inventor implemented during the product design stage.

FI Practice 12: the tools and techniques of the prototype testing stage include early field-testing

During the prototype testing stage, the TCM water filter was sent not only to NGOs, but it was also shared with close friends and neighbours before going into the next phase. These techniques helped gathering critical feedback from the market. By sending it to local NGOs, the inventor realised the impracticality of the ceramic container from the negative feedback received. Following this issue, the inventor swapped the ceramic container with a plastic one, which was then shared with close friends, leading to modifying the external design of the TCM water filter. Moreover, a TCM water filter order was also sent to NGOs across Indonesia (including across different islands), influencing further changes to the ceramic pot design. These could have been time-consuming and costly if it occurred in later stages of development, as these changes would have modified the entire product testing processes.

At first, the inventor chose a ceramic container for the TCM water filter design, which was, in fact, impractical and received negative feedback from local NGOs. The inventor realised the issues associated with the heavy weight of the product, making it difficult to transport:

> In the past I made three or four different packaging [containers]. The last one is ceramics, but this one is not easy because . . . [it is] still leaking . . . secondly, it's very heavy, you cannot move it easily. Some of the NGOs were not very [interested].
>
> (Tirta Inventor)

Among various designs, the ceramic container received negative feedback from NGOs due to its impracticality. Receiving such feedback at this prototype testing stage was highly beneficial for the inventor, as he discontinued the development of the ceramic container and shifted his focus to plastic containers. The inventor swapped the ceramic material constituting the TCM water filter container for a plastic bucket, as according to him, this was the most common form of low-cost water filter for BOP markets worldwide.

The TCM water filter design with a plastic bucket was then shared with the close friends and neighbours of the inventor and marketing manager to receive further feedback for any additional revisions needed. For example, feedback on the product was received through using the product in real-life conditions. The marketing manager used the product daily and showed the advantages of using the TCM water filter in consumers' daily life to groups of close friends and neighbours: "Because I use it every day, I can show them that . . . it's good, no deposit and bacteria, it is faster than boiling . . . It's clean, not like the burning from boiling water" (Tirta Marketing Manager). The marketing manager also had contact with potential consumers through sharing the product with close colleagues and neighbours as part of this NPDP stage.

Approaching potential consumers at this stage generated critical feedback leading to modifying the external design of the TCM water filter. Consumers prioritised aesthetic over price, and they had various perceptions regarding drinking safe water. For example, depending on where the product was sold, people would have specific aesthetic preferences such as the colours of the container. The marketing manager reflected on this:

> If I'm the buyer, I will buy the cheapest one, which has the same quality basically . . . but the people I talked to is different. The people varied from one to another. . . . People in the village prefer the Lion Star type (fancier due to its colour) to the white one, because it looks better; the white one is like a paint bucket.
>
> (Tirta Marketing Manager)

Consumers had different preferences with the TCM water filter, preferring to buy a less cheap product to acquire a product with a more attractive external design. Although the plastic bucket chosen by the inventor was the most common form of low-cost water filter, Indonesian consumers did not feel safe to drink water from it:

> It says PP05 [on the bucket]; this means that [the bucket] is fine for water and food and beverage. Not many people know because this bucket can also be used for painting, for oil.
>
> (Tirta Inventor)

By putting the product in the hands of potential consumers, Indonesian consumers expressed their feeling of insecurity when using this type of plastic container. As this type of plastic container was the cheapest, which made the TCM water filter affordable for those who cannot afford a more expensive product, through this field-testing, the inventor realised the importance of providing two options. To satisfy diverse BOP consumers' preferences, he adapted its product design requirements, offering a cheap option and a more expensive option of the TCM water filter.

Other important feedback leading to product design modifications was consumers' 'bad' feeling towards drinking water from a filter without a locked lid. Indeed, the ceramic pot filter was noticeable from outside, even when the lid was on, a detail that did not appeal to consumers:

> Before . . . we had bigger pot. . . . It was not good because otherwise when you put the [lid], people cannot close, people don't like it. This one [another container and lid] however when you close it, it looks safer you know, in terms of what's coming in.
>
> (Tirta Inventor)

With the product in the hands of consumers, the inventor enhanced his understanding of consumers' perception on the TCM product design such as the loose lid. By sharing the products with consumers, the inventor and the marketing manager received critical feedback leading to modifying the external design of the TCM water filter. If there was a poor interaction with intended consumers, the revised external design might not have occurred before full production started.

The inventor also avoided later product failure when he shared the TCM product with NGOs across Indonesia. Putting the TCM water filter under real-life situations revealed the weaknesses in local infrastructure and rough roads, leading the ceramic pot filters to be damaged when carried through usual means of transportation. The inventor concluded that the ceramic pot filters were too fragile and thus changed its design refocusing on its durability (or robustness):

> I found [the pot type]'s very fragile, you cannot send it easily outside Java. I have had an experience with some NGOs. They ordered me a dozen of it and sent it to the eastern island, so 50% broke and I got loss because of this. So I redesign this. First of all, I made it thicker, and then slimmer, longer, I mean higher . . . and more stable, I tried to send it outside to Surabaya (East Java) and to Pontianak (Kalimantan Island) and it was okay.
>
> (Tirta Inventor)

While sending the product to NGOs incurred financial loss due to breakage, putting the product in a real-life scenario avoided more losses than if this had occurred during higher volumes of production and distribution. It allowed the inventor to test the product durability in the Indonesian context and redesign the ceramic pot with a more robust shape: "This one breaks easily (it's bigger but it's also longer and thinner). And this one smaller, thus thicker" (Tirta Inventor). This was a significant discovery, as, in the laboratory, the inventor had overlooked the importance of the shape of the ceramic pot filter.

As a result of modifying the shape of the ceramic filter pot, the testing in the laboratory had to be modified as well. This was because the technical tests relied on checking the sound emitted from each ceramic filter pot and checking the filtration speed rate. The measurements of these tests were established during the development of a specific pot design. The production quality tester reflected:

> Yes, part of it . . . [is to test it by the sound, how it resonates] . . . and then by measuring the rate. Every single pot, I have to measure by rate. If rate is not good I have to discard it.
>
> (Tirta Production Quality Tester)

The sound and filtration rate testing were the two most important methods used before the product could be sold (these pots were also sent to a laboratory for more 'formal' testing). However, if the shape of the ceramic pot changed, the associated laboratory testing also required different measurements. Due to the extensiveness of the laboratory testing, the inventor explained how cost and time intensive these tests were, if they required to be modified:

> The filtering rate has to be from 1.5 to 3.5, so if you make it [the pot] in a different shape, the filtering rate would not be within that range; thus it takes time as you cannot just make it and have it tomorrow, you have to first of all, make it [the ceramic pot] in a mould, fire it and after a month you can have the product and you don't do one, you do 100 and when the production is not good, you have to throw away everything, just for testing.
>
> (Tirta Inventor)

To test ceramic pot filters, each pot had to undergo a sequence of processes that involved time intensive and costly actions. Because the TCM product was sent into the field early during the prototype testing, where only a few TCM water filters were produced, the inventor could make modifications before going for further production without experiencing significant costs.

Phase 4: commercialisation for frugal innovation

The final phase, the commercialisation phase, instigates further and more extensive testing at the market and production levels. With regard to frugal innovation, three key frugal innovation practices have emerged from the literature related to the two stages within this phase, the market testing and production ramp-up. The first two frugal innovation practices in the commercialisation phase, frugal innovation Practice 13 and Practice 14, focus on the promotion and distribution strategies employed when reaching BOP consumers.

Frugal innovation Practice 13 focuses on leveraging locally established networks through Word-Of-Mouth (WOM), local groups and NGOs to reach and distribute a product across various BOP communities. Frugal innovation Practice 14 emphasises the important role of product demonstration and training in the promotion of the product to BOP consumers. Practice 15, the final frugal innovation practice, relates to the production ramp-up stage and indicates the importance of remaining at small-scale production for a longer period to ensure high-quality standards.

FI Practice 13: the market testing stage involves testing distribution and promotion of the new product through existing local networks

Tirta's promotion and distribution activities were undertaken through leveraging collaboration using diverse networks that were locally established. These included NGOs and social gatherings through the WOM technique. In addition to collaborating with NGOs to access their networks, these NGOs also provided less financial uncertainty for Tirta for undertaking further market testing. The inventor also reached out to local research institutions by publishing research in environmental engineering journals. Another way of promoting the benefits of the TCM water filter was through establishing and joining 'communities of interest' around the potential of ceramic filters in addressing global water issues. The inventor also sought government support to support his activities during this stage.

Looking first at Tirta's initiatives in market testing the TCM water filter, the inventor and the marketing manager successfully used locally established networks from NGOs and local social gathering through WOM. They first spread awareness of the TCM water filter by leveraging NGOs' networks: "At the beginning, I was trying to contact all the NGOs in Jakarta" (Tirta Inventor). Reaching out to NGOs was critical, as Tirta could not have communicated with such dispersed BOP consumers in Indonesia: "They are everywhere and rather untouched, but . . . you have to go to NGO, they have more contact with them, [with] villages under cooperation" (Tirta Inventor). Leveraging NGOs' network was beneficial in increasing consumers' awareness and trust of the TCM water filter, due to the genuine cooperation existing between villagers and NGOs.

Tirta would have struggled reaching low-income consumers if it used just traditional promotional methods and did not have the help of trustworthy relationships built between the NGOs with local communities. In particular, as their networks were based on long-term relationships and trust, relying on WOM had a dramatic effect, as the inventor reflects:

> If you talk to a NGO – I talk to one person only and it can be spread it out easily. That's the way we are doing . . . It worked so far. Last time they bought a lot.
>
> (Tirta Inventor)

Leveraging locally established networks clearly offered time efficiency in spreading awareness of the TCM water filter across Indonesian consumers. For example, in 2012, the inventor reached communities in Purwakarta and Bogor regencies by selling 200–300 TCM water filters per month. This was possible through the collaboration with an international NGO located in Indonesia, as this option offered the possibility to rely on WOM to increase spread of the TCM water filter across various communities.

Another benefit from collaborating with NGOs was less financial uncertainty during the promotion and distribution of the product. At this stage, Tirta was not making money: "I cannot earn money out of my selling . . . At least, the income could pay for the staff [with the 200 units that the NGO bought]; if you sell less, you have less income" (Tirta Inventor). This caused the inventor to slow down the production while working through the last phase of development. With financial security in mind, the inventor aimed at selling his product in bulk rather than directly to consumers, as consumers generally utilise smaller payments, such as 1 USD a month for their purchase, thus, less financial security for Tirta:

> Usually people don't buy it at once, but they do by instalments. I'm still looking at distributors, the one who can buy from me in bulk, and they can sell it to the people . . . with instalments spread in 10 months or something, so the price is, say, 10 USD, so every month they have to pay 1 USD, so it's not that difficult for them [the distributors].
>
> (Tirta Inventor)

As the Indonesian consumers generally made their purchase in small quantities, collaborating with NGOs allowed the inventor to sell his products with bigger volume, overcoming the risks associated with uncertain revenues. While consumers could not pay for the product immediately, NGOs could enable the implementation of a payment instalment method. Collaborating with local NGOs also addressed the transporting costs linked to the geographical environment (e.g. widespread Indonesian islands). Local NGOs could reach remote areas for further market testing, which would have been difficult for Tirta, as sending TCM water filter in low quantities would have affected its affordability:

> I think the most challenging is promotion. . . . If you send it outside Java, you have to add more cost. Also, this is heavy like 10kg for Lion Star, and 7,000 IDR per kg by Tiki, by expedition.
>
> (Tirta Inventor)

Collaborating with local NGOs enabled Tirta to leverage the NGOs' local channels and avoid the high tariffs of transportation.

Other trusted networks used by Tirta were through social gathering, a key approach in the promotion and distribution of the TCM water filter. In Indonesia, these local networks are named 'Arisan', a type of microfinance group in the Indonesian culture where women gather, save money and discuss at each other's homes on a monthly basis. The marketing manager explained: "Everyone puts money and they shuffle it, also to save money; not only that, also talking about something else, or sometimes people promote something" (Tirta Marketing Manager). Utilising social gatherings to promote a product was a usual practice in the Indonesian culture. This became an advantage for Tirta, as they could suggest the TCM product to friends and family members in a much higher number than on one-to-one approach:

> This is famous; it is for chatting and communicating. . . . I also use this opportunity to share this [TCM product] with others, bring this thing and demonstrate to others that I can drink it.
>
> (Tirta Marketing Manager)

By utilising informal social gatherings to demonstrate the product quality, greater awareness and potential adoption of the product occurred within local communities. This was particularly true as WOM had a substantial impact in achieving this outcome: "If you talk to this group, you are in an easier position because you can just tell them very briefly, and then let them talk about this to others" (Tirta Marketing Manager). This closeness with local communities increased the trust among potential consumers that filtered water was drinkable and engendered people talking about the TCM water filter.

Additional ways of promoting the product included through research activities, and establishing and joining "communities of interest" (Tirta Inventor). The inventor reached out to Indonesian research institutions such as LIPI Indonesian Institute of Science to diffuse knowledge of the ceramic water filter effectiveness to address clean water access in Indonesia. Initially, the inventor published the advantages of ceramic water filter within the Indonesian context through engineering journals. These were mostly related to environment and hygiene, such as The Association of Indonesian Environmental Health and Engineering Specialists (IATPI), the Sanitary Engineering (TP) and the Environmental Engineering (TL):

> One of the publications is issued by the IATPI . . . and they are quite active; every year they make a seminar but mostly for researchers. I always participate in this. One of my articles is here.
>
> (Tirta Inventor)

The inventor published his academic research to raise awareness about the advantages of using ceramic water filter in Indonesia. The aim of going through academic research was to increase the worldwide awareness of available solutions providing drinkable water to poor families, and in particular about the potential to use a ceramic filter as a household water treatment process.

To raise further awareness, the inventor and marketing manager also decided to create a ceramic filter community and to join other groups. They first created the "Komunitas Saringan Keramik Indonesia, a community of Ceramic Filter Indonesia" (Tirta Marketing Manager). Their aim was the promotion of the product as well as gauging people's interest around the technology of the ceramic filter. In addition to creating a 'community of interest', Tirta reached out to a group of women, through Dharma Wanita, who empowered women through education, economic and socio-cultural activities, to promote the TCM water filter. In 2012, Dharma Wanita introduced and demonstrated the TCM water filter to several members of their internal and external networks (Tirta Marketing Manager). Continually reaching local associations and leveraging their networks appeared as a key foundation for the market testing stage.

Last, Tirta promoted the TCM water filter by seeking Indonesian government support in 2014, and in particular through the Ministry of Research, Technology and Higher Education. This approach was strategic, as the inventor was aware of the possibility to reach other groups of people through the Government such as Islamic educational centres: "I went there to present for the people at the Minister of Research like Islamic group people. I presented this and the minister drank [the water]; this was . . . a year ago" (Tirta Inventor). Having access to the Indonesian government and associated groups provided the inventor with further support and promotion of the TCM water filter. As the inventor shared earlier, local people might not trust new products that are developed locally; however, having government support appeared as a distinctive promotional benefit for the TCM water filter.

FI Practice 14: the market testing stage includes product demonstration and training as key promotional strategy

As part of the market testing stage, the inventor utilised both traditional and more engaged methods of promotion including demonstration and face-to-face training. The inventor supported that demonstration was a more adapted approach of promotion for low-income people than traditional methods such as selling in shopping malls or with brochures only. The inventor and the marketing manager undertook demonstrations to local communities with the assistance of a local NGO. Numerous benefits stemmed from demonstrating 'face-to-face' the product to BOP consumers, including developing brand awareness and trust among local communities and receiving feedback.

When looking at traditional methods to promote the TCM water filter, the inventor emphasised the inefficiency of displaying the product in shopping malls and giving brochures only. When the inventor worked with a local NGO, which supported the development, distribution and promotion of the TCM water filter, they recommended various methods, including traditional marketing strategies. They suggested to use "many ways of marketing; not only using one method . . . [in order to] compete with modern [products]" (Tirta Inventor). The product was thus displayed in shopping malls across Jakarta along with brochures, explaining how the product worked and responding to common questions: "If they ask questions, . . . there is a FAQ [Frequently Asked Questions] [in the brochure]. They can just read it" (Tirta Inventor). The inventor described that people were attracted by the display and showed interest in the TCM water filter, though did not buy it: "[The aim was] . . . just to sell it to people. But people are not really interested, they like the idea but they don't buy it" (Tirta Inventor). So the result from putting the TCM water filter in shopping malls was rather negative, as Tirta did not achieve many sales from this promotion method.

The brochures were also not sufficient, requiring complement by another approach: "I'm informing [them too, because] . . . the piece of brochure is not enough. Sometimes brochure is not even read by people. They just get it and throw it away" (Tirta Inventor). Brochures were not engaging enough to low-income consumers; it was important to educate them though instructions about how to operate the product, as they did not see or use any products like that before. The inventor then became involved in demonstrating the product with local NGOs:

> Distributing the brochure . . . doesn't help much as compared to do it your-self and you're demonstrated in front of the people. . . . we had some coop-eration with other NGOs, we went to the villages, we ask to get together, and then in front of them, I would start talking about this product. And then I would use the water from their well, take the water and drink the water myself. Many people bought it.
>
> (Tirta Inventor)

The inventor asserted that the increase of the TCM water filter sales came from showing the product operating in a face-to-face environment with consumers who could observe the effectiveness of the product in front of them. Similarly, promoting the TCM water filter through Arisan was beneficial as this approach enabled the marketing manager to train consumers and build their trust in the product:

> First of all, I become the example. I try to drink in front of my friends – the people who buy it. . . . I bring the sample to Arisan, . . . women gather-ing . . . neighbours; we have monthly gathering for Arisan.
>
> (Tirta Marketing Manager)

Being a member of Arisan groups made the marketing manager a reliable 'tester' of TCM water filter samples. Using demonstration, she illustrated the product quality in front of potential consumers (close friends, neighbours and other members of the group). The marketing manager explained that BOP con-sumers needed to trust the product effectiveness:

> You have to learn from the customers, what do they want. Here, demonstra-tion is key, if you demonstrate you drink yourself, and people start to believe [in the product].
>
> (Tirta Marketing Manager)

Discussing and demonstrating the product to potential consumers had sev-eral benefits, including enhancing the trust relationship and trust in the brand. A potential reason for this was that BOP consumers did not often believe in locally made products:

> People maybe don't trust the product because it's locally made, it's very simple and they don't believe that it's actually treating the water and that they can drink directly.
>
> (Tirta Marketing Manager)

Because of the origin of new products, local BOP consumers tended to be influenced in their perception that the products would be low quality. This meant that it was important to develop trust with the local consumers and be in direct contact with them. Strong examples of the benefits of the demonstration strategy exist, including noticing consumers utilising the product in different ways than expected. When consumers drank water filtered by the TCM water filter, they would still boil water afterwards even though the filtered water was drinkable. This informed the marketing manager that consumers neither fully trusted new products nor did they understand how the TCM product functioned:

> We found also people . . . [using water] for something else [than drinking]. They don't use it for drinking. But if they want to drink, they boil again . . . Maybe they don't trust it. You know, gaining people trust is a difficult part of the process.
>
> (Tirta Marketing Manager)

This finding that consumers did not trust the quality of the water (and boiled it even after being filtered) reinforced the idea that using a face-to-face approach for product demonstration was essential. Another example illustrating the benefits of product demonstration was in ensuring consumers understood how to get rid of the ceramic smell in the water before drinking from the TCM water filter. For this, consumers had to follow a simple procedure of filling the pot with water three times before consuming the water. However, it was important to show consumers in villages how to do it, so that they could use the product according to their water taste:

> In the villages, we must tell them because this is the first time they use it, so they have to fill [the TCM water filter] first and [do it] . . . three times; after the fourth, they can drink it. That's to reduce the smell; some people don't like the smell of ceramic.
>
> (Tirta Marketing Manager)

The method of removing the taste of ceramic was explained through comprehensive demonstrations to BOP consumers. Over time, the inventor saw that consumers started to accept the TCM water filter and understood how to use it: "Gradually, people, it's not easy but, they understand; people who already use it are satisfied" (Tirta Inventor). The inventor emphasised that it took time to understand and adopt the TCM water filter; thus, getting a more hands-on approach, such as through demonstration, was critical during this market testing stage.

Finally, the marketing manager also received positive and constructive comments about the product. For example, consumers commented on how utilising TCM water filter changed their spending habits on buying water: "I like those who say: that's good, I don't need to buy water, that feels good" (Tirta Marketing Manager). By receiving these comments, the marketing manager confirmed that the TCM water filter was appealing to consumers. Confirming consumers' appeal for the TCM water filter was important for the planning of further distribution and promotion, which was the following step in Tirta's NPDP: "I don't have time now . . . but I have to set a team to go around and that's the next step" (Tirta Inventor). The information collected throughout the market testing stage helped the inventor to measure expected sales, supporting the expansion of further promotion and sales as part of this NPDP stage.

FI Practice 15: the production ramp-up stage factors in low-volume production timelines for longer periods, which benefits quality standards such as QA/QC and workforce training

Looking at the production ramp-up stage, Tirta followed a small-scale strategy since 2008, preferring in-house production processes, easy adaptability to the local context and stricter quality control over learning and labour training. One of the main reasons for remaining small scale was keeping control over production variables, even though it meant starting from 'scratch'. In-house production processes were also possible due to choosing simple and more traditional manufacturing processes. These were beneficial, as it simplified learning and training of local labours, adaptation to the local context and flexibility of production capabilities. More recently, the inventor had thought of scaling up through cooperatives networks across the Indonesian islands.

At first, the production volume remained small scale up until the interview, giving time towards understanding the production processes and implementing training programs for local labour. In 2008, the inventor first developed his own production processes from 'scratch' in a local car shop before deploying these processes to a more centralised factory in Purwakarta. As part of centralising the production in-house, the inventor also bought equipment and constructed a kiln in 2010. As a result of this, the inventor's priority was not to achieve a rapid scale-up but rather taking time and keeping direct control over all production processes. Taking the extra time during this process was beneficial, as the inventor could train labours for these particular production activities:

> I started to make my factory here in Purwakarta. This factory, at the beginning, of course, you have to face the fact that it is not easy to build a factory, especially when you start from zero, from scratch, nobody knows how to do it, so I have to start training people to make it.
>
> (Tirta Inventor)

As making his own factory from scratch takes time and involved training of employees on new tools and processes, the production outputs remained small scale.

There were four key advantages of establishing in-house production processes and remaining at a smaller scale for a longer period. The first one was leveraging local employees' knowledge. Despite taking the time for training local employees, buying local equipment also enabled the inventor to leverage employees' local knowledge. For example, the new equipment for grinding the clay for the ceramic production had to be adapted to Tirta's production's requirements. In line with this, the production manager, a local employee and the inventor's family had knowledge of local repair shops and quickly addressed this issue:

> In the beginning, I had to think about the machines that grind the clay and hash. . . . I found difficulties with the [grinding and mixing] machine, [as] you know clay is sticky, so you cannot have much water, you cannot have less water. You must have balance in terms of amount of water . . . [we] had to cut some blade, just to adjust to make it work. Because nobody used it before. . . . And my younger brother in law he . . . fixes cars and engines so he has lots of contacts with garages.
>
> (Tirta Inventor)

By establishing the production site in-house, there were issues arising from new equipment, but the inventor and his team leveraged employees' local knowledge and were able to make quick improvements during the initial stage of production ramp-up. This was reflected, for example, in using local equipment for better machine efficiency, as the production manager reflected: "I made some modifications on the motor . . . we replaced it with electric motor. Not diesel motor . . . to make the engine effective" (Tirta Production Manager). This decision differentiated the production efficiency (electricity versus diesel) as well as the atmosphere (less noisy) in which ceramic filters were produced. Other detailed knowledge from the production manager addressed the issues of access to raw materials:

> Some materials are not easily found. That's why I try to explore. I know the places. I know where to buy them. Like the good wood for firing, from rambutan tree, it is the best wood for burning.
>
> (Tirta Production Manager)

The production manager was highly knowledgeable such as when finding an adequate burning wood to make the furnace more efficient. Bringing the various production processes under the control of the inventor and the production manager, as well as employing local skilled labour, brought clear advantages despite the production remaining small scale for a longer period of time.

The second advantage was with regard to ensuring quality standards. By building his own furnace in 2010, the inventor ensured quality of production outputs. Despite the production processes requiring more time and costs, the decision to build the furnace originated from the risks of working with local pottery equipment. These had been shown to experience a high failure rate in the quality of the ceramic firing process. This required getting overseas knowledge from looking at furnaces that were built in Cambodia and South America, as well as from the ceramic community in Canada, and adapting this knowledge to the local context:

I copied Cambodia, South America, and I'm also a member of Potters Without Borders, an organisation based in Canada . . . [it's a] global community online . . . sharing experience, knowledge. . . . [W]hen I designed . . . the firing place, I consulted them, they gave me a lot of advices for adjustments on my own design and with my people who know better the situation in Indonesia.

(Tirta Inventor)

Developing an in-house furnace was an extensive process that involved sharing and learning from worldwide practices before adapting them to the local context that included working with local labourers. This led to a more extensive and longer period during this stage, where learning was a necessary part of the process to refine and ensure high quality of production outputs. While having his own factory could increase the production costs, the inventor was focused on ensuring that they did not compromise the quality of the product.

The third advantage was the simplicity of the production processes, which proved more efficient and benefitted labourers' learning processes and thus quality standards. The simplicity of the production processes stemmed from not requiring advanced machines and focusing rather on more traditional processes. According to the inventor, it would have otherwise affected production variables such as slower time to market and higher direct costs. For example, the inventor discussed the testing process of the TCM water filter and compared existing approaches with the way Tirta undertook the measurement of the filtration rate. The inventor described that a more sophisticated process would have slowed down the quantity of production outputs:

You know this is the method for accuracy. The more difficult and complicated you have the formula, the more accurate you find the result. But then the process becomes very slow. So you have to wait for a week . . . to come up with the results.

(Tirta Inventor)

While more sophisticated measurement methods would have provided results that may be more precise, the inventor still preferred prioritising time efficiency and simplicity during the production ramp-up stage. In fact, even a sophisticated testing for filtration rates of the ceramic pots would not have been extremely accurate, according to the product testing manager. This was because this type of testing generally relied on human observation, implying a higher possibility of a margin of error occurring:

With this one . . . [i]t is a very simple spreadsheet. . . . I think it's accurate enough. Even measuring with this [complex technique], you cannot make it very accurate. The water level is seen by eye. . . . I don't think they can see it accurately. For instance, this is one centimetre each, maybe one-half a centimetre. They probably just guess – it's near one or two.

(Tirta Product Testing Manager)

The simplicity of Tirta's production processes, in particular in the testing of the filtration rates, provided enough accuracy. Indeed, sophisticated methods would have been more complex to use and not necessarily have provided a more precise accurate reading process. While the inventor did compromise the quality of this testing, he emphasised the need to balance decisions linked to time and costs between using more sophisticated and simpler methods: "The inaccuracy in calculating [should be] compensated by the inaccuracy in reading . . . I think you should have a balance" (Tirta Inventor). For the inventor, there was no point in utilising sophisticated processes to ensure strict accuracy in the calculation if there were already inaccuracies in the reading process.

While simpler methods might have given less accurate calculations, sophisticated methods would still have been difficult for the local context. The inventor reflected on how methods utilised overseas were often complex and difficult to use in the local context (including due to low-skilled labourers):

> I found that other groups of people – from China, and maybe other places, South America – they made [the measurements] from a very complicated calculation of . . . the average velocity. I followed that logic but it is very difficult to understand. So I modified it to make it simpler . . . [b]ecause for him [the product testing manager] it's more difficult to do because he had to understand the concept behind.
>
> (Tirta Inventor)

For the inventor, it was not essential to integrate more sophisticated calculation processes for measuring the filtration rate of the TCM water filter, as their use was also inappropriate for the skills of local labourers. The inventor, however, strongly believed that training the local workers was an essential aspect of Tirta production, as it was the start of new production processes and local workers did not have a highly skilled background.

The importance of training labourers was principally due to having a local production site where equipment, materials and components were available locally, suggesting that local employees could be hired easily. With traditional production processes, hiring local labourers involved training skills for this specific job: "I can see that component can be made locally. Also, the skills can be trained" (Tirta Inventor). As resources could be available locally, it was then implied that local labourers would be familiar with manipulating these resources and the inventor would just train them for particular production processes linked with the product.

For example, testing the quality of the pot involved a popular method, which consisted of checking "the sound [of the pot, which] is very common for ceramic" (Tirta Inventor). This process, however, required experimentation to have discernment of good versus bad quality pots:

> This is the test quality [for a good ceramic filter] and there is also the physical quality. . . . If the sound [by knocking on the pot] is not good, sometimes you have to think to discard or not . . . basically just to have a sense

of whether it is good or not. If the sound is very strong, then it is good. If the sound is not good, it may mean that the firing was not good. If so, the certification is not reached yet. It means that inside the filter, there may have some carbon residue.

(Tirta Product Testing Manager)

Despite the simplicity of the testing process, the product testing manager still highlighted the need for a 'sense' of good quality, which implied expertise and experience in the testing process. The simplicity of the production process still implied learning and training of employees, though providing a more adapted working context for local labourers.

The fourth benefit of in-house production processes was the flexibility in making changes or improvements in the product as well as with the production capabilities (the number of employees and product demand). First, the inventor could try various changes with production processes that were in-house. This led him to test or ask to make changes to the product extremely quickly and easily: "It depends on my instructions. If I ask for this, they will make this" (Tirta Inventor). Remaining at small-scale, in-house production and using simple techniques enabled the inventor and his team to have flexibility in decisions and to learn throughout the production ramp-up stage.

In addition to flexibility in production processes, there was flexibility in the number of employees. The simplicity in production was beneficial, as less sophisticated machines might not require the same level of maintenance, care and complexity in use. The number of employees was adjusted in accordance with the demand for the TCM water filter:

There is one key person – the person who knows everything from the beginning – and the helpers. . . . So if we produce a lot, we ask more helpers to . . . [join]. But if we produce less, maybe we only need one to three persons.

(Tirta Inventor)

The flexibility with the number of employees allowed the inventor to respond to product demand increases progressively, which avoided constraints created by a larger number of employees when not needed.

More recently, the inventor thought of scaling up through cooperative networks across the Indonesian islands. The inventor started discussing with local groups, including cooperatives and microfinance groups, to promote the financing and expansion of Tirta's factories across Indonesia. With the goal to provide wider access to water filtering solution across Indonesia, the inventor was willing to leverage these networks for wider scale production through different production factories:

I started to talk with a group of people in Lamongan . . . the union in one small city in East Java . . . This cooperative has money because they have members who have to pay fee every month. . . . If this money is accumulated, it becomes big enough so, they would start a factory. That's what I have in mind to guide them to make a factory. So their factory can produce this filter by themselves and distribute it to the members. It can be produced freely . . . I can lease fair my innovation to the people, so more people can have access to water.

(Tirta Inventor)

The inventor wanted to share his knowledge of the production process for faster scaling of production through these cooperatives' networks. One of the main reasons was that the inventor was limited physically and financially if he wanted to increase the volume of production and distribution at the time of the interview:

I'm talking about the way that this product could be mass produced. You cannot just rely on my team and me because we're very limited. And also in terms of distribution, it will be very limited only. If you have to send this to Pontianak or Kalimantan, or Sumatra [Indonesian Islands], it will cost more for travel, for transportation, so it increases the price of the product.

(Tirta Inventor)

This decision was based on his understanding that local networks would be clearly beneficial to sustain Tirta business. These would be less expensive and would provide closer production sites across the Indonesian islands than the factory in Purwakarta. The idea of the inventor was to promote the water filter through cooperative members, in particular sharing knowledge on the ceramic filter production across the Indonesian Islands.

Tirta summary

In summary, the Tirta case study identified, clarified and exemplified the majority of the NPDP frugal innovation practices. The analysis described for the four NPDP phases of Tirta confirms that the NPDP framework for frugal innovation has clear relevance to Indonesian start-ups targeting Indonesian BOP consumers' problems. An overview of the four NPDP phases discussed earlier are summarised in Table 5.2.

Table 5.2 Tirta NPDP summary

NPDP stages	Tirta
Opportunity and idea discovery	*FI Practice 1: The opportunity and idea discovery stage has a market-pull approach that is limited within the scope of BOP market constraints.*
	■ **Market-pull:** Identified problems stemming from the local water infrastructure
	■ **BOP constraints:** Not many options for the low-income consumer market to access clean water

NPDP stages	Tirta
	FI Practice 2: The tools and techniques of the opportunity and idea discovery stage allow external idea sources.
	■ **External sources such as knowledge from local presence:** Living in Jakarta, working for the Government's water and sanitation department and consulting for the World Bank gave the inventor clear external insights in regard to the lack of access to clean drinking water
Opportunity and idea screening	*FI Practice 3: The opportunity and idea screening stage focuses on market information, in particular appraisals of BOP consumers' unmet needs.*
	■ **Quality and price of three available products:** Piped water, bottled water and refilled water remained expensive and did not guarantee potable water
	■ **Consumer access to clean water:** Poor access to drinkable water
	FI Practice 4: The opportunity and idea screening stage focuses on business information linked with internal and external capabilities.
	■ **Internal expertise:** Education and personal and professional knowledge in regard to water and sanitation increased the inventor's confidence in further exploring the TCM project
	■ **No external capabilities assessments:** The TCM NPD project was a 'hobby' and a side project for the inventor; he did not feel comfortable using his personal network within the Governmental department where he used to work
Market study	*FI Practice 5: The market study stage has a focus on BOP consumer information related to affordability, complementary needs and product usage context.*
	■ **Meaning of affordability:** Consideration of affordability beyond the product price, including: – The difference between 'too cheap' and 'affordable' – Creating the foundation for an affordable product based on the low quality of the water provided by piped and refilled water, which led consumers to buy expensive bottled water or to boil water, spending on gas
	■ **Product usage context:** Did not consider product usage context, though the inventor sought access to clean water in consumers' homes
	■ **Complementary needs:** Considered basic needs such as daily intake of water
	FI Practice 6: The tools and techniques of the market study stage focus on a firm's immersion with targeted consumers for deeper insights.
	■ **No formal tools and techniques**
	■ **Local embeddedness:** Informal observation and living locally
	■ **Recognised the importance of marketing activities across the concept development phase**
	+ Lack of time and NPDP guidance and expertise in marketing

(*Continued*)

Table 5.2 (Continued)

NPDP stages	Tirta

Technical study	*FI Practice 7: The technical study stage focuses on primary product functionality and business model specifications.*
	■ **Primary product functionality, linked to:**
	  – Quality of water by ensuring efficient removal of the main disease-causing bacteria
	  – Speed of the filtering process to match consumers' preferences
	■ **Business model specifications:**
	  – Easy and cost-effective manufacture of the materials composing the technology of the TCM concept
	  – Many materials options that can be locally grown raw materials (e.g. rice, sawdust and coffee husks)
	FI Practice 8: The tools and techniques of the technical study stage involve seeking basic technological principles and/or architecture and components from existing products.
	■ **Basic technology:**
	  – Sought basic science principles to sieve water and found an old ceramic technology
	  – Use of gravity
	+ **Benefits:** Led to simpler, more accepted and more suitable product to the local context (production costs and local workers' knowledge)

Concept evaluation	*FI Practice 9: The tools and techniques of the concept evaluation stage integrate a set of criteria and/or simple physical version to test concept acceptance.* ■ **No concept testing:** Only considered later the importance of introducing a physical version to BOP consumers ■ **Use of quality criteria:** Reachability and affordability + Possibly due to restrained budget and lack of guidance

Product design stage	*FI Practice 10: The product design stage prioritises local outsourcing weighted off with costs and performance.*
	■ **Prioritised local resource:**
	  – Leveraged already-made ceramic container
	  – Worked with local potteries
	  – Adapted the ceramic composition to local raw materials and utilised a local tap found in rural areas
	■ **Performance–cost ratio:** Used locally designed ceramic container, which did not comply to the inventor's standards; he decided to change to plastic container as well as make his own ceramic pot filter
	+ **Benefits:** Decreased logistic and product development costs
	+ **Coping with costs increase**: More expensive tap but available in rural areas at very low cost
	FI Practice 11: The tools and techniques of the product design stage include DfX techniques specifically aimed at frugal design strategies.

NPDP stages	Tirta

	■ **No formal DfX techniques**
	■ **Pattern of strategic design (and for customisation):**
	  – **Design for easy maintenance:** Removable ceramic pot filter and local tap removable in case of breaking or damage
	  – **Design for easy cleaning:** As any ceramic technology required to be cleaned, the ceramic pot filter was the most adapted technology for BOP consumers (the candle type had an impractical screw that jeopardised the technology performance)
	  – **Design for customisation:** Offered two options of containers

Prototype testing	*FI Practice 12: The tools and techniques of the prototype testing stage include early field-testing.* ■ **No formal testing:** Shared TCM water filter with friends and neighbours ■ **Order sent to NGOs:** First showed impractical ceramic container and also demonstrated fragility of ceramic pot filter, leading to change of pot shape and associated laboratory testing + Required quick ROI to support further R&D

Market testing	*FI Practice 13: The market testing stage involves testing distribution and promotion of the new product through existing local networks.*
	■ **Locally established network:**
	  – Reached local organisations
	  – Used NGOs and social gatherings through WOM (e.g. Arisan)
	  – Sought support from the Ministry of Research, Technology and Higher Education to reach out internal groups such as Islamic educational centres
	■ **Established and joined 'communities of interest' around the potential of ceramic filters in addressing global water issues:**
	  – Reached out Dharma Wanita group
	  – Joined research institutions publishing in environmental engineering journals and The Association of Indonesian Environmental Health and Engineering Specialists (IATPI), the Sanitary Engineering (TP) and the Environmental Engineering (TL)
	  – Established Komunitas Saringan Keramik Indonesia, a community of Ceramic Filter Indonesia
	+ **Benefits of selling to NGOs:** Allowed to connect Tirta to diverse communities of consumers and faster; less financial uncertainties due to buying in bulk (avoiding local pricing strategy through instalments) and due to transporting costs linked to the geographical environment (e.g. widespread Indonesian islands), which could have affected its affordability

(*Continued*)

Table 5.2 (Continued)

NPDP stages	Tirta

	FI Practice 14: The market testing stage includes product demonstration and training as key promotional strategy.
	■ **Brochure and product demonstration:**
	  – Brochure to ensure the right product use and maintenance
	  – Showed filtered water was drinkable
	  – Explained how to clean and get the taste of the water without ceramic taste/smell
	+ **Benefits:** Building trust, understanding of the product functioning to satisfy their taste
	■ **Product training:** Kept on demonstrating to ensure consumers were educated enough regarding how to get tasteless water and how to clean
	+ As pricing strategy via instalments was risky, working with NGOs helped reducing investment risks

Production ramp-up	*FI Practice 15: The production ramp-up stage factors in low-volume production timelines for longer periods, which benefits quality standards such as QA/QC and workforce training.*
	■ **Long-term small scale:**
	  – Small-scale facility (2008–2015 interview)
	  – Simple and traditional methods
	  – Outsourced through re-using equipment and then built in-house production
	+ **Benefits:** Less time and capital start-up costs; adapted to local context; flexibility of production capabilities; flexibility according to product demand; fewer requirements for maintenance care and complexity in use; quickly tested and altered product
	■ **Quality standards:** Decision to bring in-house production process to keep control over quality outputs, despite requiring more time
	  – Did not compromise the pot filter burning process, ensuring strict quality standards
	  – Simple production methods meant adaptation for local labour through training
	  – Local labour's familiarity with experimenting good quality pots for product testing
	+ Flexibility for ongoing learning, product and production modifications

Notes

1 Although TCM (by name) was invented by Risyana Sukarma, the technology was based on the design from Potter for Peace (PfP), which was first developed by Dr. Fernando Mazariegos from Guatemala in 1981.

2 The first prototype of the TCM water filter was composed of a ceramic container, which was stopped due to its heavy weight and leakage problems. The inventor more recently decided to work on the ceramic container design again (2015–current) (see Klaten type) (tcm-filter 2018a).

3 "The category 'improved drinking water sources' includes sources that, by nature of their construction or through active intervention, are protected from outside contamination, particularly faecal matter" (WHO 2008).

References

Asian Development Bank 2016, *Indonesia country water assessment*, Manilla, Philippines, Asian Development Bank, viewed 1 September 2018, <www.adb.org/sites/default/files/institutional-document/183339/ino-water-assessment.pdf>.

Bain, R, Cronk, R, Wright, J, Yang, H, Slaymaker, T & Bartram, J 2014, 'Fecal contamination of drinking-water in low-and middle-income countries: A systematic review and meta-analysis', *PLoS Medicine*, vol. 11, no. 5, pp. e1001644-1–e1001644-23.

MIT 2008, *Global water & sanitation projects – ceramic water filter technologies*, viewed <http://web.mit.edu/watsan/tech_hwts_particle_ceramicfilters.html>.

tcm-filter 2018a, *TCM products available today*, viewed 1 August 2018, <www.tcm-filter.com/info-produk.html>.

tcm-filter 2018b, *Who we are*, viewed 1 September 2018, <www.tcm-filter.com/general-info-eng.html>.

UNICEF 2014, *Water and sanitation: Challenges*, viewed 7 August 2018, <www.unicef.org/indonesia/wes.html>.

Water.org 2018, *Indonesia: Indonesia's water and sanitation crisis*, viewed 7 August 2018, <https://water.org/our-impact/indonesia/>.

WHO 2008, *Drinking water*, viewed 1 September 2018, <www.who.int/water_sanitation_health/monitoring/water.pdf>.

WHO 2018, *Drinking-water: Key facts*, viewed 7 August 2018, <www.who.int/news-room/fact-sheets/detail/drinking-water>.

WHO/UNICEF 2017, *Progress on drinking water, sanitation and hygiene 2017: Update and SDG baselines*, viewed 8 August 2018, <www.who.int/mediacentre/news/releases/2017/launch-version-report-jmp-water-sanitation-hygiene.pdf>.

WHO/UNICEF 2017, *Safely managed drinking water – Thematic report on drinking water 2017*, World Health Organization, Geneva, Switzerland.

WHO/UNICEF Joint Monitoring Programme for Water Supply and Sanitation 2017, *Indonesia: Drinking water*, viewed 7 August 2018, <https://washdata.org/data#!/idn>.

World Bank 2017, *Population total: Indonesia*, viewed 7 August 2018, <https://data.worldbank.org/indicator/SP.POP.TOTL?locations=ID>.

6 The NPDP for frugal innovation

Introduction

With the prevalence of pressing global challenges illuminated by the recent introduction of the Sustainable Development Goals by the United Nations, this book has focused on examining how two start-ups went about addressing problems related to traditional cooking methods and access to clean drinking water, two particularly significant global challenges. In doing so, this book has focused on unravelling the process for how these frugal products are developed, providing a potential pathway from which other major global challenges can be engaged with through the development of frugal innovation.

Frugal innovation is a modern NPD approach increasingly addressing issues in developing, emerging and developed countries, and holds the promise of not only addressing the needs of BOP markets and those living under 8 USD/day,[1] but also transforming their progress towards sustainable development. With the aim to facilitate firms, governments and investors in understanding the frugal innovation phenomenon, this study has looked at the way frugal innovators manage the NPD process of frugal innovation.

Underpinning this study has been the development of the NPD process for frugal innovation (see Figure 6.1). This involved a systematic examination of traditional approaches to the NPDP, drawing together a generic framework to describe the main phases and stages within this process. This has been contextualised through the examination of a range of publications, including detailed case studies on frugal innovation. These studies have been linked with the traditional NPDP, providing insights – where possible – on the types of practices that frugal innovators might implement when adopting a process for the development of their frugal products. This approach led to not only a more systematic conceptualisation of the NPDP, but also the identification of 15 key frugal innovation practices to be examined through the two cases within this study.

With a focus on Indonesia as a major emerging economy in Asia with significant development challenges, this book has examined how two frugal innovators – Prime and Tirta – have engaged with the issues of traditional cooking methods and access to clean drinking water within the Indonesian context. Building on insights from the detailed examination of the practices of these two Indonesian frugal innovators, this closing chapter both refines and highlights the important NPDP decisions across the four phases and nine stages of the NPDP framework for frugal innovation.

In the following sections of this chapter, each NPDP phase will be examined with a focus on identifying and describing the key decisions undertaken by the frugal innovators within this study. This will be framed around the associated stages within each NPDP phase, synthesising the important frugal innovation practices, drawing from the empirical analysis within Chapter 4 and Chapter 5. The two case studies supported almost all the frugal innovation practices established in Chapter 3. However, before looking into more depth at the NPDP framework for frugal innovation, it is important to remind readers this framework does not discuss the flow occurring between the phases and stages of the NPDP. Rather, this is focused on the decisions made by frugal innovators at each of the NPDP stages.

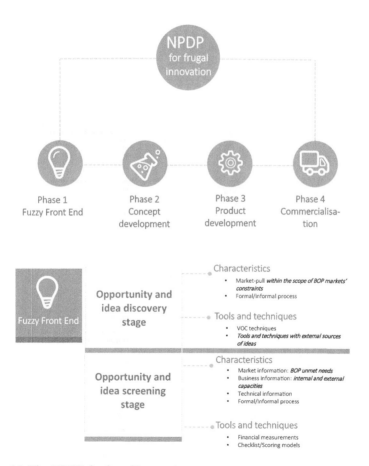

Figure 6.1 The NPDP for frugal innovation

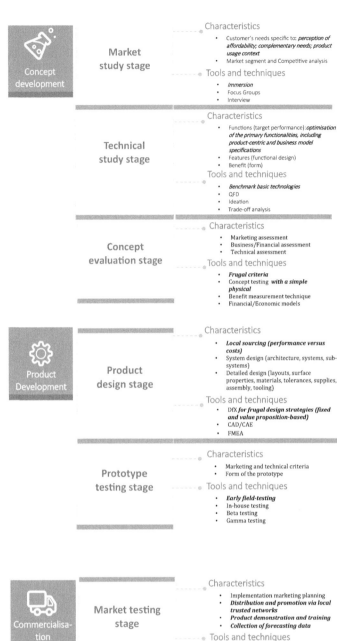

Concept development

Market study stage

Characteristics
- Customer's needs specific to: *perception of affordability; complementary needs; product usage context*
- Market segment and Competitive analysis

Tools and techniques
- *Immersion*
- Focus Groups
- Interview

Technical study stage

Characteristics
- Functions (target performance): *optimisation of the primary functionalities, including product-centric and business model specifications*
- Features (functional design)
- Benefit (form)

Tools and techniques
- *Benchmark basic technologies*
- QFD
- Ideation
- Trade-off analysis

Concept evaluation stage

Characteristics
- Marketing assessment
- Business/Financial assessment
- Technical assessment

Tools and techniques
- *Frugal criteria*
- Concept testing *with a simple physical*
- Benefit measurement technique
- Financial/Economic models

Product Development

Product design stage

Characteristics
- *Local sourcing (performance versus costs)*
- System design (architecture, systems, sub-systems)
- Detailed design (layouts, surface properties, materials, tolerances, supplies, assembly, tooling)

Tools and techniques
- DfX *for frugal design strategies (fixed and value proposition-based)*
- CAD/CAE
- FMEA

Prototype testing stage

Characteristics
- Marketing and technical criteria
- Form of the prototype

Tools and techniques
- *Early field-testing*
- In-house testing
- Beta testing
- Gamma testing

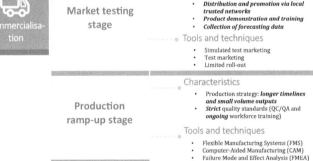

Commercialisation

Market testing stage

Characteristics
- Implementation marketing planning
- *Distribution and promotion via local trusted networks*
- *Product demonstration and training*
- *Collection of forecasting data*

Tools and techniques
- Simulated test marketing
- Test marketing
- Limited roll-out

Production ramp-up stage

Characteristics
- Production strategy: *longer timelines and small volume outputs*
- *Strict* quality standards (QC/QA and *ongoing* workforce training)

Tools and techniques
- Flexible Manufacturing Systems (FMS)
- Computer-Aided Manufacturing (CAM)
- Failure Mode and Effect Analysis (FMEA)

Figure 6.1 (Continued)

In delineating activities and decisions made at each stage, this study seeks to provide a clearer picture of the key practices necessary to develop frugal products. While this is particularly useful in presenting a clear, structured process from which to inform practice, it is worth noting that the NPDP is also characterised by informal, concurrent and iterative practices. This is reflected in the insights provided by the two Indonesian frugal innovators within this study, who did not clearly delineate these decisions across distinct phases and stages of the NPDP. With this context, this study provides a valuable basis for collecting, interpreting and classifying Indonesian frugal innovators' practices, increasing practitioners understanding of the necessary practices at the firm level. To conclude this study, the final sections of this chapter examine the theoretical and practical contributions along with the limitations of this study.

Phase 1: the fuzzy front end for frugal innovation

The fuzzy front end for frugal innovation is the phase when firms instigate their activities aimed at the discovery of new product opportunities. This is focused, in particular, on the key problems and constraints encountered by BOP consumers in developing countries. During this iterative and fuzzy phase, firms evaluate the new product opportunities to ensure they pursue one that has the right fit for what they seek to achieve. In general, frugal innovators aim to ensure the new product opportunity is meaningful for those who need this innovation and that their business will be sustainable. Two stages constitute the fuzzy front end phase: the opportunity and idea discovery stage and the opportunity and idea screening stage – around which the discussion ahead is structured.

Opportunity and idea discovery stage

Looking first at the opportunity and idea discovery stage, the traditional NPDP literature shows that most firms have two potential innovation approaches as part of the discovery stage for developed countries: technology-push and/or market-pull (e.g. Brem & Voigt 2009; Whitney 2007). This study suggests that new frugal product opportunities are generally based on a market-pull approach shaped by the constrained environment in which frugal innovators operate – which forms the first key frugal innovation practice.

When looking at the tools and techniques utilised during the opportunity and idea discovery stage, the NPDP literature highlights three common tools: brainstorming, industry assessments and VOC (e.g. Cooper & Edgett 2008; Koen, Bertels & Kleinschmidt 2014; Yeh, Yang & Pai 2010). This study, however, demonstrates the techniques for frugal innovations should rather facilitate the input of ideas and new product opportunities from outside the firms – forming the second key frugal innovation practice. This can include looking at existing products failing to be accepted by BOP consumers, observing the local environment and checking the Sustainable Development Goals and Government's calls to action.

The VOC technique can also be relevant, as it is an ideation technique driven by consumer needs and preferences (e.g. focus groups, lead users, social networks)

(Cooper & Edgett 2008; Crawford & Di Benedetto 2011; Markham & Lee 2013). While this could be somewhat relevant to frugal innovators, this has a drawback when applied by start-ups targeting BOP markets in developing countries. Impediments like the costs of focus groups and/or customer visits to BOP markets might not be suitable to budget-constrained firms or to the trusting pattern often existing within communities. Lead users and social networks may also be hard to identify in markets often lacking existing NPD and/or experiencing limiting dissemination of technology knowledge, thus limiting data to help firms increase their understanding of consumer routines (Aranda Jan, Jagtap & Moultrie 2016; Prahalad 2012). Figure 6.2 summarises the opportunity and idea stage for frugal innovation. Both frugal innovation Practice 1 and Practice 2 are further clarified ahead with conceptual and empirical examples.

FI Practice 1: the opportunity and idea discovery stage has a market-pull approach that is limited within the scope of BOP market constraints

When frugal innovators consider BOP problems, the approach adopted has been shown to originate within the distinct constraints of the BOP consumers' environment (Nakata & Berger 2011; Prahalad 2012). Rather than nurturing ideas from a wider NPD search and market problems, narrowing the scope of identification by considering BOP constraints enables the identification of new frugal product opportunities during this opportunity and idea discovery stage. This is because the constraints that bound BOP consumers can reveal distinct gaps in the market, revealing potential new frugal product opportunities. Evidence from M-PESA, Prime and Tirta case studies exemplify this market-pull approach, focused within the existing constraints of BOP consumers.

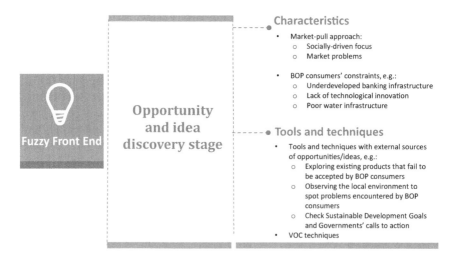

Figure 6.2 Opportunity and idea discovery stage for frugal innovation

Looking at M-PESA, a cash transfer system in Kenya, Hughes[2] first focused on addressing poverty in developing countries, and in particular looking at the MDGs (Hughes & Lonie 2007). Building from this, Hughes identified the UK Government's FDCF, a grant focusing on financial innovation, which narrowed his focus to financial problems encountered by low-income people in developing countries. Hughes understood that the under-developed banking infrastructure was a major barrier for local entrepreneurs, as they could not easily transfer money (Hughes & Lonie 2007). Driving his NPDP from the MDGs, Hughes responded to common infrastructure problems in developing countries, illustrating a market-pull approach (Hughes & Lonie 2007).

The two Indonesian firms within this study also illustrated the importance of market factors linked with constraints present in Indonesia, influencing the NPDP focus for both frugal innovators. The Prime inventor, for example, had a specific NPD goal of resolving problems with "direct impact with people here in Indonesia" (Prime Inventor), illustrating a clear market-pull approach. One of these market problems was the inventor's observation of Indonesians' dependency on unsustainable fuel usage, as he was also involved in researching, lecturing and innovating locally with a focus on renewable energy. Prime's NPD discovery was also connected with technological constraints of local BOP consumers. Realising that Indonesian BOP consumers were often constrained by a low rate of innovation addressing their everyday issues, Prime focused on developing innovations focused on Indonesian needs. In particular, the inventor was interested in solving a local problem through a technological product that relied on more sustainable fuels.

Similarly, Tirta also had a clear market-pull approach that was shaped through the inventor's observation that Indonesian BOP consumers could not easily access clean drinking water, limiting their daily water intake. With this in mind, the inventor approached the NPD with a focus on providing a solution to Indonesian water problems. The inventor focused on responding to local consumers' problems with water access while also recognising the limited water infrastructure in Indonesia. He was keenly aware of the inadequate local infrastructure and in particular the distinct limitations associated with basic water services such as expensive piped water, which did not even guarantee water quality to end users. These constraints shaped his idea of finding an affordable and accessible solution for those who could not afford, and did not have access to, safe drinking water on a daily basis.

Hence, when considering the approaches adopted by frugal innovator, there is a strong focus on market problem identification and social value-added innovation. This approach to NPDP highlights a market-pull approach. During the opportunity and idea discovery stage, this study, therefore, recommends that frugal innovators delimit the scope of their search within the constraints encountered by BOP consumers. These constraints reduced the scope of focus at the outset of frugal innovators' NPDP and on problems encountered in BOP markets specifically.

FI Practice 2: the tools and techniques of the opportunity and idea discovery stage allow external idea sources

This study proposes that most frugal innovations stem from recognising the unmet needs of BOP consumers at the opportunity and idea discovery stage. A reason for this approach is that BOP consumers are often classified as being under-served, seeking alternative solutions that are better adapted to specific demographics and characteristics (Zeschky, Widenmayer & Gassmann 2011). Using techniques querying about unmet needs reflects frugal innovators' bottom-up approach that has been recognised in the literature. It contrasts with the traditional approaches of firms using brainstorming or industry assessment tools to identify new product opportunities. These are dictated by firms' needs in the search of new product opportunities, like a top-down approach suggests.

In this study, a bottom-up approach where frugal innovators discover new product opportunities is emphasised, with firms looking at identifying BOP unmet needs. A range of different frugal products emphasises this, including the Jaipur Foot, Prime and Tirta. The Jaipur Foot team, for example, identified that patients who were fitted with imported Western designed prosthetics did not wear them, potentially because they were unadapted and lacked key usability features suited for the Indian context (Disability and Development Partners 2013; Macke, Misra & Sharma 2003). This inadequacy of existing product solutions fuelled the idea for a new, better adapted prosthetic device to suit the context of the Indian market and consumers.

Similarly, the two Indonesian inventors within this study showed how their discovery of new frugal product opportunities was inspired by external sources, implying looking outside their firms. For example, Prime's focus was clearly set on searching for external problems to solve when the Prime inventor recognised the drawbacks of existing product offerings. This led to the discovery of the Indonesian Government's call for action to address recurring explosions of LPG stoves through offering an alternative product.

With a similar approach, through Tirta inventor's strong local presence and experience, it was discovered how unreliable the access to safe water was for Indonesians. Living in Jakarta, working in the water and sanitation field and, more recently, undertaking consulting work with the World Bank offered external knowledge to the inventor regarding current problems faced by Indonesians. Stimulating the inventor's ideas for the new product, the external environment in which he was embedded helped him in sourcing his ideas within this stage, and in particular in understanding the breadth of the water access problem.

This study thus points to the discovery of new frugal product opportunities coming from observing the environment in which BOP consumers live. This helps in the identification of problems that inspire the future development of frugal innovations. This can include considering products/services that are too expensive, unadapted or unaccepted by BOP consumers. Also, frugal innovators that are locally embedded can observe how BOP consumers live and notice their daily problems. Moreover, the Sustainable Development Goals and Government's calls to action are also options for frugal innovators to be inspired to start their NPDP with new frugal product opportunities.

Opportunity and idea screening stage

When looking at the NPDP literature related to the opportunity and idea screening stage, firms assess and eliminate new product opportunities that are not worthy of further investment for both consumers and the firm (Cooper 2011; Ulrich & Eppinger 2012). This preliminary evaluation generally targets technical, market and business information (Cooper 2011; Girotra, Terwiesch & Ulrich 2010). While each of these targets add value to firms' optimal screening of new product opportunities, this study determined the importance of investigating BOP consumers' unmet needs and firms' business capabilities as pivotal.

The first one is in regard to BOP consumers' unmet needs to ensure size of the targeted market and real value of an alternative product (Practice 3). The second one is linked to external and internal business capabilities to ensure a viable business model (Practice 4). While financial and technical assessments also have their role during the opportunity and idea screening stage, it is often accommodating firms' strategic budgets for their NPD projects (Hughes & Lonie 2007; Markham & Lee 2013). Figure 6.3 summarises these two practices linked with the opportunity and idea screening stage for frugal innovation. Then the following discussion is structured around frugal innovation Practice 3 and Practice 4.

FI Practice 3: the opportunity and idea screening stage focuses on market information, in particular appraisals of BOP consumers' unmet needs

During the opportunity and idea screening stage, frugal innovators should clarify further BOP consumers unmet needs in order to explore the size of the targeted market and the real value of offering an alternative product. Obtaining a deeper

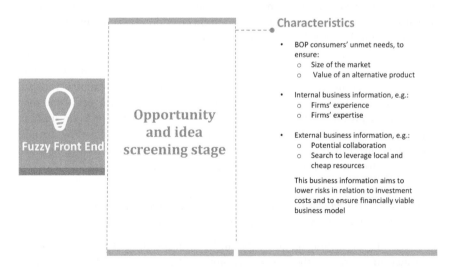

Figure 6.3 Opportunity and idea screening stage for frugal innovation

understanding of the market problems at the fuzzy front end assists in evaluating the degree to which consumers basic needs are not met (e.g. McManus et al. 2008). The goal is to select a problem and aim to respond to BOP consumers' basic needs. The emphasis is on screening new product opportunities on the basis of the problems they address, rather than on firms' prioritised criteria (e.g. Markham & Lee 2013).

The Jaipur Foot, Prime and Tirta exemplify this aspect of the opportunity and idea screening stage for frugal innovation. For example, the founders of the Jaipur Foot sought to understand why amputees were not using available prosthetic limbs, which revealed that the only options available to them were impractical and expensive prosthetics (Disability and Development Partners 2013). This was critical information to move forward to further investigate a more adapted prosthetic product. The Prime inventor sought to understand consumers' problems with LPG stoves, researching both why existing products fail and the value of pursuing an alternative solution. For example, these consumers' lives were first at stake with increased LPG explosions. Additionally, the inventor noticed that LPG stoves were inaccessible and unaffordable in some areas of Indonesia and BOP consumers lived without alternatives for cooking. Finally, government subsidies given to BOP consumers to buy LPG fuel were at risk of diminishing, leaving them with even fewer options for cooking.

The inventor of the TCM filter examined why existing products did not meet consumers' needs, leading to the screening of three key products: piped water, bottled water and refilled water. This investigation revealed critical problems with price, accessibility and water quality, all of which influenced the inventor in conceptualising a more affordable product that would allow better access to quality water than current available options. In addition, the inventor's focus on market criteria, in particular BOP consumers' unmet needs, was reflected in his socially oriented decision, where he put financial outcomes second: "It's not only because we are trying to get some profit . . . also we want to help people" (Tirta Inventor). It was clear that the inventor sought to address existing problems and made sure of it during this screening of new product opportunities.

It is, therefore, argued that the screening of new frugal product opportunities prioritises market assessments, and in particular investigating the unmet needs of the BOP consumers. At this stage, the main focus is understanding the size of the targeted market who is experiencing the problem and the real value that an alternative product will offer to these consumers. In other words, during this opportunity and idea screening stage, frugal innovators assess how low-income consumers currently respond to their basic needs, and the aim is to highlight the importance for the development of a frugal innovation alternative.

FI Practice 4: the opportunity and idea screening stage focuses on business information linked with internal and external capabilities

The second type of information that can be critical during the screening stage for frugal innovators is the business feasibility of a future frugal product. This involves the screening of both internal and external capabilities, which support and strengthen the viability of pursuing such prospects (e.g. Hughes & Lonie 2007). Looking at the NPDP literature, this includes financial information, which is frequently utilised as a screening criterion. Like traditional NPDP, frugal innovators also investigate business capabilities to ensure the frugal product is financially viable. Evidence from the M-PESA, Prime and Tirta cases all emphasise the importance of responding to new product opportunities with firms' available internal skills and expertise as well as external resources. External resources can include collaborative partnerships and locally available, cheap resources, both of which lower risks associated with investment costs.

Looking at internal capabilities in the M-PESA case, Hughes considered the M-PESA project as feasible due to the strong expertise in telecommunications networks that Vodafone has (Hughes & Lonie 2007). Similarly, both inventors from Prime and Tirta considered the scope and breadth of their internal capabilities, with focus on the relevance of their expertise for the NPD project they sought to pursue. Prime's inventor took account of his background in laser technology and various innovations he had previously developed, which increased his confidence to engage further with the local cookstove problems. It was also evident for the Tirta inventor that his educational background and strong expertise in the water and sanitation field gave him the ability to explore further the possibility of a water filter.

Looking at the importance of external capabilities, the collaboration with Safaricom in Kenya was a key basis for pursuing the M-PESA project, as it helped Vodafone in gaining access to market knowledge to establish local operations (Hughes & Lonie 2007). Similarly, Prime emphasised the important role of existing small factories in the local area of their operations, including the ability to undertake quick and cheap R&D on the future cookstove concept. This information –being able to undertake quick and cheap experiments – was pivotal in the Prime inventor's decision because it helped lower the financial risk for the Prime cookstove project. This was particularly important as the inventor did not want to borrow money or seek investment, avoiding outside obligations on project decisions: "Most of my research is self-financed; [so that] we have no responsibility to the [investors]" (Prime Inventor).

The Tirta inventor did not explore external capabilities filter because this project was initially a personal 'hobby' and was not a priority at the time. Pursuing this project informally at home, the inventor did not perceive the need to screen locally for available resources. However, he was aware of the potential to leverage his strong personal network of government colleagues, although he did not feel comfortable to integrate his past relationships in this NPD project. While the Tirta inventor did not explore available business capabilities at this stage, Tirta engaged with collaborators at later NPDP phases such as through local ceramic workshops and NGOs.

What is generally clear for frugal innovators is the importance of assessing available business capabilities before pursuing a viable NPD project into more resource-intensive phases of development. The key goal is to limit uncertainties and risks by exploring both internally to the firm and externally through collaborations and existing local resources access. While financial issues/preferences such as the unwillingness to seek external investment or tackling low capital requirement are evident, it is not consistent across the Indonesian cases or existing research.

Phase 2: concept development for frugal innovation

The concept development phase for frugal innovation is the exploration of market, technical and economic aspects of a NPD project. There are generally three key stages – market study, technical study and concept evaluation – across which preferences for frugal innovation are spelled out. Starting with the market study stage, frugal innovators undertake an in-depth exploration of three consumers' needs: affordability, complementary needs and product usage context. Furthermore, immersive tools and techniques come along this stage, enabling development team to be embedded into BOP consumers' environment.

In the technical study of a frugal innovation, development team refines their focus on the primary functionalities of the product as well as on its business model specifications. This study also suggests a technique enhancing frugal outcomes, the role of benchmarking existing basic technologies. Finally, the concept evaluation stage prioritises the combination of important criteria and concept testing with a physical version of the product while still needing further empirical research. The three key stages of the concept development phases will be discussed ahead.

Market study stage

During the market study stage, firms generally seek to identify consumer needs, wants and preferences along with detailed search and analysis of quantitative and qualitative market data (Cooper 2011; Griffin 2012). The firms' purpose is to seek the VOC to help establish consumer requirements to integrate them into the future design of the product (Otto & Wood 2000; Ulrich & Eppinger 2012). In the case of frugal innovation, this study illustrates the important role of three key BOP consumers' needs, which is frugal innovation Practice 5. To facilitate this market study stage, the NPDP literature also suggests the use of tools and techniques, such as focus groups, interviews and consumer visits/observations (Cooper 2011; Ulrich & Eppinger 2012; Urban & Hauser 1993).

While to some extent these tools and techniques are beneficial, this study demonstrates that using more practical/field-based tools and techniques is more relevant and insightful for frugal innovation, as suggested by the frugal innovation Practice 6. In particular, a suitable value proposition is largely dependent on the development team's ability to understand and translate consumer perceptions and needs into technical and design attributes (Cooper 2011; Griffin & Page 1996), which is thus highly relevant for frugal innovation. Figure 6.4 shows a practical summary of the market study stage for frugal innovation. Both frugal

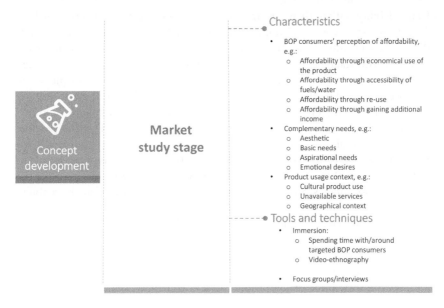

Figure 6.4 Market study stage for frugal innovation

innovation Practice 5 and Practice 6 are further clarified ahead with conceptual and empirical examples.

FI practice 5: the market study stage has a focus on BOP consumer information related to affordability, complementary needs and product usage context

As part of the market study stage for frugal innovation, this study shows the key role of exploring three types of consumers' needs along with market and competitor analysis. In particular, evidence from existing studies and the two case studies in this book highlight that when frugal innovators make decisions at the market study level, three key consumer needs are considered: consumers' perceptions of affordability, complementary needs and the context linked to the product usage.

When looking at affordability for frugal innovation, this study demonstrates that a price-point ratio should go beyond the frugal product price and includes additional cost-effective advantages (e.g. Ramdorai & Herstatt 2017). This implies that investigating affordability revolves around not only financial aspects, but also the way BOP consumers perceive and value the product offering. For example, the ChotuKool fridge was set at a low price but also offered Indian BOP shop-sellers additional income streams from being able to use this product to sell fresh food and water on the side of the road (Whitney 2010).

The price-point ratio in this case was inclusive of consumers' perceptions of affordability, rather than basing it only on firms' costs perspective such as when using target costing (Cooper 2011; Prahalad 2012; Weyrauch & Herstatt 2017). The ChotuKool had a critical advantage in functionality for its price when compared with standard fridges; consumers did not want to pay for a big fridge because it was not useful to them. They preferred the possibility to move the ChotuKool around the house (or side of the road) according to their needs.

In the same vein, Prime guaranteed that affordability advantages stemmed from more than just the cookstove's price (initially, 17–24 USD). The product was more economical to use through high fuel efficiency and the possibility to re-use burnt wood as fertiliser. The way that BOP consumers were going to use the stove was thus valuable in framing how they were going to perceive the affordability advantages. Similarly, Mukerjee (2012, p. 1) stated that affordability is about "what customers feel is an affordable price".

This is also reflected with Tirta, who developed an affordable water filter solution by going beyond offering a low-cost water filter. The inventor first defined what was perceived as too cheap and as 'affordable', and investigated competitors' product offerings to create the price foundation for an affordable product. Going beyond the price of the product, the affordability was influenced by the quality of the water provided by existing solutions, such as piped and refilled water. Piped or refilled water did not guarantee water quality, leading consumers to buy expensive bottled water as well as spending on gas to boil water. These issues resulted in indirect costs for BOP consumers in accessing clean and safe water, thus adding another meaning to affordability when consumers' perception was considered.

Looking at complementary needs, frugal innovators also go beyond traditional consumer needs, aware of other aspirational, critical and desirable needs. Frugal innovators consider other needs than just the inadequacy and/or impracticality needs during this stage; they understand that the product has to resonate with how BOP consumers live (Viswanathan & Sridharan 2012). For example, harsh environments often lead BOP consumers to prefer long-term investment when making purchase decisions (Viswanathan & Sridharan 2012). Also, BOP consumers often do not aspire to own a cheap-looking product that does not fit their lifestyle ambitions (Pitta, Subrahmanyan & Tomas Gomez-Arias 2008; Prahalad 2012).

Prahalad's (2012) cookstove developed in India illustrates this by taking account of BOP consumers' self-esteem. The cookstove needed to be a more stylish product than other cookstoves in India (Prahalad 2012). Comparably, the failure to consider Indonesians' preference for aesthetic during the market study stage of Prime had later consequences on the product acceptance. However, aesthetics attributes were included in later product refinement as Prime received consumer feedback about this, emphasising the aspirational preferences needed to be considered for product acceptance. Similarly, in the conceptualisation of the TCM water filter, the inventor integrated human beings' need to access the daily minimum of two litres of water a day. The inventor ensured the consumers' needs were broadly investigated from a human-centred perspective, integrating more than traditional needs.

Finally, looking at the product usage context, this study demonstrates that frugal innovators investigate the social, cultural and geographical contexts in which the product will be used. As a key aspect of the market study stage, market information related to the context of usage generally integrates the resource-poor context in which BOP consumers live as well as their cultural and geographical heterogeneity (Mattson & Wood 2014; Prahalad 2012; Whitney 2010). This has been demonstrated in previous studies, for example with the product usage context in the Jaipur Foot case. Uneven grounds in villages and/or rice fields made walking, praying and working uncomfortable when Indian BOP amputees wore available (Western) prosthetic products (Gollakota, Gupta & Bork 2010). Failing to consider where the product was used would have led Jaipur Foot's development team to miss some important consumer requirements in the design of the Jaipur Foot to accommodate the context of use.

The product usage context was also factored into the market study stage of the Prime cookstove. For example, local consumers' need for a new cookstove included the practicality of not repeatedly adding fuel while cooking. Underlying this was a cultural trait as where the person cooking is often multitasking while cooking their food for long hours, in particular when cooking rice. Prime's competitors did not integrate this aspect into their product development and subsequently failed in getting product acceptance within the Indonesian market. While Tirta did not put emphasise on the product usage context, the inventor still understood the lack of access to clean water and had the goal that BOP consumers get clean water at home. The inventor took into account of the BOP water accessibility needs. Another example of the product usage context that the inventor considered in later phases of development was when he realised the impracticality of moving a heavy and larger sized water filter across Indonesia. This emerged from the Indonesian geographic context where products need to be shipped long distances and across islands, thus reaching rural consumers' homes across inconsistent and poorly developed infrastructure such as roads.

Thus, this study highlights the importance of considering three key consumer needs when developing successful frugal products. First, developing a low-cost frugal product goes beyond the financial aspects of affordability and takes into account the cost of owning the product, such as being cost-effective to use, easy access to fuel and easy to repair. Second, complementary needs should be integrated in the design the concept such as life aspirations, aesthetics, basic needs and other non-traditional consumers' needs. Not considering complementary needs in the development of frugal products could lead to later failures when entering the market. As a final aspect, the context in which BOP consumers live, such as the cultural, geographical and social environment, influences strongly how consumers will interact with the product and its likely success.

FI Practice 6: the tools and techniques of the market study stage focus on a firm's immersion with targeted consumers for deeper insights

During the market study stage, it is pivotal for frugal innovators to have a deeper understanding of BOP consumers' needs and to utilise immersive techniques, such as field-based investigations. Immersive techniques such as being locally embedded focuses frugal innovators on spending time with their target market, and aims to provide an understanding of local culture and context in which the product will be used. While this allows greater engagement and relationship development, it also offers the opportunity to better understand consumers, their routines and contextual settings that influence the product development (Aranda-Jan, Jagtap & Moultrie 2016; Prahalad 2012).

A range of studies, such as in Whitney (2010) and Wood and Mattson (2014), recommends comprehensive field-based techniques due to the lack of available BOP market data. Other reasons supporting the use of immersive techniques include the need to investigate consumers' needs before attempting to find a solution (Hughes & Lonie 2007). Spending time "on the ground assessing customers' needs well ahead of designing the functional specification of any technology-based solution" is critical during the concept development phase (Hughes & Lonie 2007, p. 80). Viswanathan, Yassine and Clarke (2011, p. 567) also recommend "deep listening and understanding of customer needs", however, without further details of how to do it. The case study of Prahalad (2012) suggests video-ethnography and content/cluster analysis as part of this market study stage.

This study demonstrates that being 'present' in the targeted market, in combination with additional tools and techniques, can strongly facilitate the collection of important information for this NPDP stage. For example, the Prime inventor was embedded in the Indonesian context for many decades and had deep insights into local consumers' cooking needs. The Prime inventor also informally observed users' preferences and lifestyles to better understand competitors' failure. Reinforcing the importance of deep immersion techniques were missing data that the inventor did not acquire at this stage, such as in relation to product aesthetics, indicating that further direct contact with BOP consumers could have been instrumental during this stage. Even though techniques to collect market information were used, it was clear that Prime had limited capabilities to undertake this stage efficiently. Prime's budget was limited, so the inventor leveraged his background and ongoing local presence in deciding not to use formal tools and techniques.

Tirta did not utilise any formal tools and techniques; yet, based on his local presence, the inventor also built his understanding of the local context and BOP consumers' needs to further conceptualise the TCM water filter. The inventor was locally embedded, as he worked and lived in Indonesia for many decades. The inventor recognised stronger marketing activities could have been done across the concept development phase. Similar to Prime, the market study stage of the TCM project was also affected by the lack of time, and guidance and expertise in marketing.

It is, therefore, clear that although the Prime cookstove's and TCM's market study stage did not integrate formal immersion into BOP consumer lifestyles, they are both examples of the importance to spend time in the local settings. Expanded budgets for this stage and more guidance in how to undertake the market study could have allowed both firms to formally embed themselves in their targeted markets and get consumers' insights during this market study stage. The weakness in not doing this was addressed at later stages of their NPDP, highlighting this as a key consideration for frugal innovators when undertaking their product development.

Technical study stage

During the technical study stage, most NPD development teams generate conceptual designs based on three main characteristics: functions, features and benefits (Krishnan & Ulrich 2001; Pahl, Wallace & Blessing 2007; Ulrich & Eppinger 2012). For frugal innovation, this study concentrates on the targeted performance (or the product functions) of the frugal concept. Informing 'what' the product should do in a measurable way, frugal innovators focus on primary product functionality and business model specifications – which relates to the seventh key frugal innovation practice. This encourages the prioritisation of these two product functions before seeking to address secondary product specifications.

In addition, the NPDP literature suggests the most common tools and techniques for the technical study stage include QFD, ideation and trade-off analysis (e.g. Crawford & Di Benedetto 2014; Pahl, Wallace & Blessing 2007; Ulrich & Eppinger 2012). While these tools and techniques might be relevant to a certain extent, this study indicates that benchmarking similar performance outputs in basic technologies can help generate concepts with the right value proposition for frugal innovation. This eighth key frugal innovation practice focuses on basic technologies as these are found to deliver many benefits, such as reduced operating costs and complexity of use, including training staff and better product acceptance. Figure 6.5 summarises the technical study stage for frugal innovations. The following discussion is structured around frugal innovation Practice 7 and Practice 8.

FI Practice 7: the technical study stage focuses on primary product functionality and business model specifications

The technical study stage allows the development team to deconstruct targeted performance into functions, features and benefits. Among those three, frugal innovation NPD team distinctly prioritises primary functionalities and business model specifications. Looking first at primary functionalities, Prahalad (2012), Rao (2013) and Zeschky, Winterhalter and Gassmann (2014) support the importance of narrowing the development team's focus on 'must have' functions and features. This is really about finding the right solution without the need for a perfect concept (Praceus & Herstatt 2017). This approach helps in the optimisation of performance requirements that are critical for BOP consumer acceptance, allowing the avoidance of 'non-value-adding' functions and/or the optimisation of less important targeted performance. Such a focus does not reduce performance levels; instead, it leads to satisfactory performance of the core functionality of the product, as illustrated by this study and previous research.

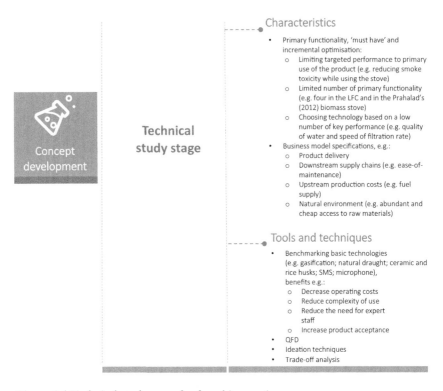

Figure 6.5 Technical study stage for frugal innovation

For example, both the development teams of the Prahalad's (2012) cookstove and the LFC wheelchair restrained their focus on four primary performance areas (Winter 2013; Winter & Govindarajan 2015). If one of these functionalities were not considered, the product could not have offered the successful value propositions for both products. The Prime case also emphasises this, with the inventor clearly focused on the primary product functionality. As part of this, it was a focus on the product feature that consumers should not breathe smoke while cooking with the stove. The choice of a technology was, therefore, based on the goal to reduce toxic smoke only during the cooking time. This contrasted with the technology used in LPG stoves that did not emit smoke also after turning the stove off.

Focusing on primary functional goals helped to avoid over-optimising the targeted performance related to the smoke emitted (the key goal was to avoid smoke emission when people are cooking such as when cooking indoor). An over-optimised technology like in the LPG stove was also too expensive and had issues, as discussed earlier. Further indications of the inventor's focus on primary functionality were that aesthetics were not a prioritised performance requirement. The inventor simply re-used an external stove design that was commonly accepted among BOP consumers worldwide.

The inventor of the TCM water filter also illustrated how his choice of technology stemmed from a narrow focus on two product primary functions, linked to the quality of water and speed of the filtering process. The inventor sought to achieve acceptable (adequate) filtration performance. The inventor first narrowed the technical study to optimise performance requirements linked to efficient removal of the main disease-causing bacteria. The second primary functionality was achieving a fast enough filtering process to match consumers' preferences for the speed of water filtrated. Consumers had strict preferences in being able to drink water faster than when they boiled water. However, a 'too fast' filtration rate could have diminished the water quality, in particular in filtering bacteria.

Looking at the importance of business model specifications, this is linked to the need to overcome local constraints (e.g. infrastructure, education or energy needs) and reach BOP consumers, which is pivotal for frugal innovation (Gassmann et al. 2017; Lehner & Gausemeier 2016; Simanis 2011). Prioritising business model specifications helps NPD development teams to anticipate a solution to these local constraints early in the technical study. For example, the Prahalad's (2012) cookstove had a primary functionality around the ease-of-use, which was an aspect related to the product as well as to the business model. On this basis, the development team ensured downstream services, such as a convenient way for consumers to access the stove's fuel.

Such considerations of business model specifications at the technical study stage are also evident with both Prime's and Tirta's NPDP. From Prime cookstove's specifications, these were linked to BOP consumers' access to the fuel and its price. This also went further into the fuel production cost, which influenced the choice of the technology. Due to the abundant forests in Indonesia, the inventor developed his technology around the accessibility to free wood, instead of relying on industrial production of other fuels. Seeking and incorporating business model–centric information allowed greater incorporation of convenience and affordability features for consumers of the Prime cookstove.

Tirta also considered business model specifications around the materials composing the ceramic technology of the TCM concept; he made sure it could be easily and cost-effectively manufactured. Considering these types of business model specifications at this stage revealed that the ceramic clay ingredients could be combined with many types of husks, opening options to adapt to locally grown raw materials. By considering such specifications as part of the key performance criteria, the TCM was easier to produce, and thus more accessible and affordable for consumers.

This study, therefore, highlights that frugal innovators concentrate on a limited number of targeted performance areas linked to primary product functionality and business model specifications. This first implies that frugal innovators focus on essential functions and avoid exceeding BOP consumers' expectations. It is not about achieving optimal results during the technical study stage, as BOP consumers do not have such expectations; rather, it is about frugal innovators recognising that their consumers are instead focused only on an optimised solution to their core problems. Second, the consideration of business model specifications allows development teams to anticipate the future constraints of the BOP market context. Taking account of the local infrastructure, available raw materials, accessibility of such supply and its production costs all increase the product acceptance due to being more practical and inexpensive to use.

FI Practice 8: the tools and techniques of the technical study involve seeking basic technological principles and/or architecture and components from existing products

The key approach this study indicates as relevant to the technical study stage for frugal innovators is the benchmarking of similar performance outputs in the basic technologies. Doing so can help generate the right value proposition for a frugal concept being developed. The aim is to get the benefits of re-using existing technologies in a new and imaginative way. Unique insights from this study illustrate the use of basic technologies in reducing costs, without having to actively seek cost reduction, as has been argued for in a previous study (i.e. Rao 2013). Evidence in this study shows the use of basic technologies lowers operational costs, reduces complexity of use for consumers, avoids high expertise of staff, circumvents unnecessary functions and features, and increases product acceptance.

Examples of frugal concept where the development teams have explored basic technologies include the M-PESA and the Siemens Fetal Heart Monitor. Both cases incorporated basic technologies (SMS and microphone, respectively) in their new products (Agnihotri 2015; Hughes & Lonie 2007). Rather than striving for breakthrough technological innovation, the M-PESA team instead looked for basic technologies, in particular mobile technologies that were already applicable in East Africa to re-use and re-apply in the context of Kenya (Hughes & Lonie 2007). Siemens also did not consider advanced technologies like ultrasound technology due to its potential cost impediments and complexity of use (Löscher 2011; Prahalad 2012).

Sourcing basic technologies was also one of the key foundations for Prime and Tirta's technical study stage. In the case of Prime, this search related to gasification technology, which was determined to be appropriate in addressing targeted performance requirements. This technology was based on technical principles that could increase the flame duration and decrease the smoke toxicity, almost comparable performance as if the product had an electrical blower, an impractical extra feature. This gasification technology relied on natural draft and did not require electricity inputs like what would be required with an electric blower. The gasification technology was, in fact, simpler, more practical and more accepted by BOP consumers in the Indonesian context.

In the technical study of the TCM water filter, the inventor explored filtering technologies that were simple in the sieving of the water, and he identified an old ceramic technology. The inventor identified its use in the UK in the 1800s and more recently in Cambodia, where the technical feasibility was already successfully established for filtering the local polluted water. He realised that the way this technology operated fitted with his goals. Using this technology also included the use of 'gravity', which also circumvented the use of additional features, such as adding a pressure mechanism. Similar to Prime, with the use of basic gasification principles, the use of an old ceramic technology had several benefits. The use of the ceramic technology allowed a simpler design and use of the product, and was more accepted by BOP consumers as well as more suitable to the local context, including reducing production costs and accessing local workers' knowledge.

This study, therefore, indicates the use of tools and techniques for the technical study stage for the inventors, or development teams, is to benchmark existing basic technologies and assess how they fit with their targeted performance. Finding basic technology instead of a sophisticated one offers several benefits such as decreasing product costs and complexity of use, avoiding expert staff handling the product, unnecessary functions and features, increasing product acceptance and more adaptation to the local context.

Concept evaluation stage

Through the concept evaluation stage, firms investigate market, technical and business/economic feasibilities of the concept under development (Cooper 2011; Murphy & Kumar 1996). Such investigations often involve evaluation criteria based on technical performance, business and financial relevance (e.g. strategic, financial and resource-fit), and market benefits (e.g. positioning, benefits, potential sales targets) (Cooper 1988; Crawford & Di Benedetto 2014). The three most common tools and techniques identified in the NPDP literature are benefit measurement techniques, financial/economic models and concept testing (e.g. Cooper & Sommer 2016; Crawford & Di Benedetto 2014; Markham & Lee 2013).

For frugal innovation, however, this study illustrates the importance of integrating consumers into the evaluation of frugal concepts. As the ninth frugal innovation practice, the use of criteria in combination with a physical version is seen critical for the concept evaluation stage of frugal innovation (e.g. Bingham, Whitehead & Evans 2016; Mattson & Wood 2014; Simanis 2011). Despite existing evidence of this frugal innovation practice, further empirical research should be undertaken regarding how frugal innovators can better evaluate frugal concept during the concept evaluation stage. This is because even though the inventor of one of our case studies emphasises the importance of having a simple physical version at this stage, the actions observed in his concept evaluation stage were not clearly showing this decision. Figure 6.6 provides a practical summary of the concept evaluation stage for frugal innovation. The following discussion focuses on frugal innovation Practice 9.

FI Practice 9: the tools and techniques of the concept evaluation stage integrate a set of criteria and/or simple physical version to test concept acceptance

During the concept evaluation stage, firms evaluate market, technical and business/economic assessments. This study indicates frugal innovators will have a

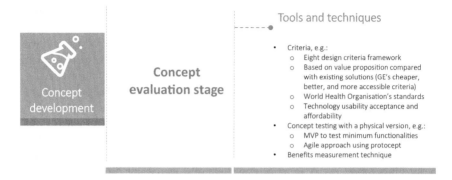

Figure 6.6 Concept evaluation stage for frugal innovation

focus on a combination of key product criteria and a physical version of the product that will be tested with consumers. Looking at the use of product criteria, several studies show the efficiency of using criteria to evaluate a frugal concept, such as the eight design criteria developed by Bingham, Whitehead and Evans (2016). They suggest questioning whether the product responds to key consumers' needs, wants and preferences, including "Does the BOP consumers have emotional connection with the product?" and "Is the product easy to repair?".

Other approaches, such as from GE and KAF, also revolve around key product criteria. GE developed a validating process before undertaking further development on healthcare innovations, using three key criteria for the value proposition: cheaper, better and more accessible healthcare solution than current available products (GE Healthcare 2017; Ramdorai & Herstatt 2017). Before implementing this formal evaluation process, GE decreased its focus on financial criteria, influencing the testing and development of the electrocardiogram (ECG) Mac 400 (Singh 2011). In the KAF example, a water filtering technology for the arsenic-tainted water of Nepal, the role of criteria as well as the use of early prototypes allowed eight technologies out of 50 to be chosen, including the KAF. These were screened by technical, financial and social design criteria, including meeting the World Health Organization (WHO) standards, and technology usability, acceptance and affordability for BOP consumers on less than 1 USD a day (Murcott 2007). In line with these earlier studies, Prime and Tirta both focused on targeting technical and market aspects related to key quality criteria. For example, the inventor of the Prime cookstove focused on safety, toxicity and comfort, whereas Tirta targeted product reachability and affordability. These criteria also included BOP consumers' preferences, such as its price and access.

Additionally, a physical version is proposed as a realistic method for testing the frugal concept, in particular to uncover additional consumer insights and increase market understanding (Mattson & Wood 2014). Early concept testing could avoid wasting resources on overdeveloped prototypes not perceived as valuable by BOP consumers. Prime demonstrated the importance of this practice when only a physical advanced version of the product developed in later phase of development received consumer feedback and led to the redesign of a more on-target concept. As the Prime cookstove failed once, this need for redesign reflects the benefits in showing the new product under development to BOP consumers. On the other hand, Tirta did not evaluate the concept with a physical version; however, the inventor admitted later the importance of showing a working product to consumers to gauge consumers' interests in the product.

It is important to understand why Prime and Tirta did not engage further consumers in concept testing. Prime's restrained budget as well as possible lack of guidance in regard to the formal NPDP could underlie this approach. The Tirta inventor also reflected that he lacked marketing efforts throughout the concept development phase, which was mainly due to its focus on addressing social problems. In this regard, several case studies, like the KAF case study, demonstrated the importance of concept testing; however, the development team had sufficient funding in their case. The test of physical versions of the KAF occurred with a multitude of grants such as 115,000 USD from the World Bank, as part of MIT projects partnering with several organisations in Nepal (e.g. Environment & Public Health Organization) (MIT 2008; Ngai et al. 2007).

In addition, Prime's neglect in developing a simple version at the concept evaluation stage parallels a common mistake start-ups make in overdeveloping their concept (Ries 2009). To address this, Ries (2009) suggests that this can be overcome with the concept of minimum viable product (MVP), which allows the testing of an early version that has the bare minimum features, based on what is most valuable to the consumers. Another concept adapted to this scenario could be the agile approach prescribed by Cooper and Sommer (2016, p. 523), with the development of a 'protocept', a type of prototype "to seek customer feedback and validation often, early, and cheaply". These approaches are highly relevant to frugal innovation, as the frugal product prioritises only the primary targeted performance. As frugal innovations are generally simple at this NPDP stage, the physical concept can be a simpler and cheaper version of the concept.

This study highlights the need for further research on the role of criteria and the use of a physical version during the concept evaluation stage. Initial evidence from the Tirta case was not clear whether a simple physical model tested with BOP consumers was useful in their concept evaluation stage. Despite this, insights from GE, KAF and Prime are supportive of the importance of both types of criteria and a physical version of a concept for the concept evaluation stage of frugal innovation. The idea of the MVP and agile approach in this NPDP stage could also be worthy of further investigation in the context of frugal innovation.

Phase 3: product development for frugal innovation

The product development phase focuses on the physical development of a new product and is considered as the back end of the NPDP. This phase is more resource-intensive and less flexible, and constitutes two main stages: product design and prototype testing. This highlights specific decisions by frugal innovators regarding the origins of material sourcing and the use of specific tools and techniques for frugal innovation.

In the first stage, frugal innovators tend to prefer local outsourcing of the design of components and the use of materials. While frugal innovators seek a reasonable performance–cost ratio, they prioritise performance over costs if the local resources jeopardise the quality of the product. A specific technique used by frugal innovators is DfX, where X stands for frugal design strategies including mandatory and value proposition–based design. In the prototype testing stage, frugal innovators have preferences for early field-testing as a complementary testing to laboratory testing in real settings with various stakeholders. The following discussion focuses on these two key stages.

Product design stage

During the product design stage, the development team advances the engineering parameters of a chosen concept, enabling the shaping of its physical design bounded by formerly established technical, market and economic requirements (Pahl & Beitz 2013). From the traditional NPDP literature, this stage is defined by both the product system and detailed design characteristics. These include decisions around the product architecture, components, systems, materials and tolerances. These decisions are pivotal for the manufacturing costs, assembly planning, supply chain decisions and the reliability and performance of the product (Osteras, Murthy & Rausand 2006).

For frugal innovators, this study illustrates these aspects of the product design stage should balance out local make-or-buy decisions with the right level of performance and costs – forming the tenth frugal innovation practice. While in this stage frugal innovators seek cost reduction, they would not compromise the core functionality of the product over costs if the local resources do not meet the set standards.

The NPDP literature also suggests various commonly used tools and techniques for this product design stage, such as DfM, DfA, CAD/CAE and FMEA (Graner & Mißler-Behr 2013; Pahl & Beitz 2013; Ulrich & Eppinger 2012). While these latter tools and techniques are somewhat relevant, DfM and DfA, on the other hand, tend to prioritise firms' manufacturing and assembly costs and time-effectiveness. This study highlights that DfX techniques for frugal innovation should relate to frugal design strategies that prioritise both the BOP consumers and the firms. X represents any design strategy that guides the development team to handle existing resources accordingly (Eastman 2012).

While clarity can be improved around the use of DfX techniques, this study identifies two types of DfX, including fixed DfX and DfX based on the product value proposition, as the 11th frugal innovation practice. Figure 6.7 provides a practical summary of the frugal innovation practices across the characteristics, tools and techniques of the product design stage. Following this, the discussion focuses on the product design stage for frugal innovation structured around frugal innovation Practice 10 and Practice 11.

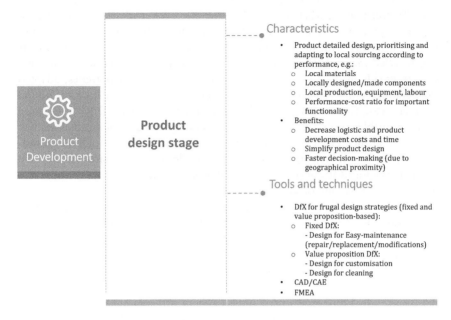

Characteristics

- Product detailed design, prioritising and adapting to local sourcing according to performance, e.g.:
  o Local materials
  o Locally designed/made components
  o Local production, equipment, labour
  o Performance-cost ratio for important functionality
- Benefits:
  o Decrease logistic and product development costs and time
  o Simplify product design
  o Faster decision-making (due to geographical proximity)

Tools and techniques

- DfX for frugal design strategies (fixed and value proposition-based):
  o Fixed DfX:
    - Design for Easy-maintenance (repair/replacement/modifications)
  o Value proposition DfX:
    - Design for customisation
    - Design for cleaning
- CAD/CAE
- FMEA

Product design stage

Product Development

Figure 6.7 Product design stage for frugal innovation

FI Practice 10: the product design stage prioritises local outsourcing weighted off with costs and performance

In the product design stage for frugal innovation, this study illustrates that design decisions prioritise local resources that fit with a satisfying performance-cost ratio. In case performance does not reach set standards, frugal innovators do not compromise the quality of the product over costs. Several benefits stem from integrating locally available resources across the frugal product design, in particular for firms' product development and production (e.g. Numminen & Lund 2017; Ray & Ray 2011; Winter 2013; Winter et al. 2010). Evidence shows these include cost reduction, simplicity of design, adaptation of locally available production sites and faster decision-making through geographical proximity. This study also reveals that cost is not prioritised over the characteristics linked to the core functionality of the frugal product.

Evidence of the importance and benefits of considering locally available resources was observed in the product design decisions of several existing case studies. For example, the ECG Mac 400 case highlighted that leveraging local resources, such as using existing 'ready-made' parts, overcame the need to design new ones. The LFC wheelchair case study also stresses the costs and simple design benefits from using bike parts in the design of the wheelchair, as those were made locally. This was also echoed in the study of Prime and Tirta. Both used local production facilities and/or equipment, and both adapted their product design decisions according to local components.

The Prime inventor had a clear preference for local resources due to cost benefits: "I prefer using what we can do here . . . even if it's a bit more expensive than if we produce in China" (Prime Inventor). He also took into account of a local factory with its machinery, skilled labour, existing stove components and recycled materials in his design decisions. Similarly, the Tirta inventor leveraged already-made ceramic containers, worked with local potteries, adapted the ceramic composition to local raw materials and utilised a local tap found in rural areas. The two inventors also pinpointed the benefits from prioritising locally available resources, both at the product development and production levels. These included cost reductions for logistics and product development, simplicity of design and adaptation of locally available production sites for low-cost maintenance for BOP consumers. It also allows faster decision-making due to the geographical proximity of suppliers.

Frugal innovators also prioritise the set standards for the product performance over costs; their key goal is to ensure that the product functionality meets the right performance and avoid considering costs (e.g. Ramdorai & Herstatt 2017; Rao 2013; Weyrauch & Herstatt 2017). Such decisions were clearly observed in both Prime and Tirta. For example, Prime's initial use of local recycled materials to design most of the Prime cookstove's components led to low product durability. As a result, Prime substituted some of them with more expensive materials such as with imported stainless steel. To compensate for the increase of price and thus ensure that the Prime cookstove remained affordable, more expensive materials were used only for those components where quality was more critical.

While Tirta benefitted from logistics, practical and cost advantages in using locally available resources, the inventor did not compromise quality. He avoided relying on local potteries for the ceramic pot filter due to not meeting his quality standards, choosing instead to establish an in-house production process for the ceramic filter. He could also have chosen a cheap tap for the TCM water filter, though if the tap were leaking and bad quality, the core functionality of the product would have been ruined. He did not compromise this and chose a better quality tap. To compensate for the cost increase, with the example of the tap, Tirta ensured that the tap was available in rural areas at very low cost. However, previous studies, such as Rao (2013), have placed more emphasis on cost reduction during the product design stage, which was less of a priority at the start of the product design of the Indonesian firms. They both intuitively started with locally available resources, as they found some satisfying performance in sourcing locally, which eventually led to cost reductions (Numminen & Lund 2017; Tiwari & Herstatt 2012).

So it is clear that frugal innovators prioritise locally available resources at both the product and production stages. Doing so leads to several benefits such as cost reductions in logistics and product development, simplicity of design and adaptation of locally available production sites. Moreover, it allows faster decision-making through geographical proximity. Nonetheless, despite their cost advantages, frugal innovators still prioritise performance if local resources are not up to the standards they seek and would modify the source of supply as a result.

Potential ways of offsetting the increase of costs include trading off between components requiring better materials and availability of a component close to BOP consumers' product use.

FI Practice 11: the tools and techniques of the product design stage include DfX for frugal design strategies

For frugal innovators, this study highlights that DfX techniques for frugal innovation should specifically relate to frugal design strategies. DfX techniques can help frugal innovators during the product design stage to anticipate the development costs and processes of the frugal product. In particular, this study illustrated some new insights into how to prioritise DfX techniques for frugal design strategies, including through establishing fixed and value proposition-dependent design for frugal innovation.

Looking first at fixed (or necessary) DfX techniques, this relates to frugal design strategies commonly found across a wide variety of studies. For example, Viswanathan and Sridharan (2012) suggest a multitude of DfX techniques that should be integrated as part of the product design stage of frugal innovation, such as design for Multiple Purposes, for Customisation, for Low Literate Users and for Local Sustainability. Ray and Ray (2011) propose Design for Modularity, where a modular system design integrates removable parts of the products to adjust the original product design to ongoing. This also relates to the concept behind Viswanathan and Sridharan's (2012) Design for Multiple Purposes, which designs a product that is "multifunctional and contextually malleable" (p. 62).

Despite Prime and Tirta not demonstrating a formal use of such techniques, they both displayed patterns of modular architecture, with the layout of some components removable when required. Both aimed at enabling easy replacement/repair/improvement of the most important and damaged components to lower the costs of ownership on BOP consumers. The design of the Prime cookstove integrated a replaceable combustion chamber, the product's engine, to avoid changing the whole product, and only the part that was often broken. Similarly, Tirta's TCM water filter was designed to be both easy to maintain and to repair in the event of damage or misuse by making the ceramic pot filter replaceable.

One of the main advantages of this technique, which we can call 'design for easy maintenance', is the cost-effectiveness both for the firm and the BOP consumers for repairing, improving and/or maintaining damaged components without changing the whole product. This study also shows this can be an additional strategy to keep the frugal product affordable, on top of the prioritisation of local resources (Tiwari, Kalogerakis & Herstatt 2014; Viswanathan & Sridharan 2012). For example, such a design kept both Prime's and Tirta's product affordable via cost-effective ownership. It allowed the repair/replacement of the damaged combustion chamber and ceramic pot filter rather than the whole product. It has also allowed continuous performance improvement of the removable components without requiring major production changes.

When looking at the DfX techniques dependent on the value proposition, this technique reflects a design strategy that is customised to key BOP consumers' needs. For Prime and Tirta, not only did "Design for Easy Maintenance" allow for easy repair and replacement, but also practicality for consumers was sought to facilitate the cleaning of the Prime cookstove and TCM water filter. In particular for Tirta, the inventor chose the design structure of the ceramic pot filter on the basis of the condition it was easy to scrub often. Providing that ceramic technologies – ceramic pot and candle type – require a monthly scrub, the candle type could have jeopardised the technology performance due to a screw in the system design that is impractical to remove. For Prime, the removable component was also practical for retrieving the charcoal from burnt wood, adding value to the product usability and therefore product acceptance. Tirta also used another strategic "Design for Customisation", which was linked to the TCM's value proposition. The TCM was developed to offer two options of containers, which meant Tirta ensured the product design integrated the possibility to change the containers.

In summary, frugal innovators develop the product design of frugal innovation following certain patterns that DfX techniques related to frugal design strategies can facilitate. This study shows that patterns of product design can be fixed or dependent on the value proposition. Some DfX, like Design for Easy Maintenance, should be part of the product design stage, whereas other DfX such as Design for Customisation can be dependent on the value proposition of the frugal innovation. While clarity around this could be further investigated, this study illustrates that such technique provides cost and time benefits to frugal innovators and better target BOP consumers. This is because when using such techniques, the development team can anticipate necessary frugal design strategies before further resource-intensive activities are undertaken on the product.

Prototype testing stage

The prototype testing stage facilitates the product testing as well as the refinement and validation of the desired benefits and performance (Cooper 2011; Crawford & Di Benedetto 2014). At this stage, both the technical and marketing aspects are generally assessed. The key characteristics of this stage leads a firm to consider the types of information required to test the product and the form of the prototype chosen for this testing. Moreover, the NPDP literature suggests three common tools and techniques to facilitate this process: in-house testing, beta testing and gamma testing (e.g. Cooper 2011; Gaubinger et al. 2014; Markham & Lee 2013).

While frugal innovators should acknowledge these tools and techniques, implying they could do testing on a beta and gamma (advanced) version, this study rather highlights that the frugal product should go into the field as early as possible – forming the 12th frugal innovation practice. For financially constrained firms, such as start-ups, this study highlights the value of collaborating with NGOs or seeking supportive funding for these activities. Figure 6.8 summarises

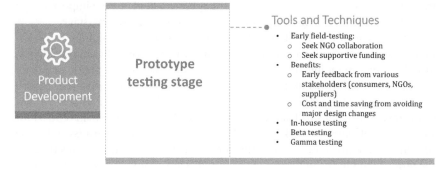

Figure 6.8 Prototype testing stage for frugal innovation

this practice the prototype testing for frugal innovation. Following which, the discussion focuses on frugal innovation Practice 12.

FI Practice 12: the tools and techniques of the prototype testing stage include early field-testing

Looking at the prototype testing for frugal innovators, this study reveals that early field-testing is a pivotal technique to ensure that the frugal product is put among BOP consumers and in their environmental context. The consequences of not undertaking field-testing in early product development, such as rectifying critical product design issues, can be avoided prior to further production through this technique (Mattson and Wood 2014; Radjou & Prabhu 2015). Evidence of this is seen across several case studies within this study. For example, the Barefoot Power Go Lamp and KAF case studies, as well as the research by Mattson and Wood (2014), Radjou and Prabhu (2015) and Wood and Mattson (2016), high-lighted the importance of iterating product design in the context of the targeted BOP consumers and early in the product development phase.

This also resonated with both Indonesian firms. Prime suffered the conse-quences of not undertaking extensive field-testing in the product development phase and had to modify the cookstove design once production ramp-up had started. The Prime cookstove was shared only with close friends, which was determined as a sufficient evaluation before moving to the production ramp-up stage. However, moving forward meant the production and distribution of more than 1,000 Prime cookstoves to Indonesian BOP consumers was initiated with-out field-testing.

Using the stove in the BOP market environment, critical feedback was then given to the development team on the shape, durability and flame duration of the stove. These product design issues could have been addressed prior to fur-ther production if field-testing had been undertaken, especially as these further changes led to successful acceptance of the Prime cookstove in Indonesia. The decision by Prime not to undertake field-testing, and the later benefits stemming from the interaction of consumers with the product, allude to the importance of deploying the field-testing technique during the prototype testing stage.

The inventor of the TCM also shared the product with close friends, neighbours and NGOs, from which the development team received critical feedback, including understanding the consumers' sense of safety with a plastic container and the way the lid was designed. They also highlighted their preferences with the simple versus fancier plastic container. The use of field-testing reflects the idea of the inventor that a small and careful entry in BOP markets remains critical for success: "Small entry in market should be small at first due to trust issue, in case of failure at the first entry" (Tirta Inventor). He was aware that it takes time for the product and its technology to be accepted. Tirta additionally sent some products to NGOs across Java Island, which saved the inventor from further critical design changes. The first TCM water filter designed with a ceramic container was found to be impractical when sent to NGOs, with them giving negative feedback on the product. The inventor realised the fragility of the ceramic pots during transportation when an order was sent to NGOs across Indonesia, leading to changing the design of the ceramic pot.

Considering this change of pot design meant that redesigning and adapting the shape of the pot filter as early as during the product development phase saved Tirta the time and costs associated. In particular, if the shape of the pot filter changed, the product testing processes associated to the pots required modifications too. Thus, undertaking testing under real-life contexts allowed the inventor to make changes to the product and production processes before moving to the commercialisation phase. Nonetheless, while being close to potential consumers at this prototype testing stage helped the Tirta inventor refine some of the TCM water filter's design, more field-based prototype testing could have provided additional feedback.

A key finding in this study extending the frugal innovation literature is from these two Indonesian start-ups reflecting the need for funding. Both of them sold their products as soon as possible for ROI, which could explain why they did not take time to deepen their field-testing technique. Prime's lack of extensive prototype testing with BOP consumers stemmed from its need to acquire ROI as quickly as possible via sales: "We were able to sell the stove, then we could get profit. Otherwise we had no profit" (Prime Inventor). Selling the Prime cookstove enabled financial sustainability. However, this happened after the prototype testing stage and meant that time and costs spent on product design changes were not as refined as they could have been prior to further production. Only after further production of stoves did Prime receive funding support from a local non-for-profit organisation.

For the inventor of the TCM, collaborating with local NGOs provided less financial uncertainty during the market testing stage, as Tirta was not making money yet: "I cannot earn money out of my selling . . . At least, the income could pay for the staff [with the 200 units that the NGO bought]; if you sell less, you have less income" (Tirta Inventor). This finding about how financial constraints have impacted on the two Indonesian case studies provides a unique insight into the prototype testing stage of frugal innovators in developing countries. It is, therefore, suggested that start-ups should seek funding assistance or potential collaboration with local not-for-profit organisations or NGOs to ensure the prototype testing stage is not overlooked.

In summary, frugal innovators benefit from putting their new product in the field for testing before moving to the commercialisation phase. In contrast to laboratory testing where the settings are different from the contextual environment in which BOP consumers live, field-testing allows the product to interact with the BOP market environment. There are clearly benefits in putting the prototype under real-life contexts such as the early product feedback, potential cost and time saving from overcoming major changes in the product design and related production processes.

Phase 4: commercialisation for frugal innovation

The commercialisation phase is the final phase of the NPDP for frugal innovation when the new product is introduced into the market in higher volume of production. The focus of this stage is to ensure the introduction of the right product among BOP consumers while managing frugal innovators' production facilities. This phase is divided into two key stages – market testing and production ramp-up – and offers insights into three key frugal innovation practices.

During the market testing stage, frugal innovators overcome the lack of promotion and distribution channels by leveraging local networks, which enable the dissemination of frugal products through WOM and social-based infrastructure. In addition to relying on existing networks of people, frugal innovators complement the promotion and distribution strategy with a more engaged approach that includes product demonstration and training. Finally in the production ramp-up stage, the production timescale and volume strategy are intertwined, as frugal innovators tend to remain small scale for a longer period of time. This strategy during the production ramp-up stage has several benefits including cost-effectiveness, adaptation to the local context, flexibility in production capabilities, ongoing learning and strict QA/QC. In the following sections, this phase focused on these two key stages – market testing and production ramp-up.

Market testing stage

The market testing stage allows the final testing and validation of the product in real life as well as the testing of associated marketing planning (Cooper 2011; Griffin & Somermeyer 2007; Ozer 1999). One of this stage's characteristics relates to the assessment of a firm's marketing strategy, with the NPDP literature highlighting several relevant aspects such as place, promotion, price and product (Awa 2010; Kotler 2016). Another characteristic of this stage is the broader group of consumers that this testing stage includes as compared with the earlier stages, which allow for the collection of forecasting data in regards to purchase intent, future sales and market share (Kotler 2016; Ulrich & Eppinger 2012).

Across these two characteristics, for frugal innovators it appears that the marketing strategy should be adjusted from traditional promotion and distribution strategies – translating into frugal innovation Practice 13 and Practice 14. Practice 13 illustrates how frugal innovators can leverage locally established networks as a promotion and distribution channel. This involves leveraging the effect of WOM and the social infrastructure across a wide variety of groups. Practice 14 relates to the role of a more engaged promotion strategy with BOP consumers, including product demonstration and training, ensuring BOP consumers understand the value and functioning of the product. Figure 6.9 summarises these frugal innovation practices for the market testing stage of frugal innovation.

The NPDP literature also discusses the most common tools and techniques such as simulated test marketing, test marketing and limited roll-out (Cooper 2011; Crawford & Di Benedetto 2014; Kotler 2016), which can be used alone or in combination.

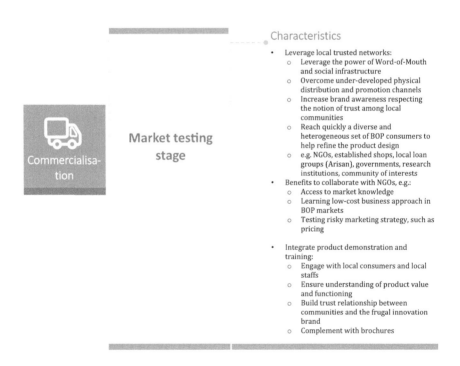

Figure 6.9 Market testing stage for frugal innovation

FI Practice 13: the market testing stage involves testing distribution and promotion of the new product through existing local networks

Looking first at frugal innovation Practice 13, it is clear that local trusted networks are pivotal to disseminating frugal products, and increasing awareness and attractiveness among BOP consumers and distribution agents. Through local networks of people, frugal innovators can reach BOP consumers easier, as these consumers often receive information about new technologies or products through these channels (Sharma & Iyer 2012). This approach leverages the power of WOM and the social infrastructure underlying these local trusted networks, which is critical for the market testing stage for frugal innovation for three reasons.

First, leveraging local trusted networks helps overcoming under-developed physical distribution and promotion channels characterising developing countries (Radjou & Prabhu 2015; Sharma & Iyer 2012; Weidner, Rosa & Viswanathan 2010). Second, the importance of establishing brand awareness through locally established networks originates from the notion of trust existing within local communities. Finally, reaching a diverse set of BOP consumers and gaining an understanding of their heterogeneous preferences can help firms refining the frugal product design before full roll-out.

Examples of such networks can include collaborating or selling the product through NGOs, established shops, local groups of interest and the government. The use of local established networks can be observed in several case studies. This includes in the product testing and associated marketing strategy of the ChotuKool fridge, which was adapted after showing the product to village gatherings involving more than 600 local women (Furr & Dyer 2015). This case also highlighted distribution points integrating a trusted network among Indian postal shops to reach local Indian BOP consumers (Furr & Dyer 2015; Innosight 2017). This approach removed the need for expensive marketing campaigns, with the WOM increasing the awareness of the ChotuKool at minimal cost (Furr & Dyer 2015; Whitney 2010).

Both Indonesian firms show evidence of successful product promotion and distribution by tapping into established and trusted networks to access their targeted markets. This study supports the arguments of Brugmann and Prahalad (2007) with how frugal innovators can benefit from such groups, and in particular, NGOs. These include capitalising on the NGO's local knowledge, low-cost budgeting and adapted marketing techniques (such as pricing strategy), while also minimising the risks of investment and indirect costs for market testing.

For example, selling and distributing to NGOs, both Prime and Tirta were able to reach a wider range of consumers across remote communities. Other notable findings are in relation to the benefits of collaborating with NGOs. NGO channels enabled access to a diversity of consumers, and thus more expansive and diverse feedback on the product from the communities' heterogeneity. For Prime, reaching out to differing communities highlighted that the Prime cookstove was not suitable for all wood houses across different regions in Indonesia, leading to the readjustment of the stove legs. Moreover, frugal innovators can capitalise on the NGO's local knowledge, as well as low-cost budgeting and adapted marketing techniques such as pricing strategy, while also minimising risks of investment and indirect costs for market testing. For Tirta, this meant being able to overcome the revenue uncertainty that stemmed from selling to individuals through instalments and instead sold to NGOs in bulk.

Other trusted networks observed in both Indonesian case studies were the benefits found in reaching out to the Indonesian Government. This approach led the Prime cookstove to promote locally from a trusted source and the TCM water filter to reach out to internal established groups linked to the government such as Islamic education centres. Tirta also used local 'communities of interest' as part of its distribution and promotion strategy, including joining research institutions and founding their own 'community of interest' around the benefits of ceramics for water filter.

Hence, when considering the market testing stage for frugal innovators, one of the important decisions for the promotion and distribution strategy is to include local trusted networks of people established within the BOP markets. This acts as a powerful WOM technique, leveraging the social infrastructure that has replaced the under-developed physical infrastructure existing in developing countries. Frugal innovators can reach out to several types of groups, including NGOs, local loan groups, established shops, communities of interest and government. Specific benefits stem from working with NGOs: increasing access for frugal innovators to further market knowledge, learning low-cost business approaches and taking investment risks while testing marketing strategy (e.g. pricing strategy).

FI Practice 14: the market testing stage includes product demonstration and training as key promotional strategy

Moving to the second frugal innovation practice of the market testing stage, this study highlights that frugal innovators complement the testing of their marketing strategy with product demonstrations and training. This is an engaged approach with local consumers and staff, such as distribution agents, that better guarantees the value and functioning of the products are correctly understood (Weidner, Rosa & Viswanathan 2010). This encourages local consumers and distribution agents, and demonstrates and teaches about the product and its associated benefits (e.g. Nakata & Weidner 2012; Radjou & Prabhu 2015). This study demonstrates that integrating product demonstration and training in the promotion and distribution strategy avoids product misuse and potential misconceptions. Engaging through this way also brings a notion of trust within local communities (Radjou & Prabhu 2015; Simanis 2011), as observed in the case studies discussed ahead.

In the M-PESA case, the development team implemented familiarisation training to distribution agents and consumers (Hughes & Lonie 2007). Due to the M-PESA novelty, the potential misunderstanding of this product's benefits was particularly high, which influenced the team to integrate demonstration and training in their market testing. When developing a new financial platform for

Kenyan BOP consumers, the implementation of training was pivotal to learn how to navigate the M-PESA application.

On the basis of similar reasons, the promotional strategy for both Prime and Tirta market testing included product demonstrations and further training. For example, such demonstrations helped in promoting the Prime cookstove as a credible product: "Nobody would buy the cookstove until they see how it works . . . even if they see nice pictures and explanations" (Prime former BDM). As part of their product demonstrations, both firms engaged with stakeholders through product training and education (e.g. distribution agents, consumers). To guarantee local consumers understood the benefits of the Prime cookstove, local distribution agents and BOP consumers were trained on how to use and look after the stove to minimise misuse of the product.

At Tirta, the development team talked a lot about trust building, which involved demonstrating and educating consumers on how to use the TCM water filter. In both cases, doing so was focused on not only selling the product but also educating consumers to understand the functioning and the value of the product. Additional findings show that both firms also complemented these engaging approaches with brochures to ensure that consumers remember the right product use and maintenance approaches with their product.

The market testing stage for frugal innovators should thus integrate product demonstration and training to engage further with local consumers and staff, along with brochures. This study shows how pivotal these two approaches were to promote and raise awareness of the product functioning, maintenance and its value among local stakeholders. Spending time demonstrating the product among local communities also enabled building relationships between consumers and the brand.

Production ramp-up stage

The production ramp-up stage relates to the planning, testing and finalisation of manufacturing and assembly processes, including both the production and product performance (Murthy, Rausand & Østerås 2008; Ulrich & Eppinger 2012). The importance of this stage stems from the effective management of all the variables moderating firm's production outcomes, including quantity and quality losses, manufacturing costs and delay in time-to-market (Almgren 2000; Brauner et al. 2016).

The NPDP literature advocates two key characteristics to consider during this stage including the production strategy (including timelines and volume goals) and quality standards (including QA/QC and workforce training). In the NPDP literature, Winkler, Heins and Nyhuis (2007) argued that running production at small scale for too long can be less efficient, delivering less output and requiring a high amount of resources.

However, as the final and 15th frugal innovation practice, this study highlights that frugal innovators are more inclined to long-term and small-scale production, as opposed to seeking rapid production scale-up as it is often done in traditional

NPDP. There are several benefits to undertaking this strategy, and one of the most important is that the preference for small-scale outputs is intertwined with the search for ongoing quality standards. This often occurs through employee training and strict QA/QC mechanisms. While human resources have often factored in traditional production ramp-ups (e.g. Glock, Jaber & Zolfaghari 2012; Winkler, Heins & Nyhuis 2007), it is also a pivotal requirement for frugal innovators due to the (often) absence of sophisticated machines. Figure 6.10 provides a practical summary of the production ramp-up stage for frugal innovation, including all the benefits stemming from choosing a small scale for longer periods. This preference refers to the frugal innovation Practice 15 and is discussed ahead.

FI Practice 15: the production ramp-up stage factors in low-volume production timelines for longer periods, which benefits quality standards such as QA/QC and workforce training

Looking at the production ramp-up stage, frugal innovators tend to choose small-scale manufacturing plants without rushing to upscale production outputs. Despite sparse frugal innovation literature on the topic (e.g. Donaldson 2006; Gassmann et al. 2017), this study highlights numerous benefits of a small-scale production approach for frugal innovators. Small-scale production size offers a cost-effective advantage due to the possibility of accessing local and more traditional production, including labour, know-how and equipment. This is cost-effective due to smaller start-up investment and a faster time to market due to less time spent on developing sophisticated production facilities. In addition, small scale also provides flexible production capacities, including being adaptable to consumer demand and feedback for product and production changes, and enabling ongoing learning. Also, small-scale production increases frugal innovators' time to enforce strict quality standards through QA/QC and ongoing employees' training.

Small-scale production was used by both Prime (2010–2015) and Tirta (2010–present). The production of the Prime cookstove relied on a local small-scale

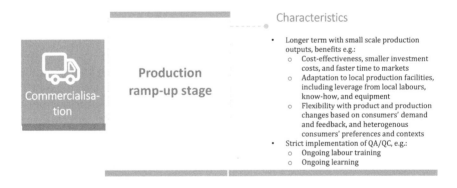

Figure 6.10 Production ramp-up stage for frugal innovation

factory until Prime decided to outsource production to a larger Indonesian producer. The TCM water filter production was also initiated and remained small scale, with the production processes built from scratch in a local car repair workshop before centralising them in-house.

The numerous advantages of doing so were evident from the literature and in these two cases. The frugal innovation literature discusses how having a small-scale production enables cost-effective access to locally and simpler production site including equipment, labour and know-how (e.g. Gollakota, Gupta & Bork 2010; Ray & Ray 2011; Seghal, Dehoff & Panneer 2010). Gassmann et al. (2017) highlighted the importance of faster time to market when developing frugal innovation for BOP markets, rather than seeking high-quality standards through production sophistication. In the same vein, the study of Ray and Ray (2011) on the Tata Nano case illustrates the preference for local cheap labour and less automated equipment due to the cost benefits. Sehgal, Dehoff and Panneer (2010) also highlighted the advantages of using local production resources, leveraging the expert local labour and available equipment.

In the production ramp-up stage of Prime, the inventor also used a local small factory, adapting his production needs to the equipment, labour and know-how for cookstove production. This small-scale production was also readily available and had the sufficient capacity to adapt to Prime's first intended sales at low-costs. Similarly for Tirta, using a local small facility was also adequate for its initial production needs. It was cost-effective, as the production processes remained simple and traditional, and adapted to the local context. Simpler production methods implied less time and less capital invested at the outset of this NPDP stage when compared with more sophisticated methods of production.

In addition, remaining at a small scale allowed flexible production capacities for both Indonesian firms. This includes remaining adaptable to potential product and production changes as well as allowing ongoing learning. Evidence from the frugal innovation literature highlights the key reasons for this, including the high probability that frugal products require changes from varying preferences and behaviours within BOP communities (Viswanathan, Yassine & Clarke 2011; Whitney 2010). This leads frugal innovators to prefer small-scale plants for the minimisation of financial risks (Donaldson 2006), the flexibility to adapt to changing market needs and in addressing consumers' feedback.

When Prime decided to work with a bigger producer, the small-scale strategy enabled faster decision-making on production processes. Their approach was to go 'step by step', supporting ongoing learning throughout the production ramp-up stage. Similarly, Tirta's smaller-sized factory helped keeping flexible production capabilities, such as offering the possibility to test and alter the product extremely quickly and easily. Additionally, less sophisticated machines led to fewer requirements for maintenance, care and complexity in use, meaning employees could be trained on an ongoing basis and the number of employees could be adjusted in accordance with the TCM water filter demand.

Furthermore, this small-scale production can also enhance the commitment to quality standards, including via QA/QC and ongoing employees' training. This study's findings illustrated the implementation of strong quality standards through QA/QC and intensive training of local labour was particularly important in the production ramp-up stage for frugal innovation. This is in line with the core difference between cost-innovation, which is cheaper than traditional innovation (Williamson 2010), and frugal innovation, which is cheaper but still highly optimised when addressing BOP consumers' problems. Indeed, Gassmann et al. (2017) points out an important quality standard at the production ramp-up stage is to meet consumers' expectations.

Both Indonesian firms' choice of small-scale production gave them more control over production variables such as ensuring strict quality standards via QA/QC and workforce training to deliver a quality product. For example, QA/QC was critical across Prime's entire production ramp-up stage. The local presence of Prime enabled close management during the Prime cookstove's production, including the inventor's strict monitoring on production outputs' details, such as detailed checks on welded components. Such attention to detail was still evident at the larger manufacturing facility. For example, regardless of the modern, cost-effective and systematic machines of the production partner, QC was maintained through disassembly and reassembly of the Prime cookstove that the manufacturing partner produced. Such double-checking shows that Prime did not adopt increased production outputs at the risk of reducing overall quality standards.

Similarly, Tirta also shows evident commitment to quality standards for the TCM water filter. The inventor's decisions to bring production processes in-house allowed control of all the variables moderating the TCM quality. For example, on the basis of his previous experience with a local pottery furnace, the inventor preferred to build his own furnace to ensure quality of production outputs, despite being less time-efficient. Also, training the local workers for these particular production processes was enabled during the time spent in building the production processes in-house. The simplicity of these processes also allowed bringing in traditional testing processes to check the quality of the ceramic pot filters. This process, however, required experimentation and discernment for good quality pots. While generally there is a lack of local regulation in developing countries, these two Indonesian firms demonstrate that they still enforced strict quality standards irrespective of the absence of local regulations.

Hence, this study extends the sparse frugal innovation literature on frugal innovators' production ramp-up stage by supporting that a longer timescale should be combined with a small volume strategy. The reasons for this are the benefits stemming from this choice, including cost-effectiveness, speed to market, flexibility of production capacities and enforcement of strict quality standards.

Having examined the key management practices exemplified by both the case studies involved in this study, as well as previous studies, the following section will describe the limitations on this study's findings. These have been cautiously managed across the development of this explorative study. Following the limitations, theoretical and practical implications will be discussed to enable businesses, investors and government to understand how they can use this NPDP for frugal innovation, before concluding with a list of suggested future research.

Limitations of this research

While this study contributes to existing knowledge within this research domain, four key limitations should be recognised. The first limitation relates to the limited number of studies available on the concept of frugal innovation (Agarwal et al. 2017). While innovation, and in particular NPDP, has been studied extensively since the 1950s, the concept of frugal innovation as an academic field can be considered nascent, including a lack of research from a NPDP angle (Cunha et al. 2014). This lack of existing research limited this study's literature review, due to the restricted number of peer-reviewed articles and highly influential journals. This limitation led to the consideration of a broader diversity of sources that were both academic and non-academic, also allowing triangulation of data using literature and case studies (discussed in Chapter 3).

A second limitation is that this study has defined frugal innovation at the product and market levels – which might reduce the sampling results for Indonesian frugal products. However, this definition was leveraged from the most accepted consensus on frugal innovation definition (e.g. Zeschky, Winterhalter & Gassmann 2014), which means this study has contributed to the foundations of this research and practical stream.

Third, the case studies analysed in this study involved two start-up firms, which limits the extent of generalisability. However, while the issue of generalisation (or transferability) was also rigorously considered in Chapter 3, it was also surmised that case study design is not generally aimed at generalisation outside the framework developed in this study. This is also particularly justifiable within the context of this study due to the nascent state of the frugal innovation field and the lack of studies on frugal innovation in Indonesia. These two case studies make a strong contribution to the validity of the NPDP framework for frugal innovation within the Indonesian context. In addition, these bring unique insights not only through collecting primary data such as interviews and field observation, but also using secondary data such as materials provided by participants and online materials in the data analysis.

The final limitation related to the data collected from Indonesian managers and supervisors. With a focus on Indonesia, the empirical findings might not have captured broader management practices. While the empirical findings for this study were limited to Indonesia only, the frugal innovation literature in this review, however, encompasses case studies from around the world including India, China, Cambodia and Kenya. Furthermore, as the frugal innovation literature mostly covers India and China (Hossain 2017), studying frugal innovation in other developing countries such as Indonesia clearly adds knowledge to the field.

Theoretical implications from this study

This study has made several research contributions, including first to the NPDP and frugal innovation literatures, and the concept of frugal innovation from a NPDP perspective. First, this study has aggregated existing knowledge within the

NPDP literature by consolidating a multidisciplinary NPDP framework with the most commonly accepted phases (see Chapter 2). Along with this consolidated framework, the various terms and jargon utilised to discuss the same concept in the NPDP literature have been clarified in this study via the development of nine commonly accepted innovation stages. This holistic NPDP framework aimed to better clarify the foundations of NPDP practices among frugal innovators.

Second, this study's in-depth review of the frugal innovation literature (see Chapter 2 and Chapter 3) contributes to a field that has been recognised as nascent and under-researched. For example, the frugal innovation literature from a NPDP angle was sparse and the underlying processes to develop frugal innovation were scattered. Thus, this study has made a theoretical contribution to the frugal innovation by aggregating both theoretical and empirical studies into a conceptual framework from a NPDP perspective.

Third, this study is also unique, as it offers a clearer pathway for better understanding the development of frugal innovation from an NPDP perspective. The emphasis on NPDP intertwined with frugal innovation has enabled the generation of a more accurate framework that offers insights into the managerial practices of frugal innovators in other developing countries as well as Indonesia. The understanding of frugal innovation structured around the key decisions in stages, including characteristics, tools and techniques, also addresses a key gap in the literature. From an extensive review of the literature, there were few existing theoretical and empirical studies on the production ramp-up stage, to which this study clearly added empirical knowledge through the two Indonesian case studies. This study has also contributed to the innovation management community and its understanding of start-ups firms' NPDP in developing countries.

Practical implications from this study

This study's findings also have practical implications for firms (innovators), investors and governments. First, developing a NPDP framework from scholarly discourse and frugal innovators' practices, and empirically testing this in Indonesia may encourage firms to consider BOP market opportunities. While this framework needs to be tested further within similar and different contexts, it provides a useful pathway for any innovator who hopes to develop new frugal products for BOP consumers in developing countries.

It provides clear information about the various areas of the NPDP as well as key decisions that should be carefully considered to develop frugal products, including the reasons for these decisions through insights provided by two detailed Indonesian case studies. This NPDP framework for frugal innovation also gives frugal innovators the foundations to adapt the framework to their specific situations/goals in a multidisciplinary and holistic way, from opportunity and idea discovery to production ramp-up stages.

It could be especially informative for frugal innovators who do not have full NPDP expertise or are not necessarily aware that their practices can be related to formal new product management like NPDP. Frugal innovators could become more competitive and efficient in responding to the specific needs of BOP markets. In the same vein, this study's framework could also motivate innovators to become frugal innovators. Firms could subsequently increase their market share while providing products that increase the standard of living and capabilities of those under-served through existing products.

Second, this research also reveals how two start-ups in Indonesia have successfully developed new products for BOP consumers, offering insights for external institutions like NGOs, business angels and/or business incubators. In particular, these Indonesian case studies have highlighted how their constrained budgets across various NPDP phases slowed their successful product acceptance. External institutions such as financial investors will have a better understanding of the key NPDP practices of frugal innovators. They will consequently be able to recognise those firms involved in developing frugal innovations aligned with practices that lead to more successful outcomes.

Third, in addition to these implications for firms and investors, this framework could also be beneficial for government agencies and bodies in relation to the presence of frugal innovators in their countries. This research indicates that governments could support frugal innovators at the policy level by providing funding opportunities, such as the European Horizon 2020 prize for Affordable High-Tech for Humanitarian Aid (European Commission 2017). This may be particularly useful, given the international agenda to address Sustainable Development Goals – and how this has translated into national policy agendas. On the basis of these contributions, suggestions for further research are discussed in the next section.

Suggestions for further research and concluding comments

This study has provided insights into the key decisions at each NPDP stage, including characteristics, tools and techniques used by frugal innovators across their NPDP based on conceptual and empirical insights. While these implications for theory and practice are unique, the frugal innovation literature remains a nascent and under-developed academic field, implying the importance for ongoing studies and discussions. The limitations of this study and the field lead to the development of the following suggestions for further research.

First, the low number of case studies has limited these research findings, even though qualitative studies and case study design are often recommended where a paucity of literature exists. Further qualitative research could, therefore, be undertaken that replicates this study, incorporating other insights from the literature and more case studies on frugal innovators decisions, tools and techniques to strengthen the quality of this study's findings.

Second, this study was unique due to its empirical focus on Indonesia as compared with the majority of studies done in China and India (Agarwal et al. 2017). The conceptual framework could, therefore, be tested among other Southeast Asia countries such as Vietnam, the Philippines and Myanmar, to be able to compare management practices between these neighbouring countries with additional case studies and thereby improve the transferability of this study.

Third, as proposed by Agarwal et al. (2017), another avenue for further study would be understanding the NPDP back end where frugal innovations are being diffused in the BOP markets, including assessing the development impact of frugal innovation at the local level (Leliveld & Knorringa 2018). This could address the critiques raised by authors such as Karnani (2007, 2017) with regard to the positive influence of frugal innovation, including practices such as using local resources on the economic and social development of populations in developing countries.

Fourth, future research could also concentrate on developing a specific NPDP for frugal innovation for a specific sector, similarly to the study of Winterhalter et al. (2017). In their study, Winterhalter et al. (2017) develop commonly found aspects of business models in the medical sector that could offer key guidance for firms willing to enter BOP markets within this sector.

Fifth, future research could also consider how the use of modern, cost-effective NPD tools could fit with the purpose of each stage, to help the different development stages become more cost- and time-efficient. Relevant tools include agile methods and 3D printing, which could facilitate cheaper development costs across the concept and development phase than using trial-and-error and/ or physical prototyping. For example, the Jaipur Foot team later collaborated with high-tech companies (e.g. Dow Chemicals) and used "computer-controlled injection-moulding process" in the reduction of the foot weight materials (Council on Foundations n.d.).

Last, in the previous practical implications section, the role of this study's NPDP framework was discussed with regard to enhancing investor understanding of frugal innovators to provide better support for their NPDP. This research emphasised that the financial restraints often encountered by start-ups developing frugal products created NPDP impediments. Another avenue for further research would, therefore, be in relation to the role of financial and other advisory support for start-up firms seeking to develop frugal products. Such research could help to understand how this support may encourage firms to undertake frugal innovation and positively influence existing frugal innovator outcomes. Within this context, the focus could be on identifying the most relevant phase of development to receive funding and other support such as training in marketing tools or workshops in relation to concept development.

In conclusion, it is hoped that this study makes a valuable contribution to both academics and practitioners within frugal innovation, and encourages research to further explore some of the potential NPD areas for the BOP markets in developing countries. This includes exploring further areas of research, such as increasing qualitative studies in the field and across Southeast Asia, towards the development area, with specific sectors, in cost-effective NPDP tools and techniques, and investor's and other advisory supports for local start-up firms. This study has made efforts to propel this research agenda with a specific focus on the Indonesian context and the entire NPDP for frugal innovation.

Notes

1 In this study, frugal innovation has been delimited to developing and emerging countries.
2 The key executive, who identified M-PESA opportunity, operated on behalf of Vodafone.

References

Agarwal, N, Grottke, M, Mishra, S & Brem, A 2017, 'A systematic literature review of constraint-based innovations: State of the art and future perspectives', *IEEE Transactions on Engineering Management*, vol. 64, no. 1, pp. 3–15.

Agnihotri, A 2015, 'Low-cost innovation in emerging markets', *Journal of Strategic Marketing*, vol. 23, no. 5, pp. 399–411.

Almgren, H 2000, 'Pilot production and manufacturing start-up: The case of Volvo S80', *International Journal of Production Research*, vol. 38, no. 17, pp. 4577–4588.

Aranda-Jan, CB, Jagtap, S & Moultrie, J 2016, 'Towards a framework for holistic contextual design for low-resource settings', *International Journal of Design*, vol. 10, no. 3, pp. 43–63.

Awa, HO 2010, 'Democratizing the new product development process: A new dimension of value creation and marketing concept', *International Business Research*, vol. 3, no. 2, pp. 49–59.

Bingham, G, Whitehead, T & Evans, M 2016, 'Design tool for enhanced new product development in low income economies', *Proceedings of DRS2016: Design + Research + Society – Future-Focused Thinking*, pp. 2241–2256.

Brauner, P, Philipsen, R, Fels, A, Fuhrmann, M, Ngo, QH, Stiller, S, Schmitt, R & Ziefle, M 2016, 'A game-based approach to raise quality awareness in ramp-up processes', *The Quality Management Journal*, vol. 23, no. 1, pp. 55–69.

Brem, A & Voigt, K-I 2009, 'Integration of market pull and technology push in the corporate front end and innovation management – insights from the German software industry', *Technovation*, vol. 29, no. 5, pp. 351–367.

Brugmann, J & Prahalad, CK 2007, 'Cocreating business's new social compact', *Harvard Business Review*, vol. 85, no. 2, pp. 80–90.

Cooper, RG 1988, 'Predevelopment activities determine new product success', *Industrial Marketing Management*, vol. 17, no. 3, pp. 237–247.

Cooper, RG 2011, *Winning at new products: Creating value through innovation*, Basic Books.

Cooper, RG & Edgett, S 2008, 'Ideation for product innovation: What are the best methods', *PDMA Visions Magazine*, vol. 1, no. 1, pp. 12–17.

Cooper, RG & Sommer, AF 2016, 'The agile – stage-gate hybrid model: A promising new approach and a new research opportunity', *Journal of Product Innovation Management*, vol. 33, no. 5, pp. 513–526.

Council on Foundations n.d., *Case study: Giving the disabled the power of mobility*, viewed 25 December 2017, <www.cof.org/sites/default/files/documents/files/casestudy-DowChemicalJaipurFoot.pdf>.

Crawford, CM & Di Benedetto, CA 2011, *New products management*, 10th edn., McGraw-Hill Irwin, Boston, MA.

Crawford, CM & Di Benedetto, CA 2014, *New products management*, 11th edn., McGraw-Hill Education, New York.

Cunha, MPE, Rego, A, Oliveira, P, Rosado, P & Habib, N 2014, 'Product innovation in resource-poor environments: Three research streams', *Journal of Product Innovation Management*, vol. 31, no. 2, pp. 202–210.

Disability and Development Partners 2013, *Dr Pramod Karan Sethi: The Jaipur foot – history and controversy*, viewed 15 January 2018, <http://ddpuk.org/drsethi.html>.

Donaldson, K 2006, 'Product design in less industrialized economies: Constraints and opportunities in Kenya', *Research in Engineering Design*, vol. 17, no. 3, pp. 135–155.

Eastman, CM 2012, *Design for X: Concurrent engineering imperatives*, Springer Science & Business Media.

European Commission 2017, *Funding opportunities – TOPIC: EIC horizon prize for "Affordable high-tech for humanitarian aid"*, viewed 15 December 2017, <http://ec.europa.eu/research/participants/portal/desktop/en/opportunities/h2020/topics/humanitarianaid-eicprize-2020.html>.

Furr, N & Dyer, J 2015, *How Godrej became an innovation star*, viewed 18 January 2018, <www.forbes.com/sites/innovatorsdna/2015/05/13/how-godrej-became-an-innovation-star/#34835f77fd3d>.

Gassmann, O, Neumann, L, Knapp, O & Zollenkop, M 2017, 'Frugal: Simply a smart solution', *Roland Berger Focus*, Roland Berger GmbH.

Gaubinger, K, Rabl, M, Swan, S & Werani, T 2014, 'Integrated innovation and product management: A process oriented framework', in *Innovation and product management*, Springer, Berlin, Heidelberg, pp. 27–42.

GE Healthcare 2017, *Making healthymagination a reality*, viewed 5 December 2017, <healthymagination.gehealthcare.com/en/process>.

Girotra, K, Terwiesch, C & Ulrich, KT 2010, 'Idea generation and the quality of the best idea', *Management Science*, vol. 56, no. 4, pp. 591–605.

Glock, CH, Jaber, MY & Zolfaghari, S 2012, 'Production planning for a ramp-up process with learning in production and growth in demand', *International Journal of Production Research*, vol. 50, no. 20, pp. 5707–5718.

Gollakota, K, Gupta, V & Bork, JT 2010, 'Reaching customers at the base of the pyramid – a two-stage business strategy', *Thunderbird International Business Review*, vol. 52, no. 5, pp. 355–367.

Graner, M & Mißler-Behr, M 2013, 'Key determinants of the successful adoption of new product development methods', *European Journal of Innovation Management*, vol. 16, no. 3, pp. 301–316.

Griffin, A 2012, 'Obtaining customer needs for product development', in *The PDMA handbook of new product development*, John Wiley & Sons, Inc., pp. 211–230.

Griffin, A & Page, AL 1996, 'PDMA success measurement project: Recommended measures for product development success and failure', *The Journal of Product Innovation Management*, vol. 13, no. 6, Nov, pp. 478–496.

Griffin, A & Somermeyer, S 2007, *The PDMA toolbook 3 for new product development*, John Wiley & Sons, Inc., Hoboken, NJ.

Hossain, M 2017, 'Mapping the frugal innovation phenomenon', *Technology in Society*, vol. 51, pp. 199–208.

Hughes, N & Lonie, S 2007, 'M-PESA: Mobile money for the "unbanked" turning cellphones into 24-hour tellers in Kenya', *Innovations*, vol. 2, no. 1–2, pp. 63–81.

Innosight 2017, *Godrej – co-creating with rural consumers helps achieve inclusive growth*, viewed 18 October 2017, <www.innosight.com/wp-content/uploads/2016/01/Client-Impact-Story-PDF-Godrej.pdf>.

Karnani, A 2007, 'The mirage of marketing to the bottom of the pyramid: How the private sector can help alleviate poverty', *California Management Review*, vol. 49, no. 4, pp. 90–111.

Karnani, A 2017, 'Marketing and poverty alleviation: The perspective of the poor', *Markets, Globalization & Development Review*, vol. 2, no. 1.

Koen, PA, Bertels, HMJ & Kleinschmidt, EJ 2014, 'Managing the front end of innovation – Part II', *Research Technology Management*, vol. 57, no. 3, p. 25.

Kotler, P 2016, *A framework for marketing management*, 6th edn., Pearson, Boston, MA.

Krishnan, V & Ulrich, KT 2001, 'Product development decisions: A review of the literature', *Management Science*, vol. 47, no. 1, pp. 1–21.

Lehner, A-C & Gausemeier, J 2016, 'A pattern-based approach to the development of frugal innovations', *Technology Innovation Management Review*, vol. 6, no. 3, pp. 13–21.

Leliveld, A & Knorringa, P 2018, 'Frugal innovation and development research', *The European Journal of Development Research*, vol. 30, no. 1, pp. 1–16.

Löscher, P 2011, 'Less is more', *The Economist*, viewed 2 December 2017, <www.economist.com/node/21537984>.

Macke, S, Misra, R & Sharma, A 2003, *Jaipur foot: Challenging convention*, Case Study Series, University Michigan Business School, Ann Arbor, MI.

Markham, SK & Lee, H 2013, 'Product development and management association's 2012 comparative performance assessment study', *Journal of Product Innovation Management*, vol. 30, no. 3, pp. 408–429.

Mattson, CA & Wood, AE 2014, 'Nine principles for design for the developing world as derived from the engineering literature', *Journal of Mechanical Design*, vol. 136, no. 12, p. 121403.

McManus, T, Holtzman, Y, Lazarus, H, Chandra, M & Neelankavil, JP 2008, 'Product development and innovation for developing countries: Potential and challenges', *Journal of Management Development*, vol. 27, no. 10, pp. 1017–1025.

MIT 2008, *Global water & sanitation projects: KanchanTM arsenic filter project for rural Nepal*, viewed 4 January 2018, <http://web.mit.edu/watsan/worldbank_summary.html>.

Mukerjee, K 2012, 'Frugal innovation: The key to penetrating emerging markets', *Ivey Business Journal*, viewed 5 February 2018, <www.iveybusinessjournal.com/uncategorized/frugal-innovation-the-key-to-penetrating-emerging-markets#.VH_3AzGUfzh>.

Murcott, S 2007, 'Co-evolutional design for development: Influences shaping engineering design and implementation in Nepal and the global village', *Journal of International Development*, vol. 19, no. 1, pp. 123–144.

Murphy, SA & Kumar, V 1996, 'The role of predevelopment activities and firm attributes in new product success', *Technovation*, vol. 16, no. 8, pp. 431–449.

Murthy, DP, Rausand, M & Østerås, T 2008, *Product reliability: Specification and performance*, Springer Science & Business Media.

Nakata, CC & Berger, E 2011, 'Chapter 18 new product development for the base of the pyramid: A theory-and case-based framework', in *Handbook of research in international marketing*, 2nd edn., Edward Elgar Publishing, UK, pp. 349–375.

Nakata, CC & Weidner, K 2012, 'Enhancing new product adoption at the base of the pyramid: A contextualized model', *Journal of Product Innovation Management*, vol. 29, no. 1, pp. 21–32.

Ngai, T, Shrestha, R, Dangol, B, Maharjan, M & Murcott, S 2007, 'Design for sustainable development – household drinking water filter for arsenic and pathogen treatment in Nepal', *Journal of Environmental Science and Health – Part A Toxic/Hazardous Substances Environmental Engineering*, vol. 42, no. 12, pp. 1879–1888.

Numminen, S & Lund, PD 2017, 'Frugal energy innovations for developing countries – a framework', *Global Challenges*, vol. 1, no. 1, pp. 9–19.

Osteras, T, Murthy, DNP & Rausand, M 2006, 'Product performance and specification in new product development', *Journal of Engineering Design*, vol. 17, no. 2, pp. 177–192.

Otto, KN & Wood, KL 2000, *Product design: Techniques in reverse engineering and new product development*, Prentice Hall, Pearson College.

Ozer, M 1999, 'A survey of new product evaluation models', *Journal of Product Innovation Management*, vol. 16, no. 1, pp. 77–94.

Pahl, G & Beitz, W 2013, *Engineering design: A systematic approach*, Springer Science & Business Media.

Pahl, G, Wallace, K & Blessing, L 2007, *Engineering design: A systematic approach*, 3rd edn., Springer, London.

Pitta, D, Subrahmanyan, S & Tomas Gomez-Arias, J 2008, 'Integrated approach to understanding consumer behavior at bottom of pyramid', *Journal of Consumer Marketing*, vol. 25, no. 7, pp. 402–412.

Praceus, S & Herstatt, C 2017, 'Consumer innovation in the poor versus rich world: Some differences and similarities', in *Lead market India*, Springer, Cham, pp. 97–117.

Prahalad, CK 2012, 'Bottom of the pyramid as a source of breakthrough innovations', *Journal of Product Innovation Management*, vol. 29, no. 1, pp. 6–12.

Radjou, N & Prabhu, J 2015, *Frugal innovation: How to do more with less*, Profile Books, London.

Ramdorai, A & Herstatt, C 2017, 'Lessons from low-cost healthcare innovations for the base-of the pyramid markets: How incumbents can systematically create disruptive innovations', in C Herstatt and R Tiwari (eds), *Lead market India*, Springer, pp. 119–144.

Rao, BC 2013, 'How disruptive is frugal?' *Technology in Society*, vol. 35, no. 1, pp. 65–73.

Ray, S & Ray, P 2011, 'Product innovation for the people's car in an emerging economy', *Technovation*, vol. 31, no. 5–6, pp. 216–227.

Ries, E 2009, *Minimum viable product: A guide*, viewed 4 January 2017, <http://solo way.pbworks.com/w/file/fetch/85897603/1%2B%20Lessons%20Learned_%20 Minimum%20Viable%20Product_%20a%20guide2.pdf>.

Sehgal, V, Dehoff, K & Panneer, G 2010, 'The importance of frugal engineering', *Strategy + Business*, Summer 2010, no. 59, pp. 1–4.

Sharma, A & Iyer, GR 2012, 'Resource-constrained product development: Implications for green marketing and green supply chains', *Industrial Marketing Management*, vol. 41, no. 4, pp. 599–608.

Simanis, E 2011, 'Needs, needs, everywhere, but not a BoP market to tap', *Next Generation Business Strategies for the Base of the Pyramid*, pp. 103–126.

Singh, J 2011, 'GE healthcare: Innovating for emerging markets', INSEAD Case Study.

Tiwari, R & Herstatt, C 2012, 'Assessing India's lead market potential for cost-effective innovations', *Journal of Indian Business Research*, vol. 4, no. 2, pp. 97–115.

Tiwari, R, Kalogerakis, K & Herstatt, C 2014, 'Frugal innovation and analogies: Some propositions for product development in emerging economies', Working Paper, Technologie-und Innovationsmanagement, Technische Universität Hamburg-Harburg.

Ulrich, KT & Eppinger, SD 2012, *Product design and development*, 5th edn., McGraw-Hill Higher Education, New York.

Urban, GL & Hauser, JR 1993, *Design and marketing of new products*, 2nd edn., Prentice Hall, Englewood Cliffs, NJ.

Viswanathan, M & Sridharan, S 2012, 'Product development for the BoP: Insights on concept and prototype development from university-based student projects in India', *Journal of Product Innovation Management*, vol. 29, no. 1, pp. 52–69.

Viswanathan, M, Yassine, A & Clarke, J 2011, 'Sustainable product and market development for subsistence marketplaces: Creating educational initiatives in radically different contexts*', *Journal of Product Innovation Management*, vol. 28, no. 4, pp. 558–569.

Weidner, KL, Rosa, JA & Viswanathan, M 2010, 'Marketing to subsistence consumers: Lessons from practice', *Journal of Business Research*, vol. 63, no. 6, pp. 559–569.

Weyrauch, T & Herstatt, C 2017, 'What is frugal innovation? Three defining criteria', *Journal of Frugal Innovation*, vol. 2, no. 1, pp. 1–17.

Whitney, DE 2007, 'Assemble a technology development toolkit', *Research Technology Management*, vol. 50, no. 5, pp. 52–58.

Whitney, P 2010, 'Reframing design for the base of the pyramid', in T London and SL Hart (eds), *Next generation business strategies for the base of the pyramid: New approaches for building mutual value*, FT Press, Upper Saddle River, NJ, pp. 165–192.

Williamson, PJ 2010, 'Cost innovation: Preparing for a "value-for-money" revolution', *Long Range Planning*, vol. 43, no. 2, pp. 343–353.

Winkler, H, Heins, M & Nyhuis, P 2007, 'A controlling system based on cause – effect relationships for the ramp-up of production systems', *Production Engineering*, vol. 1, no. 1, pp. 103–111.

Winter, AG 2013, 'Helping the disabled get off-road and on with their lives (Case study)', *Mechanical Engineering-CIME*, vol. 135, no. 11, p. S18.

Winter, AG, Bollini, MA, DeLatte, DH, Judge, BM, O'Hanley, HF, Pearlman, JL & Scolnik, NK 2010, 'The design, fabrication, and performance of the east african trial leveraged freedom chair', ASME 2010 International Design Engineering Technical Conferences and Computers and Information in Engineering Conference, pp. 753–760.

Winter, AG & Govindarajan, V 2015, 'Engineering reverse innovations: Principles for creating successful products for emerging markets', *Harvard Business Review*, vol. 93, no. 7–8, pp. 80–89.

Winterhalter, S, Zeschky, MB, Neumann, L & Gassmann, O 2017, 'Business 'models for frugal innovation in emerging markets: The case of the medical device and laboratory equipment industry', *Technovation*, vol. 66, pp. 3–13.

Wood, AE & Mattson, CA 2014, 'A method for determining customer needs in the developing world', ASME 2014 International Design Engineering Technical Conferences and Computers and Information in Engineering Conference, American Society of Mechanical Engineers, pp. V02AT03A047.

Wood, AE & Mattson, CA 2016, 'Design for the developing world: Common pitfalls and how to avoid them', *Journal of Mechanical Design*, vol. 138, no. 3, p. 031101.

Yeh, T, Yang, C & Pai, F 2010, 'Performance improvement in new product development with effective tools and techniques adoption for high-tech industries', *Quality and Quantity*, vol. 44, no. 1, pp. 131–152.

Zeschky, MB, Widenmayer, B & Gassmann, O 2011, 'Frugal innovation in emerging markets: The case of Mettler Toledo', *Research-Technology Management*, vol. 54, no. 4, pp. 38–45.

Zeschky, MB, Winterhalter, S & Gassmann, O 2014, 'From cost to frugal and reverse innovation: Mapping the field and implications for global competitiveness', *Research-Technology Management*, vol. 57, no. 4, pp. 20–27.

Index

Note: **Bold** face page references indicate tables. *Italic* references indicate figures.

For Product Safety Concerns and Information please contact our EU
representative GPSR@taylorandfrancis.com Taylor & Francis Verlag GmbH,
Kaufingerstraße 24, 80331 München, Germany

Printed and bound by CPI Group (UK) Ltd, Croydon, CR0 4YY
01/05/2025
01858422-0010